# SHAKESPEARE SURVEY

# ADVISORY BOARD

1 Shakespeare and his Stage
2 Shakespearian Production
3 The Man and the Writer
4 Interpretation
5 Textual Criticism
6 The Histories
7 Style and Language
8 The Comedies
9 *Hamlet*
10 The Roman Plays
11 The Last Plays (with an index to *Surveys 1–10*)
12 The Elizabethan Theatre
13 *King Lear*
14 Shakespeare and his Contemporaries
15 The Poems and Music
16 Shakespeare in the Modern World
17 Shakespeare in his Own Age
18 Shakespeare Then Till Now
19 *Macbeth*
20 Shakespearian and Other Tragedy
21 *Othello* (with an index to *Surveys 11–20*)

22 Aspects of Shakespearian Comedy
23 Shakespeare's Language
24 Shakespeare: Theatre Poet
25 Shakespeare's Problem Plays
26 Shakespeare's Jacobean Tragedies
27 Shakespeare's Early Tragedies
28 Shakespeare and the Ideas of his Time
29 Shakespeare's Last Plays
30 *Henry IV* to *Hamlet*
31 Shakespeare and the Classical World (with an index to *Surveys 21–30*)
32 The Middle Comedies
33 *King Lear*
34 Characterization in Shakespeare
35 Shakespeare in the Nineteenth Century
36 Shakespeare in the Twentieth Century
37 Shakespeare's Earlier Comedies
38 Shakespeare and History
39 Shakespeare on Film and Television

Aspects of *Macbeth*
Aspects of *Othello*
Aspects of *Hamlet*
Aspects of *King Lear*
Aspects of Shakespeare's 'Problem Plays'

# SHAKESPEARE SURVEY

## AN ANNUAL SURVEY OF

## SHAKESPEARIAN STUDY AND PRODUCTION

---

## 39

EDITED BY

## STANLEY WELLS

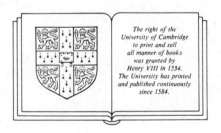

The right of the
University of Cambridge
to print and sell
all manner of books
was granted by
Henry VIII in 1534.
The University has printed
and published continuously
since 1584.

## CAMBRIDGE UNIVERSITY PRESS

CAMBRIDGE

LONDON   NEW YORK   NEW ROCHELLE

MELBOURNE   SYDNEY

Published by the Press Syndicate of the University of Cambridge
The Pitt Building, Trumpington Street, Cambridge CB2 1RP
32 East 57th Street, New York, NY 10022, USA
10 Stamford Road, Oakleigh, Melbourne 3166, Australia

First published 1987
Reprinted 1987

Printed in Great Britain at the University Press, Cambridge

Library of Congress catalogue card number: 49–1639

*British Library cataloguing in publication data*
Shakespeare survey: an annual survey of
Shakespearian study and production.
39.
1. Shakespeare, William – Societies,
periodicals, etc.
822.3'3   PR2885

ISBN 0 521 32757 1

# EDITOR'S NOTE

Volume 40 of *Shakespeare Survey* (which will be at press by the time this volume appears) will be concerned with current approaches to Shakespeare through language, text, and theatre. Volume 41 will be on 'Shakespearian Stages and Staging'. Submissions should be addressed to the Editor at Cambridge University Press, The Edinburgh Building, Shaftesbury Road, Cambridge CB2 2RU, to arrive by 1 September 1987 at the latest. Many articles are considered before the deadline, so those that arrive earlier stand a greater chance of acceptance. Please either enclose return postage (overseas, in International Reply Coupons) or send a non-returnable xerox. A style sheet is available on request. All articles submitted are read by the Editor and by one or more members of the Advisory Board, whose indispensable assistance the Editor gratefully acknowledges.

With this volume we welcome Richard Dutton as reviewer of work on Shakespeare's Life, Times and Stage.

In attempting to survey the ever-increasing bulk of Shakespeare publications our reviewers have inevitably to exercise some selection. Review copies of books should be addressed to the Editor, as above. We are also very pleased to receive offprints of articles, which help to draw our reviewers' attention to relevant material.

S.W.W.

# CONTRIBUTORS

DAVID R. ARMITAGE, *Research Scholar of St Catharine's College, Cambridge*
LORNE M. BUCHMAN, *Assistant Professor of Dramatic Art, University of California, Berkeley*
ANTHONY DAVIES, *Professor of English, University of Fort Hare*
RICHARD DUTTON, *Lecturer in English Literature, University of Lancaster*
STUART EVANS, *London*
BRIAN GIBBONS, *Professor of English, University of Zürich*
JAMES GIBBS, *Bristol*
ROBERT HAPGOOD, *Professor of English, University of New Hampshire*
GRAHAM HOLDERNESS, *Tutor in Literature and Drama, University College of Swansea*
MACDONALD P. JACKSON, *Associate Professor of English, University of Auckland*
ROSALIND KING, *Lecturer in English Language and Literature, Queen Mary College, London*
CHRISTOPHER MCCULLOUGH, *Lecturer in Drama, University College of Swansea*
E. PEARLMAN, *Professor of English, University of Colorado at Denver*
EDWARD PECHTER, *Associate Professor of English, Concordia University, Montreal*
KENNETH S. ROTHWELL, *Professor of English, University of Vermont*
NICHOLAS SHRIMPTON, *Fellow of Lady Margaret Hall and Lecturer in English, University of Oxford*
NEIL TAYLOR, *Principal Lecturer in English, Froebel Institute College, Roehampton Institute of Higher Education, London*
ROGER WARREN, *Lecturer in English, University of Leicester*
MICHÈLE WILLEMS, *Lecturer in English Drama, University of Haute Normandie*
ROBERT WILTENBURG, *Professor of English, Washington University, St Louis*

# CONTENTS

*List of Illustrations*                                                                *page*  ix

Shakespeare and the Media of Film, Radio and Television: A Retrospect
  *by* ANTHONY DAVIES                                                                            I

Shakespeare on the Screen: A Selective Filmography
  *compiled by* GRAHAM HOLDERNESS *and* CHRISTOPHER MCCULLOUGH                                  13

*Chimes at Midnight* from Stage to Screen: The Art of Adaptation *by* ROBERT HAPGOOD          39

Orson Welles's *Othello*: A Study of Time in Shakespeare's Tragedy
  *by* LORNE M. BUCHMAN                                                                        53

*Macbeth* on Film: Politics *by* E. PEARLMAN                                                   67

Representing *King Lear* on Screen: From Metatheatre to 'Meta-cinema' *by*
  KENNETH S. ROTHWELL                                                                          75

Verbal-Visual, Verbal-Pictorial or Textual-Televisual? Reflections on the BBC
  Shakespeare Series *by* MICHÈLE WILLEMS                                                       91

Two Types of Television Shakespeare *by* NEIL TAYLOR                                          103

Shakespeare on Radio *by* STUART EVANS                                                        113

The Dismemberment of Orpheus: Mythic Elements in Shakespeare's Romances
  *by* DAVID ARMITAGE                                                                          123

Remembering *Hamlet*: Or, How it Feels to Go Like a Crab Backwards
  *by* EDWARD PECHTER                                                                          135

'Then murder's out of tune': The Music and Structure of *Othello* *by* ROSALIND KING         149

The '*Aeneid*' in '*The Tempest*' *by* ROBERT WILTENBURG                                      159

The Living Dramatist and Shakespeare: A Study of Shakespeare's Influence on
  Wole Soyinka *by* JAMES GIBBS                                                               169

Shakespeare at Stratford, Ontario: The John Hirsch Years *by* ROGER WARREN                   179

Shakespeare Performances in London and Stratford-upon-Avon 1984–5
  *by* NICHOLAS SHRIMPTON                                                                      191

The Year's Contributions to Shakespearian Study:
  1   Critical Studies *reviewed by* BRIAN GIBBONS                                            207
  2   Shakespeare's Life, Times, and Stage *reviewed by* RICHARD DUTTON                       223
  3   Editions and Textual Studies *reviewed by* MacDONALD P. JACKSON                         236

*Index*                                                                                      253

# ILLUSTRATIONS

1   Orson Welles as Falstaff in the staged version of *Chimes at Midnight*   page  41
    [*By courtesy of Thelma Ruby*]

2   Sketches by Orson Welles for *Chimes at Midnight*                         48

3   Frederick B. Warde as King Lear on tour in the United States in the early part of
    this century                                                             76
    [*Billy Rose Theatre Collection, The New York Public Library at Lincoln Center; Astor,
    Lenox, and Tilden Foundations*]

4   Frederick B. Warde as King Lear banishes Cordelia (Lorraine Huling), while the
    Fool (Ernest Warde) looks on                                             78
    [*By permission of Robert H. Ball, from 'Moving Picture World', 4 November 1916*]

5   A long shot of Lear's train showing the bleak landscape in the Peter Brook 1970
    film version                                                             80
    [*By permission of Columbia Pictures*]

6   In the Kozintsev 1970 *King Lear*, Lear (Yuri Yarvet) and Cordelia (V. Shendri-
    kova) are led off to prison                                              84
    [*By permission of Corinth Films*]

7   Penelope Wilton (centre), Gillian Barge (right) play the wicked sisters in the 1982
    BBC production with Brenda Blethyn (left foreground) as Cordelia          87
    [*By permission of The Shakespeare Plays*]

8   Michael Hordern as a grizzled King Lear with Frank Middlemass as the Fool in the
    1982 BBC production directed by Jonathan Miller                          88
    (*By permission of The Shakespeare Plays*)

9   Laurence Olivier as King Lear with Diana Rigg as Regan in the 1982 Granada
    Television production                                                    89
    [*By permission of Granada Television*]

10  *The Tempest*. Stratford, Ontario, 1982. Len Cariou as Prospero          180
    [*Photo: Robert Ragsdale*]

11  *A Midsummer Night's Dream*. Stratford, Ontario, 1984. Titania (Patricia Conolly),
    Oberon (Nicholas Pennell), Puck (Diego Matamoros)                        182
    [*Photo: David Cooper*]

12  *The Merry Wives of Windsor*. Stratford, Ontario, 1982. Susan Wright as Mistress
    Page and Pat Galloway as Mistress Ford                                   184
    [*Photo: Robert Ragsdale*]

# ILLUSTRATIONS

13  *The Merchant of Venice*. Stratford, Ontario, 1984. Domini Blythe as Portia and Heather Macdonald as Nerissa                                                                    186
    [*Photo: David Cooper*]

14  *Love's Labour's Lost*. Stratford, Ontario, 1984. John Neville as Armado                    187
    [*Photo: David Cooper*]

15  *The Two Gentlemen of Verona*. Stratford, Ontario, 1984. The Outlaws (John Moffatt, Kevin Anderson, Laurence Rosso) with Valentine (Rob McClure) and Speed (David Johnson)                                                                                   189
    [*Photo: David Cooper*]

16  *Coriolanus*. National Theatre, 1984. Ian McKellen as Coriolanus                            192
    [*Photo: John Haynes*]

17  *Coriolanus*. National Theatre, 1984. Menenius Agrippa (Frederick Treves) with Volumnia (Irene Worth) and Virgilia (Wendy Morgan)                                           194
    [*Photo: John Haynes*]

18  *Coriolanus*. National Theatre, 1984. Menenius Agrippa (Frederick Treves, centre) addresses the Tribunes, Sicinius Velutus (David Ryall, left) and Junius Brutus (James Hayes)                                                                                   195
    [*Photo: John Haynes*]

19  *Hamlet* (First Quarto). Orange Tree Theatre, Richmond, 1985. Peter Guinness as Hamlet                                                                                         196
    [*Photo: Co-op, London*]

20  *The Merry Wives of Windsor*. Royal Shakespeare Theatre, 1985. The Host of the Garter Inn (Trevor Martin) and Falstaff (Peter Jeffrey)                                       196
    [*Photo: Joe Cocks*]

21  *The Merry Wives of Windsor*. Royal Shakespeare Theatre, 1985. Ford's house, act 3, scene 3. Dr Caius (David Bradley), Page (Paul Webster), Ford (Nicky Henson), Mistress Page (Janet Dale), Mistress Ford (Lindsay Duncan)                               198
    [*Photo: Joe Cocks*]

22  *As You Like It*. Royal Shakespeare Theatre, 1985. Orlando (Hilton McRae) and Rosalind (Juliet Stevenson) in act 5, scene 2                                                  201
    [*Photo: Joe Cocks*]

23  *Troilus and Cressida*. Royal Shakespeare Theatre, 1985. The Greek generals in conference: Nestor (Mark Dignam) and Agamemnon (Joseph O'Conor) seated, with Ulysses (Peter Jeffrey, standing right)                                                    202
    [*Photo: Joe Cocks*]

24  *Troilus and Cressida*. Royal Shakespeare Theatre, 1985. Pandarus (Clive Merrison) and Cressida (Juliet Stevenson) in act 1, scene 2                                         204
    [*Photo: Joe Cocks*]

25  *Othello*. Royal Shakespeare Theatre, 1985. Iago (David Suchet) and Othello (Ben Kingsley)                                                                                    204
    [*Photo: Joe Cocks*]

# SHAKESPEARE AND THE MEDIA OF FILM, RADIO AND TELEVISION: A RETROSPECT

## ANTHONY DAVIES

### I

When in 1916 Hugo Münsterberg claimed that the photoplay overcomes 'the forms of the outer world ... by adjusting events to the forms of the inner world', he perceived the major shift from the theatre stage to the cinema screen as being psychological rather than technological.[1] Any survey of available criticism in the field of Shakespeare and film tends not only to confirm that perception but to suggest that it persists not merely as an aesthetic issue but as an issue affecting the collective critical mind. While theatre remains the legitimate expressive medium for authentic Shakespeare, kept alive by a scattering of theatrical companies playing to audiences for whom theatre is both accessible and familiar, only comparatively recently has it become respectable to concentrate serious discussion on the media of cinema, radio and more especially television. These media have become the most practical means of making Shakespeare's plays in performance a world heritage rather than a national one passed on through educational systems.

The widely scattered and often tentative nature of critical writing on Shakespearian film is the result of three distinctly psychological legacies. Firstly, the motives behind the production of all films were seen to be brashly commercial, so that Richard Watts could write in his response to the Reinhardt–Dieterle film of *A Midsummer Night's Dream* (1936) that

'almost every film company makes what it calls "prestige" pictures [which are] planned by magnates ... as proofs that they are artists as well as businessmen'.[2] Secondly, the historical moment of cinema's meeting with theatre was especially traumatic. As Nicholas Vardac makes clear, just when the spectacular extravagance of the late nineteenth-century theatre was breaking down, the cinema arrived as a new and effective rival, forcing theatre back upon itself in order to compete commercially in the production of massive visual effects.[3] Cinema was seen, therefore, as the betrayer of a movement that would otherwise have redirected theatre towards its original essentials. Finally, cinema was quickly perceived as posing a threat to traditional aesthetic distinctions. Not only did it dissolve the demarcations between the actor and the inanimate spatial detail within the cinema frame, but it also manipulated the relationship of the perceiver with the fictional world of the film.[4] Furthermore, as Suzanne Langer suggests, cinema's omnivorous capacity 'to assimilate

---

[1] Hugo Münsterberg, 'The Means of the Photoplay', in *Film Theory and Criticism* (1st ed.), edited by Gerald Mast and Marshal Cohen, 239–48; p. 240.

[2] Richard Watts, 'Films of a Moonstruck World', in *Focus on Shakespearean Film*, edited by Charles W. Eckert (Englewood Cliffs, NJ, 1972), 47–52; p. 48.

[3] Nicholas Vardac, *Stage to Screen* (New York, 1968), p. xxvi.

[4] Béla Balázs, *Theory of Film: Character and Growth of a New Art* (London, 1953), p. 412.

the most diverse materials and turn them into elements of its own' appeared to threaten with extinction what had formerly seemed clearly separate artistic disciplines.[5]

II

The middle 1930s were significant years both for Shakespearian film and for the development of critical writing in the field. Not only were three films (Reinhardt's *A Midsummer Night's Dream*, Cukor's *Romeo and Juliet*, and Paul Czinner's *As You Like It*) released, but Allardyce Nicoll's perceptive book, *Film and Theatre*, was published. Early in the book, Nicoll argues that the social and economic forces governing the production of films in the 1930s were not so very different from those which promoted the theatrical fare of Shakespeare's day. 'The theatrical managers', he maintains, 'exploited freely whatever came uppermost at the moment, heaping ghosts upon the stage when the going of ghosts was good and mad ladies in white linen when ghosts began to pall.'[6] Nicoll asserts himself as no enemy to the cinema. Recognizing that literacy had changed the ear's alertness to the complexities of the spoken word since Shakespeare's plays were first produced, he suggests that the expressive potential of cinema 'may merely be supplying something that will bring us nearer to the conditions of the original spectators for whom Shakespeare wrote'. Nicoll further rightly discerns one difficulty in adapting theatrical material for film when he distinguishes the cinematic – as opposed to the theatrical – development of character. While the theatre stage can accommodate and effectively present characters who bear 'the lineaments of universal humanity', the realism of the cinema tends to deal with characters as individuals without exceptional stature.[7]

In 1936, there also emerged a vigorous debate between Harley Granville-Barker and Alfred Hitchcock. Granville-Barker is prompted, in his reactions to the films of Reinhardt and Cukor, to draw attention to the visual images in Shakespeare's dialogue and to castigate Reinhardt and Cukor for unnecessary pictorial indulgence. He reaches the conclusion that cinema and theatre 'are in their nature and their methods ... radically and fatally opposed'. He does, however, see cinema's potential as a narrative art and suggests that cinema should exploit Shakespeare stories 'to suit its pictorial purpose, without respect to him.... Shakespeare in the cinema will do – with Shakespeare left out'.[8] Alfred Hitchcock's vehement reply is at once an attack on what he sees as a purist and pedantic attitude to Shakespeare as well as an assertion of cinema's right to afford Shakespeare's dramatic action realistic locations.[9]

The exchange between Granville-Barker and Hitchcock is chiefly interesting in its revelation that up until the Second World War the most lively debate about Shakespearian film centred upon issues that were in essence extensions of that conflict which had erupted within the realm of theatre some fifty years before.

III

The critical response to Shakespearian film began to take on a more impressive stature as cinematic technology improved and the adaptive endeavour could become more versatile. The year 1944 was a major turning point in both the creation and the public acceptance of Shakespearian film. Laurence Olivier's *Henry V* was released in that year, and for the first time critics and reviewers were faced with a

[5] Suzanne Langer, *Feeling and Form: A Theory of Art* (London, 1953), p. 412.
[6] Allardyce Nicoll, *Film and Theatre* (London, 1936), p. 20.
[7] Allardyce Nicoll, 'Film Reality: The Cinema and the Theatre', in *Focus on Film and Theatre*, edited by James Hurt (Englewood Cliffs, 1974), 29–50; p. 48.
[8] Harley Granville-Barker, 'Alas Poor Will!' *The Listener* (3 March 1936), 387–9, 425–6; p. 425.
[9] Alfred Hitchcock, 'Much Ado About Nothing? I', *The Listener* (10 March 1936), 448–50; p. 448.

cinematic adaptation which operates on too many levels to be patronizingly dismissed or glibly celebrated. James Agee's ebullient eulogy, while it does not attempt to be analytical, shows an awareness of cinematic complexity when he considers the film 'essentially less visual than musical', and he recurrently refers to the powerful impact throughout the film of Shakespeare's language.[10]

Olivier's *Hamlet*, released in 1948, has attracted a greater volume of critical literature than any other Shakespearian film. Bosley Crowther not only wrote a carefully considered review for the *New York Times*, but promoted critical dialogue by inviting comment and discussion in the paper's columns, from readers.[11] Simultaneous with the release of the film, a book, *'Hamlet', the Film and the Play*, was published. Together with the screenplay dialogue, a foreword by Olivier, and an essay on editing the text by Alan Dent, there is an illuminating essay by Roger Furse, which discusses the relation between the film's set design and its dramatic action. The priorities of the film designer are made unambiguously clear when Furse asserts that 'the essence of the film is that it is *not* still. It is in motion, and . . . the designer's business is to do everything he can to assist the mobility and flow; not to freeze it into a series of orderly compositions.'[12] Not only does this essay suggest some of the spatial intentions within this particular film, but it opens the way to intelligent criticism of other Shakespearian films.

Orson Welles's *Macbeth*, also released in 1948, attracted a different strand of critical response. Whereas Olivier's films had been considered by most reviewers as extensions of theatre, Welles's first Shakespearian film rightly attracted interest as cinema rather than as Shakespeare. The French critics quickly pursued a specifically cinematic line. André Bazin wrote of 'those strange settings trickling with water, shrouded in mists which obscure a sky in which the existence of stars is inconceiv-able, literally form a prehistoric universe . . . a prehistory of the conscience'.[13] And Claude Beylie describes the décor as 'veritably "telluric", almost sublunar, a décor that is essentially the pathetic reflection of the conscious, or rather the unconscious, of the hero'.[14]

The essay by Furse and the critical reviews by Bazin and Beylie point to spatial strategy as being more important than authenticity of location, and cinematically more crucial than the actor's performance.

IV

With the release of Welles's *Othello* in 1952 there emerged the first complete volume devoted to the making of a Shakespearian film by a single author. The diary account written by Micheál MacLiammóir, who played Iago, covers the shooting of the film from January 1949 until March 1950. Despite the occasionally indulgent subjectivity of the account and its eschewing of technical details, it is an intelligent and essential contribution to the body of writing in this field. The entries are written from the point of view of a stage actor feeling his way before the film director and the camera. 'One's first job', writes MacLiammóir, 'is to forget every single lesson one ever learned on the stage: all projection of the personality, build-up of a speech, and sustaining for more than a few seconds of an emotion are not only unnecessary but superfluous.'[15]

---

[10] James Agee, 'Henry V', in *Film Theory and Criticism*, 333–6; p. 334.

[11] Bosley Crowther, *New York Times* (3 and 7 October 1948), Section 2, p. x.

[12] Roger Furse, 'Designing the Film *Hamlet*', in *'Hamlet', the Film and the Play* (London, 1948), unpaged.

[13] André Bazin, *Orson Welles: A Critical Review* (London, 1978), p. 101.

[14] Claude Beylie, '*Macbeth*, or the Magical Depths', in *Focus on Shakespearean Film*, edited by Charles W. Eckert (Englewood Cliffs, NJ, 1972), 72–5; p. 72.

[15] Micheál MacLiammóir, *Put Money in Thy Purse: The Filming of Orson Welles's 'Othello'* (London, 1952), pp. 96–100.

In 1968 appeared the first volume to essay a survey of Shakespearian film. Robert Hamilton Ball's *Shakespeare on Silent Film* is at once a meticulously documented and scholarly history of the development of silent cinematic adaptations as well as an amusing and stimulating account with a lively sense of personal interest. It covers the period from 1899 (the year in which the first recorded Shakespearian film, Herbert Beerbohm Tree's *King John* scene, was made) to 1929 when the first synchronized-sound adaptation, Sam Taylor's notorious *The Taming of the Shrew*, was released. Tree, the first established stage actor to be filmed in a Shakespearian role, is quoted as finding film acting something of an adventure. 'One throws oneself into the thing as one goes into a submarine. You take a dive – a plunge as it were – into the unknown, and calmly await the result.' Also quoted at some length is the report of a Chicago police lieutenant on the Vitagraph film of *Macbeth* (1908). It is perhaps unfortunate that the report was offered in the interests of censorship because it might otherwise stand unabashed as the first piece of intelligent criticism in the field of Shakespearian film. In selecting for special mention the film's visualizing of Duncan's murder, in which 'you see the dagger enter and come out and see the blood flow and the wound that's left', the censor was reacting as many reputable critics have since reacted to Polanski's film of 1969. Ball's historical survey is interesting, not least for its suggestion that cinema's search for respectability was a major impulse towards the endeavour to adapt Shakespeare's plays for the screen.[16]

In 1971 the first survey of sound-film adaptations, Roger Manvell's *Shakespeare and the Film*, was published. It is a most useful volume, which gives interesting background information on some twenty-five films made between 1929 and 1970, when Brook's film of *King Lear* was released. The text is accompanied by well-produced stills, and includes extensive verbatim interviews with Akira Kurosawa on his Japanese adaptation of *Macbeth*, *Throne of Blood* (1957), and with Laurence Olivier who, unlike MacLiammóir, believes 'there is much less difference between film acting and stage acting than people think – much less'.[17]

The complex cinematic achievement of Olivier's *Henry V* was first given just treatment in the slim, compact volume written by Harry Geduld and published in 1973. Among other issues, the analysis of the film contained in the book examines the major spatial transitions, the deliberate mixture of cinematic styles, the relation of the film to its source, its generic affinities, and the nature of Olivier's specific directorial intrusion.[18] This short but penetrating volume stands apart from others devoted to individual films in being an objective analysis by a writer not involved in the making of the film.

In 1977 two very different volumes on Shakespearian film were published, Jack Jorgens's *Shakespeare on Film* and the English translation of Grigori Kozintsev's *King Lear: The Space of Tragedy*. Jorgens attempts, with more academic and analytical emphasis, to do what Manvell had first done in 1971, though he limits his field to seventeen Shakespearian films, each considered in more detail than in Manvell's survey. In his introductory chapter, Jorgens notes a distinction in filming Shakespearian material which John Russell Taylor had emphasized in 1960 when he maintained that it is 'the film-maker's job' either 'to record Shakespeare' or 'to put the requirements for the film medium first'.[19] Jorgens advances the

---

[16] Robert Hamilton Ball, *Shakespeare on Silent Film* (London, 1968), pp. 42 and 82.

[17] Roger Manvell, *Shakespeare and the Film* (London, 1971), pp. 37–8.

[18] Harry Geduld, *Film Guide to 'Henry V'* (Bloomington, 1973).

[19] John Russell Taylor, 'Shakespeare in Film, Radio and Television', in *Shakespeare: A Celebration*, edited by T. J. B. Spencer (Harmondsworth, 1964), 97–113; p. 104.

distinction into three essential cinematic modes: the 'theatrical mode', which 'uses film as a transparent medium' to encapsulate theatrical space and performance, the 'realistic mode', which 'shifts the emphasis from the actors to actors-in-a-setting', and the 'filmic mode', which 'is the mode of the film poet whose works bear the same relationship to the surfaces of reality that poems do to ordinary conversation'.[20] Where Manvell's text concentrates on background information on the selected films, Jorgens illuminates, with considerable success, the capturing of each play's essence on film. A surprising omission is any extended discussion of Yutkevich's *Othello* (1955).

The volume of diary entries on the making of his *King Lear* (1970) by Grigori Kozintsev is perhaps the most engaging of all written works in the field of Shakespearian film, revealing, as it so clearly does, the creative mind of its author, his love and reverence for Shakespeare the dramatist, and the intelligence with which he strove to transpose *King Lear* to the medium of cinema. The book's material remains in its rough-hewn diary-note form, and of the twenty-four chapters five have titles which give interesting if cryptic indications of the creative processes of the author's mind. The theatrical influence on Kozintsev comes through very strongly, and his grasp of the theories of Meyerhold and Gordon Craig clearly enables him to relate the dramatic language of the theatre stage to that of the cinema screen. Kozintsev's perception of the devising of a spatial strategy as the essence of cinematic adaptation emerges clearly in his notes on the making of his own *Hamlet* (1964), when he writes that 'the time strata must seem to be laid bare in the visual development of Elsinore ... like the rings on a huge cross section of a tree' and suggests that the medieval, Renaissance and modern layers in the play, associated respectively with old King Hamlet, the prince and Claudius, should be visually articulated.[21]

As its title suggests, the central chapters in the *King Lear* diary are those which deal with the cinematic dramatization of the Lear universe. 'In choosing the location for a film', writes Kozintsev, 'you have to consider every possibility. You go on fantastic journeys ... We had begun by fighting the theatrical, trying to find means of showing reality on the screen – not copies of historical ornaments but the everyday life of history – we had cleared the décor, leaving only genuine material ... This was not a case of overcoming the conventionalities of the studio, but of uncovering nature's hidden significance.'[22]

More esoteric, partly because of its somewhat singular approach and partly because of its extended comparisons with particular paintings (reproductions of which are not given with the text), is Dale Silviria's book, *Laurence Olivier and the Art of Film Making*.[23] This is the most recently published volume devoted to Shakespearian film and though it tends to analyse moments in Olivier's Shakespeare films in theatrical terms, it eschews any sustained discussion of the relationship of film to theatre. It is divided into four lengthy chapters, the last three (dealing with the Shakespeare films) being the most rewarding, with close observation of moments like Gertrude's drinking of the poisoned wine, and detailed comparisons, like that of the Agincourt battle in *Henry V*, with other memorable battles on film.

Perhaps the major disappointment of the book is its attempt to give to Olivier's Shakespeare films a hermeticism incompatible with the forces which have made the films endure as classic adaptations. Neither its style nor its

---

[20] Jack J. Jorgens, *Shakespeare on Film* (Bloomington, 1977), p. 10.

[21] Grigori Kozintsev, *Shakespeare, Time and Conscience* (London, 1967), p. 265.

[22] Grigori Kozintsev, *King Lear: The Space of Tragedy* (London, 1977), p. 132.

[23] Dale Silviria, *Laurence Olivier and the Art of Film Making* (Rutherford, 1985).

underlying assumptions make it a particularly accessible volume for the reader whose interest in Shakespeare is essentially either theatrical or literary. The attempt to pay tribute to Olivier purely as a film director and to view the films as autonomous works of art is not entirely successful, but it does place the volume in a category different from its forerunners.

v

The growth of interest in Shakespearian film evidenced in the emergence of whole volumes devoted to the subject was matched by an increasing versatility in the critical material which began to appear in a widening variety of journals between the late 1950s and the early 1980s.

In 1965, John Blumenthal argued that Kurosawa's *Throne of Blood* (1957) 'is the only work, to my knowledge, that has ever completely succeeded in transforming a play of Shakespeare's into a film', and also drew attention to Kurosawa's use of the forest as a visual expression of the Macbeth mind.[24] Eight years later, John Gerlach, in a deliberate response to Blumenthal, maintained that in disrupting Shakespeare's balance between action and reflection, and in trapping Washizu (Kurosawa's Macbeth figure) within an ordained prophetic framework, Kurasawa 'betrayed the power of the play'.[25] The question of a film's fidelity to the play was taken up again in 1978 when Gorman Beauchamp revealed in convincing detail the extent to which Olivier's *Henry V* is a distortion of the play's view of war. While the play's only direct reflection of the battle is the inglorious encounter between Pistol and M. le Fer, Olivier depicts the battle as 'bloodless, beautiful and in technicolour'.[26]

For the most part, penetrating critical essays of Shakespearian film remain widely scattered. In 1972 Charles Eckert edited a volume which includes judiciously selected essays on important Shakespearian films made between 1935

and 1966.[27] A much more general volume on cinema published in 1974 includes a section on Shakespearian film, and reprints material by Peter Brook, who maintains that so far cinema has not found a language 'so as to reflect the mobility of thought that blank verse demands',[28] and by Frank Kermode who, in a reference to Brook's *King Lear* (1970), sees cinema as a medium ensuring that the greatness of the Shakespeare plays can only be retained if their dramatic potential is 'reborn in the imagination of another'.[29]

Two questions remain to be answered. Has the gradual accumulation of writing on Shakespearian film thrown up any clear statement about the difficulties of moving Shakespeare from the stage to the cinema screen? And can methods of enquiry employed in the relatively new specialism of film studies be brought fruitfully to bear upon cinematic adaptations of the plays?

J. L. Styan has written of the theatre audience's special situation, which allows it to make 'simultaneous perceptions' which are 'the basis for interpretation by an audience . . . To relate and synthesise what is perceived from moment to moment is to make drama meaningful.' The camera's selection, he continues, is really the director's controlling of our perception and our thinking. The loss of simultaneity is the loss of 'the very basis of tension felt in the audience'. Styan's essay, illustrated with judicious reference to the 'play'

---

[24] John Blumenthal, '*Macbeth into Throne of Blood*', in *Film Theory and Criticism*, 340–51; p. 340.

[25] John Gerlach, 'Shakespeare, Kurosawa and *Macbeth*: A Response to J. Blumenthal', *Literature/Film Quarterly*, 1 (1973), 352–9; p. 352.

[26] Gorman Beauchamp, 'Henry V: Myth, Movie, Play', *College Literature*, 5 (1978), 228–38; p. 232.

[27] Charles W. Eckert, ed., *Focus on Shakespearean Film* (Englewood Cliffs, NJ, 1972).

[28] Geoffrey Reeves, 'Finding Shakespeare on Film: From an Interview with Peter Brook', in *Film Theory and Criticism*, 316–21; p. 321.

[29] Frank Kermode, 'Shakespeare in the Movies', in *Film Theory and Criticism*, 322–332; p. 332.

scene in *Hamlet*, is the most lucid identification of an essentially theatrical experience which is inevitably lost in the cinema.[30] Paul Acker's 1980 article on Brook's *King Lear* (1970) is the clearest evidence that much can be learned about a director's treatment of a play on the screen simply by examining the use of rudimentary cinematic conventions. Acker maintains that in stretching conventions of dialogue and framing beyond their customary application, Brook deliberately creates a tension which enforces upon the cinema audience a new and disturbing encounter with Shakespeare's tragedy.[31] But it is perhaps well to remember that Brook's *King Lear* is unique among Shakespearian films in the expressions of disenchantment as well as the profound admiration it has elicited.

VI

Unlike cinema, radio and television adaptations had to await those technological developments which made it possible not only to capture performance but also to broadcast it to a domestic audience. Margaret Horsfield observes that 1923, the first full year of broadcasting by the BBC, included excerpts from Shakespeare's plays as initial drama broadcasts,[32] and John Drakakis claims that the first full production of a Shakespeare play to be broadcast was on 28 May of that year, though one's confidence in his pronouncement that the play was *Twelfth Night* is somewhat shaken by his subsequent assertion that the cast included 'Arthur Bourchier as Shylock'.[33]

Harley Granville-Barker had kinder words for radio than he had had for cinema as a medium for Shakespearian drama, when he complained that 'it is not, as is the cinema, demonstrably at cross-purposes with Shakespeare. The cinema adds much to the plays that is not wanted, and grossly offends in so doing. But the radio subtracts much.' Yet he suggests that the earlier plays, 'which abound in lyric beauty and lengths of fine rhetoric', are more suited to radio than the 'maturer work of the great tragedies', because in these later plays Shakespeare has made 'the situations in a play as effective – and more so – than the dialogue which reinforces them'.[34]

Val Gielgud, in his response to Barker, makes two significant observations. He draws attention to the distinction between a theatrical and a domestic radio audience, and asserts 'that of all effects in the BBC armoury, there is no effect in all broadcasting that can be so eloquent as ... silence ... '[35]

The matter of the suitability of certain plays for radio, raised by Granville-Barker, was apparently a vexed issue from the outset when it was decided that *The Comedy of Errors* 'would not work well on radio because of its reliance upon intractably visual material',[36] a conclusion which is strangely at odds with the choice of *Twelfth Night* as the first complete play to be broadcast. In a review of a BBC production of *Twelfth Night* during March 1947, Philip Hope-Wallace drew attention to '*Twelfth Night*'s inevitable shortcomings as a radio drama', and asks, 'Could any scenes belong more inalienably to the visual theatre than those where Malvolio is fooled or where Viola, shrinking in her disguise as a young gallant, must fight a duel with the epicene Sir Andrew? To say that we can well imagine the

[30] J. L. Styan, 'Sight and Space: The Perception of Shakespeare on Stage and Screen', in *Shakespeare, Pattern of Excelling Nature*, edited by Bevington and Halio (Newark, 1978), 198–209; pp. 205–6.

[31] Paul Acker, 'Conventions for Dialogue in Peter Brook's *King Lear*', *Literature/Film Quarterly*, 8 (1980), 219–24.

[32] Margaret Horsfield, 'All Tongues Speak of Him', *The Listener* (27 September 1979), p. 428.

[33] John Drakakis, 'The Essence That's Not Seen', in *Radio Drama*, edited by Peter Lewis (London, 1981), 111–33; p. 115.

[34] Granville-Barker, 'Alas Poor Will!', pp. 425–6.

[35] Val Gielgud, 'Much Ado About Nothing? II', *The Listener* (10 March 1936), p. 450.

[36] Drakakis, 'The Essence That's Not Seen', p. 116.

fact (and keep it in mind) that Viola is disguised as a boy surely rather begs the question.'[37]

The difficulty of relinquishing entirely the need for a visual dimension in Shakespeare's plays is discussed at some length by Drakakis, who points out that in order to make a listening audience aware of exits and entrances there must occasionally be a non-Shakespearian interpolation, and that various forms of narrator can be effective in setting a scene or in announcing a change in location, the difficulty with narration, however, being its tendency to point to rather than transcend the limitations of the medium.[38] Because of the factors governing their development, both radio and television have, from their inception as dramatic media, been far more conscious of their obligations to a heterogeneous domestic audience than has the cinema and its attracted public. Yet there has developed between radio and its audience a changed relationship. On the one hand, radio adaptations set out originally to reach a wide audience and to aspire towards the status of a truly 'national theatre'.[39] On the other, because radio drama is so wholly aural its adaptations of Shakespeare have appealed increasingly to a distinctly literary audience, and while it may be an exaggeration to claim, as John Russell Taylor does, that 'the new media best calculated to swallow Shakespeare whole without indigestion are the purely aural ones, radio and the gramophone record', there is no doubt that the power of radio as an adaptive medium lies in its capacity to become theatre of the mind.[40] Despite the advent and growing attraction of television, radio adaptations of the Shakespeare plays have retained their proportionate share of the radio audience since the peak, when the BBC's 1951 production of *Macbeth* claimed an estimated listening audience 'of more than five million', until 1979 when 'productions every year ... are estimated to draw between 100,000 and 200,000 listeners'.[41]

## VII

In December 1932, Filson Young suggested that the BBC prepare to broadcast the entire cycle of Shakespeare plays as an attempt to provide 'the highest kind of entertainment combined with high educative and cultural value'.[42] The project was not undertaken on radio, but the now famous BBC television cycle which commenced in 1978 and was completed in 1985 has constituted a dramatic achievement of the greatest signficance. While it has been generally agreed that the individual productions in the series vary in their effectiveness, the project has promoted the most intelligent critical debate about the accessibility of classical drama in our time and about the problems inherent in transposing Shakespeare from the theatre to the domestic television screen. The natural dynamic development of such a debate has been given added impetus by two other impulses. One is the policy of *The Times Literary Supplement* in approaching academics for reviews of the television productions. The other is the growth of interest, manifested in numerous academic journals, in the study of plays in performance.

Until the mid-1980s the predominant thrust in critical writing about televised Shakespeare was directed at performance, and television's achievement was measured by the extent to which it managed or failed to promote the sense of a *theatrical* experience. It has been during the last six years that there has emerged sustained, probing, and vigorous discussion about such issues as the nature of the television audience, the nature of the television idiom,

---

[37] Philip Hope-Wallace, 'Critic on the Hearth', *The Listener* (13 March, 1947), p. 395.

[38] Drakakis, 'The Essence That's Not Seen', p. 125.

[39] Val Gielgud, 'Much Ado About Nothing? II', p. 450.

[40] Russell Taylor, 'Shakespeare in Film, Radio and Television', p. 100.

[41] Horsfield, 'All Tongues Speak of Him', p. 428.

[42] Drakakis, 'The Essence That's Not Seen', p. 116.

and the relation of artistic to realistic presentation in that medium.

*Film Quarterly* gives prominence to 1953 as an important year for televised Shakespeare in the United States and, in drawing conclusions in his review of four television adaptations broadcast during that year, Marvin Rosenberg focuses necessary, though brief, attention to two aesthetic problems which beset the respective directors. He recognizes first the compulsively selective nature of television, suggesting that 'in the close relationship TV establishes, a brilliant clarity can often be given to the music of the verse as well as to its meaning', but complaining that where a character's action requires wide visual context, such as Lear's entrance with the dead Cordelia, the small screen can have the effect of making a moment 'ludicrous'. Secondly he discerns the danger of 'background clutter' as 'poison to complex drama'.[43] He also discusses the vexed problem of trying to contain a play's dramatic substance within a slotted playing time ordained by a television network, though he does not rail against the necessary dramatic truncation in such despondent tones as Flora Rheta Schreiber does.[44] Nor does he protest with such vehemence as Frank Wadsworth, who concludes his review of Peter Brook's Omnibus *King Lear* (1953) with an assertion that the director's 'cuts and revision of material' resulted in a production that 'was not only an abridgement of Shakespeare's great tragedy, but a perversion as well'.[45]

John Russell Taylor gives a useful chronological outline of the major adaptations screened by the BBC from 1938, the year of 'the first full-scale Shakespeare production on television ... the BBC's modern-dress *Julius Caesar*', until 1963, and he highlights two composite projects which treated groups of plays as 'coherent sequences with a continuity of theme'. The first, *An Age of Kings* (1960), combined the English history plays; the second was a unified arrangement of 'the classical history plays ... under the title, *The Spread of the Eagle*' (1963). Concluding that *An Age of Kings* 'probably offers the fairest ground to date for judging television's potential in adapting Shakespeare', he maintains that 'even if the effect of Shakespeare on the television screen is, even at its very best, considerably less than is a passable stage performance, television production still has a number of advantages', these being the increased audience size 'and the durability' of a taped production as a record.[46]

VIII

Despite fleeting judgements on television's particular strengths and weaknesses as a medium for Shakespeare in scattered critical response in the 1950s and 1960s, the overall tendency was to write about adaptations as second-division theatre, and to consider the likely viewers as people who, in all probability, would go to see Shakespeare in a theatre if they could. It is only in the early 1980s that there begins to surface a wholly new approach in the critical discussion of television as a potential medium for Shakespeare, not the least significant aspect of which is the fact that the discussion engaged the minds and pens of academics and directors whose opinions had not been prominent in this field before. Apart from the series of volumes published concurrently with the broadcasts by the BBC, which contain introductions by John Wilders and production comments by individual directors, there was published in 1981 an absorbing

---

[43] Marvin Rosenberg, 'Shakespeare on TV: An Optimistic Survey', *Film Quarterly*, 9 (1953), 116–74; esp. pp. 166, 169 and 172.

[44] Flora Rheta Schreiber, 'Television's *Hamlet*', *Film Quarterly*, 8 (1953), 150–6; p. 156.

[45] Frank W. Wadsworth, ' "Sound and Fury" – *King Lear* on Television', *Film Quarterly*, 8 (1953), 254–68; p. 267.

[46] Russell Taylor, 'Shakespeare in Film, Radio and Television', pp. 101–3.

interview with Jonathan Miller.[47] With characteristic precision and insight, Jonathan Miller gave the long awaited answer to those who in the early days of cinema had clashed over the issue of authentic locations. Of the setting for *Antony and Cleopatra* he says, 'What details you do introduce must remind the audience of the sixteenth-century imagination, not of the archaeologically accurate Egypt and Rome to which the play nominally, and only nominally refers.' And, in considering the question of television's realistic idiom, he concedes that 'as soon as you put Shakespeare on that box where . . . people are accustomed to seeing naturalistic events presented, you are more or less obliged to present the thing as naturally as you can'. The limits to realism have to be established, however, because the language of Shakespeare's dialogue 'comes from the past' and 'it doesn't come from the naturalistic past. It comes from the artistic past, with a style and an idiom of its own which can't be violated.'[48]

Also in 1981 appeared Sheldon Zitner's article, which deals with 'some consequent differences between the situations of the theatre and the television audiences'. In the shift from that 'ceremony, generating expectations, attitudes, behaviour' which Zitner calls 'the stage play ritual', to the relatively casual group before the television set which 'transforms all drama to closet drama, to plays for ones, if not for one', significant factors modify the relationship of the audience to the dramatic presentation. The inevitable 'de-ritualization' which television effects upon the viewing situation must in significant ways alter the nature of a Shakespeare play, though it will not necessarily reduce 'the depth of feeling one can expect from televised versions'. The alteration is rather one produced by the absence 'of the flywheel effect of live audience reaction'.[49] This point is stressed, too, by Stanley Wells in what is certainly the most comprehensive and carefully considered discussion of the BBC Shakespeare project.[50] When Wells originally delivered his lecture, in April 1982, the series was little more than half complete, but one of the conclusions which emerges (and which is endorsed in Wells's later comments in 1985),[51] is that 'a general problem . . . is the difficulty of achieving a really comic effect on television with Shakespeare's comic episodes . . . Concerted comic scenes seem far less likely to work well, and I suspect that this is because one important participant is invariably missing: the reacting audience.'[52]

IX

Perhaps the most penetrating questions which Wells raises concern the 'degree of permanence' which the productions can be expected to enjoy as a consequence of each being a part of 'a grand, perhaps grandiose scheme . . . Has there ever, in the whole history of television (such as it is), been a production of Shakespeare which has borne repetition more than a few years after it was made?' It is a question which must be asked, particularly in view of the enthusiasm with which the sale of the videotapes has been envisaged for educational purposes, and it can probably only be answered as Wells suggests. In time, the productions will, like cinematic adaptations, retain a value 'as period pieces, of interest as documents' of television history, 'or as records of performances' by particular actors or perhaps of productions by particular directors.[53]

Both Wells and John Wilders (the literary consultant on the BBC series) discuss impor-

[47] Tim Hallinan, 'Interview: Jonathan Miller on the Shakespeare Plays', *Shakespeare Quarterly*, 32 (1981), 134–45.
[48] Hallinan, 'Interview', pp. 136 and 134.
[49] Sheldon P. Zitner, 'Wooden O's in Plastic Boxes: Shakespeare and Television', *University of Toronto Quarterly*, 51, no. 1 (1981), 1–12; pp. 1–3.
[50] Stanley Wells, 'Television Shakespeare', *Shakespeare Quarterly*, 33 (1982), 261–77.
[51] Stanley Wells, 'The Canon in the Can', *Times Literary Supplement* (10 May 1985), p. 522.
[52] Wells, 'Television Shakespeare', p. 272.
[53] Wells, 'Television Shakespeare', p. 264.

tant areas of understandable conflict, such as text cutting and dramatic location. Both agree that despite the series' attempt to provide authoritative Shakespeare, some cutting, in the interests both of the medium and of its particular audience, is justified, Wilders maintaining that some dialogue could, to a modern domestic audience, be so mystifying that it might prompt 'the very people in whom we hoped to arouse enthusiasm for Shakespeare ... to switch off'. Of the various styles and locations used for setting the action of the plays, Wilders regards the attempt 'to make the productions look like paintings ... as the most satisfactory answer the directors have yet found',[54] though such a tendency, as Wells clearly perceives, carries with it the danger of inhibiting action and freezing camera movement.[55]

The question as to whether some plays are more suited to the medium than others is perhaps not so insistent in the light of a major project which sets out to televise the whole canon. However, H. R. Coursen in a review of the BBC–TV *Measure for Measure* writes that 'it seems almost to have been written for television. Not only is it melodramatic and episodic, but, as episodic narratives often are, it is a series of vivid one-on-one confrontations. Such scenes work very well within the limited space of (a) studio, and (b) a picture tube.'[56]

Jack Jorgens concluded his review of the first six plays of the BBC series with a sombre verdict:

As a culture we have apparently decided to invest in the convenience and cheapness of TV as compared to the relative expense of the theatrical film. In place of the clarity, subtle colours, and carefully controlled light values of the motion picture, we have decided to accept nervous, ill-defined images, comic-book colours, and blurred night scenes. In place of the fine image- and sound-making and meaningful technique of good films, we have decided to settle for mindless zooming and dollying, sloppy editing and compositions, crude music and sound effects.[57]

He is to some extent right. Cinema is beyond doubt a more versatile medium, affording a wider range of creative resources than television in the adaptation of drama which operates on so many and such complex levels as Shakespeare. And Wells, too, is largely right when he concludes, of the BBC series, that 'few of these productions would grip a reluctant viewer by the throat, nor do they comprehensively tackle – let alone solve – the problems of adapting Shakespeare to the television medium'.[58] But no one can regret the attempt to bring Shakespeare to vastly increased audiences, and no one can discount the value of the critical debate which televised Shakespeare has promoted.

The extent to which film and television do have the potential to re-establish Shakespeare as a popular dramatist and the degree to which various cultural authorities will continue to attempt the imposition of a traditional Shakespeare orthodoxy is the subject of an absorbing essay by Graham Holderness. It is certainly one of the most challenging issues to arise from the media's adoption of Shakespeare and it will assuredly continue to provoke dynamic debate. For when Holderness proposes that 'the most promising space for cultural intervention remains, despite systematic attacks on the system, that of education' he is locating the debate where it ought to be, but he is also commending it into the hands of what might be seen as the most legitimate cultural authority.[59]

---

[54] John Wilders, 'Shakespeare on the Small Screen', *Deutsche Shakespeare-Gesellschaft West Jahrbuch* (1982), 56–62; pp. 57 and 59.

[55] Wells, 'Television Shakespeare', p. 268.

[56] H. R. Coursen, 'Why *Measure for Measure*?', *Literature Film Quarterly*, 12 (1984), 65–9; p. 67.

[57] Jack J. Jorgens, 'The BBC–TV Shakespeare', *Shakespeare Quarterly*, 30 (1979), 411–15; p. 415.

[58] Wells, 'The Canon in the Can', p. 522.

[59] Graham Holderness, 'Radical Potentiality and Institutional Closure: Shakespeare in Film and Television', in *Political Shakespeare*, edited by Jonathan Dollimore and Alan Sinfield (Manchester, 1985), 182–201; p. 200.

# SHAKESPEARE ON THE SCREEN:
# A SELECTIVE FILMOGRAPHY

*compiled by* GRAHAM HOLDERNESS AND CHRISTOPHER

McCULLOUGH

This filmography is a reference list of 'complete', straightforward versions of Shakespeare's plays in film, television and videotape form.[1] It specifically *excludes* free adaptations;[2] film and television programmes containing insets of recorded performance;[3] educational films based on pedagogic manipulations of Shakespeare's texts;[4] material recording rehearsals, workshops, conversations with actors and directors;[5] and all operatic and balletic adaptations. There is much material in all these categories of great potential interest to researchers; this modest compilation should be regarded as the provision of basic information rather than the establishing of a comprehensive reference source.

We have listed international film, and English-language television versions, providing in each case title, date, format and medium;[6] production company (where known); producer (where applicable); director; designer (where known); and a selective cast list. Where the film is currently available for purchase or rental we have supplied the name and address of the distributor, and indicated its whereabouts if stored in an archive. It should be emphasized that specific enquiries to any distributor or archive should be undertaken to establish availability or accessibility of any individual item.

We wish to thank the following people and institutions for assistance in gathering information: the British Film Institute, the National Film Archive, the British Universities Film and Video Council, the BBC Data Enquiry Service, Thames Television, Granada Television; Russell Jackson, Kenneth Richards, Kenneth Rothwell, Carol Evans. We gratefully acknowledge the receipt of a research grant from University College, Swansea.

This filmography is dedicated to the memory of Orson Welles (1915–1985).

---

[1] 'Complete' may in itself be misleading if it is taken to mean an *uncut* version of the received texts. Many screenplays are cut drastically – Olivier's *Henry V* by approximately one-half. Early silent versions were usually 'condensed'. We interpret 'complete' as a full though possibly abridged version of the play's action.

[2] Except where, as in the case of Kurosawa's *Throne of Blood*, the film has been placed at the centre of critical debate on the screening of Shakespeare.

[3] E.g. a programme made for the Open University's Arts Foundation course contains filmed extracts from Peter Brook's production of *A Midsummer Night's Dream*: 'Interpreting a Dream' presented by Arnold Kettle, produced by Paul Kafno, BBC/Open University (1978).

[4] Many such programmes are made by the Open University. Those still extant are listed by the British Universities Film and Video Council.

[5] E.g. series of televised workshops such as John Barton's *Playing Shakespeare* (1984) and Michael Bogdanov's *Shakespeare Lives!* (1983).

[6] Modern conditions of production are rendering the distinction between 'film' and 'television programme' ambiguous: as their respective techniques become more akin, independent film and national television companies enter into closer relationship and films made for television (e.g. by Channel 4) are initially released in cinemas. We have attempted to preserve a distinction between a film made specifically for theatrical distribution and one made for television transmission.

## Abbreviations Used

| | |
|---|---|
| ARC | archive |
| AVP | Audio-Visual Productions |
| BD | Blue Dolphin |
| BFI | British Film Institute |
| BMX | Betamax |
| b/w | black and white |
| CEMIW | Columbia–EMI–Warner |
| col. | colour |
| Cont. | Contemporary Films |
| des. | designer |
| DHS | distribution, hire or sale |
| dir. | director |
| FL | foreign language |
| FSL | Folger Shakespeare Library |
| GTV | Granada Television |
| HF | Harris Films |
| IPC | IPC Video Ltd |
| NFA | National Film Archive |
| NT | National Theatre |
| NYT | National Youth Theatre |
| p.c. | production company |
| PD | Peter Darville Associates |
| pro. | producer |
| RFL | Rank Film Library |
| RSC | Royal Shakespeare Company |
| sil. | silent |
| SMT | Shakespeare Memorial Theatre |
| SUM | Sony-U-Matic |
| TTV | Thames Television |
| v.c. | videocassette |
| v.t. | videotape |
| VU | Vision Unlimited |

## Index of distributors and Archives

Audio-Visual Productions
Hocker Hill House
Chepstow, Gwent

Blue Dolphin
15–17 Old Compton Street
London W1

Columbia–EMI–Warner *see* Harris Films

Contemporary Films *see* Harris Films

Peter Darville Associates
280 Chartbridge Lane
Chesham, Bucks

Folger Shakespeare Library
Washington DC 20003, USA

Granada Television Ltd
Manchester 3

Harris Films Ltd
Glenbuck House
Glenbuck Road
Surbiton, Surrey

IPC Video Ltd
Surrey House
Throwley Way
Sutton, Surrey

National Film Archive
81 Dean Street
London W1

Rank Film Library *see* Harris Films

Shakespeare Centre
Henley Street
Stratford-upon-Avon, Warwickshire

Thames Television Ltd
306 Euston Road
London NW1

Vision Unlimited
Patrick House
West Quay Road
Poole, Dorset

## ALL'S WELL THAT ENDS WELL

*All's Well that Ends Well*
(GB, 1968): TV, b/w
p.c.: RSC/BBC
pro.: Ronald Travers
dir: Claude Watham (BBC), John Barton (RSC)
des.: Timothy O'Brien
Bertram, Ian Richardson; Helena, Lynn Farleigh; Countess, Catherine Lacey; King of France, Sebastian Shaw
ARC: BBC, v.t.

*All's Well that Ends Well*
(GB/USA, 1981): TV, col.

p.c.: BBC/Time-Life TV
pro.: Jonathan Miller
dir.: Elijah Moshinsky
des.: David Myerscough-Jones
Countess, Celia Johnson; Bertram, Ian Charleson; Helena, Angela Down; King of France, Donald Sinden
DHS: BBC, 16mm, v.c. VHS/BMX/SUM
ARC: BBC, v.t.

## ANTONY AND CLEOPATRA

*Antony and Cleopatra*
(USA, 1908): Film, b/w, sil.
pro./dir.: J. Stuart Blackton
Maurice Costello, Florence Lawrence, Paul Panzer, William V. Ranous, Earle Williams

*Antony and Cleopatra*
(USA, 1908): Film, b/w, sil.
p.c.: Vitagraph
dir.: Charles Kent
Cleopatra, Betty Kent; Antony, Charles Chapman

*Antony and Cleopatra*
(France, 1910): Film, b/w, sil.
p.c.: Pathe
pro./dir.: Henry Andreani
Cleopatra, Madeleine Roche; Le Messager, Stacia de Napierkowska

*Antony and Cleopatra*
(GB, 1951): Film, b/w
p.c.: Parthian Productions
Cleopatra, Pauline Letts; Antony, Robert Speaight

*The Spread of the Eagle*: Part 7, 'The Serpent', Part 8, 'The Alliance', Part 9 'The Monument'
(GB, 1963): TV, b/w
p.c.: BBC
pro./dir.: Peter Dews
des.: Clifford Hatts
Antony, Keith Michell; Cleopatra, Mary Morris; George Selway, David William
ARC: BBC, 35mm

*Antony and Cleopatra*
(Switzerland/Spain/GB, 1972): Film/col.
p.c.: Transac (Zurich)/Izaro (Madrid)/Folio Films (London)
pro.: Peter Snell
dir.: Charlton Heston
des.: Maurice Pelling
Antony, Charlton Heston; Cleopatra, Hildegard Neil; Enobarbus, Eric Porter; Octavius, John Castle

DHS: VU, v.c.
ARC: FSL (USA), 35 mm

*Antony and Cleopatra*
(GB, 1972): v.t./col.
p.c.: RSC/Audio-Visual Productions
pro.: Jon Scofield (AVP)
dir.: Trevor Nunn, Buzz Goodbody, Euan Smith (RSC)
des.: Christopher Morley, et al.
Antony, Richard Johnson; Cleopatra, Janet Suzman; Enobarbus, Patrick Stewart; Octavius, Corin Redgrave
DHS: AVP, v.c. VHS/BMX

*Antony and Cleopatra*
(GB/USA, 1981): TV/col.
p.c.: BBC/Time-Life TV
pro./dir.: Jonathan Miller
des.: Colin Lowrey
Antony, Colin Blakely; Cleopatra, Jane Lapotaire; Octavius, Ian Charleson; Enobarbus, Emrys James
DHS: BBC, 16mm, v.c. VHS/BMX/SUM

## AS YOU LIKE IT

*As You Like It*
(USA, 1908): Film, b/w, sil.
p.c.: Kalem Co.
pro./dir.: Kenean Buel

*As You Like It*
(USA, 1912): Film, b/w, sil.
pro.: J. Stuart Blackton
dir.: James Young
Orlando, Maurice Costello; Rosalind, Rose Coghlan; Celia, Rosemary Theby

*As You Like It*
(USA, 1912): Film, b/w, sil.
p.c.: Vitagraph
pro./dir.: Charles Kent
Rosalind, Rose Coghlan; Orlando, Maurice Costello

*As You Like It*
(GB, 1936): Film, b/w
p.c.: Inter-Allied
pro./dir.: Paul Czinner
des.: Lazare Meerson
Duke, Henry Ainley; Orlando, Laurence Olivier; Jaques, Leon Quartermaine; Rosalind, Elisabeth Bergner; Celia, Sophie Stewart
ARC: FSL (USA), 35mm; NFA, 16mm

*As You Like It*
(GB, 1946): TV, b/w
p.c.: BBC
pro.: Robert Atkins
dir.: Ian Atkins
Bankside Players

*As You Like It*
(GB, 1953): TV, b/w
p.c.: BBC
pro.: Campbell Logan
dir.: Peter Ebert
des.: Stephen Bundy
Duke, Walter Hudd; Rosalind, Margaret Leighton;
Orlando, Laurence Harvey; Celia, Isabel Dean

*As You Like It*
(GB, 1963): TV, b/w
p.c.: RSC/BBC
pro.: Richard Eyre (BBC)
dir.: Michael Elliott (RSC)
des.: Richard Negri (RSC), Andrée Welstead
(BBC)
Rosalind, Vanessa Redgrave; Orlando, David
Buck; Duke, Patrick Allen; Patrick Wymark
ARC: BBC, 35mm

*As You Like It*
(GB/USA, 1978): TV, col.
p.c.: BBC/Time-Life TV
pro.: Cedric Messina
dir.: Basil Coleman
des.: Don Taylor
Duke, Tony Church; Orlando, Brian Stirner; Rosalind, Helen Mirren; Celia, Angharad Rees
DHS: BBC, 16mm, v.c. VHS/BMX/SUM

## THE COMEDY OF ERRORS

*The Comedy of Errors*
(GB, 1954): TV, b/w
p.c.: BBC
pro./dir.: Lionel Harris
des.: James Bould
Solinus, Gerald Cross; Antipholus of Ephesus,
David Peel; Antipholus of Syracuse, Paul Hansard;
Adriana, Joan Plowright; Luciana, Jane Wenham

*The Comedy of Errors*
(GB, 1964): TV, b/w
p.c.: BBC
pro.: Peter Luke
dir.: Clifford Williams (RSC), Peter Duguid (BBC)
Antipholus of Ephesus, Ian Richardson; Antipholus

of Syracuse, Alec McCowen; Solinus, Donald
Sinden; Aegeon, John Welsh; Adriana, Susan Engel;
Luciana, Tina Packer
ARC: BBC, 35mm

*The Comedy of Errors*
(FDR, 1964) Film, b/w, FL
p.c.: Bavaria Atelier GmbH
dir.: Hans Dieter Schwarze
des.: Walter Blokesch
Erik Schumann, Clauss Biederstaedt, Ruth Kahler,
Irene Marhold, Klaus Schwarzkopf, Manfred
Lichtenfeld

*The Comedy of Errors*
(GB, 1976): v.t., col.
p.c.: RSC/Audio-Visual Productions
pro.: Philip Casson (AVP)
dir.: Trevor Nunn (RSC)
des.: John Napier
Adriana, Judi Dench; Luciana, Francesca Annis;
Solinus, Brian Coburn; Antipholus of Syracuse,
Roger Rees; Antipholus of Ephesus, Mike Gwilym
DHS: AVP, v.c. VHS/BMX

*The Comedy of Errors*
(GB/USA, 1984): TV, col.
p.c.: BBC/Time-Life TV
pro.: Shaun Sutton
dir.: James Cellan Jones
des.: Don Homfray
Aegeon, Cyril Cusack; Solinus, Charles Gray; Antipholus, Michael Kitchen; Dromio, Roger Daltrey;
Adriana, Suzanne Bertish; Luciana, Joanne Pearce
DHS: BBC, 16mm, v.c. VHS/BMX/SUM

## CORIOLANUS

*The Spread of the Eagle*: Part 1, 'The Hero', Part 2,
'The Voices', Part 3, 'The Outcast'
(GB, 1963): TV, b/w
p.c.: BBC
pro./dir.: Peter Dews
des.: Clifford Hatts
Coriolanus, Robert Hardy; Volumnia, Beatrix
Lehmann; Menenius, Roland Culver
ARC: BBC, 35mm

*Coriolanus*
(GB, 1965): TV, b/w
p.c.: NYT/BBC
pro.: Bernard Hepton
dir.: Roger Jenkins
des.: Christopher Lawrence
Coriolanus, John Nightingale; Volumnia, Mary

Grimes; Cominius, Timothy Block; Menenius, David Stockton

*Coriolanus*
(GB/USA, 1984): TV, col.
p.c.: BBC/Time-Life TV
pro.: Shaun Sutton
dir.: Elijah Moshinsky
des.: Dick Coles
Coriolanus, Alan Howard; Volumnia, Irene Worth; Menenius, Joss Ackland
DHS: BBC, v.c. VHS

## CYMBELINE

*Cymbeline*
(USA, 1913): Film, b/w, sil.
p.c.: Thanhouser
pro./dir.: Frederic Sullivan
Imogen, Florence La Badie; Leonatus, James Cruze; William Russell, William Garwood, Jean Darnell

*Cymbeline*
(Germany, 1925): Film, b/w, sil.
dir.: Ludwig Berger

*Cymbeline*
(GB/USA, 1984): TV, col.
p.c.: BBC/Time-Life TV
pro.: Shaun Sutton
dir.: Elijah Moshinsky
des.: Barbara Gosnold
Cymbeline, Richard Johnson; Queen, Claire Bloom; Imogen, Helen Mirren; Posthumus, Michael Pennington; Iachimo, Robert Lindsay
DHS: BBC, 16mm, v.c. VHS/BMX/SUM

## HAMLET

*Hamlet*
(France, 1900): Film, b/w, sil.
pro./dir.: Clement Maurice
Hamlet, Sarah Bernhardt; Laertes, Pierre Magnier

*Amleto*
(Italy, 1908): Film, b/w, sil.
p.c.: Cines
pro.: Guiseppe de Liguoro

*Amleto*
(Italy, 1908): Film, b/w, sil.
p.c.: Milano
dir.: Luca Comerio
ARC: NFA, 35mm (incomplete; German titles)

*Hamlet*
(France, 1909): Film, b/w, sil.
p.c.: Lux
Hamlet, Mounet-Sully

*Amleto*
(Italy, 1910): Film, b/w, sil.
p.c.: Cines
pro./dir.: Mario Caserini
Hamlet, Dante Capelli; Maria Gasperini

*Hamlet*
(Denmark, 1910): Film, b/w, sil.
p.c.: Nordisk
pro./dir.: August Blom
Hamlet, Alwin Neusz; Ophelia, Emilie Sannom; Claudius, Aage Hertel; Gertrude, Ella La Cour

*Hamlet*
(GB, 1910): Film, b/w, sil.
pro./dir.: William G. Barker
Hamlet, Charles Raymond

*Hamlet*
(France, 1910): Film, b/w, sil.
p.c.: Eclipse Film
pro./dir.: Henri Desfontaines
Hamlet, Jaques Gretillat; Gertrude, Colanna Romano

*Hamlet*
(GB, 1913): Film, b/w, sil.
p.c.: Hepworth Mfg. Co. (for British Gaumont)
pro./dir.: E. Hay Plumb
Hamlet, Sir Johnston Forbes-Robertson; Ophelia, Gertrude Elliott; Claudius, Adeline Bourne; Horatio, S. A. Cookson
ARC: NFA, 35mm

*Hamlet*
(Italy, 1914): Film, b/w, sil.
pro./dir.: Arturo Ambrosio
Hamlet, A. Hamilton Revelle

*Hamlet*
(Italy, 1917): Film, b/w, sil.
p.c.: Cines
pro./dir.: Eleuterio Rodolfi
Hamlet, Ruggoro Ruggeri; Ophelia, Helena Makowska; Claudius, Martelli; Gertrude, Mercedes Brignone

*Hamlet*
(Germany, 1920): Film, b/w, sil.

p.c.: Art Film
dir.: Sven Gade
Hamlet, Asta Nielsen; Ophelia, Lilly Jacobsson;
Claudius, Eduard von Winterstein; Gertrude,
Mathilde Brandt
ARC: NFA, 35mm

*Khoon Ka Khoon*
(India, 1935): Film, b/w, FL
p.c.: Minerva Movietone
pro./dir.: Sohrab Modi
Hamlet, Sohrab Modi

*Hamlet*
(GB, 1947): TV, b/w
pro.: George More O'Ferrall
dir.: Basil Adams

*Hamlet*
(GB, 1948): Film, b/w
p.c.: Two Cities Film/Olivier/Rank
pro./dir.: Laurence Olivier
Hamlet, Laurence Olivier; Claudius, Basil Sydney;
Gertrude, Eileen Herlie; Ophelia, Jean Simmons;
Horatio, Norman Wooland
DHS: RFL, 16 mm, v.c.
ARC: NFA, 35 mm

*Hamlet*
(India, 1954): Film, b/w, FL
p.c.: Hindustan Chitra
pro./dir.: Kishore Sahu
Kishore Sahu; Mala Sinha; Venus Banerji

*Moi, Hamlet*
(Italy, 1952): Film, FL
pro./dir.: Giorgio C. Simonelli
Erminio Macario, Rossana Podesta, Franca Marzi,
Luigi Parese, Adriano Rimoldi, Elena Giusti

*Hamlet*
(FDR, 1960): Film, b/w, FL, dubbed
p.c.: Bavaria Atelier GmbH
pro.: Hans Gottschalk
dir.: Franz Peter Wirth
Hamlet, Maximilian Schell; Claudius, Hans Caninenberg; Gertrude, Wand Roth; Ophelia, Dunja
Movar

*Hamlet*
(USSR, 1964): Film, b/w, FL
p.c.: Lenfilm
dir.: Grigori Kozintsev
des.: Evgeni Enei, G. Kropachev
Hamlet, Innokenti Smoktounovski; Ophelia,

Anastasia Vertinskaia; Claudius, Mikhail Nazva-
nov; Gertrude, Elza Radzin-Szolkonis; Polonius,
Iouri Tolubeyev
DHS: HF, 16mm
ARC: NFA, 35 mm (English subtitles)

*Hamlet at Elsinore*
(GB, 1964): TV, b/w
p.c.: BBC/Danmarks Radio
pro.: Peter Luke
dir.: Philip Saville
des.: Paul Arnt Thomsen
Hamlet, Christopher Plummer; Claudius, Robert
Shaw; Ophelia, Jo Maxwell Muller; Horatio,
Michael Caine
ARC: BBC, 35mm

*Hamile*
(Ghana, 1964): Film
p.c.: Ghana Film Industry Co.
dir.: Terry Bishop
Joe Akonor, Kofi Middetan-Mends, Ernest Abbe-
quaye, Frances Sey, Mary Yirenkyi

*Hamlet*
(USA, 1964): Film, b/w
p.c.: Electronovision
pro.: William Sargent Jr., Alfred W. Crown, John
Heyman
dir.: John Gielgud (Stage), Bill Colleran (Electronovision)
des.: Ben Edwards
Hamlet, Richard Burton; Ophelia, Linda March;
Claudius, Alfred Drake; Gertrude, Eileen Herlie
ARC: NFA, 35mm

*Hamlet*
(GB, 1969): Film, col.
p.c.: Woodfall Production Co.
pro.: Neil Hartley
dir.: Tony Richardson
des.: Jocelyn Herbert
Hamlet, Nicol Williamson; Claudius, Anthony
Hopkins; Gertrude, Judy Parfitt; Ophelia, Marianne Faithfull
DHS: HF
ARC: FSL (USA), 35mm; NFA, 35mm

*Hamlet*
(USA, 1970): TV, col.
p.c.: Hallmark Hall of Fame, NBC
pro.: George Le Maire
dir.: Peter Wood
Hamlet, Richard Chamberlain; Ophelia, Ciaran
Madden; Gertrude, Margaret Leighton; Claudius,

Richard Johnson; Polonius, Michael Redgrave; Ghost, John Gielgud

*Heranca*
(Brazil, 1970): Film, FL
p.c.: Longfilm Produtora Cinematografica
David Cardoso, Barbara Fazio, Rosalva Cacador, America Taricano, Deoclides Gouveia

*Hamlet*
(GB/USA, 1972): TV, col.
p.c.: Prospect Theatre Co./BBC
pro.: Eddie Kulukundis
dir.: David Giles
Hamlet, Ian McKellen; Faith Brook, John Woodvine, Susan Fleetwood
ARC: BBC, v.t.

*Hamlet*
(Canada, 1973): Film, col.
p.c.: Toronto Theatre Co./Crawley Films
dir.: René Bonnière

*Hamlet*
(GB, 1976): Film, col.
p.c.: Essential Cinema
dir.: Celestino Coronada
Hamlet and Laertes, Anthony and David Meyer; Ophelia and Gertrude, Helen Mirren; Polonius, Quentin Crisp

*Hamlet*
(GB/USA, 1980): TV, col.
p.c.: BBC/Time-Life TV
pro.: Cedric Messina
dir.: Rodney Bennett
des.: Don Homfray
Hamlet, Derek Jacobi; Gertrude, Claire Bloom; Claudius, Patrick Stewart; Ophelia, Lalla Ward; Polonius, Eric Porter
DHS: BBC, 16mm, v.c. VHS
ARC: BBC, v.c.

## HENRY IV, PART ONE

*An Age of Kings*: Part 3, 'Rebellion from the North', Part 4, 'The Road to Shrewsbury'
(GB, 1960): TV, b/w
p.c.: BBC/TV
pro.: Peter Dews
dir.: Michael Hayes
des.: Stanley Morris
Henry IV, Tom Fleming; Prince, Robert Hardy; Hotspur, Sean Connery; Falstaff, Frank Pettingell
ARC: BBC, 16mm (two parts)

*Falstaff (Chimes at Midnight)*
(Spain/Switzerland, 1965): Film, b/w
p.c.: International Films Espagnol Alpine
pro.: Emiliano Piedra, Angel Escoloano
dir.: Orson Welles
des.: Jose Antonio de la Guerra, Mariana Erdorza
Falstaff, Orson Welles; Hal, Keith Baxter; Henry IV, John Gielgud; Mistress Quickly, Margaret Rutherford; Doll Tearsheet, Jeanne Moreau
DHS: HF
ARC: FSL (USA), 35mm

*Henry IV, Part One*
(GB/USA, 1979); TV, col.
p.c.: BBC/Time-Life TV
pro.: Cedric Messina
dir.: David Giles
des.: Don Homfray
Henry IV, Jon Finch; Prince, David Gwillim; Falstaff, Anthony Quayle
DHS: BBC, 16mm, v.c. VHS
ARC: BBC, v.c.

## HENRY IV, PART TWO

*An Age of Kings*: Part 5, 'The New Conspiracy', Part 6, 'Uneasy Lies the Head'
(GB, 1960): TV, b/w
p.c.: BBC/TV
pro.: Peter Dews
dir.: Michael Hayes
des.: Stanley Morris
Henry IV, Tom Fleming; Prince, Robert Hardy; Falstaff, Frank Pettingell; Hotspur, Sean Connery
ARC: BBC, 16mm (two parts)

*Henry IV, Part Two*
(GB/USA, 1979): TV, col.
p.c.: BBC/Time-Life TV
pro.: Cedric Messina
dir.: David Giles
des.: Don Homfray
Henry IV, Jon Finch; Prince, David Gwillim; Falstaff, Anthony Quayle
DHS: BBC, 16mm, v.c. VHS/BMX/SUM

## HENRY V

*Henry V*
(GB, 1944): Film, col.
p.c.: Two Cities Films
pro./dir.: Laurence Olivier
des.: Paul Sheriff, Roger Furse
Henry V, Laurence Olivier; Chorus, Leslie Banks;

Princess Katherine, Renée Asherson; Pistol, Robert
Newton
DHS: RFL, 16mm, vc.

*Henry V*
(GB, 1951): TV, b/w
p.c.: BBC
pro./dir.: Royston Morley, Leonard Brett
des.: Barry Learoyd
Henry V, Clement McCallin; French King,
Norman Claridge; Pistol, Willoughby Gray;
Princess Katherine, Varvara Pitöeff

*Henry V*
(GB, 1953): TV, b/w
p.c.: BBC
pro./dir.: Peter Watts
Henry V, John Clements; Princess Katherine, Kay
Hammond; French King, John Garside; Pistol, John
Laurie

*The Life of Henry V*
(GB, 1957): TV, b/w
p.c.: BBC
pro./dir.: Peter Dews
des.: Guy Sheppard
Henry V, John Neville; Fluellen, Dudley Jones;
Pistol, Geoffrey Bayldon; Bardolph, Michael Bates
ARC: BBC, 35mm

*An Age of Kings*: Part 7, 'Signs of War', Part 8,
'The Band of Brothers'
(GB, 1960): TV, b/w
p.c.: BBC
pro.: Peter Dews
dir.: Michael Hayes
des.: Stanley Morris
Henry V, Robert Hardy; Chorus, William Squire;
Bardolph, Gordon Gostelow; Princess Katherine,
Judi Dench
ARC: BBC, 16mm (two parts)

*Henry V*
(Canada, 1966): TV, col.
p.c.: CFTO/TV, Toronto (for CTV)
dir.: Michael Langham (stage), Lorne Freed (TV)
des.: Desmond Heeley
Henry V, Douglas Rain; William Hutt, Bernard
Behrens, Tony Van Bridge, Jean Gascon

*Henry V*
(GB/USA, 1979): TV, col.
p.c.: BBC/Time-Life TV
pro.: Cedric Messina
dir.: David Giles

des.: Don Homfray
Henry V, David Gwillim; Pistol, Bryan Pringle;
Katherine, Jocelyne Boisseau; Chorus, Alec
McCowen
DHS: BBC, 16mm, v.c. VHS/BMX/SUM

## HENRY VI, PART ONE

*An Age of Kings*: Part 9, 'The Red Rose and the
White'
(GB, 1960): TV, b/w
p.c.: BBC
pro.: Peter Dews
dir.: Michael Hayes
des.: Stanley Morris
Henry VI, Terry Scully; Margaret, Mary Morris;
Bedford, Patrick Garland; Gloucester, John
Ringham; Joan la Pucelle, Eileen Atkins; Charles
the Dauphin, Jerome Willis
ARC: BBC, 16mm

*The Wars of the Roses*: Part 1, 'Henry VI'
(GB, 1965): TV, b/w
p.c.: RSC/BBC
pro.: Michael Barry (BBC)
dir.: Peter Hall, John Barton (RSC), Robin
Midgley, Michael Hayes (BBC)
des.: John Bury
Henry VI, David Warner; Margaret, Peggy Ashcroft; Joan, Janet Suzman; Talbot, Clive Morton;
Winchester, Nicholas Selby
ARC: BBC, 35mm

*Henry VI, Part One*
(GB/USA, 1983): TV, col.
p.c.: BBC/Time-Life TV
pro.: Jonathan Miller
dir.: Jane Howell
des.: Oliver Bayldon
Henry VI, Peter Benson; Talbot, Trevor Peacock;
Joan, Brenda Blethyn; Margaret, Julia Foster; Gloucester, David Burke
DHS: BBC, 16mm, v.c. VHS/BMX/SUM

## HENRY VI, PART TWO

*An Age of Kings*: Part 10 'The Fall of a Protector',
Part 11, 'The Rabble from Kent'
(GB, 1960): TV, b/w
p.c.: BBC
pro.: Peter Dews
dir.: Michael Hayes
des.: Stanley Morris
Henry VI, Terry Scully; Margaret, Mary Morris;

Gloucester, John Ringham; York, Jack May; Eleanor, Duchess of Gloucester, Nancie Jackson; Cade, Esmond Knight
ARC: BBC, 16mm

*The Wars of the Roses*: Part 1, 'Henry VI', Part 2, 'Edward IV'
(GB, 1964): TV, b/w
p.c.: RSC/BBC
pro.: Michael Barry (BBC)
dir.: Peter Hall, John Barton (RSC), Robin Midgley, Michael Hayes (BBC)
des.: John Bury
Henry VI, David Warner; Margaret, Peggy Ashcroft; York, Donald Sinden; Gloucester, Ian Holm; Cade, Roy Dotrice
ARC: BBC, 35mm

*Henry VI, Part Two*
(GB/USA, 1983): TV, col.
p.c.: BBC/Time-Life TV
pro.: Jonathan Miller
dir.: Jane Howell
des.: Oliver Bayldon
Henry VI, Peter Benson; Gloucester, David Burke; York, Bernard Hill; Cade, Trevor Peacock
DHS: BBC, 16mm, v.c. VHS/BMX/SUM

### HENRY VI, PART THREE

*An Age of Kings*: Part 12, 'The Morning's War', Part 13, 'The Sun in Splendour'
(GB, 1960): TV, b/w
p.c.: BBC
pro.: Peter Dews
dir.: Michael Hayes
des.: Stanley Morris
Henry VI, Terry Scully; York, Jack May; Clifford, Jerome Willis; Edward, Julian Glover; Clarence, Patrick Garland; Gloucester, Paul Daneman
ARC: BBC, 16mm

*The Wars of the Roses*: Part 2, 'Edward IV', Part 3, 'Richard III'
(GB, 1964): TV, b/w
p.c.: RSC/BBC
pro.: Michael Barry (BBC)
dir.: Peter Hall, John Barton (RSC), Robin Midgley, Michael Hayes (BBC)
des.: John Bury
Henry VI, David Warner; Margaret, Peggy Ashcroft; Clifford, John Corvin; York, Donald Sinden; Edward IV, Roy Dotrice; Clarence, Charles Kay; Gloucester, Ian Holm
ARC: BBC, 16mm

*Henry VI, Part Three*
(GB/USA, 1983): TV, col.
p.c.: BBC/Time-Life TV
pro.: Shaun Sutton
dir.: Jane Howell
des.: Oliver Bayldon
Henry VI, Peter Benson; Edward IV, Brian Protheroe; Margaret, Julia Foster; York, Bernard Hill
DHS: BBC, 16mm, v.c. VHS/BMX/SUM

### HENRY VIII

*Henry VIII*
(GB, 1911): Film, b/w, sil.
p.c.: Barker Motion Photography
dir.: William G. B. Barker
Henry VIII, Arthur Bourchier; Wolsey, Herbert Beerbohm Tree; Katherine, Violet Vanbrugh; Buckingham, Henry Ainley

*Henry VIII*
(GB/USA, 1979): TV, col.
p.c.: BBC/Time-Life TV
pro.: Cedric Messina
dir.: Kevin Billington
des.: Alun Hughes
Henry VIII, John Stride; Wolsey, Timothy West; Katharine, Claire Bloom
DHS: BBC, 16mm, v.c. VHS/BMX/SUM
ARC: BBC, v.t.

### JULIUS CAESAR

*Julius Caesar*
(USA, 1908): Film, b/w, sil.
p.c.: Vitagraph
pro./dir.: William V. Ranous
Julius Caesar, William V. Ranous

*Julius Caesar*
(USA, 1908): Film, b/w (tinted), sil.
p.c.: Vitagraph
pro./dir.: J. Stuart Blackton
Julius Caesar, Charles Kent; Mark Antony, William V. Ranous; Florence Lawrence, Paul Panzer, Earle Williams

*Julius Caesar*
(GB, 1911): Film, b/w, sil.
p.c.: Co-operative Cinematograph
dir.: F. R. Benson
Julius Caesar, Guy Rathbone; Mark Antony, F. R. Benson; Brutus, Murray Carrington; Portia, Mrs Benson; Cassius, Eric Maxim

*Giulio Cesare*
(Italy, 1914): Film, b/w, sil.
p.c.: Cines
pro./dir.: Enrico Guazzoni
Amleto Novelli, Gianna Terribili-Gonzales,
Ignazio Lupi, Lea Orlandini, Bruto Castellini

*Julius Caesar*
(GB, 1938): TV, b/w
p.c.: BBC
pro./dir.: Dallas Bower
des.: Malcolm Baker-Smith
Julius Caesar, Ernest Milton; Mark Antony, D. A.
Clarke-Smith; Brutus, Sebastian Shaw; Cassius,
Anthony Ireland

*Julius Caesar*
(GB, 1945): Film, b/w
p.c.: Theatrecraft
dir.: Henry Cass
ARC: NFA, 35mm

*Julius Caesar*
(USA, 1949): Film, b/w
p.c.: Avon Productions
pro.: Robert Keigher, David Bradley
dir.: David Bradley
Julius Caesar, Harold Tasker; Brutus, David
Bradley; Cassius, Grosvenor Glenn; Mark Antony,
Charlton Heston; Portia, Molly Darr
ARC: FSL (USA), 16mm

*Julius Caesar*
(GB, 1951): Film, b/w
p.c.: Parthian Productions
Robert Speaight, Cecil Trouncer

*Julius Caesar*
(GB, 1951): TV, b/w
p.c.: BBC
pro.: Stephen Harrison
dir.: Leonard Brett
des.: Barry Learoyd
Julius Caesar, Walter Hudd; Octavius, Richard
Bebb; Mark Antony, Anthony Hawtrey; Brutus,
Patrick Barr; Portia, Margaret Diamond

*Julius Caesar*
(USA, 1953): Film, b/w
p.c.: MGM
pro.: John Houseman
dir.: Joseph Mankiewicz
des.: Cedric Gibbons, Edward Carfagno
Julius Caesar, Louis Calhern; Mark Antony,

Marlon Brando; Brutus, James Mason; Cassius,
John Gielgud
DHS: HF, 16mm
ARC: FSL (USA), 35mm

*Julius Caesar*
(GB, 1959): TV, b/w
p.c.: BBC
pro./dir.: Stuart Burge
des.: Barry Learoyd
Eric Porter, Michael Gough, William Sylvester
ARC: BBC, 35mm

*Julius Caesar*
(GB, 1960): TV, b/w
p.c.: BBC
pro./dir.: Richard Eyre
des.: Austen Spriggs
Ralph Michael, James Maxwell, Michael Goodliffe,
Ellen McIntosh, John Laurie, Tim Seely
ARC: BBC, 16mm (Parts 1–3), 35mm (Part 4)

*The Spread of the Eagle*: Part 4, 'The Colossus',
Part 5, 'The Fifteenth', Part 6, 'The Revenge'
(GB, 1963): TV, b/w
p.c.: BBC
pro./dir.: Peter Dews
des.: Clifford Hatts
Caesar, Barry Jones; Mark Antony, Keith Michell;
Cassius, Peter Cushing; Paul Eddington, David
William
ARC: BBC, 35mm

*Julius Caesar*
(GB, 1964): TV, b/w
p.c.: BBC
pro.: John Vernon (BBC)
dir.: Michael Croft (NYT)
des.: Christopher Lawrence
National Youth Theatre
ARC: BBC, 16mm

*Julius Caesar*
(GB, 1969): TV, b/w
p.c.: BBC
pro.: Cedric Messina
dir.: Alan Bridges
des.: Spencer Chapman
Robert Stephens, Frank Finlay, Maurice Denham,
Edward Woodward
ARC: BBC, 16mm, v.c.

*Julius Caesar*
(GB, 1969): Film, col.
p.c.: Commonwealth United

pro.: Peter Snell
dir.: Stuart Burge
des.: Julia Trevelyan Oman
Mark Antony, Charlton Heston; Brutus, Jason Robards; Julius Caesar, John Gielgud
DHS: HF, 16mm
ARC: FSL (USA), 35mm

*Julius Caesar*
(GB/USA, 1979): TV, col.
p.c.: BBC/Time-Life TV
pro.: Cedric Messina
dir.: Herbert Wise
des.: Tony Abbott
Caesar, Charles Gray; Brutus, Richard Pasco; Calphurnia, Elizabeth Spriggs; Antony, Keith Michell
DHS: BBC, 16mm, v.c. VHS/BMX/SUM

## KING JOHN

*King John*
(GB, 1899): Film, b/w, sil.
p.c.: His Majesty's Theatre, London
dir.: Herbert Beerbohm Tree
King John, Herbert Beerbohm Tree

*King John*
(GB, 1951): TV, b/w
p.c.: BBC
pro./dir.: Stephen Harrison
des.: Barry Learoyd
King John, Donald Wolfit; Queen Elinor, Una Venning; Prince Arthur, Michael Croudson; Faulconbridge, John Southworth

*King John*
(GB/USA, 1984): TV, col.
p.c.: BBC/Time-Life TV
pro.: Shaun Sutton
dir.: David Giles
des.: Chris Pemsel
King John, Leonard Rossiter; Constance, Claire Bloom; Hubert, John Thaw; Blanch, Janet Maw
DHS: BBC, 16mm, v.c. VHS
ARC: BBC, v.c.

## KING LEAR

*King Lear*
(USA, 1909): Film, b/w, sil.
p.c.: Vitagraph
pro./dir.: William V. Ranous
King Lear, William V. Ranous; Thomas H. Ince

*King Lear*
(USA, 1909): Film, b/w, sil.
pro./dir.: J. Stuart Blackton
King Lear, Maurice Costello; Julia Arthur, Edith Storey, Mary Fuller

*Re Lear*
(Italy, 1910): Film, b/w, sil.
p.c.: Milano
pro./dir.: Guiseppe De Liguoro
King Lear, Guiseppe De Liguoro; Arturo Padovani

*Re Lear*
(Italy, 1910): Film, b/w, sil.
p.c.: Film d'Arte Italiana
dir.: Gerolamo Lo Savio
King Lear, Ermete Novelli; Cordelia, Francesca Bertini; Giannina Chiantoni

*King Lear*
(USA, 1916): Film, b/w, sil.
p.c.: Thanhouser/Pathe
dir.: Ernest Warde
King Lear, Frederick Warde; Cordelia, Lorraine Huling; King of France, Boyd Marshall; Edgar, Ernest Warde

*King Lear*
(GB, 1948): TV, b/w
p.c.: BBC
pro./dir.: Royston Morley

*King Lear*
(USA, 1953): TV, b/w
p.c.: CBS/Omnibus
pro.: Fred Rickey
dir.: Andrew McCullough/Peter Brook
des.: Georges Wakhevitch
King Lear, Orson Welles; Cordelia, Natasha Parry; Albany, Arnold Moss; Goneril, Beatrice Straight
ARC: FSL (USA)

*King Lear*
(GB/Denmark, 1969): Film, b/w
p.c.: Filmways (London), Athena/Laterna Films (Copenhagen)
pro.: Michael Birkett
dir.: Peter Brook
des.: Georges Wakhevitch
King Lear, Paul Scofield; Goneril, Irene Worth; Regan, Susan Engel; Cordelia, Anelise Gabold; Gloucester, Alan Webb
DHS: HF, 16mm
ARC: FSL (USA), 35mm

*Korol Lir*
(USSR, 1970): Film, b/w, FL
p.c.: Lenfilm
dir.: Grigori Kozintsev
des.: Evgeni Enei
King Lear, Yuri Yarvet; Goneril, Elza Radzins; Regan, Galina Volchek; Cordelia, Valentina Shendrikova; Edmund, Regimanias Adamaitis; Fool, Ofar Dal
DHS: Cont. 16/35mm
ARC: FSL (USA), 35mm

*King Lear*
(GB, 1975): TV, col.
p.c.: BBC
pro./dir.: Jonathan Miller
des.: Vic Symonds
King Lear, Michael Hordern; Cordelia, Angela Down; Fool, Frank Middlemass; Goneril, Sarah Badel; Regan, Penelope Wilton; Edgar, Ronald Pickup; Edmund, Michael Jayston
ARC: BBC, v.t.

*King Lear*
(GB, 1976): Film, col.
p.c.: Triple Action Theatre/BFI
dir.: Steve Rumbelow
Chris Aurache, Genzig Saner, Monica Buford, Helena Paul
ARC: NFA

*King Lear*
(GB/USA, 1982): TV, col.
p.c.: BBC/Time-Life TV
pro.: Shaun Sutton
dir.: Jonathan Miller
des.: Colin Lowrey
King Lear, Michael Hordern; Goneril, Gillian Barge; Regan, Penelope Wilton; Cordelia, Brenda Blethyn; Fool, Frank Middlemass
DHS: BBC, v.c. VHS

*King Lear*
(GB, 1984): TV, col.
p.c.: Granada TV
pro.: David Plowright
dir.: Michael Elliott
King Lear, Laurence Olivier; Fool, John Hurt; Regan, Diana Rigg; Goneril, Dorothy Tutin
DHS: GTV, v.c. VHS

### LOVE'S LABOUR'S LOST

*Love's Labour's Lost*
(GB, 1965): TV, b/w

p.c.: BBC
pro.: George R. Foa
dir.: Roger Jenkins
Berowne, Richard Pasco; Rosaline, Barbara Leigh-Hunt; Princess of France, Eithne Dunn; Costard, Russell Hunter

*Love's Labour's Lost*
(GB/USA, 1985): TV, col.
p.c.: BBC/Time-Life TV
pro.: Shaun Sutton
dir.: Elijah Moshinsky
des.: Barbara Gosnold
King, Jonathan Kent; Longaville, Christopher Blake; Dumain, Geoffrey Burridge; Berowne, Mike Gwilym; Princess of France, Maureen Lipman; Maria, Katy Behean; Katharine, Petra Markham; Rosaline, Jenny Agutter

### MACBETH

*Macbeth*
(USA, 1908): Film, b/w, sil.
p.c.: Vitagraph
dir.: William V. Ranous
Macbeth, William V. Ranous; Lady Macbeth, Miss Carver; Macduff, Paul Panzer

*Macbeth*
(Italy, 1909): Film, b/w, sil.
p.c.: Cines
dir.: Mario Caserini
Macbeth, Dante Capelli; Lady Macbeth, Maria Gasperini; Amleto Palormi

*Macbeth*
(France, 1910): Film, b/w, sil.
p.c.: Film d'Art
dir.: Andre Calmettes
Macbeth, Paul Mounet; Lady Macbeth, Joanne Delvair

*Macbeth*
(GB, 1911): Film, b/w, sil.
p.c.: Co-operative Cinematograph
dir.: Frank R. Benson
Macbeth, Frank R. Benson; Lady Macbeth, Mrs Benson; Guy Rathbone, Murray Carrington

*Macbeth*
(Germany, 1913): Film, b/w, sil.
p.c.: Filmindustrie Gesellschaft Heidelberg
dir.: Arthur Bourchier
Macbeth, Arthur Bourchier; Lady Macbeth, Violet Vanbrugh

*Macbeth*
(France, 1916): Film, b/w, sil.
p.c.: Eclair
Lady Macbeth, Georgette Leblanc-Maeterlink; Severin Mars

*Macbeth*
(USA, 1916): Film, b/w, sil.
p.c.: Triangle Reliance
dir.: John Emerson, D. W. Griffith
Macbeth, Herbert Beerbohm Tree; Lady Macbeth, Constance Collier; Macduff, Wilfred Lucas; Banquo, Ralph Lewis

*Macbeth*
(Germany, 1922): Film, b/w, sil.
p.c.: Elel Film/Filmindustrie, Heidelberg
dir.: Heinz Schall

*Macbeth*
(GB, 1945): Film, b/w
p.c.: Theatrecraft
dir.: Henry Cass
ARC: NFA, 35mm

*Macbeth*
(USA, 1946): Film, b/w
p.c.: Willow
pro.: David Bradley
dir.: Thomas A. Blair
des.: Charlton Heston
Macbeth, David Bradley; Jain Wilimorsky, William Bartholmay, Louis Northrop
ARC: FSL (USA), 16mm; NFA, 16mm

*Macbeth*
(USA, 1948): Film, b/w
p.c.: Mercury Films and Republic Pictures
pro./dir.: Orson Welles
des.: John McCarthy Jr, James Redd
Macbeth, Orson Welles; Lady Macbeth, Jeanette Nolan; Duncan, Erskine Sanford; Macduff, Dan O'Herlihy; the Three Witches, Lurene Tuttle, Brainerd Duffield, Peggy Webber; Malcolm, Roddy McDowall
DHS: HF, 16mm; IPC, v.c.
ARC: FSL (USA), 35mm; NFA, 35mm

*Macbeth*
(GB, 1949): TV, b/w
p.c.: BBC
pro./dir.: George More O'Ferrall

*Macbeth*
(USA, 1951): Film, col.

p.c.: Unusual Films, Bob Jones University
dir.: Katherine Stenholm
Members of the university faculty
ARC: FSL (USA), 16mm

*Macbeth*
(USA, 1954): Film, b/w
p.c.: Hallmark, Hall of Fame NBC
dir.: Maurice Evans
Macbeth, Maurice Evans; Lady Macbeth, Judith Anderson

*Kumonosu-Djo (Throne of Blood)*
(Japan, 1957): Film, b/w, FL
p.c.: Toho
dir.: Akira Kurosawa
des.: Yoshiro Murai
Macbeth/Taketoki Washizu, Toshiro Mifune; Lady Macbeth/Asaji, Isuzu Yamada; Duncan/Kunihara Tsuzuki, Takamaru Sasaki
DHS: HF, 16mm
ARC: FSL (USA), 35mm

*Macbeth*
(GB/USA, 1960): Film, col.
p.c.: Grand Prize Films
pro.: Phil C. Samuel
dir.: George Schaefer
des.: Edward Carrick
Macbeth, Maurice Evans; Lady Macbeth, Judith Anderson; Macduff, Ian Bannen; Duncan, Malcolm Keen
ARC: FSL (USA), 35mm

*Macbeth*
(GB, 1966): TV, b/w
p.c.: BBC
pro.: Michael Simpson
des.: Charles Lawrence
Macbeth, Andrew Keir; Lady Macbeth, Ruth Meyer; Duncan, Donald Eccles; Macduff, Anthony Bate
ARC: BBC, 35mm

*Macbeth*
(GB, 1970): TV, col.
p.c.: BBC
pro.: Cedric Messina
dir.: John Gorrie
des.: Natasha Kroll
Macbeth, Eric Porter; Lady Macbeth, Janet Suzman; John Alderton
ARC: BBC, 16mm, v.c.

*Macbeth*
(GB, 1971): Film, col.
p.c.: Playboy Productions/Caliban Films
pro.: Andrew Braunsberg
dir.: Roman Polanski
des.: Wilfrid Shingleton
Macbeth, Jon Finch; Lady Macbeth, Francesca Annis; Banquo, Martin Shaw; Macduff, Terence Bayler
DHS: HF, 16mm
ARC: FSL (USA), 35mm

*Macbeth*
(GB, 1979): TV, col.
p.c.: RSC/Thames TV
pro.: Philip Casson
dir.: Trevor Nunn
des.: John Napier (RSC)
Macbeth, Ian McKellen; Lady Macbeth, Judi Dench; Duncan, Griffith Jones; Malcolm, Roger Rees; Macduff, Bob Peck
DHS: TTV, v.c.
ARC: NFA, SUM

*Macbeth*
(GB/USA, 1983): TV, col.
p.c.: BBC/Time-Life TV
pro.: Shaun Sutton
dir.: Jack Gold
des.: Gerry Scott
Macbeth, Nicol Williamson; Duncan, Mark Dignam; Lady Macbeth, Jane Lapotaire
DHS: BBC, v.c. VHS

### MEASURE FOR MEASURE

*Dente per Dente*
(Italy, 1942): Film, b/w, FL
p.c.: Atlas (Artisti Associati)
dir.: Marco Elter
Carlo Tamberlani, Caterina Boratto, Oswaldo Genazzani, Memo Bennassi, Lamberto Picasso, Amelia Chellini

*Zweierlei Mass*
(FDR, 1963): Film, b/w, FL
p.c.: Bavaria Atelier GmbH
dir.: Paul Verhoeven
des.: Walter Blokesch
Hans Caninenberg, Lothar Blumhagen, Martin Berliner, Erik Schumann

*Measure for Measure*
(GB/USA, 1979): TV, col.
p.c.: BBC/Time-Life TV
pro.: Cedric Messina

dir.: Desmond Davis
des.: Odette Barrow
Duke, Kenneth Colley; Isabella, Kate Nelligan; Angelo, Tim Piggot-Smith
DHS: BBC, 16mm, v.c. VHS/BMX/SUM

### THE MERCHANT OF VENICE

*The Merchant of Venice*
(USA, 1908): Film, b/w, sil.
p.c.: Vitagraph
dir.: William V. Ranous
Shylock, William V. Ranous; Portia, Julia Swayne-Gordon; Jessica, Florence Turner

*Il Mercante di Venezia*
(Italy, 1910): Film, b/w, sil.
p.c.: Film d'Arte Italiana
dir.: Gerolamo Lo Savio
Shylock, Ermete Novelli; Portia, Francesca Bertini; Olga Giannini Novelli
ARC: NFA, 35mm

*The Merchant of Venice*
(USA, 1912): Film, b/w, sil.
p.c.: Thanhouser
dir.: Barry O'Neil
Shylock, William J. Bowman; Portia, Florence La Badie; Bassanio, Harry Benham; Antonio, William Russell; Jessica, Mignon Anderson

*The Merchant of Venice*
(USA, 1914): Film b/w, sil.
p.c.: Universal Pictures
dir.: Phillips Smalley, Lois Weber
Shylock, Phillips Smalley; Portia, Lois Weber; Bassanio, Douglas Gerrard; Antonio, Rupert Julian; Jessica, Edna Maison

*The Merchant of Venice*
(GB, 1916): Film, b/w, sil.
p.c.: Broadwest Film Co.
dir.: Walter West
Shylock, Matheson Lang; Portia, Hutin Britton; Bassanio, J. R. Tozer; Antonio, George Skillan; Jessica, Kathleen Hazel Jones

*Der Kaufmann von Venedig*
(Germany, 1923): Film, b/w, sil.
dir.: Peter Paul Felner
ARC: NFA, 35mm

*The Merchant of Venice*
(GB, 1947): TV, b/w
p.c.: BBC
pro./dir.: George More O'Ferrall

*Le Marchand de Venise/Il Mercante di Venezia*
(France/Italy, 1952): Film, b/w, FL
p.c.: Venturini Films/Elysées Films
dir.: Pierre Billon
des.: G. C. Bartolini-Salimbeni
Shylock, Michel Simon; Portia, Andrée Debar;
Antonio, Massimo Serato

*The Merchant of Venice*
(GB, 1955): TV, b/w
p.c.: BBC
pro./dir.: Hal Burton

*The Merchant of Venice*
(GB, 1969): VT, col.
p.c.: Audio-Visual Productions
dir.: Jonathan Miller
Shylock, Laurence Olivier; Portia, Joan Plowright
DHS: AVP, v.c. VHS/BMX

*The Merchant of Venice*
(GB, 1972): TV, col.
p.c.: BBC
pro.: Gerald Savory
dir.: Cedric Messina
des.: Tony Abbott
Shylock, Frank Finlay; Antonio, Charles Gray;
Portia, Maggie Smith; Bassanio, Christopher Gable
ARC: BBC, 16mm, v.t.

*The Merchant of Venice*
(GB/USA, 1980): TV, col.
p.c.: BBC/Time-Life TV
pro.: Jonathan Miller
dir.: Jack Gold
Shylock, Warren Mitchell; Portia, Gemma Jones;
Antonio, John Franklyn-Robbins; Bassanio, John
Nettles
DHS: BBC, 16mm, v.c. VHS/BMX/SUM

### THE MERRY WIVES OF WINDSOR

*The Merry Wives of Windsor*
(USA, 1910): Film, b/w, sil.
p.c.: Selig Polyscope Co.

*Die Lustigen Weiber von Windsor*
(Germany, 1917): Film, b/w, sil.
p.c.: Beck-Film
dir.: William Waner

*The Merry Wives of Windsor*
(GB, 1952): TV, b/w
p.c.: BBC
pro.: Ian Atkins

dir.: Julian Amyes
des.: James Bould
Falstaff, Robert Atkins; Page, Rupert Davies; Ford,
Anthony Sharp; Mistress Ford, Betty Huntley-
Wright; Mistress Page, Mary Kerridge

*The Merry Wives of Windsor*
(GB, 1955): TV, b/w
p.c.: BBC
pro.: Stephen Harrison
dir.: Glen Byam Shaw (SMT), Barrie Edgar (BBC)
des.: Motley
Falstaff, Anthony Quayle; Mistress Page, Angela
Baddeley; Mistress Ford, Joyce Redman
ARC: NFA

*The Merry Wives of Windsor*
(GB/USA, 1982): TV, col.
p.c.: BBC/Time-Life TV
pro.: Shaun Sutton
dir.: David Jones
des.: Don Homfray
Falstaff, Richard Griffiths; Mistress Page, Prunella
Scales; Mistress Ford, Judy Davis; Ford, Ben
Kingsley
DHS: BBC, 16mm, v.c. VHS/BMX/SUM

### A MIDSUMMER NIGHT'S DREAM

*A Midsummer Night's Dream*
(USA, 1909): Film b/w, sil.
p.c.: Vitagraph
dir.: J. Stuart Blackton
Lysander, Maurice Costello; Puck, Gladys Hulette;
Bottom, William V. Ranous
ARC: NFA, 35mm (incomplete)

*Le Songe d'une Nuit d'Été*
(France, 1909): Film, b/w, sil.
p.c.: Le Lion
Stacia de Napierkowska

*Ein Sommernachtstraum in unserer Zeit*
(Germany, 1913): Film, b/w, sil.
p.c.: Deutsche Bioscop GmbH
dir.: Stellan Rye
Puck, Grete Berger; Carl Clewing, Jean Ducret,
Anni Mewes

*A Midsummer Night's Dream*
(Italy, 1913): Film, b/w, sil.
p.c.: Gloria Films
Socrate Tommasi, Bianca Hubner

*Ein Sommernachtstraum*
(Germany, 1925): Film, b/w, sil.

p.c.: Neumann-Prod. Gmbh
dir.: Hans Neumann
Bottom, Werner Krauss; Puck, Valeska Gert;
Oberon, Tamara

*A Midsummer Night's Dream*
(USA, 1935): Film, b/w
p.c.: Warner Brothers
pro.: Max Reinhardt
dir.: Max Reinhardt, William Dieterle
des.: Anton Grot
Bottom, James Cagney; Titania, Anita Louise;
Puck, Mickey Rooney; Oberon, Victor Jory;
Hermia, Olivia de Havilland; Helena, Jean Muir;
Demetrius, Ross Alexander; Lysander, Dick Powell
DHS: RFL, 16mm
ARC: FSL (USA), 35mm; NFA, 35mm

*A Midsummer Night's Dream*
(GB, 1946): TV, b/w
p.c.: BBC
pro./dir.: Robert Atkins
Bankside Players

*A Midsummer Night's Dream*
(GB, 1947): TV, b/w
p.c.: BBC
pro.: Robert Atkins
dir.: I. Orr-Ewing
From the Open Air Theatre, Regent's Park

*A Midsummer Night's Dream*
(GB, 1958): Film, TV, b/w
p.c.: BBC
dir.: Rudolph Cartier
des.: Clifford Hatts
Bottom, Paul Rogers; Puck, Gillian Lynne; Titania,
Natasha Parry; Oberon, John Justin; Flute, Ronald
Fraser; Quince, Peter Sallis

*A Midsummer Night's Dream*
(GB, 1968): Film, col.
p.c.: RSC/Filmways
dir.: Michael Birkett
dir.: Peter Hall
des.: John Bury, Ann Curtis
Oberon, Ian Richardson; Titania, Judi Dench;
Puck, Ian Holm; Bottom, Paul Rogers; Lysander,
David Warner; Demetrius, Michael Jayston;
Helena, Diana Rigg; Hermia, Helen Mirren
DHS: FD, 16mm
ARC: FSL (USA), 35mm

*A Midsummer Night's Dream*
(GB, 1968): Film, TV, b/w

p.c.: Rediffusion TV
dir.: Joan Kemp-Welch
des.: Michael Yates
Bottom, Benny Hill; Puck, Tony Tanner; Peter
Wyngarde, Alfie Bass, Jill Bennett, Anna Massey,
Bernard Bresslaw

*A Midsummer Night's Dream*
(GB, 1971): TV, col.
p.c.: BBC
pro.: Cedric Messina
dir.: James Cellan Jones
des.: Roger Andrew
Titania, Eileen Atkins; Bottom, Ronnie Barker;
Helena, Lynn Redgrave; Oberon, Robert Stephens
ARC: BBC, v.t.

*A Midsummer Night's Dream*
(GB/USA, 1981): TV, col.
p.c.: BBC/Time-Life TV
pro.: Jonathan Miller
dir.: Elijah Moshinsky
des.: David Myerscough-Jones
Hippolyta, Estelle Kohler; Theseus, Nigel Davenport; Titania, Helen Mirren; Oberon, Peter
McEnery
DHS: BBC, 16mm

*A Midsummer Night's Dream*
(USA, 1982): TV, col.
p.c.: ABC Video Enterprises
pro.: Joseph Papp
dir.: James Lapine/Emile Ardolino
des.: Heidi Landesman/Randy Barcelo
Hippolyta, Diane Venora; Theseus, James Hurdle;
Titania, Michele Shay; Oberon, William Hurt;
Bottom, Jeffrey DeMunn; Puck, Marcel Rosenblatt

*A Midsummer Night's Dream*
(GB/Spain, 1984): TV, Film, col.
p.c.: Cabochan/Channel 4
pro.: Celestino Coronado, David Meyer
dir.: Celestino Coronado
des.: Lindsay Kemp, Mark Baldwin
The Incredible Orlando, Lindsay Kemp, Manuela
Vargas, Michael Matou, François Testorg, David
Meyer, David Haughton, Annie Huckle
DHS: HF, 16mm

## MUCH ADO ABOUT NOTHING

*Much Ado About Nothing*
(USA, 1926): Film b/w, sil.
dir.: Arthur Rosson

Raymond Griffith, Helene Costello, Bryant Washburn

*Mnogo Shuma Iz Nichego*
(USSR, 1956): Film, b/w, FL
p.c.: Moscow Studio
dir.: L. Samkovoi
des.: Ia Rapaport
Don Pedro, N. Bubnov; Don John, A. Katsynski; Claudio, N. Malishevski; Benedick, Iu Liubimov; Beatrice, L. Tselikorskaia

*Viel Larm um Nichts*
(DDR, 1963): Film, col., FL
p.c.: DEFA-Studio (for Spielfilme)
dir.: Martin Hellberg
des.: Hans Jorg Mirr
Christel Bodenstein, Rolf Ludwig, Wilfrid Ortmann

*Much Ado About Nothing*
(GB, 1967): TV, b/w
p.c.: National Theatre/BBC
pro.: Cedric Messina, Robert Stephens (BBC)
dir.: Alan Cooke (BBC), Franco Zeffirelli (NT)
Don Pedro, Derek Jacobi; Don John, Ronald Pickup; Benedick, Robert Stephens; Beatrice, Maggie Smith

*Beaucoup de Bruit pour Rien*
(USSR, 1973): Film, col., FL
dir.: Samson Samsonov
Beatrice, Galina Loguinova; Benedick, Konstantin Raikine

*Much Ado About Nothing*
(GB/USA, 1974): TV, col.
p.c.: NY Shakespeare Festival Production, BBC
ARC: NFA

*Much Ado About Nothing*
(GB/USA, 1978): TV, col.
p.c.: BBC/Time-Life TV
pro.: Cedric Messina
dir.: Donald McWhinnie
des.: Don Taylor
Don Pedro, Nigel Davenport; Don John, Ian Richardson; Claudio, Anthony Andrews; Hero, Ciaran Madden; Benedick, Michael York; Beatrice, Penelope Keith
DHS: BBC, 16mm, v.c. VHS/BMX/SUM

*Much Ado About Nothing*
(GB/USA, 1984): TV, col.
p.c.: BBC/Time-Life TV

pro.: Shaun Sutton
dir.: Stuart Burge
des.: Jan Spoczynski
Don Pedro, Jon Finch; Don John, Vernon Dobtcheff; Hero, Katharine Levy; Benedick, Robert Lindsay; Beatrice, Cherie Lunghi
DHS: BBC, 16mm, v.c. VHS/BMX/SUM

OTHELLO

*Othello*
(Germany, 1907): Film, b/w, sil.
pro.: Oskar Meszter
dir.: Franz Porten
Othello, Franz Porten; Desdemona, Henny Porten; Emilia, Rosa Porten

*Otello*
(Italy, 1907): Film, b/w, sil.
p.c.: Cines
dir.: Mario Caserini
Mario Caserini, Maria Gasperini, Ubaldo del Colle

*Othello*
(USA, 1908): Film, b/w, sil.
p.c.: Vitagraph
dir.: William V. Ranous
Othello, William V. Ranous; Desdemona, Julia Swayne-Gordon; Iago, Hector Dion; Cassio, Paul Panzer

*Otello*
(Italy, 1909): Film, b/w, sil.
p.c.: Film d'Arte/Italiana-Pathe
dir.: Gerolamo Lo Savio
Othello, Ferrucio Garavaglia; Desdemona, Vittoria Lepanto; Iago, Cesare Dondine

*Otello*
(Italy, 1914): Film, b/w, sil.
pro.: Arturo Ambrosio
dir.: Arrigo Frusta
Othello, Paslo Colaci; Desdemona, Lena Lenard; Iago, Ricardo Tolentino; Cassio, Ubaldo Stefani

*Othello*
(Germany, 1918): Film, b/w, sil.
p.c.: Max Mack-Film
dir.: Max Mack
Othello, Beni Montano; Desdemona, Ellen Korth; Rosa Valetti

*Othello*
(Germany, 1922): Film, b/w, sil.
p.c.: Worner Film

dir.: Dimitri Boukhoyietski
Othello, Emil Jannings; Desdemona, Ica de Lenkoffi; Iago, Werner Krauss
DHS: BFI, 16mm
ARC: NFA, 16mm

*Othello*
(GB, 1946): Film, b/w
p.c.: Marylebone Productions
dir.: David McKane
Othello, John Slater; Desdemona, Luanna Shaw; Iago, Sebastian Cabot; Emilia, Sheila Raynor

*Othello*
(GB, 1950): TV, b/w
p.c.: BBC
pro.: George More O'Ferrall
dir.: Kevin Sheldon

*Othello*
(Morocco/USA, 1952): Film, b/w
p.c.: Mogador-Films (Mercury)
pro./dir.: Orson Welles
des.: Alexander Trainer, Luigi Schiaccianoce, Maria de Matteis
Othello, Orson Welles; Iago, Micheál MacLiammóir; Desdemona, Suzanne Cloutier; Cassio, Michael Lawrence
DHS: BFI, 16mm
ARC: FSL (USA), 35mm; NFA, 35mm

*Othello*
(GB, 1955): TV, b/w
p.c.: BBC
pro./dir.: Tony Richardson
des.: Reece Pemberton
Othello, Gordon Heath; Iago, Paul Rogers; Desdemona, Rosemary Harris; Emilia, Daphne Anderson
ARC: BBC, 35mm

*Otello*
(USSR, 1955): Film, col., FL, dubbed
p.c.: Mosfilm
dir.: Sergei Yutkevitch
des.: A. Vaisfeld, V. Dorrer, M. Karyakin, O. Kroutchinia, N. Tchikirev
Othello, Sergei Bondarchuk; Iago, Andrei Popov; Desdemona, Irina Skobtseva; Cassio, Vladimir Soshalsky. English voices: Othello, Howard Marion Crawford; Iago, Arnold Diamond; Desdemona, Katherine Byron; Cassio, Patrick Westwood
ARC: FSL (USA), 35mm

*Othello*
(GB, 1965): Film, col.
p.c.: National Theatre/ABHE
pro.: Anthony Havelock-Allen, John Brabourne
dir.: Stuart Burge
Othello, Laurence Olivier; Iago, Frank Finlay; Desdemona, Maggie Smith; Cassio, Derek Jacobi
DHS: HF, 16mm; IPC, v.c.
ARC: FSL (USA), 35mm

*Othello*
(GB/USA, 1981): TV, col.
p.c.: BBC/Time-Life TV
pro./dir.: Jonathan Miller
des.: Colin Lowery
Othello, Anthony Hopkins; Iago, Bob Hoskins; Desdemona, Penelope Wilton; Emilia, Rosemary Leach
DHS: BBC, 16mm, v.c. VHS, BMX

## PERICLES, PRINCE OF TYRE

*Pericles, Prince of Tyre*
(GB, USA, 1983): TV, col.
p.c.: BBC/Time-Life TV
pro.: Shaun Sutton
dir.: David Jones
des.: Don Taylor
Gower, Edward Petherbridge; Antiochus, John Woodvine; Pericles, Mike Gwilym; Marina, Amanda Redman
DHS: BBC, 16mm, v.c. VHS/BMX/SUM

## RICHARD II

*Richard II*
(GB, 1950): TV, b/w
p.c.: BBC
pro./dir.: Royston Morley

*Richard II*
(USA, 1954): Film, b/w
p.c.: Hallmark Hall of Fame/NBC
dir.: Maurice Evans
Richard II, Maurice Evans; Sarah Churchill

*An Age of Kings*: Part 1, 'The Hollow Crown', Part 2, 'The Deposing of a King'
(GB, 1960): TV, b/w
p.c.: BBC/TV
pro.: Peter Dews
dir.: Michael Hayes
des.: Stanley Morris
Richard II, David William; Bolingbroke, Tom

Fleming; John of Gaunt, Edgar Wreford; York, Geoffrey Bayldon
ARC: BBC, 16mm (two parts)

*The Tragedy of King Richard II*
(GB, 1970): TV, col.
p.c.: BBC/Prospect Theatre Co.
pro.: Mark Shivas
dir.: Richard Cottrell
des.: Tony Abbot
Richard II, Ian McKellen; Bolingbroke, Timothy West; John of Gaunt, Paul Hardwick; Isabella, Lucy Fleming

*Richard II*
(GB/USA, 1978): TV, col.
p.c.: BBC/Time-Life TV
pro.: Cedric Messina
dir.: David Giles
des.: Tony Abbott
Richard II, Derek Jacobi; John of Gaunt, John Gielgud; Bolingbroke, Jon Finch; York, Charles Gray
DHS: BBC, 16mm, v.c. VHS/BMX/SUM

## RICHARD III

*Richard III*
(USA, 1908): Film, b/w, sil.
p.c.: Vitagraph
dir.: William V. Ranous
Richard III, William V. Ranous; Thomas H. Ince, Florence Turner, Julia Swayne-Gordon

*Richard III*
(GB, 1911): Film, b/w, sil.
p.c.: Co-operative Cinematograph
dir.: Frank R. Benson
Richard III, Frank R. Benson; Moffat Johnston, Constance Benson
ARC: NFA, 35mm

*The Life and Death of King Richard III*
(USA, 1913); Film, b/w, sil.
p.c.: Sterling
dir.: M. B. Dudley
Richard III, Frederick B. Warde

*Richard III*
(Germany, 1919): Film, b/w, sil.
dir.: Max Reinhardt
Conrad Veidt and the Reinhardt Co.

*Richard III*
(GB, 1955): Film, col.

p.c.: London Films
pro.: Laurence Olivier, Alexander Korda
dir.: Laurence Olivier
des.: Roger Furse, Carmen Dillon
Richard III, Laurence Olivier; Buckingham, Ralph Richardson; Clarence, John Gielgud; Lady Anne, Claire Bloom
DHS: RFL, 16mm
ARC: FSL (USA), 35mm

*An Age of Kings*: Part 14, 'The Dangerous Brother', Part 15, 'The Boar Hunt'
(GB, 1960): TV, b/w
p.c.: BBC
pro.: Peter Dews
dir.: Michael Hayes
des.: Stanley Morris
Richard III, Paul Daneman; Clarence, Patrick Garland; Lady Anne, Jill Dixon; Henry VI, Terry Scully; Buckingham, Edgar Wreford; Margaret, Mary Morris; Henry Tudor, Jerome Willis
ARC: BBC, 16mm

*The Wars of the Roses*: Part 3 'Richard III'
(GB, 1964): TV, b/w
p.c.: RSC/BBC
pro.: Michael Barry (BBC)
dir.: Peter Hall, John Barton (RSC), Robin Midgley, Michael Hayes (BBC)
des.: John Bury
Richard III, Ian Holm; Margaret, Peggy Ashcroft; Lady Anne, Janet Suzman; Edward IV, Roy Dotrice; Clarence, Charles Kay; Richmond, Eric Porter
ARC: BBC, 35mm

*Richard III*
(GB/USA, 1983)
p.c.: BBC/Time-Life TV
pro.: Shaun Sutton
dir.: Jane Howell
des.: Oliver Bayldon
Richard III, Ron Cook; Edward IV, Brian Protheroe; Buckingham, Michael Byrne; Lady Anne, Zoë Wanamaker; Margaret, Julia Foster
DHS: BBC, v.c., VHS, BMX

## ROMEO AND JULIET

*Romeo and Juliet*
(France, 1900): Film, b/w, sil.
dir.: Clement Maurice
Romeo, Emilio Cossira

*Romeo and Juliet*
(USA, 1908): Film, b/w, sil.
p.c.: Vitagraph
dir.: William V. Ranous
Romeo, Paul Panzer; Juliet, Florence Lawrence;
Tybalt, John G. Adolfi; Capulet, Charles Kent;
Montague, Charles Chapman; Friar Lawrence,
William V. Ranous

*Romeo e Giulietta*
(Italy, 1908): Film, b/w, sil.
p.c.: Cines
dir.: Mario Caserini
Romeo, Mario Caserini; Juliet, Maria Gasperini

*Romeo and Juliet*
(GB, 1908): Film, b/w, sil.
p.c.: Gaumont
Romeo, Godfrey Tearle; Juliet, Mary Malone;
Tybalt, J. Annard; Mercutio, Gordon Bailey

*Romeo and Juliet*
(USA, 1911): Film, b/w, sil.
p.c.: Thanhouser
dir.: Barry O'Neill
Romeo, George A. Lessey; Juliet, Julia M. Taylor

*Giulietta e Romeo*
(Italy, 1911): Film, b/w, sil.
p.c.: Film d'Arte/Italiana–Pathe
dir.: Gorolamo Lo Savio
Romeo, Gustav Serena; Juliet, Francesca Bertini;
Ferrucio Garavaglia

*Romeo et Juliette*
(France, 1914): Film, b/w, sil.
p.c.: Société Cinématographique des Auteurs et
Gens de Lettres

*Romeo and Juliet*
(USA, 1916): Film, b/w, sil.
p.c.: Metro Pictures
dir.: John W. Noble, Francis X. Bushman
Romeo, Francis X. Bushman; Juliet, Beverly
Bayne; Tybalt, W. Lawson Butt; Friar Lawrence,
Robert Cummings

*Romeo and Juliet*
(USA, 1916): Film, b/w, sil.
p.c.: Fox Film
dir.: J. Gordon Edwards
Juliet, Theda Bara; Romeo, Harry Hilliard; Tybalt,
John Webb Dillon; Mercutio, Glen White

*Romeo and Juliet*
(USA, 1936): Film, b/w

p.c.: MGM
pro.: Irving G. Thalberg
dir.: George Cukor
des.: Cedric Gibbons
Romeo, Leslie Howard; Juliet, Norma Shearer;
Mercutio, John Barrymore; Nurse, Edna May
Oliver; Friar Lawrence, Henry Kolker
ARC: FSL (USA), 35mm; NFA, 35mm

*Julieta y Romeo*
(Spain, 1940): Film, b/w, FL
p.c.: Cinedia
dir.: Jose Marie Castellvi
Marta Flores, Enrique Guitart

*Shuhaddaa El Gharam*
(Egypt, 1942): Film, b/w, FL
p.c.: Les Films el Nil
dir.: Kamal Selim
Leila Mourad, Ibrahim Hamouda

*Romeo and Juliet*
(GB, 1947): TV, b/w
p.c.: BBC
pro./dir.: Michael Barry

*Anjuman*
(India, 1948): Film, b/w, FL
p.c.: Nargis Art Concern
pro./dir.: Akhtar Hussein
Juliet, Nargis; Romeo, Jaraj; Durga Khole, Raj Rani

*Romeo and Juliet*
(Italy/GB, 1954): Film, col.
p.c.: Universal-Cine-Verona
pro.: Sandro Ghenzi, Joseph Janni
dir.: Renato Castellani
des.: Leonor Fini
Romeo, Laurence Harvey; Juliet, Susan Shentall;
Nurse, Flora Robson; Mercutio, Aldo Zollo; Friar
Lawrence, Mervyn Johns
DHS: RFL, 16mm
ARC: FSL (USA) 35mm

*Romeo and Juliet*
(GB, 1955): TV, b/w
p.c.: BBC
pro./dir.: Harold Clayton
des.: Roy Oxlen
Romeo, Tony Britton; Juliet, Virginia McKenna;
Nurse, Flora Robson
ARC: BBC, 35mm

*Romeo and Juliet*
(GB, 1965): Film, b/w

p.c.: RADA/Regent Street Polytechnic
pro.: Paul Emerson, John Fernald
dir.: Val Drum, Paul Lee
Romeo, Clive Francis; Juliet, Angela Scoular

*Giulietta e Romeo*
(Italy/Spain, 1964): Film, col., FL, dubbed
p.c.: Imprecine/Hispaner Film
dir.: Riccardo Freda
des.: Piero Filipponi
Romeo, Geronimo Meynier; Juliet, Rosemarie
Dexter; Mercutio, Carlos Estrada; Friar Lawrence,
Umberto Raho; Nurse, Toni Soler
ARC: FSL (USA), 35mm

*Romeo and Juliet*
(GB, 1967): TV, b/w
p.c.: BBC
pro.: Cedric Messina
dir.: Alan Cooke
des.: Eileen Diss
Romeo, Hywel Bennett; Juliet, Kika Markham;
Nurse, Thora Hird
ARC: BBC, 35mm

*Romeo and Juliet*
(Italy/GB, 1968): Film, col.
p.c.: Verona Productions/Cinematografia/Dino Di
Laurentiis
pro.: Anthony Havelock-Allen, John Brabourne
dir.: Franco Zeffirelli
des.: Renzo Mongiardino, Danilo Donati
Romeo, Leonard Whiting; Juliet, Olivia Hussey;
Friar Lawrence, Milo O'Shea; Nurse, Pat
Heywood; Mercutio, John McEnery; Tybalt,
Michael York
DHS: RFL, 16mm
ARC: FSL (USA), 35mm

*Romeo and Juliet*
(GB, 1976): TV, col.
p.c.: Thames TV (schools production)
pro.: Francis Coleman
dir.: Joan Kemp-Welch
des.: Fred Pusey/Martin Baugh
Romeo, Christopher Neame; Juliet, Ann Hasson;
Capulet, Laurence Payne; Nurse, Patsy Byrne; Friar
Lawrence, Clive Swift
ARC: TTV

*Romeo and Juliet*
(GB, 1977): TV, col.
p.c.: Television and Educational Classics Ltd.
pro.: Paul Bosner
dir.: Paul Bosner, George Murcell

des.: John Wood
Juliet, Sarah Badel; Romeo, Peter McEnery; Friar
Lawrence, Joseph O'Conor; Nurse, Elvi Hale
ARC: FSL

*Romeo and Juliet*
(GB/USA, 1978): TV, col.
p.c.: BBC/Time-Life TV
pro.: Cedric Messina
dir.: Alvin Rakoff
des.: Stuart Walker
Chorus, John Gielgud; Romeo, Patrick Ryecart;
Juliet, Rebecca Saire; Mercutio, Anthony Andrews;
Nurse, Celia Johnson
DHS: BBC, 16mm, v.c., VHS/BMX/SUM

## THE TAMING OF THE SHREW

*La Bisbetica Domata*
(Italy, 1908): Film, b/w, sil.
p.c.: Società Italiana Fratelli Pineschi
dir.: Lamberto and Azeglio Pineschi

*The Taming of the Shrew*
(USA, 1908): Film, b/w, sil.
p.c.: American Mutoscope, Biograph Co.
dir.: D. W. Griffith
Katherina, Florence Lawrence; Petruchio, Arthur
Johnson; Charles Molee, Linda Arridson

*The Taming of the Shrew*
(GB, 1911): Film, b/w, sil.
p.c.: Shakespeare Memorial Theatre Co.
dir.: F. R. Benson
F. R. Benson, SMT Co

*La Mégère Apprivoisée*
(France, 1911): Film, b/w, sil.
p.c.: Eclipse
dir.: Henri Desfontaines
Cécile Didier, Romuald Joube, Dinis d'Ines

*La Bisbetica Domata*
(Italy, 1913): Film, b/w, sil.
p.c.: Ambrosio Films
pro.: Arturo Ambrosio
dir.: Arrigo Frusta
Petruchio, Eleuterio Rodolfi; Katherina, Gigotta
Morano

*The Taming of the Shrew*
(GB, 1923): Film, b/w, sil.
p.c.: British and Colonial
dir.: Edwin J. Collins

Petruchio, Landerdale Maitland; Katherina, Mlle Dacia; Bianca, Cynthia Murtagh

*The Taming of the Shrew*
(USA, 1929): Film, b/w (re-issued 1966, Cinema Classics)
p.c.: Pickford/Elton Corporation
pro.: Matty Kemp (1966)
dir.: Sam Taylor
des.: William Cameron Menzies, Laurence Irving
Petruchio, Douglas Fairbanks; Katherina, Mary Pickford; Baptista, Edwin Maxwell
DHS: BD, 16mm
ARC: FSL, 35mm

*La Bisbetica Domata*
(Italy, 1942): Film, b/w, FL
p.c.: Excelsa Film
dir.: Ferdinando Poggioli
Lilia Silvi, Amadeo Nazzari, Carlo Romano

*The Taming of the Shrew*
(GB, 1952): TV, b/w
p.c.: BBC
pro./dir.: Desmond Davies
des.: Barry Learoyd
Petruchio, Stanley Baker; Katherina, Margaret Johnston; Baptista, Ernest Jay; Bianca, Sheila Shand-Gibbs

*La Mégère Apprivoisée/La Fierecilla Domada*
(France/Spain, 1955): Film, col., FL
p.c.: Vascos–Interproduction (Paris), Bonito Perojo (Madrid)
dir.: Antonio Roman
Carmen Serilla, Alberto Closas

*Ukroshchenie Stroptivoi*
(USSR, 1961): Film, b/w, FL
p.c.: Mosfilm
dir.: Sergei Kolosov
des.: N. Shyfrin, V. Golikov
Katherina, Ludmila Kasatkina; Petruchio, Andrei Popov

*The Taming of the Shrew*
(USA/Italy, 1966): Film, col.
p.c.: Royal Films International/FAI
pro.: Elizabeth Taylor, Richard Burton, Franco Zeffirelli
dir.: Franco Zeffirelli
des.: John de Cuir
Petruchio, Richard Burton; Katherina, Elizabeth Taylor; Bianca, Natasha Pyne; Baptista, Michael Hordern

DHS: CEMIW, 16mm
ARC: FSL (USA), 35mm

*The Taming of the Shrew*
(GB/USA, 1980): TV, col.
p.c.: BBC/Time-Life TV
pro./dir.: Jonathan Miller
des.: Colin Lowrey
Petruchio, John Cleese; Katherina, Sarah Badel; Bianca, Susan Penhaligon
DHS: BBC, 16mm, v.c. VHS/BMX/SUM

THE TEMPEST

*The Tempest*
(USA, 1911): Film, b/w, sil.
p.c.: Thanhouser
pro./dir.: Edwin Thanhouser

*La Tempête*
(France, 1912): Film, b/w, sil.
p.c.: Eclair

*The Tempest*
(GB, 1939): TV, b/w
p.c.: BBC
pro./dir.: Dallas Bower
des.: Malcolm Baker-Smith
Prospero, John Abbot; Miranda, Peggy Ashcroft; Ariel, Stephen Haggard; Caliban, George Devine; Ferdinand, Richard Ainley

*The Tempest*
(GB, 1956): TV, b/w
p.c.: BBC
pro./dir.: Ian Atkins, Robert Atkins
des.: Barry Learoyd
Prospero, Robert Eddison; Miranda, Anna Barry; Caliban, Robert Atkins; Ariel, Patti Brooks; Ferdinand, Bernard Brown
ARC: BBC, 35mm; NFA, 35mm

*The Tempest*
(USA, 1960): Film, col.
p.c.: Hallmark Hall of Fame/NBC
dir.: George Schaefer
Prospero, Maurice Evans; Miranda, Lee Remick; Caliban, Richard Burton; Ferdinand, Roddy McDowall

*The Tempest*
(GB, 1968): TV, b/w
p.c.: BBC
pro.: Cedric Messina
dir.: Basil Coleman

des.: Tony Abbott
Prospero, Michael Redgrave; Miranda, Tessa Wyatt; Caliban, Keith Michell; Ariel, Ronald Pickup; Ferdinand, Jonathan Dennis

*The Tempest*
(GB, 1980): Film, col.
p.c.: Boyd's Company
pro.: Guy Ford, Mordecai Shreiber
dir.: Derek Jarman
des.: Yolander Sonnabend
Prospero, Heathcote Williams; Miranda, Toyah Wilcox; Ferdinand, David Meyer; Caliban, Jack Birkett; Ariel, Karl Johnson
DHS: HF, 16mm, v.c.; AVP, v.c. VHS/BMX

*The Tempest*
(GB/USA, 1980): TV, col.
p.c.: BBC/Time-Life TV
pro.: Cedric Messina
dir.: John Gorrie
des.: Paul Joel
Prospero, Michael Hordern; Miranda, Pippa Guard; Caliban, Warren Clarke
DHS: BBC, 16mm, v.c. VHS/BMX/SUM

### TIMON OF ATHENS

*Timon of Athens*
(GB/USA, 1981): TV col.
p.c.: BBC/Time-Life TV
pro./dir.: Jonathan Miller
des.: Tony Abbott
Timon, Jonathan Pryce; Alcibiades, John Shrapnel; Flavius, John Welsh
DHS: BBC, 16mm., v.c. VHS/BMX/SUM

### TITUS ANDRONICUS

*Titus Andronicus*
(GB/USA, 1985): TV, col.
p.c.: BBC/Time-Life TV
pro.: Shaun Sutton
dir.: Jane Howell
des.: Tony Burrough
Titus, Trevor Peacock; Lavinia, Anna Calder-Marshall; Tamora, Eileen Atkins; Aaron, Hugh Quarshie
DHS: BBC, 16mm, v.c. VHS/BMX/SUM

### TROILUS AND CRESSIDA

*Troilus and Cressida*
(GB, 1954): TV, b/w

p.c.: BBC
pro.: Douglas Allen
dir.: George Rylands
des.: Michael Yates
Troilus, John Fraser; Cressida, Mary Watson; Hector, William Squire; Paris, Simon Lack; Pandarus, Frank Pettingell; Achilles, Geoffrey Toone; Thersites, Richard Wordsworth

*Troilus and Cressida*
(GB, 1966): TV, b/w
p.c.: National Youth Theatre/BBC
pro.: Michael Bakewell (BBC)
dir.: Paul Hill, Michael Croft (NYT); Bernard Hepton (BBC)
des.: John Buglir
Troilus, Andrew Murray; Cressida, Charlotte Womersley; Hector, Timothy Block; Achilles, Dennis Marks; Ulysses, Derek Seaton; Helen, Mary Payne; Pandarus, David Stockton
ARC: BBC, 16mm

*Troilus and Cressida*
(GB/USA): TV, col.
p.c.: BBC/Time-Life TV
pro./dir.: Jonathan Miller
Troilus, Anton Lesser; Cressida, Suzanne Burden; Pandarus, Charles Gray; Achilles, Kenneth Haigh; Ulysses, Benjamin Whitrow; Helen, Ann Pennington; Thersites, Jack Birkett
DHS: BBC, 16mm, v.c. VHS/BMX/SUM

### TWELFTH NIGHT

*Twelfth Night*
(USA, 1910): Film, b/w, sil.
p.c.: Vitagraph
pro./dir.: Edwin Thanhouser
Julia Swayne-Gordon, Florence Turner

*Twelfth Night*
(GB, 1939): TV, b/w
p.c.: BBC
pro.: Bronson Albery
dir.: Michel St Denis
Michael Redgrave, Peggy Ashcroft, Esmond Knight, George Hayes, George Devine, Vera Lindsay, Lucille Lisle

*Twelfth Night*
(GB, 1950): TV, b/w
p.c.: BBC
pro.: Robert Atkins
dir.: Harold Clayton

des.: Barry Learoyd
Orsino, Terence Morgan; Viola, Barbara Lott; Olivia, Patricia Neale; Malvolio, Geoffrey Dunn; Feste, John Gatrell

*Dvenadtsataia Noch*
(USSR, 1955): Film, col., FL
p.c.: Lenfilm
dir.: Jan Fried
des.: S. Malkin
Viola/Sebastian, Katya Luchiko; Olivia, Anna Lavianova; Sir Toby, M. Yanshim; Malvolio, V. Morkuriev; Feste, B. Friendlich
ARC: FSL (USA), 35mm

*Twelfth Night*
(GB, 1957): TV, b/w
p.c.: BBC
pro.: Michael Elliott
dir.: Caspar Wrede
des.: Stephen Taylor
Orsino, Robert Hardy; Viola, Dilys Hamlett; Olivia, Maureen Quinney; Malvolio, John Moffatt; Feste, James Maxwell

*Twelfth Night (Was Ihr Wollt)*
(FDR, 1962): Film, b/w, FL
p.c.: Bavaria Atelier GmbH
dir.: Franz Peter Wirth
des.: Walter Blokesch
Orsino, Karl Michael Vogler; Viola/Sebastian, Ingrid Andree; Karl Block, Fritz Wepper

*Twelfth Night (Was Ihr Wollt)*
(DDR, 1963): TV, b/w, FL
p.c.: DEFA-Studio für Spielfilme (for Deutscher Fernsehfunk)
dir.: Lothar Bellag
des.: Alfred Tolle
Gerry Wolff, Christel Bodenstein, Johanna Clas

*Twelfth Night*
(GB, 1969): TV, col.
p.c.: ITC
pro.: John Dexter, Cecil Clarke
dir.: John Sichel
Malvolio, Alec Guinness; Sir Toby, Ralph Richardson; Viola/Sebastian, Joan Plowright; Feste, Tommy Steele

*Twelfth Night*
(GB/USA, 1980): TV, col.
p.c.: BBC/Time-Life TV
pro.: Cedric Messina
dir.: John Gorrie

des.: Don Taylor
Orsino, Clive Arindell; Viola, Felicity Kendal; Olivia, Sinead Cusack; Sir Toby, Robert Hardy
DHS: BBC, 16mm, v.c. VHS/BMX/SUM

## THE TWO GENTLEMEN OF VERONA

*Zwei Herren Aus Verona*
(FDR, 1963): Film, b/w, FL
p.c.: Bavaria Atelier GmbH
dir.: Hans Dieter Schwarze
des.: Walter Blokesch
Hans Karl Friedrich, Norbert Hansing, Rolf Becker

*The Two Gentlemen of Verona*
(GB/USA, 1983): TV, col.
p.c.: BBC/Time-Life TV
pro.: Shaun Sutton
dir.: Don Taylor
des.: Barbara Gosnold
Duke, Paul Daneman; Valentine, John Hudson; Proteus, Tyler Butterworth; Julia, Tessa Peake-Jones; Silvia, Joanne Pearce
DHS: BBC, 16mm, v.c. VHS/BMX/SUM

## THE WINTER'S TALE

*The Winter's Tale*
(USA, 1910): Film, b/w, sil.
p.c.: Thanhouser
pro./dir.: Barry O'Neill
Leontes, Martin Faust; Hermione, Ms Rosemund; Polixenes, Frank Crane

*Tragedia alla Corte di Sicilia*
(Italy, 1914): Film, b/w, sil.
p.c.: Milano
pro.: L. Sutto
dir.: Baldessare Negroni
Leontes, V. Cocchi; Pina Fabbri
ARC: NFA, 35mm

*Das Wintermärchen*
(Germany, 1914): Film, b/w, sil.
p.c.: Belle Alliance
Senta Soneland, Albert Paulig, Richard Sonius

*The Winter's Tale*
(GB, 1962): TV, b/w
p.c.: BBC
dir.: Don Taylor
des.: Marilyn Taylor
Leontes, Robert Shaw; Hermione, Rosalie Crutchley; Florizel, Brian Smith; Perdita, Sarah Badel
ARC: BBC, 16mm

# A SELECTIVE FILMOGRAPHY

*The Winter's Tale*
(GB, 1966): Film, col.
p.c.: Cressida/Hurst Park
pro.: Peter Snell
dir.: Frank Dunlop
des.: Carl Toms
Leontes, Laurence Harvey; Hermione, Moira Redmond; Perdita, Jane Asher; Paulina, Diana Churchill

*The Winter's Tale*
(GB/USA, 1980): TV, col.
p.c.: BBC/Time-Life TV
pro.: Jonathan Miller
dir.: Jane Howell
des.: Don Homfray
Leontes, Jeremy Kemp; Hermione, Anna Calder-Marshall; Polixenes, Robert Stephens
DHS: BBC, 16mm, v.c. VHS/BMX/SUM

## ADDENDA

*Hamlet*
(BBC, 1947)
des.: Peter Bax
Hamlet, John Byron; Ophelia, Muriel Pavlow; Claudius, Sebastian Shaw; Gertrude, Margaret Rawlings; Horatio, Patrick Troughton

*Julius Caesar*
(BBC, 1959)
Caesar, Robert Perceval; Brutus, Eric Porter; Antony, William Sylvester; Cassius, Michael Gough

*Macbeth*
(BBC, 1949)
des.: Peter Bax
Macbeth, Stephen Murray; Lady Macbeth, Bernadette O'Farrell; Duncan, Arthur Wontner; Banquo, Esmond Knight; Malcolm, Patrick McNee

*Macbeth*
(USA, 1981): vc, col.
p.c.: Bard Productions Ltd.
pro.: Jack Nakano
dir.: Arthur Allan Seidelman
des.: John Retsck
Macbeth, Jeremy Brett; Lady Macbeth, Piper Laurie; Macduff, Simon MacCorkindale; Banquo, Barrie Primus
DHS: Encyclopedia Britannica, v.c. VHS/BMX

*The Merchant of Venice*
(BBC, 1947)
des.: Barry Learoyd
Antonio, Austin Trevor; Shylock, Abraham Sofaer; Bassanio, Andre Morell; Portia, Margaretta Scott; Jessica, Jill Balcon

*The Merchant of Venice*
(BBC, 1955)
des.: Hal Burton
Antonio, Raymond Westwell; Shylock, Michael Hordern; Bassanio, Denis Quilley; Portia, Rachel Gurney; Jessica, Veronica Wells

*A Midsummer Night's Dream*
(BBC, 1946)
Theseus, Desmond Llewelyn; Hippolyta, Angela Shafto; Oberon, John Byron; Titania, Vivienne Bennett; Bottom, Robert Atkins

*Othello*
(USA, 1981): vc, col.
p.c.: Bard Productions Ltd.
pro.: Jack Nakano
dir.: Franklin Melton
des.: John Retsek
Othello, William Marshall; Desdemona, Jenny Agutter; Iago, Ron Moody; Emilia, Leslic Paxton
DHS: Encyclopedia Britannica, v.c. VHS/BMX

*Romeo and Juliet*
(BBC, 1947)
Romeo, John Bailey; Juliet, Rosalie Crutchley; Nurse, Agnes Lauchlan; Tybalt, Michael Goodliffe

*The Tempest*
(USA, 1983): vc, col.
p.c.: Bard Productions Ltd.
pro.: Ken Campbell
dir.: William Woodman
des.: Donald L. Harris
Prospero, Efrem Zimbalist, Jr.; Miranda, J. E. Taylor; Caliban, William Hootkins; Ariel, Duane Black; Ferdinand, Nicholas Hammond
DHS: Encyclopedia Britannica, v.c. VHS/BMX

# 'CHIMES AT MIDNIGHT' FROM STAGE TO SCREEN: THE ART OF ADAPTATION

## ROBERT HAPGOOD

Most of the best Shakespeare films have a stage production in their background. Examples come readily to mind: Olivier had performed on stage all the plays he made into films; Kozintsev had directed both *Hamlet* and *King Lear* for the theatre before he made films of them. Zeffirelli's film of *Romeo and Juliet* put the same accent on youth as had his Old Vic production; the Peter Brook/Paul Scofield film of *King Lear* was a revised edition of their stage version. Yet this theatrical lineage of the films has received remarkably little comment. In general, film commentators have tended to play down the ties between film and theatre (they are more inclined to see parallels with narrative literature) precisely because the two are so close, theatre came first, and the commentators are concerned to maintain the integrity of film as an independent art-form.[1] That it is. Yet much can be learned from exploring the relations between the two forms of drama, as indeed Allardyce Nicoll, André Bazin, and Roger Manvell have already shown.[2] They, however, have considered the subject in general terms and have not focused on particular films and the stage productions to which they were related, whether the plays were by Shakespeare or other playwrights. Admittedly, a prior stage production may not always be an asset for a film. Most critics have felt that, on film, Olivier's portrayal of Othello would have been better if it had not so directly reflected his stage performance; what was bravura classic acting on the stage seems

stagey on the screen. A stage production should not be in the foreground of a film. But in general a stage background seems to have been an asset for most Shakespeare films, making for a maturely considered and fully crystallized interpretation. The study of this background should thus help to illuminate the film interpretation.

I

Orson Welles's film *Chimes at Midnight* is an especially interesting case in point. It has justly been praised as a 'masterpiece' or a 'near masterpiece' (flawed by a poor soundtrack) by the authors of books both on Shakespearian films and on Welles's films in general. It was preceded by two stage incarnations, neither of which was itself a success yet both of which made important contributions to the film.

The first was *Five Kings* (1938), which traced in a single, very long evening the whole career of Harry Monmouth from Prince Hal cavorting with Falstaff in the tavern to King Henry V wooing Katherine after his victory at Agin-

---

[1] Susan Sontag, *Against Interpretation* (New York, 1972), pp. 242–5.

[2] Allardyce Nicoll, *Film and Theatre* (London, 1936); André Bazin, *What is Cinema?*, trans. H. Gray (Berkeley, 1974); Roger Manvell, *Theatre and Film* (Rutherford and London, 1979). See also Andrew Horton and Joan Magretta, *Modern European Filmmakers and the Art of Adaptation* (New York, 1981).

court.[3] At twenty-three, Welles was nearing the height of the Boy Wonder phase of his career. He had already scored successes on stage with his fascist *Julius Caesar* and voodoo *Macbeth* and was about to film *Citizen Kane*. For *Five Kings* he adapted the script (selecting, condensing, and rearranging relevant portions of the two parts of *Henry IV* and *Henry V*, plus preliminary materials from *Richard II*), directed the production, and played the role of Falstaff. The result was to have been performed in tandem with a similar reworking of materials drawn from the first tetralogy of history plays. (As a schoolboy Welles had adapted and played the role of Richard III in just such a compilation called 'The Winter of Our Discontent'.)[4] Hence the promise of five kings in the title. The second project was never realized. In *Five Kings* reviewers found much to praise, especially Welles's own performance as Falstaff and his imaginative use of a revolving stage. The latter was a source of practical difficulty (its misadventures are entertainingly recounted by John Houseman),[5] but integral to Welles's conception of a 'world in motion'.[6] The production as a whole, however, could not be called either a critical or a financial success. After try-outs in Boston, Washington, DC, and Philadelphia, it folded without reaching New York.

In 1960 Welles tried again with a stage production called *Chimes at Midnight*, which played in Belfast and Dublin for a month.[7] It had much in common with *Five Kings*. The use of a narrator continued, but with material drawn exclusively from Holinshed and without additional choruses from *Henry V*. In both versions, essentially the same portions were selected from the *Henry IV* plays: Hotspur was given an important role, his farewell scene with Lady Percy was included, Worcester's role as villain was developed somewhat; but other aspects of the civil wars were totally omitted – Glendower and Douglas did not figure at all, nor did the rebels in *Part 2* apart from occasional mention of

Northumberland. All of the tavern scenes were kept, as were most of the scenes involving the king at court and on the battlefield. In both versions, newspaper reviewers agreed, the emotional highpoint was the rejection of Falstaff. Reviewers also consistently found more sadness than humour in Welles's Falstaff.[8]

What was chiefly different about the Irish version was its stronger focus on Falstaff, 'being' (as the programme put it) 'the adventures of the Fat Knight and the Prince of Wales'. As adapted by Welles, its first act was essentially an abbreviation of *Part 1* of *Henry IV*. Welles wrote to Hilton Edwards, who staged it: 'the shape and form of Part One is well nigh perfect . . . not only as a whole play, but as *an act*'; hence 'in general terms, the shape of our Act One simply must have the basic

---

[3] For details of the script of this production I have consulted the typescript bearing the name of Millie Davenport, who did the costumes for *Five Kings*, in the Billy Rose Collection of the New York Public Library at Lincoln Center.

[4] Richard France, *The Theatre of Orson Welles* (Lewisburg and London, 1977), pp. 24–6. As France discusses (pp. 72–3), Welles's film of *Macbeth* derives in many ways from his prior stage versions.

[5] John Houseman, *Run-Through* (New York, 1972), pp. 414–28. See also Jean Rosenthal, 'Five Kings', *Theatre Arts Magazine*, 23 (1939).

[6] France, *Theatre of Orson Welles*, p. 161.

[7] For details of the script of this production, which has been virtually ignored by previous commentators, I have consulted the typescript by Welles and the three booklets of production notes by Hilton Edwards in the Gate Theatre Archive, Special Collections, Northwestern University Library. These resources – along with other materials in the Archive – have not to my knowledge hitherto been brought to bear on Welles's work.

[8] An appendix of *The Theatre of Orson Welles* lists numerous reviews of *Five Kings*. I have consulted the following newspaper comments on the stage *Chimes at Midnight* in 1960: *Belfast Telegraph*, 20, 22, 24 February; *Belfast Newsletter*, 23, 24 February; *Northern Whig*, 24 February; *The Times*, 25 February; *Daily Mail* (London), 22, 24, 25 February; *Daily Express* (London), 25 February; *Irish Times*, 1 March; *Evening Mail* (Dublin), 1 March; *Evening Herald* (Dublin), 1 March; *Irish Independent*, 7 March.

shape of Shakespeare's Part One.' Welles's second act was a reworking of materials in *Part 2*, for which he did not have so high a regard: 'The scenes in Part Two are often superior to Part One ... but the shape is less good, and, thus, our cutting is going to actually help.'[9] Only Falstaff's death was included from *Henry V*.

The staged *Chimes at Midnight* was a critical success, with London as well as Belfast and Dublin reviewers, but a financial disaster. Welles himself regarded it as a 'flop' and did not take it on a contemplated tour to London and Paris.[10]

The filmed *Chimes at Midnight* (originally distributed in the United States under the title *Falstaff*) was released in 1965. It was adapted

and directed by Welles, who played Falstaff. For it Welles made essentially the same selection of materials from *Henry IV* as for the two stage versions. In content, it resembles the Irish version in drawing its text almost entirely from the two parts of *Henry IV*, without the large concern of *Five Kings* with *Henry V*. In structure, however, it resembles the treatment of *Henry IV* materials in *Five Kings*,

9 From a note 'about essentials' in the file of Edwards's correspondence with Welles in Northwestern University's Gate Theatre Archive. As here Welles often uses '...' as a mark of punctuation; in my quotations from Welles I have avoided use of three dots as a mark of ellipsis.
10 Barbara Nearing, *Orson Welles* (New York, 1985), p. 448.

1 Orson Welles as Falstaff in the staged version of *Chimes at Midnight*

taking *Part 1* as its basis and drawing on portions from *Part 2* to fill out that structure and add an extended coda to it.

In matters of detail, the film is especially close to the Irish stage production. Many of the film script's stage directions are verbatim from the stage script.[11] For instance, the film's introduction of the Percys one by one as the narrator mentions them comes directly from the Irish version. Keith Baxter played Prince Hal in both, and with the same mixture of the 'young man with a taste for practical jokes and the serious young prince aware of his own destiny'.[12] The slowly tolling bells which are a motif in the film serve the same function as did the death-march drumbeats which sounded through much of the Irish production.

It is fascinating to see how certain features in the film emerged as Welles moved from version to version. One of the funniest moments in the film comes in the midst of the prince's battlefield lament over 'dead' Falstaff (*1 Henry IV*, 5.4.102–10).[13] No sooner has he said 'I could have better spared a better man' than he sees the vapour of Falstaff's breath coming through his visor: 'Embowelled will I see thee by and by,' he taunts and goes his ways. In the Irish version, the lines between 'better man' and 'Embowelled' were cut, but without motivation. In the film script, the cut was prompted by the prince's noticing 'an involuntary heave' in the 'corpse'. In the film, the tell-tale vapour makes the effect unmistakably graphic and comic.

The successive versions show Welles practising a growing economy of means. At first he apparently felt it necessary to dramatize his use of Holinshed by showing the audience a copy of the *Chronicles*. On-stage in Ireland the narrator took a large book from a stand and read from it; in the film script: 'the screen is filled with a section of a page from "Holinshed's Chronicle History of England" showing the same words as those spoken by the narrator'. The actual film dispenses with this fuss: the titles conclude with 'Narration

based on Holinshed's Chronicles as spoken by Ralph Richardson', at which we hear Richardson's voice describing the murder of Richard II as the camera shot descends from the sky to reveal Pomfret Castle.

At times, Welles may have overdone his economies, becoming so elliptical as to be obscure. In the stage *Chimes at Midnight* he took elaborate pains to introduce the prince to the audience. He had the king ask, 'Can no man tell me of my unthrifty son?' (*Richard II*, 5.3.1–12) to which Westmoreland replied, 'The prince will, in the perfectness of time, / Cast off his followers' (*2 Henry IV*, 4.4.74–9). The Chorus then put in, 'Now for the king's son':

[*Enter Prince Hal*] Lord Henry prince of Wales . . . Indeed he was youthfully given, grown to audacity, and had chosen companions with whom he spent the time in such recreations, exercises and delights as he fancied . . .
[*Falstaff, awakening, pops his head up from behind a rostrum or chest*].

This may have been too explicit an introduction, but in the film Welles goes to the other extreme. After Hotspur has wished that his rival might be 'poisoned with a pot of ale', the image dissolves to show Hal finishing a pot of ale – and that is the extent of his introduction. The effect is direct and vivid, to be sure, but it is one of the reasons the film often seems made for an audience that already knows the plays.

Considering the closeness of the film to the stage productions, Welles was remarkably successful in respecting the idioms of the two dramatic forms. In the film, he avoids the use of stage conventions. He has all Shakespeare's soliloquies spoken as dialogue in the hearing of other characters; he gets around the conven-

---

[11] For details of this script I have consulted the copy in the Gate Theatre Archive.

[12] Betty Lowry, *Belfast Telegraph*, 24 February 1960.

[13] All line references are to *The Riverside Shakespeare*, ed. G. B. Evans *et al.* (Boston, 1974).

tion of impenetrable disguise by making Poins and Hal hidden eavesdroppers on Falstaff in the tavern rather than presenting themselves as pantlers. In his own performance as Falstaff in the Irish stage version, Welles made the most of the live situation, playing up a sense of community with the audience. As his own script writer, Welles let Falstaff in on secrets that in the original are at first known only to the audience. (He realized in advance that it was the prince who had picked his pocket and who was disguised as a pantler.) In turn, Welles as actor let the audience in on Falstaff's secrets. Reviewers delighted in the way he would confide certain of his speeches, 'sitting down with his legs dangling over the front of the stage, chatting to the audience'.[14] Appropriately, none of these stage familiarities carried over into his screen performance.

To focus so neatly on the two stage productions and the film is untrue, however, to the fecundity of Welles's response to the history plays and the fluidity of his creative process. By all accounts, *Five Kings* was in a continual state of redefinition, especially of ruthless cutting, during its time on the road. Of the Irish production, Thelma Ruby, who played Mistress Quickly, has recalled that the cast was still rehearsing at the end of the run, trying new arrangements of the material.[15] For instance, Welles experimented with taking Mistress Quickly's report of the death of Falstaff from the very end (where a reviewer had found it 'anticlimactic'),[16] and introducing it at the very beginning, thus interestingly anticipating the retrospective effect the film creates by putting the 'chimes at midnight' exchange between Falstaff and Shallow before the titles.

Beyond the examples already given, Welles's original film script differed significantly from the version that reached the screen. There were good things in the script that got lost. The 'quite symphonic' snoring that Welles called for when Falstaff is first presented is hardly more than a snuffle on the soundtrack. Falstaff was to have gone to Gadshill on a 'huge shire horse to match his size'. In the script Welles made the prince the bearer of the good news to his dying father that the rebels had been defeated; hence his initial jocularity to his weeping brother ('How now? Rain within doors, and none abroad?' – *2 Henry IV*, 4.5.9). In the film his bearing of the good news does not appear, leaving his jocularity a puzzle, especially after his solemn final departure from the tavern. Other omissions, however, were positive benefits to the film, such as the cutting of the extended treatment of Falstaff's debt and breach of promise to Mistress Quickly, which the film script had taken over bodily from the Irish stage version.

Welles's process of redefinition did not stop with the shooting of the film. Keith Baxter has pointed out that only after editing the film did Welles begin talking of it as a lament for the loss of Merrie England.[17] In this respect and others Welles's *Sight and Sound* interview about the film, which has been highly influential upon subsequent commentators, can thus be read as still another refashioning of the *Henry IV* materials.[18] For instance, James Naremore has rightly observed that Welles's claim in the interview that he intercut the famous battle scene so that 'every cut seemed to be a blow, a counter-blow, a blow received, a blow returned' does not in fact fit what we see on the screen.[19] Welles seems never to have tired of ringing new changes on the Shakespearian themes, and his film is best understood as part of this continuum of interpretation.

[14] H. R. Jeans, *Daily Mail*, 25 February 1960.

[15] In conversation with the author, July 1985.

[16] Lowry, *Belfast Telegraph*.

[17] Deborah T. Curren Aquino, '*Chimes at Midnight*: Retrospectively Elegiac', *Shakespeare on Film Newsletter*, 4 (1979).

[18] Juan Cobos and Miguel Rubio, 'Welles and Falstaff', *Sight and Sound*, 35 (1966).

[19] James Naremore, *The Magic World of Orson Welles* (Oxford, 1978), p. 271.

## II

Amid these permutations, certain hallmarks of Welles's style as an adapter of Shakespeare stand out, both in his scriptwriting and directing:

(1) *Expansion/contraction*. Obviously, the initial impulse for all the adaptations is Welles's desire to encompass as much as he can of Shakespeare's large scope but render it within a shorter form: to tell the story of Harry Monmouth in one play rather than three. Such expansiveness is to be seen at every stage of his adaptive process. Throwing back to *Five Kings*, Welles's film script called for an opening section drawn from *Richard II*; it gave an abbreviated treatment of Richard's deposition and Exton's delivery of his corpse to the horrified new king. Reportedly, Welles also shot footage of Bolingbroke's arrival from banishment.[20] All this preliminary matter was eventually omitted, thus illustrating Welles's ability to counteract his own expansiveness when it was excessive.

(2) *Dynamism*. A related impulse is Welles's desire to have more going on per dramatized moment than he found in his source. By his own acknowledgement Welles was himself 'easily bored'. Presumably he felt (as is true) that the first time we see Prince Hal and Falstaff together not very much happens beyond talk and preparation for the Gadshill incidents. In *Five Kings* he moved the pantlers episode in *2 Henry IV* up to fill this vacuum, even though the tone of the latter passage is much less playful than that of the Gadshill high jinks. The film much more successfully moves the pocket-picking (*1 Henry IV*, 2.4) up instead. And by making a single episode of the pocket-picking, which Shakespeare rather thinly spreads out over two separate scenes, Welles is able to follow through on the action to its conclusion. The incidents in the Gadshill adventure are similarly combined into a single uninterrupted sequence. Here, however, Welles overdoes the fast pace of his story-telling; his Poins never gives the audience the pleasure of hearing in advance the details of the trick to be played on Falstaff.

(3) *Pointing/counterpointing*. In general, Welles seeks an intenser impact than he finds in his Shakespeare materials. In *Five Kings* some of the vignettes suggest 'black-out' sketches.[21] At the end of the pantler episode, for example, when Falstaff is defending his dispraise of the prince to the wicked and expatiating on the wickedness of his associates, especially the Hostess, Welles cleverly stitches on Falstaff's give-and-take with the Hostess from *Part 1* (3.3.115–30) so that her 'Thou or any man knows where to have me' becomes the punch-line that ends the scene.

Often Welles rearranges dialogue for climactic emphasis. In both the stage and the film *Chimes at Midnight* he reversed the order of *2 Henry IV*, 3.1, so that the scene would end with the king's 'Uneasy lies the head that wears a crown'. In the Irish stage version he put Falstaff's praise of sherris sack (*2 Henry IV*, 4.3.86–125) at the end of the battle scene in which he had claimed credit for killing Hotspur. Confided to the audience, it made an effective end to the first act. In the film, Welles keeps the speech in this same position but to very different effect; it has become an appeal to Hal to renew their tavern conviviality, which the prince walks away from, dropping his cup as he goes.

It is very like Welles when he actually shot the lead-in to the opening credits of the film to go beyond his script's scene of 'trees like black skeletons against a leaden sky', amid which are seen some 'old gentlemen walking together in the winter orchard, talking over old times'. The film brings the talkers indoors from the orchard, past a contrastingly hot fire in a round

---

[20] Cobos and Rubio, *Welles and Falstaff*, p. 161.

[21] France, *The Theatre of Orson Welles*, p. 168, connects Welles's 'black-out' techniques in *Five Kings* with those Pauline Kael sees in *Citizen Kane* – in *The Citizen Kane Book* (Boston, 1971).

stove, to seat them in front of a still larger fire in a huge fireplace. Welles then goes on to contrast the stasis of the reminiscers recalling the chimes at midnight with the rush of a troop of horsemen riding to wild music through a street, as the titles begin.

(4) *Knitting.* Shakespeare himself likes to create a tissue of cross-references, which Welles delights in underlining. As early as *Five Kings* he went out of his way to take the prince's protestation of virtue amid bad influences ('by this hand thou thinkest me as far in the Devil's book as thou, and Falstaff' – *2 Henry IV*, 2.2.45–60) and juxtapose it with Falstaff protesting to Bardolph, 'Company, villainous company hath been the spoil of me' (*1 Henry IV*, 3.3.1–33). In the film script, the king's 'Uneasy lies the head that wears a crown' (*2 Henry IV*, 3.1.1–31) dissolves into the prince telling Poins that 'Before God, I am exceeding weary' (2.2.1). The film itself not only includes this link but begins the scene that follows with Falstaff telling Bardolph, 'I am as melancholy as a gib cat or a lugg'd bear' (*1 Henry IV*, 1.2.74). The three moments are further knit by brooding background music scored for strings.

The film threads together numerous motifs. The mourning bells that sound during the lead-in before the credits are heard at intervals throughout and turn to 'joy-bells' (as they are described in Welles's scene direction) at the coronation. Troops of horsemen repeatedly ride by, usually suggesting the imperious claim of public duty on private lives. Scene after scene ends with someone watching someone else leave, whether it is Falstaff watching the prince ride away, or Lady Percy watching her husband ride away, or Falstaff – on foot – being seen off by Doll (with kisses blown) or Justice Shallow. At the very end, after the rejection, the page watches as Falstaff, deserted by his other associates, makes his slow way out of the courtyard; after Falstaff's death, Mistress Quickly watches as his huge coffin is laboriously pushed away on its cart.

(5) *Narrative coherence.* In addition to such interstitching in the texture of his adaptations, Welles seeks to tighten the loose narrative patterns he finds in the original. This is especially notable in act 2 of the staged *Chimes at Midnight*. Having removed from it the political scenes in *Part 2*, with which Shakespeare alternates the adventures of Falstaff, Welles makes a virtuoso rearrangement and integration of what remains, resulting in a little story about Falstaff's day. First we see Hal and Poins plotting to disguise themselves as pantlers (2.2) and trick Falstaff. We are then given a further promise of problems to come for Falstaff as Mistress Quickly appears, instructing Fang and Snare to arrest him (2.1.1–37). At last Falstaff himself appears in the street, talking of how he has led his ragamuffins to where they were 'pepper'd' (*1 Henry IV*, 5.3.35–8). 'And I,' he continues, 'am I not fallen away vilely since this last action?' (*1 Henry IV*, 3.3.1–10). His servant appears, giving the doctor's report on his 'water' and leading into his remark that 'I am not only witty in myself, but the cause that wit is in other men' (*2 Henry IV*, 1.2.1–9). His servant replies, 'Sir John, you are so fretful you cannot live long' (*1 Henry IV*, 3.3.3–11) and Falstaff maintains that he is 'as virtuously given as a gentleman need to be' (ll.12–17). Then follows the first encounter between Falstaff and the Lord Chief Justice (*2 Henry IV*, 1.2.61–192), considerably cut and with Falstaff's 'gravy, gravy, gravy' (l.161) transposed as a punchline to give him the last word. Then the Hostess 'dashes onto the scene' with Fang and Snare. Unaware of their arrival, however, Falstaff instructs his servant to bear various letters, including one 'to old Mistress Ursula, whom I have weekly sworn to marry since I perceiv'd the first white hair of my chin' (ll.237–42). At this the Hostess breaks in, 'Thou didst swear to *me*' (2.1.86–92). She then urges the beadles into action and the Justice intervenes very much as in the original, except that Welles highhandedly omits all the lines reconciling Falstaff and Mistress Quickly,

apart from his 'Come hither, Hostess'. Despite the urgent news of the arrival of the prince and the king, Falstaff limps toward the tavern brooding, 'A pox of this gout, or a gout of this pox' (1.2.242–8). As he proceeds there, we see the Hostess consoling Doll (2.4.22–30), who has drunk too much canaries. Falstaff arrives, then Hal and Poins in disguise, and then Pistol. Unlike the original, Welles thus has Hal and Poins present during the Pistol episode; they in fact take the lead in driving Pistol away. Doll then babies Falstaff as in Shakespeare (ll.208–25) but Welles adds to this passage the later one in which Falstaff laments 'I am old' (ll.271–9). By doing so, Welles tightens the connection between Falstaff's insults about the prince and Poins (ll.236–54) and their discovery (ll.283–4), which thus follows immediately. The story of Falstaff's day then ends as in Shakespeare with Falstaff sending for Doll, and Quickly hurrying her off.

Much of this is in the film script, but little of it appears in the film. In the film Welles is nonetheless much concerned with small narrative continuities. He likes to develop a second ring for his circus so that by cross-cutting he can tell an incidental story, such as the repeated knocks at the door during the play-within-a-play of which the Hostess alone seems to be aware or Falstaff's visit to the water-closet ('Empty the jordan' – *2 Henry IV*, 2.4.34), which is linked to his page's report on his 'water' (1.2.1–5). Welles never lets us forget the presence of onlookers, each time showing them in a different aspect – as with the whores at the play or Poins and the prince eavesdropping from a loft on Falstaff: in separate glimpses, they 'shh' an attendant to silence, Hal bumps his head on a rafter, they spy through slats in the floor, almost fall out of the loft, before swinging down to identify themselves.

Welles is especially intent on sustaining a fluidity between scenes. In *Five Kings* he made the most of the revolving stage to keep a steady flow of action. Martin Gabel describes how Falstaff learns that Hal has been made king and sets off for the palace:

The revolve was also going, in the opposite direction ... Finally, the palace comes into view, and there's Falstaff outside the gate with all the mob (as many people as Welles had). The guard tries to keep Falstaff out, but he gets through with his one henchman. Now, the palace courtyard is raked, and as the stage revolves to bring it in front of you, two rows of nobles, all clad in ermine, come out of the coronation. The courtyard now occupies virtually the whole stage...[22]

One can see why film proved so congenial a medium for Welles. In Ireland there was no revolve, but transitions were enhanced by music and lighting. Here is the way Welles envisaged the moment after the king's soliloquy ending 'Uneasy lies the head that wears a crown':

Lights dim as the king exits ... The slow death-march beat of distant drums is heard and then in time to this (but *double* time) – a chorus of male voices offstage begins a drinking song. The tune is fierce and coarse (like 'Let me the canniken'). There is a burst of raucous laughter and a woman's shrill scream ... A small gang of vaguely military young men tumbles forward out of the darkness in pursuit of a girl ... The prince and Poins follow the group on-stage ... The girl is cut off by one of the soldiers and turning runs into the prince's arms. He kisses her a bit absent-mindedly and lets her go. She runs off pursued by the others except for Poins, who is left downstage looking at the prince sardonically. (The drinking song continues off but fades throughout the following scene, leaving only the muffled death-march drum beat) ...
*Poins.* Is it come to this?
*Prince.* [*with a slight laugh*]: Before God, I am exceeding weary.

The production notebook indicates that this transition was in fact made in just this fashion.

In dialogue as well as in plot, Welles seeks a rapid, conversational flow. He not only drastically cuts long speeches but reworks the order

---

[22] Quoted by France, p. 167.

of speeches for comic or dramatic effect. In the arrest of Falstaff in the Irish stage version, for example, he has Fang twice interrupted by Falstaff ('Away varlets') and the Hostess, who is continuing her aggrieved account of Falstaff's breach of promise (2 *Henry IV*, 2.1.93.101–2), before he can get out 'Sir John, I arrest you at the suit of Mistress Quickly' (45). Welles adds emphasis to the king's question, 'But wherefore did he take away the crown?' (2 *Henry IV*, 4.5.88) by having him address it not to the court but directly to the prince and immediately before he gives his explanation:

> *King*. But wherefore did you take away the crown?
> *Prince*. God witness with me, when I here came in,
>   And found no course of breath within your Majesty,
>   How cold it struck my heart!  (ll.149–51)

This kind of reworking is more and more pronounced in Welles's successive versions.

### III

All these features can be seen as bringing Shakespeare's text into line with the general idiom of modern drama, tightening its unity and coherence, sharpening its emphasis, speeding its pace. Welles is not so different from contemporary directors, who are not as scrupulous as he to label their work as adaptations. After all, he uses only Shakespeare's dialogue, although he may occasionally change a word or speaker. What distinguishes Welles is his boldness and flair and the extreme freedom he takes in transposing parts. He thus occupies a middle area between a director given to interpretative cutting and a free adapter (such as John Barton, Charles Marowitz, or Tom Stoppard), who writes a good deal of his own dialogue.

The feature in Welles's adaptations that most stands out is another modern preoccupation, a strong emphasis on psychology.

Both stage versions were centrally concerned with the personal relationship between the prince and the fat knight. The film gives greater prominence to the king, and to the inner workings of the resulting triangle, than do the stage productions. Welles was brilliantly right in telling Kenneth Tynan:

The richness of the triangle between the father and Falstaff and the son is without parallel: it's a complete Shakespearean creation. The other plays are good stories borrowed from other sources and made great because of what Shakespeare breathed into them. But there's nothing in the medieval chronicles that even hints at the Falstaff–Hal–King story. That's Shakespeare's story.

There is truth, too, in Welles's assertion: 'My film is entirely true to the story, although it sacrifices great parts of the plays from which the story is mined.'[23]

Visually, the film constantly contrasts the king and his court with Falstaff and the tavern. The king is spare, shaven, sharp-featured (as emphasized in profiles); Falstaff is enormous and round of body and beard. The king's ambience is vertical (full of vaults and spears), stone, stark, where Falstaff's is horizontal (low-ceilinged), wood-and-plaster, full of things and people. Welles repeatedly juxtaposes the half-timbered tavern and the walls of the fortress. Like Shakespeare, he shows an all-male court whereas the women are in the tavern, but Welles underlines the contrast by filling the tavern with whores, who at exciting moments come running déshabillé from their rooms.

In body language, too, court and tavern contrast. The king is physically remote, cold (his breath vapourizes when that of his courtiers does not – as if he were surrounded by an aura of coldness). He is often very still and indeed most effectively exerts his royal authority through a prolonged level gaze at his

---

[23] Kenneth Tynan, 'Interview with Orson Welles', *Playboy*, 14 (1967), 56.

adversaries. When he moves it is in straight lines. His attending armed soldiers always stand in long lines. Light in his court is visibly angular, as sunlight is spotlighted through

2   Sketches by Orson Welles for *Chimes at Midnight*[24]

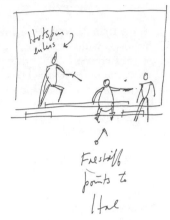

As in the film (and film script), Welles's Falstaff was at pains to make sure that Hotspur recognized Prince Hal (not himself) as his antagonist

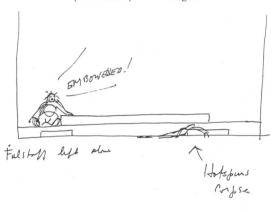

Welles's own girth, supplemented by padding, gave special point to Falstaff's expostulation

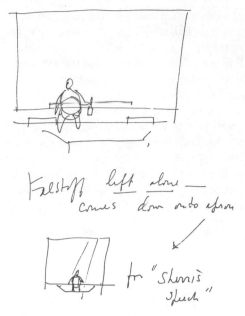

At the end of the first part, Welles's Falstaff confided his 'sherris sack' speech to the audience

high windows. Only once does the king reach out in affection to his son.

In the tavern, light is diffused. Tavern people move in circles (as does the camera in places), often spinning around. When we are introduced to Hal he spins from whore to whore before he runs up some steps to join Poins, who, after announcing 'I've picked his pocket', does a slow twirl around a post. When the prince is making his last exit from the tavern (now walking purposefully in a bee-line to his horse), Falstaff as he hurries after him is

[24] For the Irish *Chimes at Midnight*, Welles outlined in a memo to Hilton Edwards a re-blocking of the battle between Prince Hal and Hotspur. The memo was accompanied by a set of sketches, of which four are reproduced here. The new staging was designed to permit Welles, who had a long history of back trouble, to have off-stage assistance with picking up Hotspur's corpse. In archive correspondence, Edwards at first expressed resentment at Welles's re-staging but later recanted. Although the sketches were originally catalogued as the work of Edwards, they are clearly by Welles, who as a youth aspired to be a painter, and reflect the energy of his visual imagination.

caught by dancers who take him arm-in-arm and swing him in circles. Falstaff is associated with touching (he and Hal often embrace), and with warmth, making especially ironic Mrs Quickly's lament that the dead Falstaff is 'cold as any stone'.

The resulting effect approaches expressionism, so graphically do the contrasting filmed worlds project the inner attitudes of their inhabitants. Thinking literally, one might marvel at the scene in which Hotspur uses his weapon-room as a place to bathe. But in the idiom of the film the scene is a visual pun on his nickname: he is not only hot but steaming from his bath, not merely fitted with spurs but surrounded by spears and complete coats of armour – and then hurried off to the battlefield by carefully climaxed calls of one, two, four, six buglers.

Welles seems to have a special feeling for Hotspur. As he explained in a note to Hilton Edwards,[25] he sees Hotspur as more sympathetic than the prince, whom he regards as 'beady-eyed and self-regarding'.[26] Gabel, in his recollections of *Five Kings*, describes Hotspur's final battle:

the stage had started circling. Finally, upstage, half-hidden behind a mound, you saw Hal deliver the death-blow to Hotspur. At this point, the revolve stopped; the music stopped; and there was a great moment of silence. Then, slowly, the revolve brought Hotspur around in front where he delivered his last words.[27]

Along with Hotspur, the audience must have felt that 'time, that takes survey of all the world,/Must have a stop.' In the film there is a comparable overlap of inner and outer worlds when the prince mistakenly assumes that the king is dead. At this moment, Welles interposes shots of monks in the court and sounds of their chanting, as if indeed they were already mourning the dead king.

Subtextually, the film carefully traces a straight line in the relationship between the king and the prince. In Shakespeare the king repeatedly zigzags between mistrust and trust

of his son – he needs continually to be won over – as in their first interview and Hal's battlefield rescue of his father in *Part 1* and Hal's premature taking of the crown in *Part 2*. Welles cuts the battlefield rescue in all three versions. *Five Kings* simply reflected the king's other vacillations. In the staged *Chimes at Midnight* the king 'suddenly embraced' his son at 'A thousand rebels die in this' (*1 Henry IV*, 3.2.160). Welles then took care to motivate the king's renewed suspicions by inserting a choric passage from Holinshed concerning rumours of Hal's designs on the throne and his consequent banishment from court. In the film Welles cuts the 'thousand rebels' line from their first interview and the king remains distant throughout the scene. As the stage direction in the script reads: the king is 'still bleakly unconvinced', and he gives the order 'coldly': 'Harry you shall set forward.' The word 'cold' recurs three times in the stage directions and is applied to both speakers. After the battle is won and Falstaff has made his claim of killing Hotspur, the king makes an unspoken rejection of his son in the series of looks that are exchanged. The stage directions in the script make clear what is not so clear in the film; Falstaff has said, 'I look to be either Earl or Duke, I assure you':

Silence as the king moves to the body of Hotspur . . . He looks from the dead hero to his son . . . Then to Falstaff (who is, for once, a bit abashed and keeps silent) . . . Now the king turns back to the prince . . . Hal meets his father's eye, but makes no reply to the unspoken question, stubbornly refusing to spoil Falstaff's joke . . . Then suddenly weary disappointment in the king's face touches him . . . But it's too late; the king has turned away . . . Hal wants to go with his father, but stands paralysed by the hopeless distance stretching between them . . .

Only after the crown has been returned and

---

[25] In the note 'about essentials' in the Gate Theatre Archive.
[26] Tynan, 'Interview', p. 56.
[27] Quoted by France, *The Theatre of Orson Welles*, p. 167.

his death is near does the king express love for his son and put his hand on his shoulder.

The prince's attitudes toward his responsibilities as heir apparent are no less carefully charted. Each twinge of conscience is motivated. In the film script his 'I know you all' speech is prompted by Falstaff's question (interpolated from earlier in the scene), 'I prithee sweet wag, shall there be gallows standing when thou art king?' The prince does not answer, being 'lost in a sort of dream'. 'Do not thou, when thou art king, hang a thief,' Falstaff goes on. The prince responds to this but makes the joke 'with an absent air': 'thou shalt have the hanging of the thieves and so become a rare hangman'. He moves to the door:

Hal turns back, looking at Falstaff . . . What he now says is deadly serious, but he covers it with a very slight sweetening of self-parody – almost as though he were quoting some other, some more virtuous prince . . .

Although the film is not entirely clear, the script confirms that Welles intended that Falstaff should at least half overhear the prince's words. After 'unyoked humour of your idleness', Falstaff raises his wine cup 'in ironic salutation'. After 'be more wonder'd at': 'Falstaff watches him with a grin, but behind the twinkle in the old man's eye there is a faint shadow of foreknowledge.'

The actual film points Hal's motivation still more strongly. It substitutes for the 'hanging of thieves' speech Falstaff's ruminations about the squires of the night's body (ll. 23–9). This speech not only includes a reminder to Hal about his future 'when thou art king', but also refers to 'men of good government'. It is at this last phrase that Hal's expression turns sober.

Welles commented that the farewell of the prince to Falstaff is 'performed about four times during the movie'.[28] But this is not simply a series of reluctant farewells; they reflect his growing revulsion towards his low-life associates. At a crucial turning point,

Hal makes explicit his distaste for Poins, and by extension for Falstaff. Welles's treatment of this feature in the film evolved through the successive versions. In *Five Kings*, Hal's rejection of Poins was confined to a single scene (*2 Henry IV*, 2.2). In it Welles gave the rejection prominence by rearranging the dialogue so that Hal's strongest words of repudiation came at the very end of their exchange (this is true of all later versions as well): 'By this hand thou thinkest me as far in the Devil's book, as thou, and Falstaff for obduracy and persistency. Let the end try the man.' Since, in this version, the pantler-disguise episode had been transposed to the very first encounter between the prince and Falstaff, the prince never did make a final return to the tavern.

In the stage *Chimes at Midnight* this serious omission was rectified. Welles restored the pantler episode as in the original, and the prince made his exit upon hearing Peto's report that the king 'is at Westminster', and after reflecting, 'I feel me much to blame/So idly to profane the precious time.' As for the prince's earlier repudiation of Poins, Welles's stage directions suggest the tone he desired:

*Prince.* Shall I tell thee one thing, Poins? [*There is something hard and dangerous in his tone, but Poins puts a good face on it, and plays up gaily.*]
*Poins.* [*with hollow-heartiness*] Yes, faith; and let it be an excellent good thing.
*Prince.* [*with an icy smile*] It shall serve among wits of no higher breeding than thine.

In the film script, Welles sees Poins as less on the defensive, almost asking for his own repudiation:

*Prince.* Doth it now (*sic*: apparently a typographical error for 'not' that is spoken thus in the film) show vilely in me to desire small beer?
*Poins.* [*playing up, but with a cruel undertone in his joking*] How ill it follows, after you have laboured so hard, you should talk so idly! Tell

---

28 Cobos and Rubio, *Welles and Falstaff*, p. 159. See Samuel Crowl, 'The Long Goodbye', *Shakespeare Quarterly*, 31 (1980).

me, how many good young princes would do so, their fathers being so sick as yours at this time is? [*Silence . . . (Poins, feeling his days numbered, has been committing a kind of social suicide) . . . The prince looks at him . . .* ]

*Prince.* What a disgrace is it for me to remember thy name! . . . Or to know thy face tomorrow! [*Then the prince laughs – quite nicely – and Poins is quick to join the laughter*] Do you use me thus, Ned? must I marry your sister?

*Poins.* God send the wench no worse fortune – [*quickly*] but I never said so.

The passage ends with Poins '[bowing with a sour smile]': 'I am your shadow, my lord; I follow you . . . '

In the film most of the speeches of repudiation are transferred to the prince's last tavern visit. After Poins and Hal have revealed themselves and had their fun with Falstaff about his dispraising them before the wicked, Falstaff rambles on about how vilely he is fallen away (*1 Henry IV*, 3.3) and hears from his page that his 'water' shows he might have more diseases than he knew of (*2 Henry IV*, 1.2). The prince's mind is elsewhere; he reflects solemnly 'how idly I do profane the precious time'. He then talks to a wickedly grinning Poins about his father's sickness, much as in the original text (*2 Henry IV*, 2.2.35–60) except that their lines are counterpointed against Falstaff's all-too apposite comments about wisdom crying out in the street (*1 Henry IV*, 1.2.83–8) and how men should take heed of their company (*2 Henry IV*, 5.1.75–8). Thus Falstaff is audibly linked by Welles with Poins in the prince's disgust.

For Hal's last words, the soundtrack makes a refinement on the script. In the script the prince replied to Poins's 'I would think thee a most princely hypocrite', with 'It would be every man's thought; and thou art a blessed fellow to think as every man thinks . . . Never a man's thought keeps the roadway better than thine.' On the soundtrack this part is cut, leaving the prince's final 'Every man would think me a hypocrite indeed' an unsoftened, *self*-rebuke. He gives Poins a long level look

worthy of his father: 'Let the end try the man', and heads off hurriedly.

Thus Welles totally internalizes the prince's final departure from the tavern. He has made the bold choice of cutting Peto's report that the king has come to Westminster, the external factor with which Shakespeare prompted the prince's departure. In the film, this prompting is solely the result of the prince's feeling for his father in his illness, his revulsion towards his tavern associates, and his resolve to reform his own behaviour.

IV

Since Welles's rearrangements suggest different choices that Shakespeare might have made, they can provide a fresh perspective on the original text. From this vantage one is first of all struck by how much less overtly psychological Shakespeare is than Welles, and how much more political. As has just been discussed, the psychology of the prince's choice between his father and Falstaff is suggested in Shakespeare but less often than in Welles and less explicitly. Daniel Seltzer aptly writes in this respect of 'Welles' dramatization of the plays' *sub*text'.[29] In the original *text* the prince's decisive assumption of his regal responsibilities comes later than his last visit to the tavern, in act 5, scene 2 (a scene that Welles omitted from all his adaptations). Shakespeare's timing is more external than Welles's (Henry IV is actually dead and Henry V all but crowned), and his context is more political (the young king affirms the rule of law and the Lord Chief Justice's adherence to it).

In general, Shakespeare is much more interested in the civil wars than is Welles. The battle is of course one of the high points of the film, but not because it shows a meaningful struggle between the two sides. Through most of it, it

---

[29] Daniel Seltzer, 'Shakespeare's Texts and Modern Production', *Reinterpretations of Elizabethan Drama*, ed. Norman Rabkin (New York, 1969), p. 109.

is impossible to tell who is winning and who is losing. As Welles shows the increasing brutality and squalor of the fighting, indeed, his chief point seems to be the political meaninglessness of it all. This is true even of the hand-to-hand victory of the prince over Hotspur, which comes after Hotspur has driven the prince to the ground and is taken off guard while coming in for the kill. Contrast Shakespeare, where by an adversary's account the prince's 'swift wrath beat down / The never-daunted Percy to the earth / From whence with life he never more sprung up' (*2 Henry IV*, I.I.109–II).

Other features of the original stand out in contrast to Welles's adaptations. Shakespeare's delight in local colour is an instance, as in the exotic Welsh court and the Cotswold talk of Shallow and Silence. Welles's amalgamations tend to level the striking differences between the two parts of *Henry IV*, the muse of *Part 1* being youthful while that of *Part 2* is ageing, verging on senility.

Yet, outweighing these and other differences, the chief insight into Shakespeare that is yielded by Welles's work is a point of resemblance. The film and the stage adaptations make one see anew the genius of the core of the *Henry IV* plays: Shakespeare's treatment of the four-way conflicts of the king, the prince, Hotspur, and Falstaff as they move the action through the contrasting worlds of court, tavern, and battlefield. Welles did not come to a fully successful treatment of this core until he had tried tipping Shakespeare's balance in alternative directions – towards the prince in *Five Kings*, towards Falstaff in the stage *Chimes at Midnight*. Through trial and error in these stage adaptations he worked his way back to a balance in his film that is, ironically, very close to Shakespeare's own. Yet this process was not unproductive, for through it Welles gained not only a deeper insight into the original but a freer hand in reworking it and a surer touch in placing his distinctive psychological emphasis upon it.

In his 'Defense of Mixed Cinema', André Bazin argues that 'Far from being a sign of decadence, the mastering of the theatrical repertoire by the cinema is on the contrary a proof of maturity. In short, to adapt is no longer to betray but to respect.'[30] A key word in Bazin's very hopeful declaration is 'mastering'. Not all Shakespearian films show the necessary mastery. *Chimes at Midnight*, however, does. As it emerged from its stage versions to its final realization on screen, Welles's adaptation achieved, in essentials, that difficult double feat that Bazin envisages: it respects its Shakespearian theatrical original while also respecting its modern film idiom – and in such a way that, when it is at its best, Welles's vision and Shakespeare's coincide.

---

[30] Bazin, *What is Cinema?*, p. 69.

# ORSON WELLES'S 'OTHELLO': A STUDY OF TIME IN SHAKESPEARE'S TRAGEDY

## LORNE M. BUCHMAN

With the recent wave of scholarship on Shakespeare on film there is at least one important line of questioning still to pursue: can the film medium serve as a critical tool for interpreting or reinterpreting Shakespeare's work?[1] Is there something to learn, to rediscover, to see in a new light when, to borrow Walter Benjamin's phrase, we have 'the ingenious guidance of the camera' leading us through the text?[2] If, as Benjamin suggests, the camera opens up 'a new field of perception' in this age of mechanical reproduction, how can we apply his notion to the specific instance of a Shakespeare play adapted to the screen?[3]

One film that provides a particularly exciting opportunity for a critical analysis of Shakespeare's work is Orson Welles's *Othello*.[4] Of Welles's three Shakespeare films – *Macbeth* (1948), *Othello* (1952), and *Chimes at Midnight* (1965) – *Othello* has received the least critical attention and continues to be one of the most rarely seen of all cinematic adaptations of the plays. But careful study of this film illuminates a thematic aspect of the text that leads to a fresh reading of the play as a whole. Through his use of cinematic technique, Welles has produced a work that emerges as a study of time in Shakespeare's *Othello*. The insights to be gained from the film concerning this element of the play are of considerable importance for, and can contribute significantly to, scholarship on Shakespeare's great tragedy.

I

Welles spent four difficult years producing an *Othello* that, despite its technical flaws, can be placed with the finest of Shakespeare films.[5]

---

[1] To date, the most valuable and comprehensive study on Shakespeare films is Jack Jorgens's *Shakespeare on Film* (Bloomington, 1977). Other major studies include Robert Hamilton Ball, *Shakespeare on Silent Film* (New York, 1968), Roger Manvell, *Shakespeare and the Film* (New York, 1971), and Charles W. Eckert, ed., *Focus on Shakespearean Films* (New Jersey, 1972). The question as to what the cinema can tell us about the plays is not the point of enquiry for any of these works.

[2] 'The Work of Art in the Age of Mechanical Reproduction', in *Illuminations*, trans. Harry Zohn, ed. Hannah Arendt (New York, 1969), p. 236.

[3] A survey of articles on Shakespeare films written in the last few years does indicate a growing concern with what the cinematic medium can reflect about Shakespeare's dramaturgical design. See, especially, Samuel Crowl, 'The Long Goodbye: Welles and Falstaff', *Shakespeare Quarterly*, 31 (1980), 369–80, and Barbara Hodgdon, 'Kozintsev's *King Lear*: Filming a Tragic Poem', *Literature/Film Quarterly*, 5 (1977), 153–8.

[4] *Othello*, Mercury Productions, released by United Artists, 1952.

[5] Although free of the many production problems caused by the 23-day shooting period of *Macbeth*, *Othello* is not without the kind of technical negligence typical of all Welles's Shakespeare films. As with *Macbeth*, there is a serious dubbing problem in *Othello* that at moments becomes so severe one has great difficulty understanding the dialogue. The director ran out of funds during production and had to stop shooting at many points in order to raise enough money to complete the film. For an eloquent account of the erratic nature of the making of this film see Micheál MacLiammóir, *Put*

The director's commitment to the cinema as a unique vehicle for producing Shakespeare is a key to his success. After completing the film he remarked,

In *Othello* I felt that I had to choose between filming the play or continuing my own line of experimentation in adapting Shakespeare quite freely to the cinema form ... *Othello* the movie, I hope, is first and foremost a motion picture.[6]

The visuals of Welles's *Othello* attest to his considerable talents as a film-maker. His *mise-en-scène* brings important thematic concerns to the fore and is scrupulously based on ideas inherent in the text. His presentation of Venice with its stately buildings, its calm and channelled waterways, and its solid appearance, reflects well the sense of order achieved – temporarily – in the first act of Shakespeare's drama. Moreover, the visuals of the Venice world serve as a harmonious complement to the nobility and stature of the hero before he is overwhelmed by the 'green-eyed monster' of jealousy. Juxtaposed to the ordered world of Venice is Cyprus, with its jungles of arcades and pillars, its seamy underground, its narrow and winding streets, its stairways, its high and frightening cliffs and battlements, and its roaring ocean shore.[7] If Venice is the setting that corresponds to the hero, Cyprus is the complement to Iago. Within this world the villain reigns supreme, and he uses the twisted and confusing dimensions of the Cyprus environment to create an unrelenting hell for his victims.

But what is perhaps the most interesting aspect of Welles's film is the way in which he exploits the concept of time inherent in the text. Consider, for example, the prologue. The film opens with the funeral processions of both Othello and Desdemona silhouetted against the sky. Othello is carried on a bier followed by a long line of monks in black, while Desdemona is carried and followed by a line of monks in white. Although the processions are clearly separated (physically and through colour), the rhythm of the two lines is synchronized. Bells chime in a regular beat throughout the prologue, suggesting a firm and cohesive sense of time. The pace of the processions and the repetition of the accompanying chimes yields the sense of unity through compatible rhythm. Like many of Welles's films, *Othello* opens with visual images taken from the very end of the film not because the director wants to remove all suspense, but because he wants to establish a unified sequence for the whole work. In other words, the way the plot unravels takes precedence over the surprises of narrative. Moreover, by using the dominant rhythms of the processions to establish a sense of coherence and order early in the film, Welles can then illustrate how Iago shatters this tight temporal structure to bring chaos into the world of the play and its hero. Indeed, when one sees the processional image again at the end of *Othello*, one recognizes how the rhythm of time is broken and restored through the course of the tragedy.

In the opening sequence, Welles intersplices the funeral processions of Othello and Desdemona with shots of Iago dragged by chains through a crowd of screaming Cypriots. Guards throw him into an iron cage and haul him to the top of the castle walls. We witness the world momentarily from Iago's perspective; the cage spins as it hangs, the crowd screams, and, as long as we are with Iago, the stately rhythm of the processions is lost. In the prologue, Welles develops his temporal theme by realizing the opposing rhythms of Othello and Desdemona on the one hand and Iago on the other. The critic William Johnson sees

*Money in Thy Purse* (London, 1952). MacLiammóir played the part of Iago.
[6] Quoted in Peter Noble, *The Fabulous Orson Welles* (London, 1956), p. 215.
[7] Most of the film was shot in Morocco (except for the first act, which was filmed mainly on location in Venice) in the west-coast town of Mogador, where Welles ably used a castle built by the Portuguese in the sixteenth century.

the entire film as a structure of contrasting rhythms, and his sensitivity to this aspect of Welles's work is rare; in the following passage he seems to scan the rhythms of the film.

Welles sets the whole tragedy in perspective with an opening sequence that interweaves the funeral cortèges of Othello and Desdemona and the dragging of Iago to his punishment ... [But] the staccato rhythm associated with Iago gradually imposes itself on Othello's stately rhythm, and the increasing complexity of the film's movements suggests the increasing turmoil of doubt in Othello's mind.[8]

Welles uses the rhythms of time to guide the spectator through *Othello*. The film conveys an objective sense of time in the regular pattern of beating drums or chiming bells heard through a large part of the film. With this use of the soundtrack, the characters of the drama appear contained within the ordered passage of time. For example, at certain key moments in the film the spectator hears the footfalls of characters in a regular and constant rhythm, yielding the sense of the individual's participation in time's inevitable passage. Like the ticking of a bomb about to explode, however, these regular patterns erupt in corresponding sounds and images of chaos as realized by the tempest, the crashing waves of the Cyprus shore, the sudden explosion of cannon fire, the wild break of seagulls in the sky, and the uncontrolled and chaotic revels after the defeat of the Turks. In an objective sense, one recognizes an ambiguous sense of time – ordered and chaotic, constant and fragmented.

I have used the term 'objective' only to differentiate the presence of time as a force in the film as distinct from individual relationships to that force. For it is in Welles's development of the 'subjective' experiences of time that he works out his thematic concern most effectively. On the one hand, we understand time through Othello's experience; what is clear and chronologically sound in the first part of the film eventually becomes distorted and irregular as the drama progresses. As Othello's pain and jealousy increase, we lose a sense of

coherence in the film. Through the unique resources of the cinema – montage, cinematography, and the soundtrack – Welles realizes the hero's experience as he is overcome by jealousy. Early in the film the director shoots Othello in clear light, but as the film progresses we see him increasingly in shadow; through the use of montage, our sense of space disintegrates; harsh dissonant sounds eventually replace the regular and even sounds of the first part of the film. As jealousy and madness overwhelm the hero, we watch him traverse the spectrum from order to chaos, from light to shadow, and, as a result, we understand how Iago has set out to destroy his victim. He causes Othello to see only the dark, chaotic side of time – something that the hero fears and that is fundamentally against his character. 'And when I love thee not,' he says of Desdemona, 'chaos is come again.' Chaos represents a movement backwards for the hero, a state without love, a destruction of his sense of the eternal.

By contrast, Iago perceives time as an agent to control. He emerges as the master of time in the film, and the 'success' of his scheme relates to his ability to manipulate not only the 'objective' force of time but also Othello's relationship to that force. Welles develops this idea early in the action. Still in Venice, Iago is working on his gull, Roderigo, when he comes forward to the camera and says to the audience, 'I am not what I am.' Immediately following his words the scene dissolves to a close-up shot of mechanical figures striking the bells of the clock in St Mark's Square. In perfect mechanical order, these human impressions (the figures are human in shape but not in substance— i.e., not what they are) strike. Welles's use of the dissolve here forces the spectator to associate these figures with Iago as one who will hammer upon Othello's emotional balance as the figures hammer upon

---

[8] 'Orson Welles: of Time and Loss', *Film Quarterly*, 21 (1967), p. 21.

the chimes. But the specifics of the image also suggest that he will achieve his ends through a controlled use of time. As the 'Jack of the clock' – to borrow the trope of Richard II – marks time, so too will Iago orchestrate his destruction of Othello. To make this metaphor clear, Welles follows the shot of the mechanical figures with a dissolve to the bedchamber of Othello and Desdemona. Othello parts the curtains surrounding the bed and, in a high-angle shot, we see Desdemona lying on the bed with her long blonde hair spread out underneath her. Othello then speaks his lines from act 1, scene 3:

> Come Desdemona. I have but an hour
> Of love . . .
> To spend with thee. We must obey the time.
> (1.3.301–3)[9]

Eventually, one recognizes Othello's words, 'we must obey the time', as highly ironic because an obedience to time, in this film, translates into an obedience to the one who controls time – Iago. The hero bends down to kiss his bride followed by a dissolve to black. In this sequence of images Welles encapsulates the entire drama: Othello and Desdemona 'obey' time as it is orchestrated from without but, ultimately, this obedience leads to an overwhelming blackness, consuming beauty and love.

II

The question now arises as to how we can begin to use Welles's cinematic treatment of this play as a critical insight into Shakespeare's text. How does time function as a thematic device in the play? Welles's film inspires at least two important questions. Is Iago's success in destroying the hero connected to his ability to master the ebb and flow of time's rhythms? Moreover, what is Othello's sense of time and can we specify it as something that makes him particularly vulnerable to Iago's tactics? Because the major focus of this essay concerns the insights gained through seeing the

play in a new medium, I pause here to return to the text to examine the theme of time. For purposes of coherence, I delay a detailed treatment of how time works as a focal point in the film to clarify the function of time in the text.

Iago's words to Roderigo in the second act reveal his skill in manipulating time:

> Thou know'st we work by wit, and not by witchcraft;
> And wit depends on dilatory time. (2.3.366–7)

A review of Iago's speeches demonstrates that they are filled with the word 'time' and that his language is often constructed around temporal imagery. For example, in the very first scene he is angry because time has failed to bring about his expected promotion. He begins by speaking of his frustrations in Othello's service and of his jealousy of Cassio:

> This counter-caster,
> He [Cassio], in good time, must his lieutenant be,
> And I – God bless the mark! – his Moorship's ancient. (1.1.32–4)

Iago believes that he has proved himself in time but still has lost the promotion. Preferment seems to have nothing to do with loyalty in time:

> Preferment goes by letter and affection,
> And not by old gradation, where each second
> Stood heir to the first. (1.1.37–40)

Like Richard II, Iago believes that he has wasted time; but unlike the king, he will not allow time to waste him. He will not be like

> Many a duteous and knee-crooking knave
> That, in his own obsequious bondage,
> Wears out his time, much like his master's ass . . . (1.1.46–8)

Iago then calls for the bell to wake Brabantio (an image akin to the mechanical figures who

[9] David Bevington, ed., *The Complete Works of Shakespeare*, 3rd ed. (Glenview, Illinois, 1980). All subsequent quotations are from this edition.

mark time in Welles's film). He begins here to use time actively to achieve his ends.

Iago's perception of time is close to Machiavelli's notion of Fortune in *The Prince*.[10] For Machiavelli, Fortune is like a river that fluctuates between extremes of chaos and peace. But, he says, one can take precautions by building 'floodgates and embankments' in quiet times so that the violent times can be controlled. One of Machiavelli's central points in *The Prince* is his call for an easing of the control of Fortune in human affairs. If one exercises the highest Machiavellian virtue of prudence, one can learn to take control over much of one's destiny.

Iago emerges as a figure who works with time in the manner that Machiavelli prescribes. In the first scene of the play Iago tells us that he had waited for time to give him his promotion but was ultimately frustrated. Now, however, he will conquer time by taking control. Machiavelli's metaphor of the river is akin to Iago's use of images associated with pregnancy, gestation, and birth. For example, in a discussion with Roderigo towards the end of the first act, Iago tells his gull that 'There are many events in the womb of time which will be delivered' (1.3.371). In the soliloquy that ends the scene, he concludes,

> It is engendr'd. Hell and night
> Must bring this monstrous birth to the world's
> light. (1.3.404–5)

Indeed, Iago fertilizes time so that it will give birth to his desires. At a propitious moment, he will inject his poison into Othello with tales of Cassio and Desdemona: 'After some time to abuse Othello's ear / That he is too familiar with his wife' (1.3.396–7). From this point in the play he will work so that, to use his words, 'Time shall . . . favourably minister' his ends.

When next we hear of Iago we discover that he has indeed begun to conquer time. On the shores of Cyprus, the Second Gentleman remarks that Iago has fought his way through the tempest and has landed safely. Cassio remarks on how the ancient has had 'favourable and happy speed' (2.1.68). He comments approximately ten lines later that Iago has defied the expected time of his arrival. Desdemona was 'Left in the conduct of the bold Iago, / Whose footing here anticipates our thoughts / A se'nnight's speed' (2.1.76–8). It is interesting to note that at this point in the play Shakespeare juxtaposes Iago's victory over time with Othello's corresponding delay.

As I mentioned earlier, Iago's speeches are filled not only with many utterances of the word 'time' but with images of temporality as well. Curiously, Iago's victims use this word and corresponding images with increased frequency as the villain gains control. G. Wilson Knight points out that Othello eventually enters Iago's 'semantic sphere' and Jan Kott argues, 'Not only shall Othello crawl at Iago's feet; he shall talk in his language.'[11] But it is in their specific concern with issues of time and their use of temporal imagery that Iago's victims interest us here. For example, when Othello discovers Cassio, in Iago's words, in a 'time of his infirmity', he dismisses the lieutenant from his post. Interestingly, Cassio confides in Iago that what bothers him most is not that he has disillusioned the general but that his reputation will suffer. He defines that reputation as 'the immortal part of myself'. In a sense, Cassio perceives that he has lost time by losing his post. Iago 'comforts' Cassio by telling him that nothing is final – that, in time, he can gain his lieutenancy back. After all, 'you or any man may be drunk at a time, man' (2.3.307). What is most significant here is that Shakespeare expresses Iago's control by showing him to be the master of time. It is when his victims are concerned, somehow, with issues of time that they are most vulnerable to him.

---

[10] Translated by Mark Musa (New York, 1964). See especially Chapter 25.

[11] Jan Kott, *Shakespeare Our Contemporary*, translated by Boleslaw Taborski (New York, 1966), p. 112.

Shakespeare also represents vulnerability through temporal concerns in Desdemona's plea for Cassio. The former lieutenant asks Desdemona, in essence, to redeem time for him. She promises that she will speak with her husband and 'tame and talk him out of patience' (3.3.23). When she makes her request to Othello, she insists on knowing the time when he will restore Cassio.

*Desdemona.* I prithee, call him back.
*Othello.* Went he hence now?
*Desdemona.* Yes, faith, so humbled
  That he hath left part of his grief with me
  To suffer with him. Good love, call him back.
*Othello.*
  Not now, sweet Desdemon; some other time.
*Desdemona.*
  But shall it be shortly?
*Othello.*             The sooner, sweet, for you.
*Desdemona.*
  Shall't be tonight at supper?
*Othello.*             No, not tonight.
*Desdemona.*
  Tomorrow dinner, then?
*Othello.*           I shall not dine at home;
  I meet the captains at the citadel.
*Desdemona.*
  Why, then, tomorrow night, or Tuesday morn,
  On Tuesday noon, or night, on Wednesday
    morn.
  I prithee name the time, but let it not
  Exceed three days.          (3.3.51–67)

Ironically, Desdemona's insistence on naming the time is a tacit victory for the one who conquers time – Iago. She becomes an unwitting accomplice in the villain's scheme. Shakespeare's clear emphasis on naming time is a comment on the vulnerability of Iago's victims. Moreover, the great 'temptation scene' follows this sequence; now that his victims are working on his terms and using his language, Iago finds the appropriate moment to strike.

Iago's mastery over time manifests itself in a more fundamental and obvious way in Shakespeare's *Othello*. Simply put, he has superb timing and knows exactly when to strike. Like Machiavelli's brightest examples of political success (Moses, Cyrus, Romulus, Theseus), Iago receives nothing from Fortune but the occasion; and when that occasion arises, he makes optimum use of it. Emilia happens to pass by when Desdemona drops the handkerchief. Bianca conveniently arrives when Iago is with Cassio as Othello secretly watches and receives the 'ocular proof'. Roderigo happens to be in love with Desdemona and is stupid enough to abide by Iago's demands to achieve his desired ends. But, in each instance, Iago is able to exploit to the full the opportunities that his good fortune provides. Whether one is directing the play for the stage or for film, one must create situations that reveal Iago's understanding of how to take the greatest advantage of the circumstances of the moment. One can imagine the myriad ways of staging Iago's famous 'Ha, I like not that', which subtly sets off the spark of destruction in Othello's consciousness. But, in whatever way it is performed, a director must present Iago's brilliant sense of timing at that moment. And as we witness Iago's clever machinations, we are watching one of the keenest manipulators of time in the history of drama. He knows when to push and when to hold back. He knows when to further his wretched lie and when to keep silent. He knows how to build his 'evidence' and how to bring his victim to the point where he perceives what Iago wants him to perceive. And he does all this by recognizing when the opportune moments occur. Iago knows how to work with time so that time works for him.

Iago's perception of time is thus one that assumes constant change and mutability. It cannot be trusted to bring about one's desires because, like Machiavelli's river, it is fickle and erratic. For Iago, time is the 'fashionable host' that Ulysses speaks of in *Troilus and Cressida*. Indeed, to the villain of Shakespeare's *Othello*, 'Beauty, wit, / High birth, vigour of bone, desert in service, / Love, friendship, charity, are subjects all / To envious and calumniating time' (3.3.171–4). But Iago uses the fickleness of time to his own advantage; his skill lies in his ability to exploit 'calumniating time' through dissembling, plotting and Machiavellian prudence.

In contrast to Iago's perception of time as something that fluctuates and that ultimately must be conquered is Shakespeare's presentation of Othello's perception of time. For the hero, time has meaning and significance in its range and continuity. Unlike Iago, Othello perceives the world in terms of the eternal. His speeches resound with repeated use of the words 'never' and 'forever'. He asserts that he received his 'life and being / From men of royal siege'. He invests a great deal in a handkerchief given him by his mother because it represents history and links him with his past and his heritage. Othello's world is based on loyalty, history, and a sense of being rooted in time. When he vows anything, from his marriage to his vengeance, his words have an everlasting implication. To Iago he swears, 'I am bound to thee forever.' In the words of G. Wilson Knight, 'from the first to the last he loves his own romantic history'.[12] His association with the grand spectrum of time in human history also leaves one with the impression of an integrated man whose nature, to borrow A. C. Bradley's phrase, 'is all of one piece'.[13] Iago, who knows his target, refers to Othello as one with a 'constant, loving and noble nature'.

At a key moment in the play, Othello becomes so overwhelmed with Desdemona that he expresses a desire to immortalize his love for her. As Derek Traversi points out, when the hero arrives in Cyprus and is reunited with Desdemona, 'his one desire is to hold this moment to make it eternal'.[14]

> If it were now to die,
> 'Twere now to be most happy; for I fear
> My soul hath her content so absolute
> That not another comfort like to this
> Succeeds in unknown fate.     (2.1.186–90)

But Othello's belief in the possibility of absolute happiness through love also reveals his greatest point of vulnerability. Implicit in his words is a restless awareness that, until death, time has the power to destroy present emotion. Traversi clarifies the paradox:

> This precarious moment of happiness will never find its fellow, for the temporal process is . . . one of dissolution and decay. Only death can come between this temporary communion and its eclipse; but death, of course, implies the annihilation of the personality and the end of love.[15]

Unlike the realistic and sensible Rosalind, Othello reaches for the 'ever' and not the 'now' of human love. As is so often the case in Shakespeare's dramas, one's greatest desire is also the point of one's greatest vulnerability. In a way similar to Maria's exploitation of Malvolio, Iago pinpoints the spot where his revenge will 'find notable cause to work' (*Twelfth Night*, 2.3.152). Othello's statement on the manner by which he could attain eternal happiness through love exposes, by implication, his fear of the power of time's mutability; this fear becomes Iago's primary target. The villain exploits the hero's hidden anxiety and shatters his greatest hope.

Iago destroys Othello by altering his perception of the nature of time. At a number of moments in the play, Desdemona is associated with images of the divine. For Othello, she becomes 'a symbol of man's ideal, the supreme value of love . . .'[16] When Iago shows Desdemona false, Othello's sense of the eternal decays in turn. As Othello succumbs to Iago, he speaks in terms of shattered time, of a broken sense of that which holds his world

---

[12] G. Wilson Knight, *The Wheel of Fire* (London, 1960), p. 107.

[13] A. C. Bradley, *Shakespearean Tragedy*, 2nd ed. (1905; rpt. London, 1963), p. 155.

[14] Derek Traversi, *An Approach to Shakespeare*, 2nd ed. (New York, 1956), p. 138.

[15] Traversi, *Approach to Shakespeare*, p. 138.

[16] Knight, *The Wheel of Fire*, p. 109.

together. Let us return, for a moment, to that key passage early in the 'temptation' scene:

> Excellent wretch! Perdition catch my soul
> But I do love thee! And when I love thee not,
> Chaos is come again.           (3.3.92–4)

Othello's reference to 'chaos' obviously foreshadows the disintegration of his being. Chaos is time with neither order nor coherence; and by destroying Othello's sense of the constancy of experience, Iago brings chaos into his life. The concept of marriage, by its very definition, is something based on the notion of eternity. It is a gift of heaven, sanctioned by the eternal. As Othello says: 'If she be false, O, then heaven mocks itself.' When his marriage is destroyed, everything in the hero's existence seems lost in the timelessness of chaos. Iago, by contrast, thrives in chaos because he understands how to work within it, how to build the floodgates and embankments, and, therefore, how to use it to his advantage.

The emotion of jealousy is one that necessarily suggests a sense of time shattered. As that 'green-eyed monster' 'mocks the meat it feeds on', one becomes enraged because one's sense of continuity is broken. Instances of the link between jealousy and chaos are not unique to *Othello*. A similar relationship is suggested in *A Midsummer Night's Dream* when, in act 2, Titania attributes the disorder of the natural world to the dissension between the king and queen of fairies; moreover, that dissension, in her view, ultimately stems from 'jealous Oberon' and, in a larger sense, from the 'forgeries of jealousy'. Similarly, Leontes' jealousy leads to a sense of time broken as he loses the rhythm of sleep and rest: 'Nor night nor day no rest' (2.3.1). The only antidote to the poison of his jealous rage is sixteen years of penitence and faith; time in *The Winter's Tale* is restored. Jealousy belongs in Iago's domain because it is part of the capricious time of which he is the master. Othello's time – constant and ordered – is one where jealousy cannot reign. As a result, he is spoken of as 'one not easily jealous'; 'his whole nature was indisposed to jealousy'.[17] When asked whether Othello is jealous, Desdemona replies:

> Who he? I think the sun where he was born
> Drew all such humours from him.   (3.4.29–30)

It is made clear in the first half of the play that Othello's nature is 'made of no such baseness / As jealous creatures are'. He confirms that jealousy is part of changing time and that his sense of constancy has always kept him from such dis-ease. As Desdemona associates constancy with the reference to the sun, the hero associates jealousy with the changing moon:

> Think'st thou I'd make a life of jealousy,
> To follow still the changes of the moon
> With fresh suspicions?        (3.3.183–5)

When time loses its scope and becomes changeable like the moon, the result, for Othello, is madness and chaos:

> It is the very error of the moon;
> She comes more nearer earth than she was wont,
> And makes men mad.        (5.2.113–15)

As 'Iago time' takes over the play, men are made mad. Shakespeare's persistent use of temporal imagery suggests that Iago's victory is one in which he uses time to break time. In other words, his ability to manipulate time in order to achieve his ends amounts to a shattering of the constancy at the base of Othello's nobility and Desdemona's virtue. Ironically, as Othello first becomes enraged with jealousy, Iago remarks:

> My Lord, I would I might entreat your honour
> To scan this thing no further; leave it to time.
>                   (3.3.251–2)

Leaving it to time is tantamount to leaving it to Iago. Indeed, Iago's use of the term 'scan' signals once again that the villain recognizes situations by their temporal organization and examines them in terms of their rhythm. As

---

17  Bradley, *Shakespearean Tragedy*, p. 151.

the 'temptation' scene progresses, he maps out exactly what will ensue as time goes by. Finally, one recognizes Iago's victory as Othello, like Desdemona and Cassio before him, completes the pattern of all Iago's victims by demonstrating a concern with time in his lamentation of lost history and reputation:

> O, now, forever
> Farewell the tranquil mind! Farewell content!
> Farewell the plumed troop, and the big wars
> That makes ambition virtue! O, farewell!
> Farewell the neighing steed, and the shrill trump,
> The spirit-stirring drum, th' ear-piercing fife,
> The royal banner, and all quality,
> Pride, pomp, and circumstance of glorious war!
> And, O you mortal engines, whose rude throats
> Th' immortal Jove's dread clamours counterfeit,
> Farewell! Othello's occupation's gone.
>
> (3.3.352–62)

Although Iago destroys Othello's sense of time, the hero still speaks in terms of the everlasting when he vows his revenge. The villain's success, therefore, can be understood by the way in which he uses Othello's unswerving will to his own advantage. He causes the hero to translate momentary circumstance (of which Iago is the master) into terms of the eternal. Othello becomes a kind of dynamo through which Iago wreaks destruction. Once he shatters the hero's sense of time through the circumstance of the moment, Othello, in turn, translates the instant into a matter for all eternity:

> No! To be once in doubt
> Is once to be resolv'd;        (3.3.184–5)

Shakespeare has thus remained constant in his presentation of the hero even when the foundation of Othello's life has been destroyed: 'thwarted in love, his egoism will be *consistent* in revenge, decisive, irresistible . . .'[18]

Othello is clearly a man of action. The logistics of his elopement with Desdemona as well as his success as a soldier speak to this. He recognizes the calling of a moment and does something about it. But his action is always informed by his sense of time. This idealism is the key to the kind of nobility that defines Othello: he is a man of action but always has a sense of the relevance of that action to the greater order of the world. He is the opposite of a character like Hotspur even in his raving jealousies, because he believes that he will redeem time through his violent deed. Having shattered Othello's sense of the eternal, Iago spurs the man of action to wreak the most horrible vengeance on the one who supposedly precipitated the fall – Desdemona. But, in his brutal act, he is always conscious of 'the cause' as he tries to restore time. Indeed, Othello does not 'chop her into messes' as he vowed earlier in the play. Such an act would only further the victory of chaos. Othello smothers Desdemona.

Othello kills Desdemona in order to save the moral order, to restore love and faith. He kills Desdemona to be able to forgive her, so that the accounts be settled and the world returned to its equilibrium . . . He desperately wants to save the meaning of life, of his life, perhaps even the meaning of the world.[19]

In the terms I have discussed in this essay, Othello wants to restore eternity. Facing the horror of his deed, however, he speaks of all time lost – both of the constant sun and the changing moon:

> Methinks it should be now a huge eclipse
> Of sun and moon, and that th' affrighted globe
> Should yawn at alteration.        (5.2.103–5)

And in the simultaneous eclipse of sun and moon we have the death of Othello and the end of Iago's terrifying reign. Time ultimately catches up with both men in one huge eclipse.

### III

I have concentrated on Shakespeare's text in some depth because I believe Welles's film, in

---

[18] Traversi, *Approach to Shakespeare*, p. 146. Emphasis mine.

[19] Kott, *Shakespeare Our Contemporary*, p. 123.

its concern with temporal matters, inspires a fresh insight into the play. What remains is to return to the film itself in order to discover how the unique resources of the cinematic medium illuminate Shakespeare's development of this theme.

After Othello arrives in Cyprus, the Herald stands on the battlements of the castle to announce the general's order for feast and celebration (2.2), and it is within the context of the revels that Iago begins his work. Meanwhile, Welles takes us to a second bedchamber scene, where he depicts the embrace of the lovers through projected shadows on a wall. While their bodies merge in shadow we hear Othello's 'If I [*sic*] were now to die, / 'Twere now to be most happy.' The moment, as Welles presents it, is fundamentally ambiguous and realizes the paradox suggested above. The words express Othello's belief in the possibility of eternal happiness through his absolute love for Desdemona, but the shadows undercut the hero's sentiments and remind us of the ephemeral nature of their love and of its vulnerability to time. Through the contrasting juxtaposition of things seen and things heard, Welles represents the mutability of a love that the hero wishes to immortalize.

The film juxtaposes the peace and calm of the two lovers with the revels occurring outside. Welles uses the resources of the cinema to present a wild and raucous celebration, the disorder of which becomes a perfect environment for the manipulations of Iago. The montage of the celebrations forces one to feel lost in a maze of drunken revelling. After Iago encourages Cassio to drink, we watch Bianca unwittingly further the villain's plan by tempting the lieutenant to indulge again. We see dancing crowds, musicians, close-ups on the instruments as well as on the bottles and the flying goblets of the drunken crowd. Welles then uses montage to present people turning and dancing as we see face after face moving about in a dizzying sequence of images. The celebrants laugh uproariously.

Welles intersplices all this action with the only definable, rooted element – Iago. We see Iago subtly manipulating the quarrel between Roderigo and Cassio. When the fight breaks out, the celebrants seem to get even wilder, and their shouts and laughter serve as the backdrop to the encounter. A menacing feeling pervades all of this, a sense of people out of control – except for Iago, who works efficiently amidst this disorder.

At the culmination of the sequence, we follow the fighting men as Cassio chases Roderigo down into the underground of the castle, where a jungle of revellers is replaced by a jungle of vaults and pillars. In fact, Welles uses images of depths in his film to enforce a sense of a fallen world; he also contrasts such images by placing his characters in dangerously high places when they are particularly vulnerable – Iago in his cage, Cassio and Desdemona on top of the battlements after the war with the Turks, Othello and Iago on a huge cliff overlooking the sea at the culmination of the 'temptation' scene. By shooting the encounter of Cassio and Roderigo in the underworld of Cyprus, Welles creates a visual hell: a concrete net to 'enmesh them all'. The screams and laughter of the celebrants now echo off the walls of this underworld, increasing the eerie sense of a world gone mad. Chaos is unleashed on Iago's inspiration. All coherence is gone.

When Othello enters, he dismisses Cassio and apparently restores order. As the gathering breaks up, Cassio laments his dismissal by focusing on his lost reputation. As mentioned earlier, Cassio's main concern is that, with his loss of reputation – 'the immortal part' – he has also lost time. Immediately before Iago urges Cassio to work for his reinstatement through Desdemona we hear the crowing of the cock – a sign that the order of time is, temporarily, restored. In Machiavelli's terms, the river of Fortune will have its wild moments and its corresponding quiet times. When things are settled one must build the floodgates and embankments necessary for the inevitable chaotic times to come. This practice is the key to mastering time and Fortune. Thus, with the signal of the crowing cock calm is restored and Iago begins to build. Significantly, Welles uses the camera to distort Iago's shape with a low-angle shot, causing the villain to loom (as a physically exaggerated form) over Cassio. The 'huge' Iago persuades Cassio to appeal to the 'real' general of the times ('Our general's wife is now the general'). The scene concludes with the regular beating of a drum.

Welles's treatment of the 'temptation' scene (3.3) reinforces Shakespeare's representation of Iago's ability to manipulate time. Whereas we have just witnessed Iago incite chaos within the celebrations, we now witness the master of time creating chaos within Othello himself. Interestingly, Welles shoots the entire episode with a long travelling shot of the two men walking up the battlements to establish a sense of constant movement. Welles exploits the cinema's unique capacity to perform scenes in motion, and the effect of his presentation is to feel that Iago, the manipulator of time, works best on the move. Moreover, on the sound-track we distinctly hear the regular pattern of the footfalls of the two men as they walk in perfect synchronization. When they reach the top they are, significantly, on the edge of an enormous cliff as Iago leads his victim to a state of precarious balance.

The 'temptation' scene continues as the two men go inside the castle and below. Again, Welles takes us into an underworld as Othello becomes more and more enraged at the prospect of Desdemona's infidelity and as his world loses its equilibrium. During the 'I see you are moved' section of the dialogue (ll.207.ff), Iago actually helps Othello take off his armour. What must sound like a banal and obvious image when described in words is actually a very powerful moment. Iago disarms Othello, physically and spiritually, and Welles succeeds in accomplishing a strong visual statement to support this subtextual

aspect of the scene. Moreover, the shots become more and more tilted as Iago tips the balance of Othello's world.

As Iago continues to work on Othello we see, at approximately line 234 ('And yet, how nature erring from itself –'), the Moor examining himself in a mirror that seems to distort his image. As Iago shatters Othello's sense of coherency and estranges the Moor from himself, we witness the hero confront a 'shadow' of his being. But it is Iago who stands behind the mirror, making the unmistakable statement that the villain is the device through which Othello perceives not only the world but himself as well. The man who was once able to say 'My parts, my title, and my perfect soul / Shall manifest me rightly' is now beginning to confront the possibility of 'erring nature' and its distorted shadows. Othello's 'parts' are no longer integrated and the man whom Bradley saw at the beginning as 'all of one piece' is now coming apart.

Shakespeare uses images of fragmentation in his play to create a sense of a world that has lost cohesion. This idea is especially apparent in Othello's repeated references to destroying Desdemona by ripping her apart. Because Iago has destroyed the hero's sense of constancy and eternity, it follows that Othello responds with vows of revenge that are associated with dis-integration. Welles echoes these images of fragmentation in his film through montage, a quick-moving camera, and the contrasting rhythms of the soundtrack.

Towards the end of the 'temptation' scene, for example, Iago gains ground in his deception by telling Othello that he 'lay with Cassio' and that the latter, in his sleep, spoke of his love for Desdemona. Othello believes Iago's tale and becomes enraged. At this juncture, he first speaks of revenge in the short line, 'I'll tear her all to pieces' (3.3.436). Here Welles employs a powerful counterpoint to Othello's statement. During much of the 'temptation' scene the waves of the sea rhythmically beat on the fortress walls. When Othello speaks his first words of revenge, a sudden boom of the crashing sea punctuates the wrath of his exclamation. To support Shakespeare's imagery of fragmentation, Welles uses the soundtrack to suggest a break of rhythm and order with the fierce explosions of the sea. Similarly, after Othello is deceived by the 'ocular proof' that Iago provides in the contrived discussion with Cassio and Bianca, the hero vows, 'I will chop her into messes. Cuckold me?' (4.1.199). Here Welles uses montage as he cuts to cannon after cannon firing to announce the arrival of Lodovico's ship. As Iago destroys his sense of order, Othello responds with images of disintegration in his vows to revenge, and Welles uses cinematic techniques to emphasize a corresponding transition from order to chaos in the world outside.

Following the exploding cannons that announce the arrival of the Venetian ships, Welles cuts to a shot of Iago and Othello walking rapidly along the battlements, and a sequence representing the hero's trance then follows. As the dialogue of act 4, scene 1 is spoken, Welles uses quick cuts from one speaker to the other to produce a sense of approaching hysteria through the speed of the shots and the rapid gait of the characters. When Iago speaks the words 'Lie with her? Lie on her?' Othello runs into the concrete jungle below the castle; we see shadows of jail-like bars projected on his frantic body and hear frenzied electronic music sustained on the soundtrack. Suddenly, we are with Othello on top of a watchtower. Our sense of space is completely disoriented. The following shot then yields a low-angle perspective on the tower as we are now transported to a new location below. On the soundtrack we hear the heavy rhythmic breathing of Othello which, in the context of the film, yields the sense of the hero's desperate attempt to hang on to the rhythm of his life with the very air that sustains him. The next shot shows seagulls wheeling in the sky followed by a close-up of Othello's face as he lies on his back. We then assume his

perspective and another low-angle shot of the tower reveals a number of people looking down and laughing at the hero. With the use of a reverse zoom, the faces of these frightening spectators appear tiny and extremely far away. Othello mutters something about the handkerchief during which we also hear the sound of Iago's voice crying 'My Lord' as he searches for his master. The next shot is of the tower once again but this time the haunting faces are gone. Iago arrives on the scene, revives the hero, and the sequence ends with Othello's 'farewell' speech transposed from act 3, scene 3. In this sequence, Welles converts Shakespeare's stage direction 'Falls in a trance' into cinematic values that create a sense of spatial and temporal disorientation. Through this, one identifies with Othello as his world comes apart and as Iago destroys him by sabotaging his sense of order and coherence – all culminating in Othello's farewell to his own history and occupation.

Finally, Welles works with time in one more sense that has its seed in Shakespeare's text but is developed by the film-maker in a way that adds a further dimension to his interpretation. It is the concept of time that is ultimately responsible for restoring order to the world. It is a redeeming force of time beyond human manipulation. It is the kind of time that Viola speaks of in *Twelfth Night*, time which unties the complicated knot of that comedy. It is 'the old common arbitrator' that Hector refers to in *Troilus and Cressida*. In short, it is a form of time that is ultimately triumphant in *Othello*.

At the end of *Othello* Lodovico speaks to Montano of the incipient punishment for Iago:

> To you, Lord Governor,
> Remains the censure of this hellish villain,
> The time, the place, the torture. O, enforce it!
> (5.2.376–8)

Welles takes this reference at the end of Shakespeare's text and develops it into a motif apparent throughout the film. It will be recalled that the film begins with the funeral processions of

Othello and Desdemona and that Iago is simultaneously dragged by chains through the crowd, thrust into an iron cage, and hoisted to the top of the castle walls where he is left to hang. From the opening of the film, therefore, we are aware of his ultimate punishment. At four key moments during the course of the film Welles shoots the empty hanging cage, reminding the audience of how Iago will eventually be punished in time. Welles lingers with a shot of the cage during the Herald's announcement before the celebration, has Iago exit directly below it at the end of act 2, scene 3 after the line 'Dull not device by coldness and delay', pans to reveal it immediately after the villain murders Roderigo, and cuts to a shot of it at the moment Desdemona dies. The moments Welles chooses are significant. The first two occur immediately before Iago takes a major step in his attack: i.e., before the set-up of Cassio and before the 'temptation' scene (Welles places the 'temptation' scene directly after act 2, scene 3). The last two instances take place immediately after we witness the tragic consequences of his deeds in the deaths of Roderigo and Desdemona. Thus we are reminded of Iago's ultimate punishment both in the preparation and in the culmination of his evil machinations. Of course, there is a neat symmetry to Welles's choices as well: the attempt to destroy Cassio ultimately leads to the death of Roderigo (shots one and three), while the manipulations of the 'temptation' scene culminate in the death of Desdemona

(shots two and four). But what is most important to stress here is that the director exposes an aspect of time that even Iago cannot control. By opening the film with the visuals of the final moment and by demonstrating Iago's eventual doom with recurring shots of his cage, Welles suggests that even though Iago works in time to destroy time, 'the old arbitrator time' eventually triumphs and exposes his treachery.

The cinema has the capacity to inspire a fresh series of questions into the complexities of Shakespearian drama. The film medium gives the play a unique context for performance and, with its aural and visual resources, can serve as a vehicle for the examination of central thematic issues in a new light. Orson Welles's *Othello* is only one of several cinematic adaptations of Shakespeare's work. Clearly, the approach of this chapter can extend to the films of such directors as Kozintsev, Kurosawa, Polanski, Olivier, Zeffirelli, and Reinhardt. The cinema has emerged not as a 'better' way of looking at Shakespeare – it is not a question of competition – but as a means of attaining a fresh look at one of the greatest playwrights of all time. The achievement of the film medium for a study of Shakespeare is considerable, and the insights it can reveal are significant for an ever-expanding field of criticism. As foreign as the cinema was to a man writing four centuries ago, it is a peculiarly fertile medium for an investigation of his plays.

# 'MACBETH' ON FILM: POLITICS

## E. PEARLMAN

Each of the three important directors – Welles, Polanski, and Kurosawa – who attempted to recreate *Macbeth* on the screen has had to come to terms with the play's reverence for monarchy. Despite idolatrous claims that Shakespeare was not of an age but for all time, the royal play of *Macbeth* unabashedly celebrates a semi-divine monarch in terms specific to the first years of Stuart absolutism. King Duncan is thoroughly paternal, compassionate, and regal. Of him even devilish Macbeth testifies that he 'hath borne his faculties so meek, hath been / So clear in his great office, that his virtues / Will plead like angels, trumpet-tongu'd, against / The deep damnation of his taking-off' (7.17–20).[1] *Macbeth*'s politics are cyclical, and the play cannot conclude until the pure and untainted Malcolm, Duncan's son and the usurper's successor, invites home 'our exil'd friends abroad / That fled the snares of watchful tyranny' (5.9.32–3), and, invoking the 'grace of Grace', sets out to be invested at Scone. The play's satisfaction with the traditional order, though severely tested by the reign of the tyrant, is confirmed when a second exemplary monarch succeeds his father.

Shakespeare expands on the contentment with divine or semi-divine monarchy in two interpolated episodes. Both appear in the difficult but elegant scene in which the play temporarily escapes the witch-dominated claustrophobia of Scotland for redemptive England. In the initial passage, Malcolm first confesses to a variety of monstrous sins, then immediately reverses himself to assert his purity. He claims that he has pretended villainy only to test Macduff's devotion to virtuous rule. The scene is designed so that Malcolm may extol, in a parade of abstractions which sacrifices poetry to panegyric,

> The king-becoming graces,
> As Justice, Verity, Temp'rance, Stableness,
> Bounty, Perseverance, Mercy, Lowliness,
> Devotion, Patience, Courage, Fortitude
> (4.3.11–14)

Shakespeare has digressed from the principal action of the play in order to evoke a monarchic ideal which has been lost or beclouded during the reign of the tyrant. A second episode in the same scene celebrates (some suppose for a specific command performance) the thaumaturgic King Edward, who touches for the evil. Malcolm reports on a miracle he has seen with his very own eyes:

> How he solicits Heaven,
> Himself best knows; but strangely-visited
>     people,
> All swoln and ulcerous, pitiful to the eye,
> The mere despair of surgery, he cures;
> Hanging a golden stamp about their necks
> Put on with holy prayers; and 'tis spoken,
> To the succeeding royalty he leaves
> The healing benediction.     (4.3.149–56)

---

[1] Citations to *Macbeth* are to Kenneth Muir's Arden edition (London, 1951; Cambridge, Mass., 1953).

The 'succeeding royalty', as a Jacobean audience would well know, includes King James himself, a putative descendant of Banquo and a healer of scrofula. These two excrescent episodes are included only to clarify the play's royal bias.

*Macbeth* assumes that misgovernment enters the community not because of defects in the system of monarchy, but at the behest of agents of darkness. The kingdom has prospered under Duncan and will again see good days under Malcolm. The reign of Macbeth is foul but aberrant. In the end Scotland regains its good health and the play ends on an optimistic note. Even though there is always the danger that kingship may degenerate into tyranny, in the world of *Macbeth* monarchy remains the only conceivable form of government.

Although monarchy is a relic of the past, the acquisition and disposition of power is of eternal concern. Indifferent to the politics of absolutism, modern interpreters of *Macbeth* inevitably represent political ideas which are more germane to our century than to Shakespeare's. Orson Welles unsuccessfully labours to strip *Macbeth* of its political content. He eliminates the episodes crucial to a theory of monarchy and reduces both Duncan and Malcolm to ciphers. To fill the gap, he substitutes an allegorized conflict (as his own sonorous voice pronounces in a didactic voice-over prologue) between 'agents of chaos, priests of hell and magic ... [and] christian law and order'. The film's principal iconic device opposes the spindly forked twigs of the witches – a symbol of their demonism – to the crucifixes of the newly converted Scots. The overthrow of Macbeth is achieved not so much by the march of Birnam Wood as by a moving forest of Celtic crosses. Morality-play elements are clearly embodied in Welles's pedestrian 'Holy Father' – a personage conjured up of shards stolen from four of Shakespeare's minor characters. Welles even goes so far as to invent a primitive but obtrusive ceremony in which the Father leads the multitude in abjuring 'Satan and all his works'. The priest – unfortunately a trifle malevolent and greasy for the moral weight he is asked to bear – is killed when Macbeth's pagan spear pierces his heart. In spite of such murky or inexplicable moments, Welles strives valiantly to minimize politics and emphasize religion.

In defiance of this intent, the film inadvertently generates a rudimentary political vision of its own. By concentrating so exclusively on Macbeth (a devotion which shadows Welles's own achievement as producer, director, scriptwriter, costumer and principal player), the film ruthlessly subordinates all other interests to his, and turns the play into an exploration of both dictatorship and the cult of personality. Huge Macbeth dominates the foreground of innumerable frames of this egocentric production. Other characters, petty men in comparison to Welles's colossus, are pushed into corners or confined to the margins of the frame. When Macbeth encounters the witches for the second time, the camera locates him as a speck in the middle of a distant heath (or soundstage), then tracks him with single-minded intensity until the entire frame is filled with his distorted shape. Except for the dominating presence of Macbeth, the film allows little but the anarchy of faceless masses, from whom (it is presumed) no alternative government could possibly arise.

Attempting to exclude politics, Welles engendered a film in which Shakespeare's poles of monarchy and tyranny have been replaced by a right-wing world view which can admit nothing other than dictatorship or disorder. It is no surprise that he should see the world in these terms. Welles had already demonstrated his simultaneous attraction and repulsion from the *Übermensch* in a number of films, the most familiar of which is *Citizen Kane*. He again wrestles with proto-fascism in this 1948 *Macbeth*. In it, he is both (as Macbeth) the embodiment of the wicked dictator and (as director) the creator of the civilization that bulwarks us against that horror. In his hands, *Macbeth* becomes a parable of fascism narrowly averted. Yet no more than Shakespeare can Welles imagine an alternative to absolute power, and when, at the end of the film, the camera grants us one last look at its papier-mâché castle, it leaves a Scotland in which the regime of Macbeth has been overthrown, but the threat of dictatorship still looms.

At the end of the original *Macbeth*, Shakespeare's confidence in monarchy remained steadfast. Orson Welles is indifferent to monarchy and fascinated by an inchoate but primitive Christianity. He is repelled by the fascism he has figured forth, but cannot find his way to a convincing moral or political alternative.[2]

Welles's version of *Macbeth* was influenced by the bleak events of the 1930s and 40s. Roman Polanski's contact with repressive regimes has been more intimate. Displaced by the Nazis as a child, he has been in voluntary exile from Polish communism for most of his adult life. He has said that, in his *Macbeth* (1971), the superfluous brutality of the hired killers who invade Macduff's castle at Fife recalls an SS intrusion into his own home during the Second World War. If Welles creates a film in which religion is central and politics inadvertent, Polanski, whose vision is even more despairing, offers a *Macbeth* in which both Christianity and monarchy are deliberately and systematically replaced by satanism.

Shakespeare depicted a world in which dark-age mythology was overlain and perhaps even superseded by Christian morality. Polanski attempts to purge *Macbeth* of its Christianity and at the same time to amplify elements of the supernatural or uncanny. The only specific Christian reference is fleeting and irrelevant – when Fife is ravaged a huge wooden structure in the shape of a cross momentarily appears in flames. The film is otherwise without Christian content. In order to salvage a dark-age setting, Polanski even falls into the anachronism of juxtaposing late

medieval fortifications and armaments to neo-lithic religion. While Welles imagines a ceremony in which the multitude forsake pagan religion, Polanski invents a rite of coronation in which, within a ring of cardboard menhirs, Macbeth himself is lifted aloft on an improbably weightless circular stone. Such legitimate claim to kingship as Macbeth possesses seems to derive from this pseudo-druidic ceremonial. Polanski's Scots are on the whole depicted as a spiritually primitive population ripe for invasion by demons.

Stripped of Christian comfort, Scottish civilization is primarily composed of two antithetical secular elements. On the surface, the Scottish populace is depicted as healthy and prosperous. Macbeth and his wife are picture-book handsome, while Duncan looks like nothing so much as the King of Hearts. Macduff is strong and virile; Lady Macduff, in her one brief scene at Fife, a model of maternal solicitude. Seyton is a reliable soldier, the physician a responsible tradesman. Even members of the subordinate classes are healthy and attractive. When Duncan visits Macbeth's castle, Polanski lavishes a great deal of attention on preparations for the feast. Well-fed servants bustle about sweeping up and arranging the sleeping quarters. The household is apparently democratic – Lady Macbeth herself helps shake out the mattresses and strew the rushes. At the feast itself, the frame is filled with bright colours, cheerful servants, and the generous participation of musicians and singers. Unlike Welles's world, which is men-

---

[2] For general information on Welles's *Macbeth* see Jack J. Jorgens, *Shakespeare on Film* (Bloomington, 1977). The best essay on Welles's Shakespeare is James Naremore's 'The Walking Shadow: Welles' Expressionist *Macbeth*', *Literature/Film Quarterly*, 1 (1973), from which I have borrowed a number of ideas. Other useful information is contained in Charles Higham's *The Films of Orson Welles* (Berkeley, 1970), the collection of essays on *Macbeth* in the *University of Dayton Review*, 14 (1979–80), as well as the bibliographies and notes included in the valuable *Shakespeare on Film Newsletter*.

acing and brooding, or Kurosawa's spare and joyless universe, Polanski's world is characterized by song, dance, and even a degree of joy. Yet there is a sinister underside to this apparently prospering community. It is permeated by the gratuitous violence for which Polanski has become notorious. The film takes as its text Macbeth's 'I am in blood / Stepped in so far, that should I wade no more, / Returning were as tedious as go o'er'; its catalogue of bloody horrors does not require rehearsal here. Polanski's Scotland, whether under the rule of Duncan or the usurper, is as brutal as it is beautiful.

To the opposition of natural prosperity and natural cruelty, the film adds a third and dominant note – the ugliness and power of the demonic. The two aged witches in the opening scene are hideous, the younger one pocked and verrucose. Their collection of enchanted objects is even fouler to the eye than Shakespeare's list of ingredients to the ear. The massed ugliness of the naked witches in their cave is an imaginative expansion of the misogyny of the original play. The world of *Macbeth* is almost perfectly Manichean. Polanski has devised a population which is natively attractive (though violent and irreligious) but prey to a powerful and supernaturally sanctioned cult.

The only gods who matter in this *Macbeth* are the demons. They control (or seem to control) the actions of men. In the strong opening moments of the film, the witches bury a number of objects on a sandy beach, most prominently a severed arm and hand with a knife in its grasp. A few moments later a bloody battle takes place on the spot – at the command of the witches, it would seem. These witches are not fantastical; they are exactly what they seem. They do not disappear 'into the air', as do Shakespeare's fiends, but into an underground cavern. Their power overwhelms both religion and monarchy. While government and other human institutions are fragile, witchcraft is perpetual. In Polanski's film, the demonic has penetrated to the core of Scottish society and displaced all other forms of power. As a result, even Macbeth's acceptance of the prophecy, a subject of troubled soliloquy in Shakespeare's play, offers only the slightest moral qualms to Polanski. Macbeth commits himself to the witches at their first meeting when he lies to Banquo and announces that the witches have simply disappeared. While Shakespeare acknowledges the witches' power, he never forgets that goodness and truth are also native to mankind. In Polanski's version of *Macbeth*, human political institutions are regularly subordinated to demonic power.

The penetration of evil into this world is revealed by one of Polanski's principal alterations of Shakespeare's text – the change in the character of Rosse. Rosse figures in the revised plot in a number of places (he is the shadowy Third Murderer, for example), and is one of the agents by which the politics of the film is defined. When he is not granted Macduff's title after aiding in the destruction of Fife, he deserts Macbeth to join the fugitives. In the film's concluding moments, it is Rosse who picks up Macbeth's fallen crown and presents it to Malcolm. This is of the greatest political significance, for when the corrupt and venal Rosse handles so important a symbolic object he contaminates it. In Shakespeare's play, the crown is divine. In Polanski's film, it is a gift to the new king by a murderer and a machiavel. Malcolm had originally been conceived of as an 'innocent lamb'; in this film, he is just another politician, tainted by both his henchmen and his own ambition.

The climax of the film is the prolonged and undignified tussle between Macbeth and Macduff. Where tradition demands a heroic duel between superb warriors, Polanski offers a brawl which borders on farce. In Polanski's version, Macbeth does not lose because he has been betrayed by the equivocation of the fiends, nor Macduff win because the prophecy is fulfilled. Macduff's victory is not inevitable, but accidental. At the point of exhaustion, he strikes a lucky blow and happens to impale his opponent. Shakespeare's confidence in the triumph of justice has been transformed into our favourite contemporary cliché – that all events are merely accidents of an indifferent universe.

The supersession of the demonic over the divine is a reiterated theme, but for those members of the audience who might possibly have missed it, Polanski provides an unequivocal and unsubtle epilogue. Donalbain, Malcolm's brother, distinguished by his jealous glare and awkward limp, heads for the lair of the witches. He will commit himself to them and attempt to displace the reigning monarch. Just as the film began with the witches, so does it end. While Shakespeare's cycle is from one legitimate king to the next, Polanski's is from demon to demon.

In Welles's *Macbeth*, the alternative to monarchy is anarchy; in Polanski's version, the alternative is diabolism. Welles's characters are prey to their basest characteristics. Polanski's version is even bleaker, and offers even less hope for a successful polity. In his world there is no reason to build political institutions, since they are all subordinated to a powerful and uncontrollable evil. It is a remarkably pessimistic view of the world, antithetical in almost all respects to Shakespeare's.[3]

Neither Welles nor Polanski places a great deal of confidence in man's political capacity. Kurosawa's *Throne of Blood* (1957) represents politics in a far different light. At the end of his film, the question of royal succession is deliberately left unresolved, and the throne of the fallen usurper remains unclaimed. While Shakespeare offers us a pure Malcolm and Polanski a compromised one, Kurosawa breaks with tradition and precedent and brings his film to a conclusion without even bothering to instal a new monarch. Instead, he distracts our attention from the problem of succession by focusing on the fall of Washizu (Macbeth).

No viewer can forget one of the most remarkable sequences in film – that in which Washizu is assassinated by his own soldiers. Isolated on the balcony from which he has been haranguing his troops, he becomes the target of innumerable arrows. A final arrow pierces his larynx and the soundtrack becomes preternaturally silent. Washizu tumbles down a flight of wooden steps, and, still attempting to draw his sword, gapes at the camera for a long moment before collapsing. The scene is very powerful and creates a great impression of finality. But contrary to the memory of most audiences, the death of Washizu is not the last event in the film. *Throne of Blood* can be thought of as ending three times, and Washizu's death as only the first of these. The third and final conclusion is, of course, the reprise of the chant with which the film began – the lament for the ambition that leads only to death. The chorus distances the events of *Throne of Blood* by placing them somewhere in an unspecified past, and turns the inset story into a parable in which Washizu becomes the

---

[3] Other films by Polanski come to the same conclusion. *Rosemary's Baby* offers a remarkable parallel to *Macbeth*. An isolate, Rosemary Woodhouse is intrigued against by a group of elderly witches. In the last and climactic scene, Rosemary accepts the responsibility for mothering the demonic child to whom she has given birth. Evil is invested with the same continuity as is implied by the Donalbain episode. In Polanski's lone attempt at comedy, the execrable *Famous Vampire Killers*, a young woman (played by Sharon Tate), apparently rescued from vampires, reveals her newly elongated teeth and bites Alfred (Polanski himself) on the neck. A voice tells us that evil is now loosed on the world. A more subtle version of the same idea appears in the entirely secular *film noir* masterpiece *Chinatown*. Noah Cross, who is guilty of murder, incest, and the systematic perversion of the laws, and who has the semi-demonic ability to survive a bullet unscathed, is in total control of events at the picture's conclusion. The last moments of the film, according to Barbara Leaming (*Polanski, a biography* (New York, 1981), p. 147), were altered by Polanski to emphasize Cross's power (in the original film script Evelyn Mulwray had escaped with her daughter-sister).

type of the ambitious man. Yet between Washizu's grotesque death and the moment the chorus begins to sing, still another 'ending' takes place on the screen. For not more than two or three seconds, the audience is returned to the perimeter of Forest Castle to catch a brief glimpse of the attacking forces who have found their way through the natural labyrinth of the forest. They have covered themselves and their battle wagons with boughs and branches and are poised for an assault. But Kurosawa withholds the satisfaction of a climactic and conclusive battle and cuts directly and precipitously to the distancing chorus. The event which resolved the earlier films, and which all versions of *Macbeth* have traditionally offered – the battle and the crowning of a new monarch – is simply omitted. Kurosawa has frustrated our natural desire for closure. A battle at this moment would be out of place, for Kurosawa has rearranged the order of events, and Washizu has already been slain. By abandoning the story just at the moment of the assault, Kurosawa does not have to decide who should succeed to the lordship of Forest Castle, and therefore sidesteps the conventional political problems raised by *Macbeth*. When he leaves Forest Castle without a master, Kurosawa forces us to think about its social and political problems in a new way. Unlike Shakespeare's *Macbeth*, which invests monarchy with the potential for justice and morality, *Throne of Blood* does not contain the seeds of a healthy polity within its ruling élite. On the contrary, Kurosawa portrays a community so defective that it must be transformed root and branch before a legitimate government can be installed.

The distinguishing marks of the society of *Throne of Blood* are inequity, corruption, and frigidity of personal relationships. The gap between the feudal lords and the common people is so great that it often seems as though we are dealing as much with two species as with two classes. The members of the ruling élite rarely acknowledge the existence of the subordinate classes. In the occasional instance when circumstances require communication, intercourse is stylized, formal, and stilted. When messengers bring news, as they do in the opening sequence, they prostrate themselves fearfully before the generals. At one point the Lord of Forest Castle makes a surprise visit to Washizu. There is a long shot from an elevated point of view of peasants working in a field. (This may be the sole evidence of an economic base to a society totally preoccupied by war, feuds, and dynastic squabbles.) The peasants are not seen as individuals and the camera treats them rather as objects than as people. After a few seconds, a line of horse makes its way down a path while peasants on both sides of the row humbly bow their heads. The visual statement of the distance between warriors and peasants is forcefully made. On the whole, power is the monopoly of a very few, and it is used only for the benefit of those who possess it. The society of *Throne of Blood* is also deeply corrupt. Unlike *Macbeth*, where the witches invade a basically healthy universe, Kurosawa's universe is devoid of political virtue. The present master of Forest Castle, Kunihara, has become its lord not by inheritance or election but by murdering the last occupant of the office. In one emblematic scene a group of soldiers discusses the decay of Washizu's castle. The castle is shaking, they assert, because 'the foundations have long been rotting. Even the rats have begun to leave.' The allegory tells us that not only the castle but feudalism itself is rotten. In addition to being inequitable and corrupt, the community is also without warmth. Love (or even affection), loyalty, generosity, confidence, or pleasure are rarely if ever expressed. The society is characterized instead by narrow self-interest, distrust, constant fear, and the easy recourse to violence. Relationships between individuals are remarkably sterile. In one memorable scene, when Washizu and his wife Asaji converse, they sit far apart in a conventionally bare room. Propped up on the wall behind them and separating them is an unsheathed sword – a perfect metaphor for a marriage of understated but unrelieved hostility, and an expressive symbol of the distrust which seems to characterize all human relationships. There are in fact only a handful of moments in the film in which the characters make physical contact with each other; for the most part they do not touch, and when they do, it is at such moments as Asaji's wrenching Washizu's lance from his hands. Kurosawa even contrives it so that when more than one member of the feudal élite is in the frame, the images of the persons do not overlap. On the other hand, when soldiers and servants gather, as they do for periodic choral discourse, they are disposed in more informal and intimate patterns.

It is only when this film turns away from human social and political institutions that it discovers a new world of beauty and mystery. Things made by man pale in comparison to animate nature. The rigid and futile geometry of manufactured structures is continually contrasted to the fertility, magic, and riot of the forest. The most memorable scenes juxtapose frail human institutions to the greater power of the natural world. When Washizu is in the forest he is regularly photographed through a thick tangle of vines and branches. It is clear that he is merely an intruder in an enduring world. Washizu antagonizes nature and its spirits by shooting arrows into the trees, but the forest ultimately claims its revenge. The great scene of the two horsemen lost in the fog, the miraculous invasion of Forest Castle by the crows, and the slow-motion march of this film's Birnam Wood all stress the power of nature. It is as though the attempt of Japanese feudalism to impose its rigidities on this world is both doomed and hubristic. In *Throne of Blood*, tyrants come and go, but the earth abides. If the film has an occidental moral, it is not Shakespeare's but Shelley's: the forest is as permanent as the lone and level sands stretch-

ing away from the shattered statue. Even Washizu's death can be understood as a symbolic act by which the forest asserts its dominance over the tyrant. This has always been implicit in Shakespeare's fable. No event in literature so clearly sets forth the triumph of the natural world over the human than Birnam Forest picking itself up in order to expel the wicked king. Kurosawa expands the metaphor by making Washizu the victim not only of the forest itself but of arrows which combine the wood of the trees with the feathers of its birds. This is an entirely appropriate way for offended nature to regain control over an evil usurper.

It is in this context that Washizu's ghastly end acquires its fine political importance. The common people, the nameless soldiers of Washizu's army, mobilize themselves to commit not a mindless act of violence but an assassination – an act of specific political rebellion. These are the people whom the film treats as the exploited and nameless victims of Japanese feudalism. They lack authority and autonomy; they have no leaders and no individuality. In fact, when Washizu is felled, Kurosawa arranges it so that an audience is conscious not of the archers but only of their arrows. It is as though the arrows appear from nowhere, and are not launched by any specific person. Yet the arrows stand for the collective mind of the masses, who, the film seems to say, have had enough of tyranny. Washizu is not killed by one arrow, or ten, or a hundred, but by thousands. The moral is obvious: the tyrant and the rotten feudalism for which he stands cannot be brought to its knees by one individual or a hundred, but can be overcome by the people acting in concert. It is nevertheless an equivocal ending. Insofar as the assassination of Washizu can be regarded as a political act, it offers some cause for optimism; to the extent that the assassination simply expresses the opportunism of the soldiers, it is dreadfully pessimistic. The death of Washizu can therefore be conceived of as mildly exhilarating and cautiously optimistic. The film can offer no improvement over tyranny, nor can it provide a successor for Washizu, but it does suggest how the first step might be taken towards a different kind of government.[4]

Of the three films, *Throne of Blood* is the most akin to Shakespeare in the grandeur and spaciousness of its vision. While the two English-language versions of the play vie with each other in fashionable and even facile pessimism, Kurosawa grants his characters the power to challenge and refashion imprisoning social systems. *Throne of Blood* is uplifting not only for its remarkable craft, but for its confidence in human capabilities. While Kurosawa offers no easy answers, neither does he permit his film to succumb to authoritarian or demonic presences.

[4] Many of Kurosawa's films deal with feudalism, which by some reckonings survived in Japan until 1945. The critique of feudalism in film may be understood as a similitude of recent Japanese history. *Kanjincho* for example, made in 1945, and 'one of the strongest indictments of feudalism ever filmed' according to Donald Richie (*The Japanese Film*, rev. ed. (Tokyo and New York, 1982), p. 76), was suppressed until 1953. In Kurosawa's most remarkable film, the *Seven Samurai* (1954), a group of farmers employ masterless samurai, then neglect them. The film pays homage to feudal and military achievement but also regards it as slightly archaic compared to the continuing and more fundamental dramas of harvest and love. Just as Washizu is overthrown by his followers, so the samurai are superseded by the peasantry. In *Hidden Fortress* (1958), which immediately followed *Throne of Blood*, the emphasis is on the point of view of the peasants. In the end, the defection of General Hyoe dissolves feudal loyalty.

# REPRESENTING 'KING LEAR' ON SCREEN: FROM METATHEATRE TO 'META-CINEMA'

## KENNETH S. ROTHWELL

The advantage of the cinema over the theatre is not that you can even have horses, but that you can stare closer into a man's eyes; otherwise it is pointless to set up a cine camera for Shakespeare ...

Grigori Kozintsev[1]

Representing *King Lear* on screen, representing almost any Shakespearian play on film or videotape, means broadening the ancient trope of the world as stage to include the world as screen. As the idea of the screen as screen takes its place alongside the idea of the play as play, so 'meta-cinema' inevitably emerges alongside metatheatre. In making the means of representation a subject of representation, film-makers have only mimicked their stage forebears.[2] Like theatre, film may also self-referentially draw attention to itself through ironic devices, or, alternatively, it may even have sequences that are essentially movies-within-movies. Oliver's *Henry V*, by shifting from a documentary mode in the Globe playhouse to a stylized medievalism at the court of France, gives an example of the former; while the Polanski *Macbeth*, in embedding a silent movie about Ross within the talking picture about Macbeth, illustrates the latter.

In Shakespeare films, 'meta-cinema' may or may not assume the additional burden of apologizing for the film's not being a page in a printed book or a play on the public stage. The history of screened Shakespeare furnishes a special reason for this directorial breast-beating. Ever since those early silents, such as

the 1911 'epoch-making picture of *Henry VIII*, as given by Sir Herbert Tree',[3] or Sir Johnston Forbes-Robertson's 1913 *Hamlet*, for which at enormous expense a castle was constructed in Dorset's Lulworth Cove,[4] film-makers have been guilt-ridden. Movies, it was thought, were an unsuitable vehicle for the masterpieces of Shakespeare. Stanley Kauffmann, while excoriating Franco Zeffirelli's 1966 *The Taming of the Shrew* as an 'abomination', expressed a consensus when he wrote that 'the film medium and Shakespeare are born

The author expresses his thanks to Dr Thomas Berger of St Lawrence University, Candace Bothwell of the Folger Shakespeare Library, Patrick Sheehan of the Motion Picture Division of the Library of Congress, Roger Holman of the National Film Archive, and Gillian Hartnoll of the British Film Institute, without whom this work could not have been accomplished, as well as to the Graduate College, University of Vermont, for funding of travel.

1 Grigori Kozintsev, *King Lear, the Space of Tragedy*, trans Mary Mackintosh (Berkeley, 1977), p. 55.
2 For commentary on interrelationships between film and theatre, see especially Roger Manvell, *Theater and Film* (London, 1979); and A. N. Vardac, *Stage to Screen* (Cambridge, 1949), p. 129, particularly where Vardac details the intimate bond between David Belasco's 1884 *May Blossom*, starring the well-known Ben Maginley as Uncle Tom Blossom, and D. W. Griffith's first release in 1908, *Adventures of Dolly*. Among many discussions of metatheatricality is Anne Righter, *Shakespeare and the Idea of the Play* (London, 1962).
3 'Advertisement', *Bioscope* (2 March 1911), p. 21.
4 'Interview with C. Hepworth', *Bioscope* (24 July 1913), 275–9; p. 275.

antagonists'.[5] Laurence Kitchin uttered much the same thought, though less abrasively, twenty years ago in this series: 'Shakespeare's plays were written to be used by live actors in the presence of a crowd. It follows that all screen versions of them are subject to the limitations of the screen.'[6] Sensitive to these concerns, directors have sought to appease Shakespeare's praetorians in the libraries and theatres with gestures of obeisance. Insofar as these defensive strategies draw attention to the way that the film is being made, they emerge in a meta-cinematic context.

### I

Edwin Thanhouser's 1916 *King Lear*,[7] one of the best of the silents, offers a paradigm. Its opening sequence takes the 'forelock-tugging' approach. Director Ernest Warde's concern about tampering with the written text of Shakespeare's play is privileged over the *diegesis* (film narrative) itself. The opening shot reveals a man in a smoking jacket who affects a wing collar. Seated bolt upright in a wingback chair, he is reading a book. These codes signal a stereotypical Victorian gentleman – learned, haughty and stuffy. The film's anxiety about removing a Shakespearian tragedy from that context into the vulgarity of the nickelodeon is betrayed by the very next shot, a close-up of the first page of *King Lear* in what could pass for the Globe edition.

The actor seated in the chair, it so happens, is Frederick Warde, who in his day resembled an American clone to Albert Finney's 'Sir' in Peter Yates's 1983 film version of *The Dresser*, with Tom Courtenay as Norman, or Fool. Warde, described by his biographer as 'an old-fashioned, ranting performer', was an expatriate Englishman born in 1851, who toured the hinterlands of the United States as an itinerant Shakespearian, never quite making it on the New York Stage, until he 'drifted' into a film career.[8] In his regal appearance Warde embodied every nineteenth-century

3  Frederick B. Warde as King Lear on tour in the United States in the early part of this century

5 '*Romeo and Juliet*', in *Figures of Light: Film Criticism and Commentary* (New York, 1971), 112–14; p. 113.

6 'Shakespeare on the Screen', *Shakespeare Survey 18* (Cambridge, 1965), 70–4; p. 70. For other general views, see Roger Manvell, Alan Dent, Philip Hope-Wallace, 'Can Shakespeare Be Filmed? A Discussion...', a BBC Radio Programme, 1948 (typescript in British Film Institute Library); Marvin Felheim, 'Criticism and the Films of Shakespeare's Plays', *Comparative Drama*, 9 (1975), 147–55; N. McDonald, 'The Relationship Between Shakespeare's Stagecraft and Modern Film Technique', *Australian Journal of Screen Theory*, 7 (1980), 18–33; and most recently S. Giantvalley, 'Shakespeare on the Screen: A Symposium', *Quarterly Review of Film Studies*, 7, (1982), 102–3.

7 *King Lear*. USA, 1916. pro. Edwin Thanhouser; dir. Ernest Warde; with Frederick B. Warde (King Lear), Lorraine Huling (Cordelia), Ernest Warde (Fool), Ina Hammer (Goneril), Wayne Arey (Albany), Edith Deistal (Regan), Charles Brookes (Cornwall). b/w. 43 min.

8 Alan Woods, 'Frederick B. Warde: America's Greatest Forgotten Tragedian', *Educational Theatre Journal*, 29 (Oct. 1977), 333–44; p. 335.

Bardolator's ideal of an authentic Shakespearian actor. And in the next sequence of the film Warde gradually begins to dissolve in front of the audience's eyes and to turn into King Lear.[9] Once transformed into the king, Warde's position in the frame is then usurped by a lengthy subtitle:

King Lear was written in 1607 during the time when the immortal dramatist was at the height of his creative power. King Lear, a proud old man in his dotage, listened to the flattery of his treacherous daughters, and divided his kingdom between them, while he banished Cordelia, his youngest child, the only one who really loved him. On the day that King Lear assembles his court to tell them of his proposed abdication in favour of his daughters . . . [etc.]

The film struggles to free itself from the constraints of page and stage. It moves from the opening *mise-en-scène* with a man reading in a chair (which is spatial), to the close-up of the *Lear* text (which involves montage), to the Méliès-like stunt of dissolving Warde into Lear, and then to the narrative device of subtitles for telling the plot of the play. The director has privileged the world of the library (the page); used a well-known actor of the time in the title role (the stage); and literally framed his movie (the screen) between the pages of a book. Page, stage and screen, the triad of Shakespearian incarnations, momentarily interface, though the tension generated among the three inevitably favours disconnection of the filmic from page and stage. To accomplish that, the book and the reader are figuratively and literally dissolved to make room for the movie.

Admittedly, to sensible persons the whole idea of Shakespeare on silent film must seem nothing short of crazy.[10] How could Shakespeare, whose essence is the spoken English language, plausibly be represented in silent moving pictures? As the old silent Shakespeare films with a Forbes-Robertson or a Frederick Warde show, to derive any pleasure from them the audience was expected to be, or at least had

to be, familiar with the text. It has so often been said that the early film-makers exploited Shakespeare only to legitimize a sleazy art form that this point has been virtually lost to view. Forbes-Robertson's *Hamlet*, for example, was played on screen much as it was acted at the Theatre Royal, Haymarket, and in 1914 in America at Boston's Shubert Theatre and Chicago's Blackstone. Warde's Lear resembled what he had done on stage all over America in transforming himself into the very incarnation of the noblest and most monarchial-looking of kings. The silent Shakespeare films challenge the spectator to recollect what words go with what lip movements, facial expressions, and body language of the on-screen players. Thus very early in the history of filmed Shakespeare, there was a proleptic fulfilment of John Russell Taylor's belief that often the best filmed Shakespeare is based on the assumption that the audience knows the play. The film 'affirms' but does not 'record'.[11] Today's avant-garde Shakespeare films, such as the 1980 Derek Jarman *Tempest* and the 1984 Celestino Coronado *A Midsummer Night's Dream*, also attempt to affirm rather than record, though their roots lie in the underground films of an Andy Warhol rather than in the classical movies of a George Cukor. The audience should know better than to assess these films as literal representations of Shakespeare's text.

In Warde's *King Lear*, however, the visual treatment alone, even without the imagined dialogue, shows again, as it did in the eighteenth century for John Boydell's Shake-

---

[9] In much the same way, Harry Baur in *Shylock* (France 1913), dir. Clement Maurice, appears first as himself and then dissolves to the character of Shylock.

[10] Robert Hamilton Ball's *Shakespeare on Silent Film* (London and New York, 1968) pioneered in dispelling this perception.

[11] 'Shakespeare in Film, Radio and Television', in *Shakespeare: A Celebration, 1564–1616*, ed. T. J. B. Spencer (Harmondsworth and Baltimore, 1964), 97–113; p. 113.

speare Gallery of engravings, the power of Shakespeare's verbal imagination to inspire pictorial representation. For example, the 'division of the kingdom' scene is framed around the admonishing hand of the old king pointing at a Cordelia who shrinks from her father's abuse behind her protector, France. The empty space between father and daughter, contrasted with the clasped hands of Cordelia and France, signifies the shattered bond between father and daughter. In the foreground, conspicuously inconspicuous, as though he did indeed belong inside Lear's head, is the Fool. The frame thus positions the severing of the bond of trust and faith at the centre, where it belongs, but the grids surrounding the centre reflect the 'vectors' of disturbance that fall out and away from the king's rash deed. A daughter discarded, a future son-in-law alienated, a court thrown into turmoil, an inner doubt and anxiety in the old king adumbrated by the presence of the Fool, impending collapse and disintegration – all these complexities are reflected in the spatial relationships of the actors in the *mise-en-scène*. It is Shakespeare without words, indeed without montage, but it is also eloquent testimony as well to the power of the art of mime.

Where film most differs from stage, however, is in the capacity to handle the kinds of vast outdoor spectacles suggested in so many of Shakespeare's plays and embodied in *King Lear* in the struggle between the armies of France and England. Warde's *King Lear* did not offer anything quite so spectacular as, for example, the celebrated 1927 Abel Gance *Napoleon* with its triple screens and thunderous musical accompaniment, but freed, as it were, from the 'unworthy scaffold' and 'wooden O', the film revels in the great battle scene, which

4   Frederick B. Warde as King Lear banishes Cordelia (Lorraine Huling), while the Fool (Ernest Warde) looks on

was shot in and around the environs of a 'castle' located in New Rochelle, New York. For that time, when heavy equipment made cameras immobile, the results are impressive. A series of reaction shots depict a gloating Goneril and Regan ecstatic over the carnage spread out before them; dozens of extras outfitted in costume armour carry out a rousing cavalry charge while foot soldiers hack away with menacing-looking long swords or hurl boulders on the helpless wounded. Intercut are reaction shots of an angelic and anguished Cordelia. And even as the film attempts to sever the ancient bond with the theatre, the veteran actor, Warde, as did the more celebrated Forbes-Robertson in his *Hamlet*, offers a documentary of how a nineteenth-century actor approached a major Shakespearian role.

At the very end, when for no apparent reason the film abruptly terminates – after Cordelia has been strangled in prison by brutes, after Regan has been poisoned in close-up, and after Goneril has stabbed herself – Lear carries his daughter out of prison and the subtitles inform the audience that he is saying, 'She's gone forever'. Then the old king, in anticipation of the 1969 Michael Birkett/Peter Brook ending of *King Lear*, literally falls out of the frame. Whether advertent or inadvertent, this camerawork perfectly captures a cosmic truth in Lear's story. He too, like Cordelia, is 'gone forever'. He too has experienced the 'nothingness' with which the play begins and ends. It is a nothingness that is always on the edge of curving back into somethingness, like the theoretical physicist's nothing that is inherently ready to turn back into something. And that hint of grace also comes through in the stately, dignified, thoroughly old-fashioned performance of Mr Warde.

## II

As others have pointed out,[12] Peter Brook's 1970 film of *King Lear* did not spring forth from the head of its creator without gestation.[13] Not only had Brook directed the 1962 RSC stage version starring Paul Scofield, but prior to that he had acted as artistic advisor for a 1953 US television performance with Orson Welles in the title role. This expertise should have shielded him against the obloquy that descended on Sam Taylor for a reputed credit to the 1929 Douglas Fairbanks–Mary Pickford *The Taming of the Shrew*: 'with additional dialogue by Sam Taylor'. That light-hearted jest was solemnly misread as *prima facie* evidence of Taylor's innate vulgarity.[14] Despite his establishment credentials, Brook proved to be a lightning-rod for hostile criticism. If the Thanhouser–Warde *Lear* belongs to the Bardolatry school of forelock-tugging, then the Brook film has been identified with another species of body language – nose-thumbing. The reviewers developed a litany of complaints about his *King Lear*: it is 'depoeticized';[15] inept 'in handling of film medium ... a travesty';[16] 'an image, not of regeneration, but of moribundity and sad decay'.[17] Pauline

---

12 Robert A. Hetherington, 'The *Lears* of Peter Brook', *Shakespeare on Film Newsletter*, 6, no. 1 (1982), p. 7.

13 *King Lear* GB, 1970. pro. Michael Birkett; dir. Peter Brook; camera Henning Kristiansen, with Paul Scofield (King Lear), Irene Worth (Goneril), Jack MacGowran (Fool), Alan Webb (Gloucester), Cyril Cusack (Albany), Patrick Magee (Cornwall), Robert Lloyd (Edgar), Tom Fleming (Kent), Susan Engel (Regan), Anelise Gabold (Cordelia), Ian Hogg (Edmund), Barry Stanton (Oswald), Soren Elung Jensen (Burgundy). b/w. 137 min.

14 Talbot Rothwell, scriptwriter for *Carry on Cleo*, GB 1965, a travesty vaguely under the influence of Shakespeare's Roman history plays, carried the Taylor joke one step further with his credit line, 'From an original idea by William Shakespeare'.

15 Normand Berlin, 'Peter Brook's Interpretation of *King Lear*: "Nothing Will Come of Nothing"', *Literature/Film Quarterly*, 5 (1977), 299–303; p. 303.

16 William Johnson, '*King Lear* and *Macbeth*', *Film Quarterly*, 25 (1972), 41–8; p. 43.

17 Sylvia Millar, '*King Lear*', *Monthly Film Bulletin*, 38 (1971), 182–3; p. 183.

Kael didn't just 'dislike' it; she 'hated it'.[18] The complaint that Brook had made a Shakespeare movie that could not be understood by people who had not read the play surfaced again,[19] as though a Shakespeare film's only function is to serve as a glorified comic book.

Others saw matters differently: Guy Allombert wrote that 'Brook va plus loin; il connaît ses spectateurs. Il traite d'égal à égal. Son film est celui d'une certaine élite. Il la fascine. Il la séduit. Il n'émeut jamais';[20] Frank Kermode thought (though with some qualifications) that Peter Brook had made 'the best of all Shakespeare movies';[21] and the late Lillian Wilds went even further than that in a thoughtful essay that viewed the movie's alleged flaws as artistic triumphs.[22] What Brook did was simply to declare independence from the constraints of page and stage and to make a genuine effort at converting the Shake-

spearian experience into a cinematic idiom. Ideology became confused with artistry, however, and in the chorus of disapproval over his 'gray and cold' vision (has anyone ever thought of *King Lear* as cheerful?) his pioneering efforts were overlooked.

Brook's film really does not set a 'nose-thumbing' attitude against Warde's 'forelock-tugging'. Brook took seriously the mandate to find visual signifiers for what Shakespeare's words signified. The epic scale of Shake-

---

18 'Peter Brook's "Night of the Living Dead"', *The New Yorker*, 11 December 1971, 135–7; p. 136.
19 Millar, '*King Lear*', p. 183.
20 '*Le roi Lear*', *Image et Son*, 282 (March 1974), p. 103.
21 'Shakespeare in the Movies', *New York Review of Books*, 18 (4 May 1972), 18–21; p. 19.
22 'One *King Lear* for Our Time: A Bleak Film Vision by Peter Brook', *Literature/Film Quarterly*, 4 (1976), 159–64.

5　A long shot of Lear's train showing the bleak landscape in the Peter Brook 1970 film version

speare's apocalyptic tragedy demanded radical experimentation with filmic *Verfremdung* to represent the unrepresentable. That the film was not frivolously planned is evidenced in the interview with the producer of the film, Michael Birkett, in Roger Manvell's *Shakespeare and the Film*;[23] or in the 1968 draft shooting script, which painstakingly describes the blocking for each scene, though indeed many alterations from this version occurred by the time the film was actually made.[24]

Insofar as this film also is not just a representation of *King Lear* but a movie about making movies, it exploits meta-cinematic rhetoric. Unlike the Warde *Lear*, it is not in the least defensive about being a film, but instead flaunts its identify. Filmed in North Jutland, Denmark, its black-and-white starkness shows a winter world of ironic despair in grainy shots and deliberate out-of-focus frames. It is perversely cinematic in its Godardian techniques of alienation and in its deliberate break with Hollywood slickness. Like a 'New Wave' director, Brook employs discontinuities: zoom-fades, accelerated motion, rapid editing, complex reverse angle and over-the-shoulder shots, montage, jump cuts, overhead shots, silent-screen titles, eyes-only close-ups, and hand-held cameras as well as stationary, immobile ones. The influence of Jan Kott's 'Grand Mechanism' and of Bertolt Brecht's epic theatre are present also.[25] But for Brook in the late sixties all the world was no longer a 'stage' but a movie screen. At the end, a gravelly voiced Paul Scofield as the dying king literally falls out of the frame (as in the ending of the Warde silent film) to be replaced by white nothingness.

The pervasive view of Brook's film as having been shaped by Brecht and Kott as much as by Shakespeare, however, somewhat obscures the influence on the film of the earlier 1953 television version that Brook helped to produce in North America. The technical realities of television as much as ideological considerations nudged Brook more towards

the play's vision of 'death' over 'life'.[26] The tyranny of time demanded sacrifice of optimistic elements in the Gloucester subplot to compress the performance into 73 minutes. That shortened 'Omnibus' version of *King Lear*, starring the late Orson Welles, was nationally televised in the United States one Sunday afternoon in October 1953.[27] Framed between commercials for Greyhound buses, bath tissues and textiles, the commentator for the 'wraparound', a youthful Alistair Cooke, then just beginning his career as the master of making the art of introduction look easy, opined that while the Gloucester subplot had been thrown away (subplots, he said, were only in Elizabethan plays to rest the main actors anyway), 'everything that bears on the tragedy of *Lear* is in this version'.

Cooke exaggerated, though. The scrapping of the subplot with its redemptive thrust in the behaviour of Edgar, of Albany, and of Gloucester (despite his 'As flies to wanton boys are we to th' gods' (4.1.36))[28] almost guaranteed a

---

23 London, 1971; rev. ed., Cranbury (NJ), 1979; pp. 136–43.

24 Microfilm copy deposited in Folger Shakespeare Library, Washington, DC.

25 Kozintsev thought the influence of Brecht somewhat overrated: 'their [i.e. directors who thought that they had been influenced by Brecht] first teacher, whether they know it or not, was [Vsevolod] Meyerhold, and the fantastic realism of Gogol and Dostoyevsky' (*Space of Tragedy*, p. 93). Meyerhold was director of Moscow's Theatre of the Revolution in the post-revolutionary era.

26 Jack J. Jorgens, *Shakespeare on Film* (Bloomington, 1977), p. 236, makes a nice distinction between the optimistic and pessimistic sides of the play that co-exist within the same text.

27 *King Lear*, USA, 1953 pro. Fred Rickey. Staged by Peter Brook, dir. Andrew McCullough; music, Virgil Thomson; with Orson Welles (King Lear), Natasha Parry (Cordelia), Arnold Moss (Albany), Bramwell Fletcher (Kent), Margaret Phillips (Regan), Beatrice Straight (Goneril), Alan Badel (Fool), Frederick Worlock (Gloucester), Scott Forbes (Cornwall), b/w. 73 min.

28 Shakespeare quotations from the *Riverside Shakespeare*, ed. G. Blakemore Evans *et al.* (Boston, 1974).

victory of existentialism over essentialism. Cooke's introduction reductively, but nevertheless accurately, seems to have prefigured Kott's vision of the play: 'We give you *King Lear* in the hope that you may learn more from Shakespeare's pessimism than from the optimism of lesser men.'

Constraint can be and often is the mother of invention. So it was with this television version of *King Lear*. Like the 'wooden O' of the Globe, the small box of television requires ingenuity, a feel for the 'meta-cinematic', to overcome its limitations. The opening sequence of the production becomes a dumbshow for the style of representation that is to follow. A curtain with an enormous map of England painted on it is suddenly ripped apart and through the tear steps Orson Welles's King Lear to begin the division of the kingdom. The violation of the map foreshadows the violation of the text; that act of aggression signals an approach that privileges themes of power and assertiveness embodied in images of domination and subjugation.

This is a 'bondage' *King Lear*. As Marvin Rosenberg has also noticed,[29] the overtones from Alfred Hitchcock's spy thrillers are pervasive. A major influence, besides the intellectualization of despair by Brecht and Kott, is Hitchcock's obsession with human degradation. Iron gates, steel bars, hempen ropes, and other hints of sado-masochism fill the frames. A portcullis rises at Gloucester's castle, its iron bars reminiscent of the famous cage imprisoning Iago at the beginning of Orson Welles's 1952 filmed *Othello*. The prisonhouse motif persists as Regan and Cornwall are viewed peering through iron bars at a Kent caged and stocked. It continues as the Lear party takes refuge from the storm in a windmill. Ropes, grinding wheels, chains – all foreshadow 'the rack of this tough world' (5.3.315) upon which the old king will figuratively be stretched. Poor Tom, a relic of the jettisoned Gloucester plot, suddenly and inexplicably turns up. Whirling windmill blades

and Virgil Thomson's film music of muted horns and muffled drums offer visual and sonic punctuation for Lear's inner confusion. In the windmill, now clearly an emblem for the old king's spiritual bondage to a foolish appraisal of reality, Gloucester is seized, bound, and has his eyes gouged out by the venomous Cornwall, who uses his thumbs, not his spurs. A wooden-faced Regan looks on without pity.

Wellesian camera angles and imaginative ballet-like blocking of the characters, as well as Welles's own flamboyant performance, make this production from the infancy of televised Shakespeare memorable. Only Jane Howell with her recent BBC productions of the minor tetralogy has achieved nearly so much in transferring Shakespeare to television.

Had Welles lived in the nineteenth century he would have been applauded for the robust talents that make him comparable to a Forbes-Robertson or a Frederick Warde. From the first sequence, as the Fool cowers under his master's dining table while Goneril dominates the old king in a low-angle shot, to his bellowed 'Who put my man in the stocks?', to the frightening moment when his daughters circle him like wolves until he cries out his heartbreaking 'I gave you all', to the memorable closing scene when he drags poor Cordelia in (in the manner of the Italian actor Salvini before him), as though she were a rag doll[30] – Welles's performance is pitched at the highest level of energy.

Indeed the latter scene wrings the most out of primitive studio lighting conditions by correlating darkness with chaos, light with harmony. The old king's howls originate and intensify in darkness and dwindle as he moves into the light. The audience's sudden perception that the *thing* he is dragging along the ground is actually Cordelia simultaneously

---

29 'Shakespeare on TV: An Optimistic Survey', *Quarterly Film, Radio and TV*, 9 (1954–5), 166–74; p. 171.
30 Marvin Rosenberg, *The Masks of King Lear* (Berkeley, 1972), p. 312. '"Drag it" Salvini did, with failing energy; Welles would do the same . . .'

arouses pity and fear. The loyal daughter has become a rag doll, a child's toy, in the hands of a man who has himself reverted to childlike innocence. The slow movement from dark to light, as Welles painfully crawls back up to the throne that he had so foolishly given away, cinematizes the shift from isolation to community. Like Warde in the Thanhouser film and Scofield in the Brook version, the king moves into what Henry Vaughan spoke of as 'the world of light'. Albany is given the final lines; there is a slow fade; and the music comes up. Despite this performance, reviewers were harsh, even cruel. One went so far as to write that Welles resembled 'a man who had been hauled off a park bench and hastily pressed into service as Macy's Santa Claus'.[31]

### III

Paradoxically what seems most remarkable about Grigori Kozintsev's 1970 Russian-language version of *King Lear* is that it is apparently unremarkable.[32] That is to say, there is no tie to a past of page or stage hidden away in the film's rhetoric ('forelock tugging'); nor is there on the other hand the baroque style of the Brook film, which might open it up to charges of 'nose-thumbing'. Kozintsev, perhaps because of his many years of experience as a film-maker and consequent ability to resist the temptation of over-using a camera, elegantly realized the impossible task of making *King Lear* possible on screen. With Kozintsev, the camera probes as much as records; it is an x-ray, not a mirror. He accomplishes his goals through patient contemplation of the problem at hand rather than through superficial tricks. He searches for a deeper structure in Shakespeare's play that needed to be brought to the surface for effective cinema. The solution seems to be the close scrutiny of faces, all kinds of faces – those of the king, his daughters, of Kent, of Cordelia, of the Fool, of Edmund – to allow the camera to reflect the inner passions expressed in the glitter of eyes, the curl of a lip, or the toss of a head.

Essentially the only thing remarkable about the film is that the dialogue is in Russian, using Pasternak's translation. Even there, a curious anomaly lies in the fact that the star of the film, Yuri Yarvet, an Estonian non-speaker of Russian, had to force himself to learn the language to avoid the infelicity of dubbed-in speech. Yarvet was actually the last actor cast after many had been auditioned for the leading role. The subjecting of each aspirant to three entire weeks of rehearsals simply for the auditions[33] was entirely typical of the relentless pains that Kozintsev took in the pre-shooting phase.

From its famous opening shot, one that depicts hundreds of peasant feet clumping and toiling up a stony hillside that looks like some druidic boneyard, to its closing shot as Edgar silently moves forward against the backdrop of a fertile pasture, Kozintsev relates this legendary tale of shattered human trust with a serene dignity. The film's dominant motifs and images are not quickly forgotten: the sound of the Fool's bells ('a tongue stuck out against pomposity', as Kozintsev himself said)[34] before the old king enters, laughing, for the 'division of the kingdom' scene; the 'presence' (in a post-structuralist sense) of Yarvet as king, a scrawny little man who nevertheless can speak with the authority of thunder and who serves notice that his essence is not subject to usurpation; in the hearth of the great hall a

---

[31] Quoted in Hetherington, 'The *Lears* of Peter Brook', p. 7.

[32] *King Lear.* USSR 1970. dir. Grigori Kozintsev; music, Dmitri Shostakovich; trans. Boris Pasternak. c. Jonas Gricius; with Yuri Yarvet (King Lear), E. Radzins (Goneril), G. Volchek (Regan), V. Shendrikova (Cordelia), O. Dal (Fool), K. Sebris (Gloster (*sic*)), L. Merzin (Edgar), R. Adamaitis (Edmund), V. Emelyanov (Kent), A. Vokach (Cornwall), D. Banionis (Albany), A. Petrenko (Oswald). b/w. English subtitles. 139 min.

[33] *Space of Tragedy*, p. 75.

[34] *Ibid.*, p. 119.

fire through which the king is glimpsed as though he were himself in flames (as he will be) and the linking, as Kozintsev wrote, of that fire with the recurring images of flaming torches in the king's train of carts, the army campfires, the searing tar hurled at the fortress with catapults, and a gutted city that resembles Hiroshima; Lear's incendiary diatribe against Cordelia, his throwing of the map around this way and that, as he rumbles his awful wrath over her apparent ingratitude; the old king vigorously striding through the palace selecting household objects and animals for his journey – the hawks, greyhounds, setters, everything that a king with a hundred knights should have in his train; the scathing denunciation of and then spitting upon Kent, which even though uttered in Russian makes clear that Kent's sentence has gone beyond exile to the level of ritual excommunication or perhaps exorcism; and then in unexpected con-

trast the quiet, meditative speaking of the 'O reason not the need' speech in soliloquy at Gloucester's castle; the way that Regan in a white heat to possess Edmund rips off his clothing, only shortly thereafter to plant an erotic kiss full on the lips of Cornwall's corpse; the quick cut (Kozintsev prefers the cut to the dissolve) to 125 frames (5 seconds) obscenely displaying the hanged Cordelia high above the castle walls; the funeral cortège bearing the bodies of the fallen while the Fool (now transformed into a Russian village idiot) sits amidst the rubble mourning the loss of his master and of his own identity; and an over-the-shoulder shot of the king looking down on a throng of peasants and crying out (he who has himself been dragged through the mud and a hovel with Kent and Mad Tom): 'O, [you] are men of stones!' (5.3.258).

In short, Kozintsev has approached the making of a film as a sculptor who would

6    In the Kozintsev 1970 *King Lear*, Lear (Yuri Yarvet) and Cordelia (V. Shendrikova) are led off to prison

suggest rather than articulate the innermost character of his subjects. Wherein, however, is the film meta-cinematic? How does it show awareness of itself as a work of art and how does it work out the buried fear of subservience to page or stage? Is this film, too, still fettered to page and stage? The answer must be that Kozintsev moved very close to that ideal stage of film-making advocated by V. F. Perkins,[35] in which the medium informs the subject and the subject informs the medium. It is a balance that favours neither the accumulation of detail (*mise-en-scène*) nor the selection of detail (montage), but interweaves through skilful editing all elements into a coherent design. The commentary that Kozintsev makes about his film within his film is clandestine, implicit, expressed as much through what is not seen as through what is seen. If Brook is the Brecht of film-makers, then Kozintsev becomes the Pinter. Brook favours theatricality; Kozintsev, silence. This difference does not mean that Brook should be indicted as a director guilty of using 'bombast and rhetoric', but rather that two gifted film-makers have discovered different ways of capturing the extraordinary complexity of Shakespeare's greatest tragedy. To be dangerously reductive, Brook favours montage and Kozintsev *mise-en-scène*.

A major reason for Kozintsev's understated, covert rhetoric may well be that much of what he thought about the movie had already been expressed in his diaries before he began filming. His astonishing book, *King Lear: The Space of Tragedy*, is unmatched as a record of a film director's artistic struggles. The book is the meta-cinematic side of his production because all the theorizing about the film, and about the problems of making a film, went into it before the film itself was made. It made a cinema without prefixes possible. Probably its genius, its status as one of the great works of this century, has never been properly acknowledged. J. W. Lambert came close, though at the end of his review essay he

undercut his own estimation with a stock complaint of cinemaphobes: 'is the resulting experience [of film] any deeper, any stronger, any better, or even as good, as a good director with a good cast will arrive at in six weeks or so in the theatre?'[36] Studded with polished anecdotes and aphorisms, Kozintsev's book meditates on film-making as an art. It probes the configurations of the reality that shaped his awareness. The effect of a stone in a Kyoto garden, of the Hiroshima museum, of Noh drama, of the influence of Meyerhold, of Brecht, of Zen, of his own association in the early twenties with Sergei Yutkevich in FEKS ('The Factory of the Eccentric Actor'), and of the grotesqueries of Gogol and probings of Dostoevsky – all in one way or another lie behind the conception of his *King Lear*. Little is said about Marxism, though there is a tendency for some Westerners to ferret out evidence that Russian film directors employ Marxist assumptions about power relationships.[37] Kozintsev circumvents political theory in favour of timeless themes of evil and injustice. Even so, his apparent indifference to hard-core socialist realism did not prevent acclaim from Soviet as well as Western critics,[38] and through his personal appearance in 1971 at the International World Shakespeare Congress in Vancouver, Canada, Kozintsev

[35] *Film as Film: Understanding and Judging the Movies* (London, 1972), p. 24.

[36] 'Shakespeare and the Russian Soul', *Drama*, 126 (1977), 12–19; p. 19.

[37] E.g. Morris Carnovsky in *Literary Review*, 22 (1979), 408–32, p. 423. He speaks of 'what we might expect from a Soviet artist' in the 'heavy contrast between the rulers and the ruled'.

[38] See Barbara Hodgdon, 'Kozintsev's *King Lear*: Filming a Tragic Poem', *Literature/Film Quarterly*, 5 (1977), 291–8; Nigel Andrews, 'King Lear', *Sight and Sound*, 41 (1972), 171–2; and Alexander Anikst, 'Grigori Kozintsev's *King Lear*', *Soviet Literature*, (1971), 176–82. All express enthusiasm for the film, Hodgdon's essay perhaps most effectively. For mention of Kozintsev's appearance at Vancouver, see J. M. Welsh, 'To See it Feelingly: *King Lear* Through Russian Eyes', *Literature/Film Quarterly*, 4 (1976), 153–8; p. 154.

was one of the first film-makers to win a serious hearing from a wide range of Shakespeare scholars.

IV

Since the 1953 Brook–Welles *King Lear*, television has undergone a technological growth that makes it unreasonable to discuss recent and past productions as though they were of the same genre. The three major televised *King Lears* of the past two decades – those with James Earl Jones, Michael Hordern, and Laurence Olivier in the title roles[39] – have been produced using studio equipment that was unimaginable in the 1950s with its 'live' performances fraught with potential disasters: an actor doing a swaggering Petruchio could stumble on the stairs or a Lady Macbeth could muff a cue in front of millions. And yet as television approaches the technical competence of film it gains an 'air-brushed' slickness at the expense of spontaneity, ironically the same complaint that theatre advocates have always made about filmed Shakespeare.[40]

Even television reduces itself into further subsets when one considers that the 1977 broadcast in the United States of the James Earl Jones *King Lear* was actually a recording of an earlier Delacorte Theater production in New York City's Central Park. Camera becomes merely a tool or service to the stage, though even that assertion needs qualification because some recordings of stage productions have obviously been done with greater expertise than others. The Richard Burton/John Gielgud Electronovision *Hamlet*, for example, used no less than fifteen cameras,[41] which did not guarantee its success but does suggest the magnitude of the production's mechanical problems.

The chronicle of making a 'television movie' from *King Lear* will focus here on Jonathan Miller's 1982 BBC TV/Time–Life version starring Michael Hordern, and the 1983 Granada Studios *King Lear* starring Laurence

Olivier. Both these television plays appeared at almost the same time, just as the two film versions of Brook and Kozintsev made their premières within a few months of each other. Like the Brook and Kozintsev films, the Miller television version also gestated on stage before being subjected to the permanent record of the camera.

As well as in a 1975 television production, Miller had directed Hordern in a 1970 Nottingham Playhouse production of *King Lear*, which in London appearances received mixed reviews: J. W. Lambert found Hordern's 'grizzled' style and the 'grey sets' faithful to the Shakespearian intention,[42] but Eric Shorter seems to have had an opposite impression, summed up in a laconic conclusion: 'I still do not understand those costumes.'[43] The television version[44] apparently adhered very closely to the style of the stage production in its stress, as Miller put it, on an 'absence of regality' in the person of the old king. Indeed, anyone calling for 'regality' is in peril of being dismissed by Miller as a kind of lout with 'lower middle class' sensibilities.[45] There is not

---

[39] Neither the Joseph Papp production starring James Earl Jones nor the Jonathan Miller 1975 television version, which preceded the BBC production, starring Michael Hordern will be discussed here because of their current unavailability.

[40] For a thoughtful analysis of Shakespeare on television, see Sheldon P. Zitner, 'Wooden O's in Plastic Boxes: Shakespeare and Television', *University of Toronto Quarterly*, 51 (1981), 1–12.

[41] Brenda Davies, 'Hamlet', *Monthly Film Bulletin*, 39 (1972), p. 163.

[42] 'Plays in Performance,' *Drama* (Summer 1970), 15–28; p. 24.

[43] 'Plays in Performance,' *Drama* (Spring 1970), 27–31; p. 30.

[44] *King Lear*. GB, 1982. BBC TV/Time–Life Inc. pro. Shaun Sutton; dir. Jonathan Miller; with Michael Hordern (King Lear), Gillian Barge (Goneril), Penelope Wilton (Regan), Brenda Blethyn (Cordelia), Frank Middlemass (Fool), col. 1/2" VHS. 180 min.

[45] Henry Fenwick, 'The Production [of *King Lear*]', in *King Lear, The BBC TV Shakespeare*, ed. Peter Alexander *et al.* (London, 1983), p. 22.

7   Penelope Wilton (centre), Gillian Barge (right) play the wicked sisters in the 1982 BBC production with
Brenda Blethyn (left foreground) as Cordelia

8  Michael Hordern as a grizzled King Lear with Frank Middlemass as the Fool in
the 1982 BBC production directed by Jonathan Miller

room here to do full justice to Hordern's thoroughly professional and competent performance in this startlingly original conception of the old king, nor to Frank Middlemass's Fool. The measure of how far it is removed from the cliché King Lear is to think of Albert Finney's Lear in *The Dresser*, which carries all the old stereotypes to the point of a *reductio ad absurdum*. Then again, however, one recollects the wild old hirsute king of Frederick Warde's nineteenth-century America and grave doubts settle in. Has the loss of regality been bought at the expense of innate dignity? Has the Jove figure been reduced to Job?

Whatever the answers to these questions, in putting the play into a monochromatic, late Renaissance ambiance and in attempting to turn the disadvantages of acting in a television studio into advantages, Miller used the medium to serve Shakespeare's words rather then Shakespeare's words to serve the medium. At the same time, there is no defensiveness about television's being neither a play script, nor a stage play, nor a film. Quite the contrary. One senses an aggressive, even robust, relish for working with the medium. With such an attitude, the technicians on the set replace the live audience in the theatre, as Hordern once commented. There is a willingness to work with what is on hand rather than a restless search to recover the lost glories of either stage or film. As with Kozintsev, most of Miller's thoughts about making a television movie out of a Shakespearian tragedy apparently took place at the planning stage, not in production. This is not a *King Lear* that readily responds to a search for elements of either metatheatre or 'meta-television'; it both records and reaffirms the Shakespearian text. Its hidden agenda may be that the Notting-ham theatre origins partially subverted re-making of the play for television. Along the way, however, Michael Hordern, in becoming less the king-man and more the man-king, displays a special brand of competence, summed up in John J. O'Connor's homespun comment: 'While he is not overwhelming, he is mightily convincing.'[46]

v

To complete the figure, however, of meta-theatre to 'meta-cinema', the promise of my

subtitle, the Olivier/Elliott *King Lear* offers a splendid coda. What could possibly be more self-referential, more 'meta-television', than the world's greatest actor playing himself as an aged monarch in the declining years of his career?[47] More than that, the veteran sup-porting cast is virtually a real-life counter-part to the old king's hundred knights. From all accounts they also brought a Kent-like

---

46 'TV: A No-Nonsense *King Lear*', *The New York Times* (18 Oct. 1982), p. 16.

47 *King Lear*. GB, 1983. Granada Television, prod. David Plowright; dir. Michael Elliott; with Laurence Olivier (King Lear), Colin Blakely (Kent), Anna Calder-Marshall (Cordelia), John Hurt (Fool), Leo McKern (Gloucester), Diana Rigg (Regan), Dorothy Tutin (Goneril). col. 1/2″ VHS, or Beta. 158 min.

9    Laurence Olivier as King Lear with Diana Rigg as Regan in the 1983 Granada Television production

loyalty on the set to the aged monarch,[48] which in a way is reflected in the 'division of the kingdom' scene when they lie prostrate in awe of the king's majesty. A retinue of stars in their own right, they include Diana Rigg as a surprisingly reptilian Regan and Colin Blakely, a memorable Antony in the BBC *Antony and Cleopatra*, as Kent. Dorothy Tutin's Goneril is quietly degenerate but no doubt Leo McKern as a throaty Gloucester offers the most memorable of the supporting performances.

The producers also constructed a studio replica of Stonehenge to endow the play with timelessness. Enormous hunks of cowhide make up the map of England in the first scene, and a Stonehenge setting at the beginning and ending of the play hint at dark druidic mysteries of sacrifice. Moreover Stonehenge, as Tucker Orbison recently observed,[49] is set off against an oak tree to punctuate the nihilistic and regenerative side of the Lear tale.

Olivier himself never loses his gift for canny stage business, particularly in the mad scenes when, to signify his pathetic vulnerability, he washes clothes, exposes the breasts of his withered body, slaughters a rabbit and consumes its raw flesh, makes a necklace of flowers, and plays with a mouse. Shorn of his beard at the end, not even grizzled like Hordern, Olivier is the very opposite of the Warde King Lear of the nineteenth century. This King Lear of the post-holocaust era, of the post-monarchial period, of the electronic age, cannot somehow achieve the sublimity of the past. He must be made, as with the Hordern King Lear, as much man as king. And yet neither the medium nor the director is actually decisive. It is the genius of the actor that makes audiences either sit up and take notice or switch to another channel. Olivier's remarkable voice, which can turn a vowel or a diphthong into discovery of a lost chord, does not desert him even in his advanced years and guarantees the enduring viability of this production.

Having said all that, however, one is still left uneasy about this representation of Shakespeare's greatest tragedy. In spite of the expenditure of huge sums of money by Granada Television, in spite of the star quality of the cast, and in spite of the brilliance of Olivier's performance, the result still illustrates the obstacles to literal representation of Shakespearian tragedy on screen. Something undergoes a sea change from stage to screen. What works perfectly at an RSC performance in the Barbican may turn leaden on screen. Only the star-quality performance of Olivier saves this production from sinking without a trace. As one reviewer said, the cast and Olivier were simply too large for the production.[50] It would seem that all attempts at literal representation only lead back to the conclusion that Shakespeare on film is most interesting when least representational.

As we have seen then, since the early twentieth century directors have undertaken to represent the unrepresentable by putting *King Lear* on the big screen of movies and then, subsequently, also on the small screen of television. Haunted by the stage traditions of the past, self-conscious about the film and television medium of the present, and anxiety-ridden by the burden of their responsibility to the world's greatest dramatist, they have inevitably allowed their perturbations to creep into their moving pictures. In turning our attention back to the inexhaustible problems of reading, acting, producing, interpreting, and filming the canon, 'meta-cinema' offers yet another way to approach and understand the art of William Shakespeare.

---

48 Peter Cowie, 'Olivier at 75 Returns to *Lear*', *The New York Times* (1 May 1983), Entertainment sec., 1–2.

49 'The Stone and the Oak: Olivier's TV Film of *King Lear*', *CEA Critic*, 47 (1984), 67–77. See also Frank Occhiogrosso, '"Give Me Thy Hand": Manual Gesture in the Elliott–Olivier *King Lear*', *Shakespeare Bulletin*, 2.9 (1984), 16–19.

50 Lloyd Rose, 'Television: A Winter's Tale', *Atlantic* (Feb. 1983), 90–2; p. 92. The production combines 'genius and schlock'.

# VERBAL-VISUAL, VERBAL-PICTORIAL OR TEXTUAL-TELEVISUAL? REFLECTIONS ON THE BBC SHAKESPEARE SERIES

## MICHÈLE WILLEMS

The 1965 issue of *Shakespeare Survey*, entitled 'Shakespeare Then Till Now', included a short article by Laurence Kitchin which must have broken new ground at the time since it dealt with 'Shakespeare on the Screen'.[1] Writing incidentally about what he called television's 'inevitable recourse to Shakespeare', the author remarked ruefully: 'We must learn to live with the results', and concluded that 'as a trendsetter, the screen is potentially a menace. It has given Shakespeare its biggest audience. Up to a point it can lead that audience, but it is a mass audience which demands concessions.'[2]

Twenty years later, with the BBC Television Shakespeare completed, not only have we learnt to live with the results but we are learning to teach with them;[3] and we can no longer be content with dealing at one go with 'Shakespeare on the screen'; we must learn to distinguish between Shakespeare on film and Shakespeare on television. Yet, although the last twenty years have accustomed us to an ever-increasing presence of Shakespeare on the small screen, culminating in what the BBC itself describes as 'the most ambitious and expensive project in the history of television',[4] they have not brought us anything equivalent to the full-scale studies of Shakespeare on the big screen provided by Roger Manvell or Jack J. Jorgens.[5] Nor can the student find, on the theoretical front, any reflection on the televising of drama comparable to the analyses conducted by André Bazin or Albert Laffay on the filming of plays, to say nothing of the

works of Christian Metz on the semiotics of the cinema.[6] In an age so much concerned with the relation between text and spectacle or script and performance, it is surprising that the transformation of a Shakespearian play into images for the small screen should so often be approached as yet another stage production, its failure or success being mostly attributed to the quality of the acting or to the interpretation of the director.

These, it is true, can also make or mar a television film, but one should not underestimate either the specific problems attached to producing a Shakespeare play for a medium so different from that for which it was written and for the benefit of a public whose expectations and rapport with the play are so different

---

[1] L. Kitchin, 'Shakespeare on the Screen', *Shakespeare Survey 18* (Cambridge, 1965), 70–4.

[2] Kitchin, 'Shakespeare on the Screen', pp. 70 and 74.

[3] For instance, volume 35 (no. 5) of *Shakespeare Quarterly* (1984), devoted to teaching Shakespeare, includes several articles on the use of BBC Shakespeare in the classroom.

[4] *The BBC Catalogue for Schools*, p. 20. An expensive project indeed for the school that attempts to buy the series, as the export prices for each play vary between £340 and £475.

[5] Roger Manvell, *Shakespeare and the Film* (London, 1971); Jack J. Jorgens, *Shakespeare on Film* (Bloomington, 1977).

[6] André Bazin, *Qu'est-ce que le cinéma* (Paris, 1958); Albert Laffay, *Logique du cinéma* (Paris, 1964); Christian Metz, *Essais sur la signification au cinéma*, vols. 1 and 2 (Paris, 1968).

from those of its original audience. The gap between the 'wooden O' – or indeed any modern stage attempting honestly to accommodate a Shakespeare play – and the electronic square is so wide that one may wonder whether the BBC series would not have benefited from a preliminary reflection on the best ways of bridging it, instead of dealing with the problems empirically for better or for worse.[7] As far as analysis is concerned, there is no need to make the same mistake and the very concept of 'Television Shakespeare' calls for an investigation of the two systems of signs informing those two realities which have suddenly been brought together: a Shakespeare play on the one hand, a television film on the other. In both cases, we are dealing with modes of communication, either with an audience or with a viewer, and the functioning of each mode must be investigated before we can appreciate the problems posed by translation from one to the other.

Superficially, the cinema, television and the theatre all appear to rely on the layering of signs to communicate with their publics. Viewer and audience alike must apprehend a variety of signs simultaneously: aural signs such as words spoken by actors, music and other sounds; visual signs such as costumes, setting, lighting and sometimes special effects. But there the similarity ends, because the respective importance and status of these signs vary enormously from one medium to the next. On the stage all the other signs are subordinated to speech (in monologue, dialogue or aside), while on the screen words are secondary; the dialogue follows the image. It is a commonplace to say that the theatre is an aural medium whereas the cinema is primarily a visual one, a characteristic inherited and accentuated by television in spite of its smaller screen. On the stage the spoken word is prevalent; it has a primary function as it conjures up the whole universe of drama, particularly in Shakespearian drama where the language can be oratorical, formalistic, ironical, metaphori-

cal and, on rare occasions only, purely descriptive. (The few cuts in Jane Howell's *Henry VI* do away with descriptions of battles, which are turned into pictures for television.) But most of the time Shakespeare's language is charged with layers of significance; not only does it carry the dramatic energy, it is also fraught with symbols and networks of metaphors. The screen, on the contrary, addresses its public through pictures which often replace words, so much so that words may seem out of place and too much speech may be prejudicial to the effect of a film, as Albert Laffay notes about the end of Chaplin's *The Great Dictator*. And Manvell writes in his first chapter devoted to the problems on moving 'from the open stage to the screen': 'There can be no doubt that the full-scale spoken poetry of Shakespeare's stage and the continuous visual imagery of the cinema can be oil and water' (p. 15). The solution is even more difficult to obtain if the screen is a small screen, as we shall see.

But the tension between text and visuals does not in itself account for the basic incompatibility between the two media, especially as the visual element of stage productions has gained prominence over the centuries. The conversion from play to film comes up against another major contradiction, which is, in many ways, related to the different function of words in each medium: the theatre is a mode of communication based on convention, while the cinema and television are representational media. The cinema, its theoreticians like to explain, produces an impression of reality, the actual two-dimensionality of the image on the screen creating in effect an illusion of three-dimensionality, which encourages the public to enter passively a new world which they

---

[7] In his article 'Adjusting the Set' (*Times Higher Educational Supplement*, 10 July 1981, p. 13), John Wilders explains that his initial suggestion of holding a seminar before the filming began was rejected for fear of cramping the directors with a 'house style'.

perceive as real. But if the cinema thrives on realism, television's proper style is generally described as naturalistic and even domestic, the size of the screen reducing what Bazin calls 'the window open onto the world' (p. 165) offered by the big screen to what amounts to key hole peeping into a drawing-room. Indeed, the nature of the communication induced by television calls to mind the famous fourth-wall convention which describes so well the functioning of the proscenium arch. In the case of television, the screen stands for some transparent division, which enables the viewer to witness a courtroom quarrel between Hotspur and King Henry IV, or to catch Prince Hal and Falstaff at the tavern in the midst of their plans for robbery. Hence the captivated excitement of the spectator sitting at home in his armchair, but it is passive excitement which does not stop him from getting his cup of coffee in the kitchen. In the theatre, and particularly in the case of a Shakespeare play, the imaginative involvement of a live audience is required. But although active, this participation remains deliberate, complicity is mitigated by detachment. This dual response is a specific characteristic of the theatrical experience which even the confirmed theatre-goer will find difficult to recapture once he is himself in the 'viewing' situation, which, as the very word indicates, does not necessarily include listening or imagining.

Nor does viewing afford the shared experience of the theatre. Even a family of viewers does not make up an audience. The cinema is more akin to the theatre than television as far as communication with a collective public is concerned. Not many people like to see a funny film in an empty auditorium and watching a Shakespeare comedy on television with a crowd of students is preferable to viewing it on one's own. At a symposium on *The Merchant of Venice* held at Rouen University at the beginning of 1985, we showed some eighty colleagues and students the scene between Launcelot Gobbo and his father which had been omitted on French television the previous Sunday.[8] The laughs from the audience drowned part of the dialogue but reconciled Jack Gold, who was with us to discuss his film, to what he considered as a disappointing performance on the part of his Launcelot (Enn Reitel). He told us how excellent the actor had been in rehearsal as long as he was performing for the benefit of an audience of technicians, cameramen and actors but how, when silence was required in the studio for the actual filming of the scene, he became panic-stricken and the comic quality of his performance went down.

This anecdote points to another opposition between the stage and the screen: however present and real the actor may appear to be on the screen, he is actually absent, unaware of the response of the public and consequently deprived of the possibility of gauging the effect he produces. The interviews collected by Henry Fenwick for publication alongside the BBC Television texts record the frustrations and difficulties of actors normally used to a live audience when they have to perform in a silent studio and when, as Derek Jacobi explains, the experience of acting Hamlet is split up over six or seven days. The essential transience of the stage performance is transformed into something final, encapsulated once and for all, yet to be shown again and again. The advantage of acting for the cinema is the possibility of shooting and reshooting until director and actor are satisfied with the results. But this advantage was lost because of the restrictions imposed on the BBC series. Directors repeatedly bewail the obligation of filming

---

[8] This sort of thing often happens because the films have to be reduced to two and a half hours to fit into the programmes. As the plays are subtitled and the credits are not changed, the French viewer is treated at the end to a list of characters some of whom may not have appeared on his screen. Part of the discussion on Gold's *Merchant of Venice* is published in the proceedings of the symposium: *'Le marchand de Venise' et 'Le Juif de Malte', texte et représentations* (Rouen, 1985), pp. 167–75.

every play in six days, and actors such as Anthony Quayle lament the impossibility of seeing themselves to judge whether the scale of their performance is right.

Even a brief exploration of the specific characteristics of each mode of communication brings to light a number of incompatibilities between a Shakespeare play and television, and points to the necessity of what Kitchin would call concessions, or of what one might choose to call transcoding in the translation from one system of signs to the other.

Now, the BBC's project was to produce the Shakespeare canon, complete and unabridged, and this went together with the decision to use the Peter Alexander text and to take no liberties with it. The initial brief, one reads everywhere, was to cut and alter the text as little as possible, which amounted to stating that the play text would have to serve as film script. The impossibility of rephrasing, of restructuring, of substituting another sign for the prevalent verbal sign of the original meant that it was impossible to conform to the fundamental necessity of 'shifting the stress from the aural to the visual', as Kozintsev sums up the problem of filming Shakespeare.[9] Both Manvell and Jorgens show how the best Shakespeare films make free with the text the better to adapt it to the exigencies of the medium, the object being to translate the poetical effects of the original into visual imagery. One may argue that the result is another work, but in the best cases it is an adaptation which is faithful to the spirit, if not to the letter, of the original play. And if we turn to precedents in television films, we find that such series as *An Age of Kings* or *The Spread of the Eagle* did not attempt complete or exhaustive productions of the history plays or of the Roman plays. They cut, adapted, restructured, and serialized to meet the demands of the new medium. Can this account for the fact that these series had an average viewing audience of three million some twenty years ago, whereas the present audi-

ence figures for one of the BBC Shakespeares range from one to two million, at a time when a Chekhov or an Ibsen can gather five million viewers? Shaun Sutton, the third producer of the series, who provided these figures, offers this explanation: 'Shakespeare's plays are so long ... one of the main difficulties is the amount of words spoken ... In television we are used to terseness, to shortness.' Yet to the question: 'What sort of public were you aiming at?', Sutton answers: 'Everybody; students, but also ordinary people; Shakespeare wrote them for everybody.' This may well be true, but nowadays one should also take into account what Jack Gold, who had no previous experience of directing Shakespeare, stresses in order to explain his primary concern with making his BBC *Macbeth* and *The Merchant of Venice* intelligible to the general viewer: 'When I go to watch Shakespeare, people on the stage seem to be speaking in a foreign language.'[10]

In fact, the BBC's confusion between play text and film script goes together with a confusion about the public aimed at. The production of a 'definitive' version of the Shakespeare canon concerns a limited public of students, teachers, and Shakespeare lovers who may be interested in turning to 'preserved' Shakespeare for want of the real thing. Building up 'a library of Shakespeare video-productions' a definition that was suggested to Cedric Messina in an interview,[11] could justify the ruling out of such tampering with the text as is common even on the stage. But a project

---

[9] Kozintsev, quoted by Jorgens, *Shakespeare on Film*, p. 10.
[10] The interview with Shaun Sutton, as well as those with Jack Gold and David Jones, referred to at various times, were collected by our research team. Rouen University's 'Centre d'étude du théâtre anglo-saxon' (CETAS) will publish them, along with other articles, in a book of essays entitled *Shakespeare à la télévision*, some time in 1986.
[11] Quoted by Stanley Wells in 'Television Shakespeare', *Shakespeare Quarterly*, 33 (1983), 261–77; p. 263.

which involves a thousand actors, which is supported by well-known financers, widely publicized and sold to thirty-five countries, needs more to justify it than an appeal merely to students. Producing Shakespeare for what Ann Pasternak Slater, in her interview with Jonathan Miller for *Quarto*, refers to as 'the small-screen with the huge audience',[12] implies attracting to Shakespeare a public which rarely or never goes to the theatre and involving viewers who, as David Jones pointed out in a private interview, do not know how the story will end. The basic question connected with the determination of the target is formulated by Stanley Wells, when he writes in an article on 'Television Shakespeare': 'Do we want good television drama or pure Shakespeare?'[13] The fact that this question never received a proper answer is shown by the very diverse reactions of the various directors, some of whom refer to Veronese or Rembrandt to explain to Henry Fenwick how they approached the Shakespearian material, while some others allude to *Dallas* or to Northern Ireland. By not deciding clearly what the target was, which would have entailed a reflection on the best means of reaching it, or rather by aiming at too wide a target, the BBC series ran the risk of satisfying neither the few nor the many. And it has had, so far, neither the international impact of Olivier's *Richard III*, nor the critical acclaim of his *Henry V* which Bazin described as 'Shakespeare pour tous' (p. 174). Nor has anyone noted an increase in the sale of Shakespearian texts comparable to the increase in the sale of recordings of Mozart's symphonies registered in every country after the release of *Amadeus*.[14] As for the few, their enthusiasm has been more than muted, as was shown by the results of the poll organized by the Shakespeare Association of America[15] and by the various calls for a remake of the series in the States.[16]

The fluctuations in textual policy also testify to the difficulty of keeping to a party-line which has not been theoretically thought out.

More freedom to stray from devotion to the text was obviously given by Jonathan Miller than by Cedric Messina. 'It was all talk and no action' became a recurrent excuse for cutting as the series progressed, and it seemed to be more and more recognized that full-length plays acted as a deterrent for the average viewer. The fact, for instance, that *Coriolanus* was submitted to such drastic paring down that it was reduced from 3½ to 2½ hours is not perhaps to be attributed solely to Moshinsky's very personal approach to the text. From the start he contended that a Shakespearian text needed a certain amount of 'doctoring' if it was to be enjoyed by a television public, but even so his 1980 *All's Well that Ends Well* and his 1981 *A Midsummer Night's Dream* were models of textual faithfulness compared to his 1983 *Coriolanus*.[17]

However, taken as a whole, the BBC series offers the original example of using a theatrical text as a film script with only minor changes, thus assuming that a visual medium can somehow accommodate an abundance of

---

[12] *Quarto* (September 1980), 9–12; p. 9.

[13] Wells, 'Television Shakespeare', p. 266.

[14] In France, for instance, an average of 250,000 viewers watch the Sunday afternoon broadcasts of the Shakespeare series, while the viewing figures of French classics are between two and three million and the Saturday evening boulevard comedies attract an audience of up to ten million.

[15] The SAA ratings on a scale of 10 ranged from 3.2 for *Romeo and Juliet* to 8.1 for *Henry VIII*. *The Tempest* scored 4.8 and *As You Like It* 5.2.

[16] See particularly Maurice Charney, 'Shakespearian Anglophilia; the BBC-TV Series and American Audiences', *Shakespeare Quarterly*, 31 (1980) 287–92; p. 292.

[17] At the same time more efforts were made to appeal to the general public. Shaun Sutton confesses 'a show-biz approach' rather different from the more intellectual approach of his predecessor: 'I would have liked to have seen more stars on the series ... Richardson, Peggy Ashcroft, all these people ... I think the greater the star, the more chance people will watch.' There was, he explains, no financial reason for not getting the best known actors: 'Even the biggest star only gets so much on television.'

verbal signs. This confrontation between the two media is often bypassed – successfully some will argue – by resorting to filmed theatre,[18] which amounts to a superposition of the two media. But in the case of the BBC we are dealing with authentic television films produced in the studio – with the exception of two outside broadcasts – without the support of a live public. The question now is: how do these solve the problem of producing for the small screen a script in which the theatrical mode is to remain prevalent? Given the fact that, as John Wilders explains in his article 'Adjusting the Set', each director was left to find his own solutions, the responses to the problem vary from play to play but they can be classified, roughly, into three categories: naturalistic, pictorial, and stylized.

The naturalistic solution was the most commonly chosen, especially at the beginning of the series. It was presented by the people involved – directors, designers, and costume designers – as the best way of satisfying the expectations of a public who watch the news every night and thus expect battles, fights, and scuffles, among other things, to be presented with a degree of realism. In any case, the brief given by the BBC and its financers, that the plays should be set in a period which Shakespeare would have recognized, did not encourage innovation or invention, but rather threw the directors back on traditional approaches and sent the costume designers searching for reference books and even for a thesis on the clothes worn in Henry IV's reign. Indeed the early publicity for the series was in 'Hollywood style', to take up Jack Jorgens's expression in his review of *Julius Caesar*.[19] It extolled, among other things, the 'authentic recreation of Caesar's Rome', and the filming of *As You Like It* in a 'real forest'. Conversely, it congratulated itself on the exclusion of stylization and 'gimmicks'. Not unsurprisingly, what emerges from the interviews conducted by Henry Fenwick over the first two or three years of the enterprise is the directors' and designers' concern for authenticity, their preoccupation that badges, banners, and weapons should look genuine. Priority was given to historically acceptable reconstitutions: a suitably timbered tavern alternating with a period courtroom for *Henry IV*, a credible Elizabethan mansion and garden for *Twelfth Night* and, even later on in the series, a village square such as Shakespeare might have known for *The Merry Wives of Windsor*, which, much to David Jones's regret, could not be filmed on location like *Henry VIII*. The object of such productions is to present the viewer with a universe which he can accept as an authentic representation of the world of the play. And other choices logically follow: *The Tempest* opens on a real tempest; the actress taking the part of Juliet has to be fourteen – even if this is to be her major asset – because 'on television there's no way in which you can make a 25-year-old look fourteen'; for *Twelfth Night* it seems important 'to get the society of the play right' and thus to make Sir Andrew 'an even faintly plausible suitor for Olivia's hand'. If Jane Howell had opted for this approach in *The Winter's Tale*, her main problem would have been to find a geographically acceptable beach for the coast of Bohemia.

Without denying the attractiveness of many realistic productions or the visual pleasure they can produce, it must be said that the naturalistic approach often aggravates the tensions between the two media instead of solving

---

[18] This concept means different things for different people. Everyone objects to films of live performances shot from the vantage point of the spectator sitting in the stalls. In his chapter devoted to 'Théâtre et cinéma' (*Qu'est-ce que le cinéma*, pp. 130–78), A. Bazin puts forward his own conception of filmed theatre, which is epitomized by Olivier's *Henry V*. In a different perspective, in an article entitled 'BBC Television's Dull Shakespeares' ( in C. B. Cox and D. J. Palmer, eds., *Shakespeare's Wide and Universal Stage*, Manchester, 1984, pp. 48–56), Martin Banham suggests that the plays could be filmed in front of a live audience.

[19] *Shakespeare Quarterly*, 30 (1979), p. 412.

them. What happens in effect is that each mode of communication imposes its own prevalent signs, which often vie for the spectator's attention without supporting each other. Shakespeare's idiom is transported wholesale on television. The message is dense, polyvocal; layers of significance qualify and enrich the basic narration. Now naturalism, instead of trying to find ways to transpose this complex language, retaliates by superimposing its own favourite representational idiom. The visuals describe what is said by the text in successions of purely referential shots. The well-meaning desire to make the story absolutely clear often results in the reduction of a play to its story-line and to a number of characters delivering speeches which are received as too long and pointlessly verbose. As with those translations which ignore the various operations of transcoding, only the literal meaning is transcribed. The story, the information, the description get the lavish support of the visuals but the rest of the message is often wasted in the process, if only because the attention of the viewer is channelled towards the visual signs and consequently strays away from the spoken word. The text becomes submerged, devalued. When Old Capulet delivers his lines while shopping in an Italian market, the odds are that the viewer will devote more attention to what Capulet is buying than to what he is saying. The substitution of a real forest for the emblematic Forest of Arden works against the verbal poetry of the play. Real sheep, an oak and magnificent bluebells – an unlikely haunt for a lioness – take first place in the viewer's interest, before Rosalind's love-play and Touchstone's witticisms.

And the conflict between word and picture is complicated by the clash between the conventional mode and the representational one. Prince Hal sitting at a tavern table where he has just finished his breakfast with Falstaff really takes the spectator by surprise when he launches into his monologue: 'I know you all'. When Malvolio airs his dreams of grandeur in a park for the benefit of a few eavesdroppers hiding ineffectively behind a tree, the comic convention of non-discovery comes into conflict with the realistic setting. Throughout the letter scene the conventional status of protagonists-turned-spectators enjoyed by Sir Toby and his crew is totally lost as the camera tries to respond to the comedy of situation with the traditional two-shot technique. When Malvolio is on, the eavesdroppers are off, and when they are all in the picture together the tree adds to the confusion of an already cluttered-up picture. The descriptive sequence of shots characteristic of realistic productions cannot accommodate the conventional play-within-the play.

Indeed it is in comedy that the conflict between the two modes is most marked. This is so true that many directors seem to have thrown in the comic sponge before the struggle to arouse laughter in the living-rooms of thirty-five countries had even begun, preferring to offer the viewer a documentary or sociological study of Elizabethan life instead. David Jones confides to Henry Fenwick about his production of *The Merry Wives of Windsor*: 'I said right from the beginning, I am not concerned at all if the play is not funny'; and Jonathan Miller remarks to Tim Hallinan about *The Taming of the Shrew*: 'As happens with almost all of Shakespeare's comedies, it really is a more serious play than people have taken it for.'[20] Although these may sound like rationalizations after the event, such options are perfectly legitimate, and one must allow that *The Merry Wives of Windsor*, broadcast during the Christmas season, succeeded in its attempt to recreate the Merrie England spirit. But for anyone who saw Ben Kingsley on the stage and enjoyed the hilariously funny effects he drew from the character of Ford, a sense of anticlimax will prevail when watching his Ford on the screen. In fact the importance

---

[20] In an interview published in *Shakespeare Quarterly*, 32 (1981), 134–45; p. 139.

given to architectural and social realism is probably just as detrimental to the comic effect as the absence of a live public. An actor cannot cultivate his class credibility and his comic performance at the same time; insistence on the first smoothes over the excesses inherent in the second. Again the emphasis is shifted from comic convention to realistic representation. Trying to present Sir Andrew as a plausible suitor for Olivia's hand is basically at odds with the conception of the character; in the same way, the focus on Malvolio's status as a steward cannot easily be reconciled with a truly comic treatment of the character; those yellow stockings and cross-garters cannot be dismissed with a few rather unsuccessful close-ups. The emphasis on social context is part and parcel of the realistic logic. In comedy, particularly, it only reinforces the incompatibility between convention and representation at the expense of laughter.

As in writing, there is a coherence within the style of a production and a number of options are consequential to the initial choice of naturalism. Realistic diction is another one. That the actor can be heard without having to project as far as the last seat in the gallery has been repeatedly hailed as one of the advantages of a medium often described as intimate, the domestic setting being the specific response of television to the necessity of scaling down its naturalistic scenery. The small screen will favour a house rather than a town and an indoor scene rather than a street scene. Now, when speaking in chambers, antechambers or libraries – a recurrent setting in the series – the actor resorts, logically, to a conversational tone of voice to deliver his lines. This may be well adapted to some scenes, such as the beginning of *All's Well that Ends Well* where the reflective mode is served both by the beautiful interiors inspired by Dutch paintings where successive doors open on to successive rooms, and by the quiet diction which is sometimes even used to render part of a monologue voice-over. In *Measure for Measure*, too, the

traditional two shots, improved by constantly changing angles of shooting, effectively present the confrontation of Angelo and Isabella, and counter her pleading tones with his quiet determination. But the muted confidential diction does not suit all Shakespeare's speeches. Anthony Quayle shows himself aware of the difficulty of finding the right pitch and of the danger of misgauging his performance on television, and it is true that his Falstaff strikes one as too quiet and too sedate at times. Falstaff is an enormous, larger-than-life character who cannot always give his measure in confidential tones. At the other end of the scale, tragic speeches, with their rhythm, rhetoric, and imagery, hardly benefit either from everyday delivery in naturalistic surroundings. What happens to the famous *Othello* music when it is delivered in conversational tones over a desk in some sort of library? Few tragedies have been treated realistically, and in the case of *Othello* the problem seems to be more one of interpretation. The deliberately domestic bias – rendered among other things by the systematic staging of outdoor scenes in chambers and halls – is meant to stress the fact that, in Miller's terms to Fenwick, the play is not concerned 'with the fall of the great but with the disintegration of the ordinary'.

Whatever Miller's justifications, the realistic approach again results in reductiveness. Its concrete, referential, visual language is certainly effective in story-telling. It makes the most of the advantages offered by the medium in order to smooth over the inconsistencies and deal effectively with the spatial and temporal discontinuity of Shakespearian drama. But it responds to every convention by doing its best to occlude it, at the same time doing away with that unique combination of detachment and involvement which causes dramatic emotion, as well as passing off the poetical density of the blank verse as everyday informative prose.

Another approach was greeted by commentators as possibly *the* answer to the problem of translating a Shakespeare play to television. This was the pictorial solution, initiated by Miller's passion for Renaissance painting and supported by his intimate knowledge of it. In the two interviews he gave on the subject,[21] he explains how he uses paintings as source material not only for setting and costumes but to determine the general organization of space in the studio and consequently on the screen. For *Antony and Cleopatra* he agrees that 'it would have looked ludicrous to place that verse against a realistic Rome and Egypt of the first century AD', so he turned to images of Veronese to recreate a sixteenth-century version of Roman antiquity instead. For *The Taming of the Shrew* he derived his inspiration from Dutch paintings, which gave him a picture of domestic life at the beginning of the seventeenth century. De la Tour was a major influence for the costumes in this play as well as in *Othello*; and more references to Chirico or Caravaggio come to support Miller's contention that he has found a visual counterpart for the 'unscenic stage' that Shakespeare wrote for. It is indeed tempting to consider that this pictorial approach, also favoured by Elijah Moshinsky, particularly in his *All's Well that Ends Well* and in his *A Midsummer Night's Dream*, provides a specific code for the conversion of Shakespearian drama into televisual language. This, one might think, is a specifically visual response adapted to a visual medium. But the question remains of the relation between the text and the visuals. One should not confuse visual richness and visual significance. Titania in her bower beautifully suggests Rembrandt's *Danae's Bower*, and even the spectator who does not recognize the allusion will enjoy the picture, but will this help him to understand a rich and difficult text? Is there not rather a danger that the picture will interfere with the reception of the words? In *A Midsummer Night's Dream*, particularly, the abundance of visual signs would probably be more at home on the big screen than on a small screen. Even systematic filming in depth does

not manage to accommodate easily an unusual quantity of visual signs; the result is a picture which is often difficult to decipher and words which are swallowed up in visual abundance. Some unquestionably magnificent pictures seem to use the text as a pretext; they exist at the expense of the words which are often diluted in obtrusive visual detail and interfering sound.

Instead of using music to make a point or underscore an effect ('as a sign-post for the audience', to quote one of Jack Gold's expressions), Moshinsky adds beautiful background music, in keeping with the atmosphere created by the pictures, but often vying with the text for attention. The same goes for his sound effects: bird-songs, evocative of the forest, sounds of water as the lovers wade or splash, neighing when Oberon comes in riding his horse. All these realistic noises blend in with the words which the actors often speak together. The use of overlapping dialogue confirms the priority given to realism at the expense of the text: probable as it is that lovers quarrelling or artisans planning a theatrical performance should speak together and shout to make themselves heard, the result is far less likely to be comprehensible. In the same way, Moon, chanting his part in the hall where the newly married couples are enjoying their meal and passing comments on the performance, has little opportunity of making the most of his text. In such circumstances, it is not surprising that Bottom's most appreciative audience, when he does his party-piece at Ninny's tomb, should be the same Moon, but not the diners or indeed the viewers. The conventional play-within-the-play is a major hurdle for television and one which pictorial productions do not seem to negotiate any better than naturalistic ones. Jonathan Miller chose to film the taming of his shrew without a witness, doing

---

[21] Given to *Quarto* and to *Shakespeare Quarterly*, 32. The subsequent remarks are in *SQ*, 32, p. 137 and then p. 134.

away with the Induction. It is not so much that the size of the screen makes it difficult to show at once the actors and the actors-turned-spectators; what happens is that in a realistic or pictorial context the whole point is lost in any case, the significance of the theatrical metaphor being diluted in attempts to make the situation convincing.

In short, the pictorial solution does not appear as a specific solution at all. It may give more aesthetic and visual attraction to a production, but instead of solving the problem of transcoding from one medium to the other it complicates matters by transcoding twice: once from the theatre into painting and then from painting into television pictures. Instead of reconciling the verbal and the visual, it promotes a predominantly visual mode which may interfere with the reception of the text even more than in a naturalistic production. Whereas in a naturalistic production the visual sign is purely referential and channels the viewer's attention to what the text says (but not to what it means), in a pictorial production it will direct it even more to what is shown. The visual sign is then both referential and aesthetic. Even if the visual quotation is not recognized, the beauty of the picture may become an end in itself and distract from the spoken word, unless it is calculated to reveal it. But referring to pictorial codes to support an interpretation of the text is one thing; this is what Ariane Mnouchkine does when she ends her *Richard II* on a Pieta. But this is not what Miller or Moshinsky are doing when they evoke, or even quote visually, Rembrandt, Veronese, or Caravaggio. They are creating a visual atmosphere, producing a succession of beautifully decorative pictures, but these do not necessarily reveal the meaning of the text or the organic unity of the play.

Both with the naturalistic and pictorial approaches, television responds to the challenge of transposing a Shakespeare play by resorting to a cinematographic mode of expression which, in effect, often brings to light its incapacity to beat the cinema on its own ground. Filming in depth for want of width often results, unless close-ups or head-and-shoulder shots are systematically used, in a confused picture. Visual selection is felt to be a more or less gratuitous intrusion. This is due to the fact that, in a representational mode of expression, what is left out of the picture is felt to be actually missing because one expects a logical chain of references. In another context, what is off-camera can be sensed or imagined as virtually present. A realistic battle scene will only underscore the smallness of the screen, whereas in a stylized universe, like that created by Jane Howell for her *Henry VI*, an archer will be received as representing a whole army. In this case, the metonymic mode of expression brings television much nearer to the theatre. Given the obligation to use a basically unabridged, unmodified text, it appears that an approach where the visual element is used as functional or suggestive is preferable to one in which it is referential or decorative. Instead of vying for pre-eminence with the spoken discourse – when it does not completely interfere with it – the visual discourse can be made to support it or even to reveal it.

Productions like Miller's *King Lear*, Gold's *Macbeth* (and up to a point his *The Merchant of Venice*), Rodney Bennett's *Hamlet*, as well as Jane Howell's *Henry VI*, *Richard III* and *The Winter's Tale*, to name the prominent ones, have this in common: that they resort to the stylization that was the object of so much scorn in the BBC's first publicity for the series. Their settings do not attempt to represent or describe any given location. In fact they often proclaim that they are mere settings, in the first sense of the word: settings for the characters to come to life in, for the words to bounce back on. Bare boards, tall grey walls, columns without tops or even some sort of timeless recreation ground do not make any claim at authenticity (in *Henry VI* a carpet is unrolled under the viewer's eyes and a panel announces 'Part 2' or 'Part 3'); neither do they make a statement descriptive of, or liable to interfere with, the text. They provide a space for the interiorized world of tragedy. In *Macbeth* and in *Hamlet* only slits and holes open onto the outside world. In *King Lear* bare boards and a few props recreate a theatrical space. But these settings also provide a general impression that will support the interpretation of the text. Macbeth's castle is no real castle but an elementary enclosed space where passions will develop and fester. The steps to Duncan's chamber lead to a misty nowhere very suggestive of the everlasting bonfire whereas the scenes in England are filmed against blue skies. The evolution of the setting may also support the progression in the meaning. The colourful playground of *1 Henry VI* becomes gradually boarded up and more oppressive as play follows play, and as the playful skirmishes of the beginning develop into savage battle. The costumes, instead of striving at pure authenticity, fulfil a function; they become darker and more tattered as the war spreads like a disease. This goes beyond the colour coding of naturalistic productions in which the viewer can distinguish between rival factions as in a football match. With Jane Howell, the visual is not only referential, it is supportive, revealing. The same happens in *The Winter's Tale* when the dead tree of the first three acts, set in the middle of the same stylized space which is then looked at through different lenses, is seen in bloom in the second part. Yet at no time is it trying to be a real tree. It provides a visual support to the natural imagery of the play; it reveals the sterility and sickness of Sicilia at the beginning, and suggests the advent of spring and fertility with Perdita in Bohemia. Thus the reversal of tragedy into comedy is made more understandable, supported also by changes in the colours of the costumes, of the setting, and in the lighting.

This is not to say that such productions successfully negotiate all the obstacles. The statue scene in *The Winter's Tale* comes up against the difficulties incident to any last scene of a comedy, complicated in this case by what amounts to a play-within-the-play or a masque-within-the-play. The visual selection that necessarily ensues is not wholly satisfactory. But, on the whole, visual selection is received less as a constraint than as a positive choice in a stylized production. The selection of shots and their arrangement in sequences is what makes up a director's style, his own form of writing, and once the viewer has accepted stylization, he will be prepared to receive elliptic or symbolic shots without feeling frustrated or lost if he is not shown everything and everyone at once. As Jack Gold says: 'Television is not a very democratic medium; unlike what happens in the theatre, you cannot choose what you see.' But the inevitability of visual selection can be perceived positively if it is felt to be part of a pact with the director in the same way as any reader has to play the game of reading according to a number of rules implicit in the writing from the beginning. This may result in a form of participation which is still different from that expected in the theatre, but is nearer to its dual response, as some sort of active reaction is required if the viewer is to decipher the director's signs and to let himself be guided towards a better understanding of the play. Thus the play-within-the-play in *Hamlet* is visually introduced by Hamlet donning a cloak and covering his face with a mask representing a skull. He walks round the part of the floor marked by stools that will stand for the stage. The coexistence of two spaces will now be suggested by filming in depth or more exactly by layering different planes which are significant as well as descriptive. In the foreground, to the right and left of the screen are the backs of Gertrude and Claudius, metonymically standing for the public. The Players are discovered in the space between them as they walk in along a gallery with a chequered floor. They are not only distinguished by their masks and clothes but essentially by their extravagant miming, which survives after the dumb-show. Their performance is now and again interrupted by reaction shots on Gertrude and Claudius, laughing and 'paddling palms', but appearing gradually more worried and closely watched –

another series of shots cutting in – by a tense Hamlet. As the camera either travels over the changing faces of the courtiers or closes in upon Hamlet shouting his narration of the play from behind the Players, the whole scene is totally understandable. Reaction shots and close-ups inserted in a well-thought-out sequence manage to make up for the absence of space and the whole art consists in first giving the viewer a number of visual landmarks: the gallery as a background to the performance, the stools as the limits to the stage, and the public standing on three sides, with Gertrude and Claudius sitting in a central position facing the corridor. Hamlet can then move in and out of the theatrical space. The viewer will retain a mental impression of what is off-camera if its virtual presence has been established by a prior exploration of the geography of the space in which the drama is to take place.

Most of the time, however, the space provided by the screen will be entirely devoted to what is said and heard as the important conversations are recorded in close shots. The close shot, though often decried, remains the basic advantage of the medium; it helps the viewer to follow the text as the facial expressions and reactions of speaker and listener can be registered with an intensity that cannot be equalled on the stage. Many directors use triangular compositions of faces, or of faces and shoulders, to film dialogue. Both Miller and Gold prefer their actors to face the camera rather than filming profiles. In *King Lear* the speaker is often behind the listeners, whose reactions are thus registered in the foreground, as in scenes involving Goneril and Regan. This is often preferred to the not so satisfactory alternative of interrupting the flow of a speech with a reaction shot. But the use of close shots in settings reminiscent of Shakespeare's un-furnished stage will, in any case, encourage a much more theatrical diction. This choice does not exclude the possibility of playing upon a much wider range of voices than in the theatre,

where whispering tones cannot be properly used. Nicol Williamson, playing Macbeth, uses a hoarse, rasping voice for the mono-logues in which he reveals his inner tension and torture, while he remains loud and appar-ently self-assured in public. But in plays with such abundance of words, the silent shot is a means of getting relief by contrast. Sudden silence, or the use of functional music, accom-panies close shots on revealing visual signs: Macbeth's bloody hands; the witches clasping hands in a truce; Lear's tears as the camera closes in on his face at the end of the storm scene; Hamlet suddenly interrupting the verbal and physical violence against Ophelia as the camera registers the realization of his excess, and the fear travelling in his mind before he eventually pronounces, quietly, 'it *hath* made me mad'; or the sudden interruption of loud laughter and noisy reactions that accompanies the transformation of Shylock's well-known plea for his race into a call for revenge. All these are moments of dramatic intensity, which are probably very demanding on the actor but in which the significance of the text can be caught by the camera better than by the wandering and in any case distant eye of the spectator in the auditorium.

Thus visual selection can work as a peda-gogy of the text. Using the visual signs that make up the specific mode of expression of television in order to support and reveal the verbal signs which constitute Shakespeare's own mode of expression may allow the direc-tor to reconcile the two media. The theatrical and the visual may be made to merge into the televisual. On the whole, although they are often considered as 'just not on on television', stylized productions manage this better than naturalistic ones. Producing Shakespeare with the resources normally expected on the small screen has too often resulted in attracting attention to the fact that Shakespeare did *not* write for television.

# TWO TYPES OF TELEVISION SHAKESPEARE

## NEIL TAYLOR

In order to appreciate the significance of The Television Shakespeare (the BBC series which broadcast thirty-seven plays between 3 December 1978 and 27 April 1985), it is necessary to think of it not just as Shakespeare but as television.[1] Derek Longhurst wrote while the series was still in production that it 'needs to be evaluated in terms of the whole determining medium of television' and in a recent essay Graham Holderness has partly taken up this challenge.[2] My intention is more modest and more formalistic.

I shall be looking at the work of two directors, Jane Howell and Elijah Moshinsky, who between them directed eleven of the plays. Much of my evidence will be drawn from Howell's production of the first tetralogy (broadcast in England on 2, 9, 16 and 23 January 1983) and Moshinsky's production of *Cymbeline* (10 July 1983). In my opinion the originality (and success) of these directors in translating Shakespeare from one medium into another derived from a split in their allegiances. Howell publicly acknowledged a struggle between television and the theatre. Moshinsky's case is more ambiguous, but it can be interpreted that he was frequently attempting to treat television as if it were cinema. In both cases the conventions of television drama were partly assimilated, partly challenged.

Raymond Williams reckoned in 1974 that most people spent more time watching various kinds of drama on television than in preparing and eating food.[3] But if 'Drama' is distinguished, following the BBC's practice, from 'Light Entertainment' and 'Feature Films and Series', the importance of drama on BBC Television is waning, and has been for many years. In 1949–50 it represented 17.8 per cent of all broadcasting, in 1973–4 only 6.1 per cent, and in 1984–5 it was down to a mere 3.2 per cent. If one distinguishes between plays written originally for the stage and plays written specially for television, television's output of the former category has always been dominated, as one would expect, by Shakespeare. But there has been a recent marked decline in the number of broadcasts of this category of play. In 1964 there were seventy-three such broadcasts on BBC Television. When it is taken into account that some of these were serialized episodes, excerpts, or repeats, the number of different plays broadcast in that year turns out to have been fifty-three. In 1984, however, only eight different

---

[1] In the preparatory work for this article I was very grateful for the encouragement of Dr T. P. Matheson of the Shakespeare Institute.

[2] Derek Longhurst, 'Not For All Time, But For an Age', in *Re-reading English*, ed. P. Widdowson (London, 1982), p. 163; Graham Holderness, 'Radical Potentiality and Institutional Closure: Shakespeare in Film and Television', in *Political Shakespeare: New Essays in Cultural Materialism*, ed. Jonathan Dollimore and Alan Sinfield (Manchester, 1985), pp. 182–201.

[3] *Television: Technology and Cultural Form* (London, 1974), p. 60.

plays were broadcast – and of these 50 per cent were part of The Television Shakespeare.[4]

There is thus an institutional commitment to Shakespeare (no doubt because he seems to be ideologically safe and sound[5]) and yet he forms part of a genre, the stage play translated into television, whose importance is steadily diminishing. The odds would seem to be that, in terms of production-style, Shakespeare will always be subject to the predominant conventions of the medium.

What, then, are these conventions? John Ellis has argued that, instead of the single, coherent text that is found in the cinema or theatre,

broadcast TV offers relatively discrete segments: small sequential unities of images and sounds ... organised into groups, which are either simply cumulative, like news broadcast items and advertisements, or have some kind of repetitive or sequential connection, like the groups of segments that make up the serial or series.[6]

But the conventions also derive from the conditions under which programmes are made and viewing takes place. The use of multiple cameras and cross-cutting in studio time creates a sense of 'real time'. The use of direct address in non-dramatic programmes, along with the continuity of radiating sound for all broadcasts, combines with the illusion of real time to establish a very direct relationship between the image and the viewer. The result is an aesthetic which emphasizes the close-up and fast cutting. At the same time, viewing is assumed to be casual, domestic, and familial, and this affects programme content. Ellis concludes that television 'massively centres its fictional representations around the question of the family. Hence TV produces its effect of immediacy even within dramas of historically remote periods by reproducing the audience's view of itself within its fictions.'[7]

If these are, indeed, the conventions, then Shakespeare would seem to be both highly suitable and highly unsuitable for television. Jonathan Miller, who produced thirteen plays

in the series, revealed his suitability for such a role when he remarked in an interview, published in 1981, that 'Shakespeare is the great playwright of the family'.[8] Furthermore, one can see immediately that Shakespeare's plays can be regarded as costume pieces and the canon as a series. But the sustained concentration demanded by the individual plays as discrete units runs counter to television's rhythms of very short, ateleological segments. And who, had they never been put on, could have predicted that the first tetralogy and Cymbeline would have proved so royally as to attract an average audience for each broadcast of over half a million viewers?[9]

I

Jane Howell's productions within the series were The Winter's Tale (broadcast on 8 February 1981), the first tetralogy, and Titus Andronicus (27 April 1985). Her attitude to the printed text has been the same in all six productions: a remarkable fidelity, both to its

---

4 The statistics in this paragraph derive from the BBC Annual Report and Handbook (1951; 1975; 1986) and Radio Times (1964; 1984).

5 See, for instance, Rod Allen, 'International Co-Production: Cash for the Concept', Edinburgh International Television Festival Magazine (1978), pp. 22–4; Carl Gardner and John Wyver, 'The Single Play: From Reithian Reverence to Cost Accounting and Censorship', EITFM (1980), pp. 48–9. At the opening press conference for the series the Managing Director of BBC TV promised that it would be 'straight' (Birmingham Post, 2 November 1978, p. 2).

6 Visible Fictions: Cinema, Television, Video (London, 1982), p. 112.

7 Ibid., p. 135.

8 Quoted in Tim Hallinan, 'Interview: Jonathan Miller on The Shakespeare Plays', Shakespeare Quarterly, 32 (1981), 134–45; p. 140.

9 Henry VI Part 1: 800,000; Part 2: 500,000; Part 3: 500,000; Richard III: 500,000; Cymbeline: 400,000. (Source: BBC Broadcasting Research Department.) These figures must surely outstrip the total size of audience for any production of any Shakespeare play ever performed in the British theatre.

letter and to its spirit. In the case of *Titus Andronicus*, for example, she made two significant editorial interventions, opening at line 70 and thereby introducing Titus before Saturninus, and inserting a silent Young Lucius into this and a number of other scenes. But, as Stanley Wells wrote at the time, 'the text is altered here less than in most stage productions'.[10]

Furthermore, she resisted television's normal pattern of segments. The original 1965 television version of *The Wars of the Roses* kept to John Barton's heavily cut and reworked tripartite division, but it was also shown in fifty-minute episodes.[11] Cedric Messina, who conceived The Television Shakespeare and produced the first twelve plays, had begun by wanting to compress the *Henry VI* plays into two episodes.[12] His script editor was of the opinion that about 2½ hours is 'the maximum length for a television play to hold the viewer's attention'.[13] But Howell's production of the first tetralogy was four complete plays shown on consecutive Sunday nights, each broadcast averaging about 3½ hours of peak viewing time.

A consequence of playing the full tetralogy was that, when *Richard III* was reached, the usual pressure to cut it on grounds of obscurity was less forceful. David Snodin, the script editor on her production, pointed out that

Whereas in most productions of the play several references to the reign of Henry VI are omitted, they have naturally been allowed to remain in this version – as has, of course, the haunting figure of old Queen Margaret, who so dominates the *Henry VI* trilogy, but who is often removed altogether from productions of *Richard III*.[14]

Howell cut only 5 per cent of the text of the tetralogy (613 out of 11,601 lines). Such respect for the writer may be regarded as revealing theatrical thinking – after all, in the cinema the actors and the director have almost always eclipsed the author of the screenplay – but Stanley Wells believed that in the case of this production the texts were 'probably purer

than any given in the theatre since Shakespeare's time'.[15]

Because of its financial resources and because of its fragmented rehearsal and shooting schedules television can employ large, talented casts. Messina promised in 1978 that The Television Shakespeare would employ 'some of the greatest classical actors of our time'.[16] Effectively, he played the star-system, signing up big names in television, the cinema and the theatre: Claire Bloom, John Gielgud, Derek Jacobi, Celia Johnson, Penelope Keith, Alec McCowen, Keith Michell, Helen Mirren, Kate Nelligan, Anthony Quayle, John Stride, Michael York, and so on. For the tetralogy, Howell drew on eighty-one different actors but created a hard-core company of thirty-nine whom she used throughout. Despite the BBC publicity, which spoke of a 'star-studded cast',[17] her company had no stars and only one or two faces familiar to television viewers.

Instead of stars she chose actors with whom she had worked before, added to them, and tried to create 'a strong sense of family'.[18] Her target was a company whose unity derived from a corporate experience during production; the willingness and versatility to double parts enabled actors to become far more involved in the play as a whole than is normally the case in the disintegrated process

[10] 'The Canon in the Can', *Times Literary Supplement* (10 May 1985), p. 522.

[11] Stanley Wells, 'Television Shakespeare', *Shakespeare Quarterly*, 33 (1982), 261–77; p. 261.

[12] Cedric Messina, 'Cedric Messina Discusses *The Shakespeare Plays*', *Shakespeare Quarterly*, 30 (1979), p. 135.

[13] Alan Shallcross, 'The Text', *Romeo and Juliet*, The BBC TV Shakespeare (1978), p. 21.

[14] 'The Text', *Richard III*, The BBC TV Shakespeare (1983), p. 34.

[15] 'The History of the Whole Contention', *Times Literary Supplement*, 4 February 1983, p. 105.

[16] Preface to *Richard II*, The BBC TV Shakespeare (1978), p. 8.

[17] *Radio Times*, 24 December 1982.

[18] Henry Fenwick, 'The Production', *Henry VI Part 2*, The BBC TV Shakespeare (1983), p. 26.

of television filming. Altogether, twenty-six actors were required to double. The actor playing Henry (Peter Benson) appeared in all the plays in that role, but also played two other minor parts. The actor playing Richard (Ron Cook) took three other minor roles. Another actor (Derek Farr) played sixteen different roles!

Howell intended the viewer to recognize, and think about, the doubling.[19] And the actors were themselves forced to acknowledge the puzzling effects of televising the tetralogy, of exposing the plays to viewing conditions. David Burke, who played Gloucester, Dick the Butcher, and Cade, talked to Henry Fenwick about the differences between the Gloucester of *Part 1* and the Gloucester of *Part 2*:

Watching it all in one evening an audience would say, 'That actor's changed his style'. But I know that there will be a gap between the two episodes and therefore people will just have a vague memory of what he was like; hopefully they won't see a change in style, they'll just see a different aspect of him.[20]

The approach to casting was thus practical, in that it encouraged integration and cohesion between actors, and interpretative, in that the doubling exposed relationships between one role and another, and between the community of roles and the community of actors. Howell remarked that her *Richard III* was a play 'haunted by the other three plays and also by the presence of the same actors'.[21]

Part of the strength of her company derived from the conditions under which rehearsals and filming took place. Whereas most productions in the series had to make do with a month's rehearsals and a week's filming, Howell worked with her company over six months. Furthermore, the plays were made in the right chronological order and, although they were shot in the normal stretches of a week each, the same company was actually filming together for a total of twenty-nine days. Such conditions improved ensemble playing. As she herself put it, 'courage grows and people get better'.[22]

Fenwick called Howell's use of a permanent company, and the device of doubling, a 'theatrical approach' from a director with a 'strong theatrical background'.[23] Another of her decisions which was more characteristic of the theatre than of either television or the cinema was the choice of a permanent set. Indeed, in all her productions in the series, Howell used some form of permanent, semi-abstract and semicircular structure, surrounding an open acting space. It was most abstract in her first production, *The Winter's Tale*. In *Titus Andronicus* (her last) it was clearly intended to suggest the Colosseum – a theatre of cruelty. In the tetralogy the size, complexity, and flexibility of the crude wooden structure, punctuated by a number of openings, ramps, and swing-doors, created an equivalent of medieval multiple staging. The shape, bareness, and twin levels of the structure encouraged a use equivalent to Shakespeare's own experience of an Elizabethan public theatre. Finally, modernity was provided by the avowed inspiration of an urban adventure playground[24] and the use of anachronistic features – not just the swing-doors but a vast area of parquet flooring for the ground level.

Beyond all this, the set for the tetralogy called attention to itself *as a set*. Its patent artificiality was intended to help the viewer 'accept the play's artificiality of language and action'.[25] The swing-doors and the fact that, throughout the first scene of *Part Two*, the words 'HENRY VI Part Two' were written on the set itself, were sources of a Brechtian

---

[19] Fenwick, 'The Production', *Richard III*, The BBC TV Shakespeare (1983), p. 27.

[20] Fenwick, *Henry VI Part 2*, p. 29.

[21] Fenwick, *Richard III*, p. 27.

[22] Fenwick, *Henry VI Part 2*, p. 24.

[23] Fenwick, 'The Production', *Henry VI Part 1*, The BBC TV Shakespeare (1983), p. 29.

[24] *Ibid.*, p. 24.

[25] Wells, 'The History of the Whole Contention', p. 105.

alienation. Finally, the parquet flooring openly proclaimed the actual conditions under which the production was being filmed: it seemed to be saying, 'This is a television studio'.[26] Such frankness was part of a strategy to educate the viewer into an understanding of the spatial conditions under which the performance was taking place.

As well as providing an immense range of different settings, the tetralogy's set allowed Howell the pace and flexibility of the medieval or Elizabethan stages. But, as John Wilders has pointed out, television itself can 'restore to Shakespeare's plays the unbroken flow and continuity they almost certainly achieved in the renaissance theatre. By the simple process of cutting, the director can shift from one scene to another even more swiftly than was possible in Shakespeare's time.'[27] Furthermore, the camera is mobile. Thus Howell had at her disposal the physical opportunities of her set, permitting her the spatial strategies of the theatre, and the cinematic possibilities of cutting from one shot to another and, by means of the camera's own movements, 'discovering' or 'losing' an actor or a portion of the set. In the theatre the set is all there before us, but in film and television each new shot creates a new set. Howell achieved *two* sets, the *known* permanent set and the *framed* set, and she played them off against each other.

On the other hand, her spatial manipulation of the three elements – actors, camera, and permanent set – privileged the first two over the third. Although the set's residual force was part of a possible metatheatrical statement ('This is a play'), the fact that it was inconsistently naturalistic, and susceptible of merely abstract or geometrical readings, suppressed its denotative and spatial significance.

Instead, the camera concentrated on the actors and their relationships. They were blocked primarily in relation to one another and to the camera itself, and only rarely in relation to a detail of the set, such as an entrance, or a level, or a property. The set merely created an acting space, and a space for the camera to move in.

Because the camera was so mobile in this production Howell could create fertile spatial relationships not only within the studio but also within the frame. But the source of that fertility was primarily her knowledge of what can be done with blocking in the theatre.

I do find the transition from one medium to another an extra worry and burden and problem. The scenes themselves need so much work and I get so involved that often at the end of a scene I think, 'Oh blast it, Jane, you were supposed to be dashing around looking for camera shots!' But actually I was thinking about what the scene means.[28]

And, for all that on occasion Howell could use filmic techniques (there were slow-motion sequences in both the tetralogy and *Titus Andronicus*), her notion of meaning was always theatrical before it was filmic. For example, she had a problem with act 3, scene 1 of *Henry VI Part 2*.

The Parliament scene where Gloucester is baited by his enemies was a nightmare. There is something foreign about doing it on telly because you need to see them all. What is lovely is seeing all the group at once, but I know I can't do that a lot of the time. And you can't ask the actors to be somewhere just because of the camera: they've got to have their own reality.[29]

This statement makes three important points. In the first place she seems to feel that the scene is at home on the stage but not on television which, by contrast, is restricting and denying. Secondly, the actors must have their own reality, i.e. they are not Eisenstein's *types* to be co-ordinated in pictorial terms by the solely autonomous director. Thirdly, 'you need to see them all'.

---

[26] In fact, as Fenwick pointed out in *Henry VI Part 2*, p. 20, the parquet was not the studio floor but was laid specially for the production!

[27] 'Adjusting the Set', *Times Higher Educational Supplement*, 10 July 1981, p. 13.

[28] Fenwick, *Henry VI Part 2*, p. 23.

[29] *Ibid.*, p. 22.

This phrase surely indicates that Howell would like television to do what the theatre has to do, namely provide the viewer with a visible account of those present throughout a scene. And in all her productions in the series she tried to find gaps in a composition which she could fill with the heads of the silent participants in a scene. By moving the camera or moving the actors a sense of the complete cast for a particular scene could be built up. The composition of the frame was rapidly and continuously changing, through a combination of actors' regrouping, camera movement, and cutting between cameras. The actors' movements were theatrical, the camera's movements were cinematic, but the constant impulse to change the composition or the shot was televisual.

Commitment to 'seeing them all' was part of Howell's consistent desire to relate individual experience to social experience and social facts, and not to read human history in terms of those few individuals with power and authority.[30] Even in *Titus Andronicus* sympathetic identification was deflected away from the suffering Titus and on to the viewer's representative she had constructed for her production – Young Lucius. Her adherence to attitudes and techniques drawn from the theatre was both a commitment to a 'committed' theatre and an attempt to make television communal in the way that all theatre inevitably is.

II

In his attitude to the text, to casting, to *mise-en-scène*, and to the individual, Elijah Moshinsky provided a distinct contrast to Jane Howell. His productions in the series were *All's Well that Ends Well* (4 January 1981), *A Midsummer Night's Dream* (13 December 1981), *Cymbeline, Coriolanus* (21 April 1984) and *Love's Labour's Lost* (5 January 1985). These were his first work in television, but from the beginning he enunciated some bold principles: 'People think

the plays should "speak for themselves"! . . . Plays *don't* speak for themselves – you interpret them by casting, by editing, by designing. They *need* interpretation . . .'[31]

'Interpretation' is a radical procedure in Moshinsky's hands. In *Cymbeline*, which may be regarded as typical of his method, he set about creating a new structure for the play, and to this end removed 25 per cent of the lines (820 out of 3,272). Furthermore, he transposed speeches, divided scenes into smaller units and then staged them in different settings.

The cutting of speeches is not to do with the overall length of a production . . . but with the internal rhythm and excitement of it. For example when you're trying to balance different parts and different points of view it's not very good if you have long development takes . . . The best thing to do is not to have long speeches but to intercut them, so you get four or five speeches, cut in the middle and relocated in different places so that they can be done as it were simultaneously. I also think time-lapse is vital in all this because it's got to do with rhythm . . . In television I can cut within a speech to a different location and not worry about continuity: it's like a time jump.[32]

This degree of editing had ceased to be a matter of interpretation of someone else's text. A new text, effectively the product of the cinema's cutting room, had displaced Shakespeare. Moshinsky had become *l'auteur*.

The contrast between the two directors continued into the area of casting. Moshinsky went for stars, particularly in *Cymbeline*, whose cast included Claire Bloom, Richard Johnson, Robert Lindsay, Helen Mirren, and Michael Pennington. The BBC's pre-publicity used a close-up of Mirren on the *Radio Times* cover ('Helen Mirren stars as Imogen . . .') and a two-page article inside included a second

---

[30] See her remarks on Richard quoted in Fenwick, *Richard III*, p. 30.

[31] Fenwick, 'The Production', *All's Well that Ends Well*, The BBC TV Shakespeare (1980), p. 17.

[32] Fenwick, 'The Production', *Cymbeline*, The BBC TV Shakespeare (1983), p. 20.

photograph of her, occupying almost a whole page. This article, entitled 'Mirren's Imogen', took as its theme the seeming inappropriateness of her playing the part of a long-suffering, patient, and pure wife. 'But then, director Elijah Moshinsky does not see the play the way the Victorians saw it. "I wanted an actress of great sexual voltage," he declares.'[33] Thus, the star-system offered Moshinsky the opportunity to establish a tension between the actor's public image and the conventional reading of her/his role.

The producer of Moshinsky's first two plays in the series was Jonathan Miller, and Moshinsky's ideas for settings for all his productions showed the clear influence of Miller's theory and practice. In Miller's opinion, the way to unlock Shakespeare's imagination is to immerse oneself in 'the themes in which he was immersed. And the only way you can do that is by looking at the pictures which reflect the visual world of which he was a part.'[34] The television frame became a picture-frame in Moshinsky's productions, and the viewer was invited to recognize in the sets and compositions the world of Rembrandt, Hals, Vermeer, and other Dutch masters (All's Well that Ends Well and Cymbeline), and of Watteau (Love's Labour's Lost). In A Midsummer Night's Dream, the picture-frame became a picture-frame stage and even a cinema screen as the exterior scenes invoked the productions of Beerbohm Tree and Max Reinhardt. But on the whole Moshinsky's pictorialism concentrated on naturalistic interiors. Naturalistic exteriors, argued his designer for All's Well, 'look dreadful in the studio, so phoney. We deliberately eschewed any sort of exterior – not even landscapes through windows.'[35] In Love's Labour's Lost the famous eavesdropping scene in the park was set in a library and in Cymbeline so much exterior setting was lost that one reviewer complained that the play's ideas of pastoral were lost too.[36]

Naturalistic interiors in the manner of the Dutch masters not only look authentic on television but suit television's conventional pressure towards domestication. In Cymbeline even Jupiter was dressed as a Rembrandt nobleman, and merely had the advantage over the mortals of meriting a tilted camera angle – in other words, of being looked up to. Jane Howell is quoted as saying that 'Everything you put on stage is a political statement'.[37] In Coriolanus Moshinsky could see 'a curious mixture of the domestic and the political' and decided that the central theme he wanted was 'the non-political one'.[38]

Moshinsky's mise-en-scène was also quite opposed to the style of Howell's: it involved keeping actors and camera comparatively still and providing movement through montage. The drastic editing of the text and modernist fracturing of the narrative were reflected in the use of montage and rejection of development shots. Henry Fenwick remarked that, in the case of Cymbeline, this was 'a style worked out carefully to gibe with his vision of the play as a dream'.[39]

Convinced that the play is a psychological study of 'very dark motives'[40] Moshinsky provided his Cymbeline with two texts, an objective level of action and 'a subjective level of action . . . [which] is like a series of nightmares . . . The play centres round these therapeutic dreams.'[41] Moshinsky cast the viewer in the role of voyeur-cum-analyst, observing and overhearing the conscious and unconscious actions of the play. Whereas Howell had

---

[33] Fenwick, 'Mirren's Imogen', Radio Times, 9–15 July 1983, p. 4.
[34] Hallinan, 'Interview', p. 140.
[35] David Myerscough-Jones quoted in Fenwick, All's Well that Ends Well, p. 25.
[36] Katherine Duncan-Jones, 'Sitting Pretty', Times Literary Supplement, 22 July 1983, p. 773.
[37] Quoted in Ultz, Plays and Players (September 1983), p. 15.
[38] Fenwick, 'The Production', Coriolanus, The BBC TV Shakespeare (1984), p. 21.
[39] Fenwick, Cymbeline, p. 26.
[40] Ibid., p. 19.
[41] Ibid., p. 17.

deployed two modes of verbal discourse – open dialogue and soliloquy addressed directly to the camera – Moshinsky opted for three: open dialogue, voice-over, and soliloquy directed at an angle to the camera.

We have a simple relationship to characters who are engaged in open dialogue. We witness the dialogue but our existence is not acknowledged; we are voyeurs, eavesdroppers, in a way absent. Our relationship to voice-over is one in which we seem to be privileged, in direct communication with the characters' thoughts. But in the third of Moshinsky's modes, soliloquy not addressed to the camera, the viewer is in an ambiguous position, possibly absent but equally possibly known to be present but being evaded. The complex of all three modes created a gulf between viewer and actors. The concentrated study of the characters was intimate, but the viewers were unacknowledged voyeurs. Such a relationship characterizes cinema rather than theatre or television.

In order to signal the beginnings of dream sequences (Iachimo, for instance, came out of the trunk in Imogen's bedchamber both literally and, the viewer was encouraged to believe, within Imogen's dreams), naturalism was overlaid with conventional signs drawn from the cinema: 'We're very close and we move in and we do all the filmic technique of close-up and time-lapse and silhouettes and menacing shots and the suggestion of his nakedness, so he has a rather potent sexual force.'[42]

In comparison with Howell, Moshinsky went for closer shots. Her characters were almost always standing, his frequently seated and often at tables. Whereas in *Henry VI Part 2*, for example, there were 315 medium and long shots, in *Cymbeline* there were only 226; whereas *Part 2* had only 88 close-ups, *Cymbeline* had 231. The effect in *Cymbeline* was to reinforce Moshinsky's emphasis on individuals, psychological interpretations of behaviour, and subjective experience.

This emphasis was also noticeable in his *Coriolanus*. David Snodin, the script editor, explained that the massive cuts and changes to the text were effected 'in order to sustain the story's narrative energy by concentrating on the thoughts and actions of the principals'.[43] Moshinsky wished to stress the central character's intensifying isolation:

when you read it it looks as though the play has no internal monologues or discussions at all, whereas actually on television you can extract lots of Coriolanus' speeches where the sense of internal disenchantment grows; he becomes alienated ... we have these incredible close-ups where he's off-centre and we can hear the monologue of disenchantment which goes throughout the play.[44]

In his *Cymbeline* he deployed a series of devices to suggest the isolation of all the characters. As well as using the close-up he ensured that one character would be separated from another by being reflected in a mirror, or he deliberately broke the flow of the action by breaking up the text. He conceived of Posthumus as a man who 'labours entirely under guilt, the guilt of his existence ... a bitter, existential and Dostoevskian character'.[45] This existential isolation of the characters was often reinforced by the set. The windows offered no views of the outside world, and many of the characters had their backs to the walls and were out of direct communication with others. Silent, oppressively obsequious, standing or bowing, the servants and anonymous courtiers might be present but served only to focus attention on the principals.

Where Moshinsky's approach was under the greatest strain was in the final scene.

On the stage, of course, it's the whole cast assembling and telling each other what they've experienced and how their relationships have changed ... I came

---

[42] *Ibid.*, p. 17.
[43] 'The Text', *Coriolanus*, The BBC TV Shakespeare (1984), p. 31.
[44] Fenwick, *Coriolanus*, p. 22.
[45] Fenwick, *Cymbeline*, p. 25.

to the conclusion that how to do this on television
... is to deal with it not as a group scene but as a
series of individual small scenes ... It's all either
close-ups or two shots ... without too many geographical establishings of where people are. Iachimo
as it were disappears out of the scene after he's said
his piece and Posthumus comes in – he literally
walks off camera and isn't seen again until he's
needed. And we're not meant to know where he is –
he's somewhere off camera.[46]

So, this way of shooting the final scene
ensured that the architecture and topography
of the shooting conditions were not finally
intelligible to the viewer. The emphasis was on
individual characters and on the smallest units
of human interaction. Howell's tetralogy had
given a social reading within a simulated real
time (often employing long takes on a single
camera) and real place (the known set in an
implied studio). Moshinsky's *Cymbeline* was
thoroughly subjective, exploring dream interiors in dream time.

### III

Stanley Wells wrote, after The Television
Shakespeare was complete, that few of the
productions had tackled, let alone solved, the
problems of adapting Shakespeare to the television medium.[47] Howell and Moshinsky may
not have solved all the problems, but they
certainly tackled some of them, boldly. Both
drew on some of the conventions of television
(in Howell's case, the primacy of talk and a

rapid alteration of the image, for instance; in
Moshinsky's case, a preference for the seated
figure and the close-up) but rejected others
(Howell opted for stylized acting, Moshinsky
for images of intense visual detail). In addition, Howell discovered in television's
immediacy and intimacy an equivalent to the
stage actor's direct relationship with the audience. Television's ability to simulate real time
was combined with its frankness about the
physicality of things, so that a pact was made
with the viewer: these are the actors, this is the
text, this is the set, this is the space in which
we shall all be working. She operated within
the known.

Moshinsky, on the other hand, discovered
in television's sealed, iconic screen a denial of
immediacy and intimacy. He deconstructed
the text and remade it. His *mise-en-scène*
ensured that the space which the viewer saw
became a puzzle. He used television's preference for segmentation, and its ability to cut
between shots, to create a cinematic montage
that challenged the known.

Their joint achievement derived from their
ability to combine an initial conception of the
cultural form to which television could best be
assimilated – for Howell, theatre, for
Moshinsky, cinema – with a sensitivity to the
character of television as a cultural form in
itself.

---

[46] *Ibid.*, p. 26.
[47] 'The Canon in the Can', p. 522.

# SHAKESPEARE ON RADIO

## STUART EVANS

These observations are based on my experience of eighteen years at the BBC (mainly in educational broadcasting), during which time I worked on some fourteen Shakespearian productions, along with other important plays, poetry features, and literary commentaries. I aim at describing the particular advantages that radio offers, while taking into account the obvious disadvantages of a non-visual form of presentation. There are certain problems which producer, actors, and technical staff must solve; decisions to be made about the use of effects, music, and radiophonics. Most important, of course, are the specialized approach of actors to the text in question, the techniques that must be developed, and the virtues of an experienced company working together over years rather than months on many different plays: tragedies, comedies, histories and romances.

Hamlet's advice to the Players is as pertinent for radio as it is in the theatre. Of course the speech should come trippingly, and tearing a passion to tatters is all the more agonizing when only the ear and imagination are engaged: there should be no vocal sawing of the air. Just as too much 'business' on stage can disturb the flow of action and destroy the rhythms particular to tragedy and comedy as well as significantly distracting attention from the words, so too many aural tricks, over-elaborate effects, too much use of ingenious radiophonics or of music, can upset the delicate balance of a performance of Shakespeare on radio. Actors, director, and technicians must always remember that it is the verse, and perhaps less obviously the prose, delineating character and motive, describing situations, which matters most.

Experienced radio actors will have few difficulties with the longer speeches of (say) Hamlet, Macbeth, Othello, or Antony. Radio is particularly kind to soliloquies, and it might be argued that the player of Hamlet or Macbeth is able to speak them more naturally than is possible in the theatre. Othello will have most potent, grave, and reverend signors all about him – for it is worth noting that thoughtful actors in a happy cast do *not* scurry into corners to read the book page of *The Times*, do the *Guardian* crossword, or get on with the shopping list at the first opportunity. They stay at the microphone and react visually of their own accord or vocally as directed.

There are, however, long speeches which are very difficult when there is no visual response to excite the audience. The king in *Henry IV Part I* has some formidable stretches of verse at the opening, and more especially in his scene with Hal in act 3 scene 2; Ulysses in the first act of *Troilus and Cressida* must hold attention through some intricate argument; the king and Wolsey have substantial though dramatic tracts in act 2 scene 4 and act 3 scene 2 of *Henry VIII*. Mercutio's 'Queen Mab' speech can seem to some heretics (who must include Romeo) even more tedious on radio than it is on stage. Speeches such as these call for great resources of skill and variation, and it is essential to cast an actor in such parts who matches dramatic power with a subtle verse-speaking intelligence. The producer may choose to help with judicious cutting.

Prose – especially comic prose – is even more tricky. Falstaff's garrulities are sustained by the sheer comic girth of his character (requiring an actor of some ebullience) and by the responses and ad lib interpolations of Hal, Poins, Bardolph and others, or else the delightful interplay with Shallow. The dramatic force underlying the acerbic observations of the not-altogether Fool and the ramblings of Edgar as Poor Tom in *King Lear* lends its own clarity to difficult prose passages. But consider Feste's exchanges with Olivia and Viola in *Twelfth Night*, or Touchstone *passim*, or Autolycus in spate, and it will be evident that comic allusions, mocked pedantry, and inkhorn parody readily appreciated by fashionable wits in Shakespeare's time make difficult listening for most members of a twentieth-century audience, especially when deprived of accompanying movement and facial expression.

Suiting the action to the word, then, is hardly possible on radio, pointing to some of the disadvantages of presenting Shakespeare in a medium which relies entirely on sound. These are fairly obvious, so I will be brief. There can be no spatial relationship between actors – whether principals in regard to one another or to an ensemble. There can be no movement: for example, if the producer decides he might like to have a restless Iago circling round an immobile Othello. It is true that skilful use of stereo (of which more later) can go some way to achieving such effects, but the result may very well be distracting, even irritating. Most of all, actors and producers miss the opportunity of tactile contact, half-gestures of excitement or pathos, lingering glances, the shifting of position or stance to imply domination or submission. Scenic and lighting effects, acrobatics, and other visual innovations are denied in radio presentation.

Only through choice of music can a Shakespeare play be set in some other period: there are no costumes or props. And yet, while acknowledging the supremacy of the theatre, I would contend that Shakespeare on radio works more convincingly, stimulating the imagination, than on television.

So what are the advantages? First, in terms of sound effects: outdoor effects are more real on radio and may be used to enhance the impact of a particular scene. Let us take the departure of Laertes in act 1 scene 3 of *Hamlet*. Elsinore (Helsingor) is on the sea and the royal apartments are evidently close to the port from which Laertes will bend his wishes towards France. So the scene may be played out of doors with distant seabirds, seawash, perhaps the sounds of a port in action. Good studio managers delight in obliging such requests and are meticulous in their sense of 'period'. This adds a freshness to the scene when all is still well with the Polonius family and Ophelia is in a playful mood with her sententious male relatives. It also emphasizes, however mildly, the fussiness of the second leave-taking. And the irony may be made tragic if the same acoustic is used for Ophelia's mad scene in act 4 scene 5.

The 'high fantastical' comedies – *Twelfth Night*, *As You Like It*, *The Merchant of Venice*, *Much Ado About Nothing* – offer good opportunities for contrast. All are set in sunny places, so that it is legitimate enough to create the atmosphere of an idyll with its feet on the ground in Olivia's orangery or the Forest of Arden or gardens in Belmont and Messina, with birdsong, and a gentle rustle of leaves (though, if overdone, this can sometimes sound like an unseasonable shower). Effective contrasts occur in the Illyrian streets, near the harbour, where Sebastian and Antonio talk, or on the bustling Rialto as Shylock bargains with Antonio or suffers the taunting of Salerio and Solanio. This Renaissance hubbub is also part of commercial Verona, with Guelphs and Ghibellines at every corner; so that the underlying hum of potential violence emphasizes all the more the doomed peace of the Capulet garden or larks rising above the cell of gentle Friar Lawrence. Owls and nightingales, when not in literary debate, are much courted by radio producers. A skilfully placed owl-shriek in counterpoint to lyrical love can produce a chilling sense of foreboding. Of course we all know that the lovers are star-crossed and what is going to happen in all the plays; but part of the suspension of disbelief is that we pretend that we do not, and allow ourselves willingly to be thrilled.

City kerfuffle is one thing, but what radio manages lovely well (as Glendower might have had it) is crowd scenes, especially when the crowd is angry. In plays such as *Coriolanus* or *Julius Caesar*, where the mob is not so much a part of the action as a character in the development of the drama, it is reasonable to be reminded of it. Narrowing focus on to Republican Rome before the ascendancy of Caesar, there were the 'social' wars of Marius and Sulla, the street-gangs of Milo and Clodius Pulcher: the people in the streets played an active part in politics. So, from the opening scene with Flavius and Marullus, through the distant crowning while Cassius lays siege to Brutus' image of his honour, until Caesar makes his appearance on the fateful day, the audience should be reminded of the crowd – its latent violence, its undirected anger capable of demagogic manipulation. After the murder of Caesar, growing background concern as the news spreads and the rumours sprawl, can surge into panic by stages, while Antony and the conspirators play out their diplomatic hands. By the time Brutus and Antony face the crowd, there is a frenzy which is volatile and the more dangerous. Here, where the orator (demagogue) is close to them, distant effects (on disc) can be enhanced by pre-recorded closer reactions and then brought to a climax by the immediate response of the whole company (if necessary conducted by the chorus leader or Antony himself) as the speech

progresses. The culmination of this fury is the murder of Cinna the poet. Here the background turmoil may be lifted so that the immediate participants – once again the entire company – have to bawl against it, before approaching, close and vicious, for the slaughter.

Battles work well, too. Once again direct confrontation may be juxtaposed to a panoramic backcloth of carnage. Radio armies know no numbers, they are logistically sound, and the listener may be transported at the flick of a fader from savage hacking to a moment of gruesome calm. Stereo recording will suggest any number of perspectives which undoubtedly work; but is the listener's attention distracted from the lines spoken? And this matters even in battle scenes. Does the pace change, does the rhythm suffer, in the name of a technical holiday? Such reservations have nothing to do with radiophonics. It is hard to give a name to the people who combine intricate electronic skills with all kinds of aural creativity, even if their local habitation is Maida Vale. I shall refer to them as composers. Radiophonics are marvellous for magic. They may have little to contribute to the histories, the factual comedies, or the high tragedies; but when spelled upon *A Midsummer Night's Dream*, *Macbeth*, or *The Tempest*, radiophonic wizardry comes into its own.

Let us begin with that most magical of comedies, *A Midsummer Night's Dream*. An introductory phrase will suggest the sympathetic magic of a comedy and may be used, with discretion, for bridges between scenes. Song can often be lulling (if not boring) when there is no visual aid, so radiophonic music can send Titania sweetly to sleep with efficiently ethereal cadences that can in a second thrum into Oberon's sinister malice as he wishes her to wake when some vile thing is near. This, of course, is dear old Bottom. Under the spell the radiophonic rhapsody may continue as Titania suggests immortal and Bottom rather more earthy longings; until Bottom wakes in an ordinary Athenian wood from which the spirits have departed, marvelling at his dream and setting off singing tunelessly to himself. All the fairy scenes benefit from radiophonic effects. Puck throws a radiophonic girdle round the earth and has terrific fun deceiving Lysander and Demetrius; Oberon broods; Titania relaxes in erotic fancy; and eventually the ancient, potent spirits, so much wiser than the mortals, proffer blessing.

*Macbeth* is altogether different. If Oberon is sometimes sinister, there must be in *Macbeth* an oppressive sense of evil; vigorous enough in the Weird Sisters, but a dull throbbing pain in the conscience of the erstwhile hero. Owls and nightingales may have intruded into the radiophonic Athenian wood: in *Macbeth* the mixing of natural effects (thunder, icy wind, the cry of ravens and corbies) works in concert with whatever the radiophonic composer has devised. A theme of evil for the Weird Sisters might recur at various points in the production: something frenetic and malignant to contrast with the pounding of Macbeth's heavy guilt before, during, and after the event. Producer and composer may decide to keep a particular theme for all Macbeth's soliloquies: let us say an exaggerated heartbeat under an intense obsessional throb of insistent music. This to occur from 'Is this a dagger' to 'Tomorrow and tomorrow', whenever Macbeth is left to his own thoughts. Quite different the radiophonic treatment of two notably different scenes in the theatre: act 3 scene 4, where Banquo's ghost appears, and act 4 scene 1, where Macbeth seeks out the Weird Sisters and conjures the various apparitions. In the first instance, jovial Macbeth, after his brief words with the assassin, fixes on the empty stool. One radiophonic chord establishes his terror before he starts to speak, lasting through his hysterical spasm until Lady Macbeth has succeeded in (as it were) soothing him. A radio producer might then choose to use a device, most effective in Alfred Hitchcock's *Psycho*, where a musical effect alerted

almost subliminally the audience to some impending horror. So, while Macbeth, apparently restored to normal behaviour, is addressing the assembled thanery, the ghost of Banquo is already present *in his mind*, before he turns to the empty place to see the apparition a second time. Difficult but not impossible to convey on radio. The scene with the Weird Sisters, the apparitions, and Banquo's descendants is much more easily achieved on radio than in the theatre with the aid of radiophonics. The calmer the evil purpose of the Weird Sisters, the smoother and more snickeringly vile their delivery, the more shrill or sonorous the apparitions may be and the more distraught the ragings of Macbeth. But the cauldrons and their emanations are best left to the art of the composer.

*The Tempest* is a play which asks for magic. All kinds of brilliant effects have been devised for Caliban's first appearance and Ariel's liberation, especially in open-air productions. These may well be the stuff of radiophonic invention. Certainly, whenever Ariel appears, the opportunities are considerable; as they are in the masque, in Prospero's great speeches, 'Our revels now are ended' and 'Ye elves of hills, brooks, standing lakes and groves', and in Caliban's 'Be not afeard: the isle is full of noises'. Radiophonics apart, *The Tempest* is perhaps a play admirably suited to stereo. The advantages of this technique in a play where sprites flit about (not only Ariel, but Puck deluding Lysander and Demetrius), or where old moles lurk in the cellarage, will be obvious. In complex battles, where the listener moves from one camp to another in a moment (act 5 of *Julius Caesar*) it is especially useful. Storms can be tremendous: the opening of *The Tempest* or act 3 scene 4 of *King Lear*. At the same time there are distractions when voices wander about the room and it is certainly possible to argue that perspective and distancing can be as effective on mono. It is too easy and too tempting to be beguiled by technicalities at the expense of the text, by spectacle at the expense of poetry in the theatre, by elaboration rather than definite, certain purpose in any form of presentation. There are strong arguments for and against innovations of all kinds – though stereo is hardly an innovation – but, in the end, it is the words that matter, not the balance of voices related to putative distance or the optimum position for perfect hi-fi reproduction.

What then of good old-fashioned perspective? I have already said that soliloquies work very well on radio. Let us consider four examples. Falstaff on 'honour' in the last act of *Henry IV Part 1*; Antony's 'O pardon me thou bleeding piece of earth', and Macbeth and Hamlet throughout the respective plays. Extrovert Falstaff need not work too close to the microphone; he is quite capable of talking, indeed declaiming, to himself if there is no one in politic earshot, so he may deliver in normal tones, reasoning aloud. Antony presents a problem to the actor. 'O pardon me thou bleeding piece of earth' must contrast with the immensely bold (whatever we may think of Antony – and some of us are prejudiced by history) 'O mighty Caesar dost thou lie so low', where he takes on the conspirators at their most febrile moment of elation. The speech where each of them renders him his bloody hand is performance. The soliloquy before Caesar is (we must assume) sincere, as Antony's own ambitions waken. Should the actor play it 'in his head', working very close, or allow himself space and resonance for Caesar's spirit raging for revenge, crying *Havoc* and letting slip the dogs of war? On radio I would suggest temperate vindictiveness which is immeasurable: all in the head – the final lines hissed with venom of a serpentine spirit already coiled about the trunk of power.

Macbeth's tortured probing of his soul, let alone his conscience, is very much a matter for the actor. Of course, a producer will indicate this or that direction coherent with his overall view of the play and will agree with the actor

how radiophonic effects will be used, if they are used at all. But the actor must find for himself that stasis in Macbeth, the overwhelming guilt which cannot be dissipated however much he may bluster. Unlike Hamlet, Macbeth is stranded in mental and spiritual shallows where his misery, his sense of sin, his awareness of having trafficked with evil throb against his skull and hollow crown. If Macbeth's imagination dominates, Hamlet is intellectually vibrant. Various devices may be used on radio to explore this complicated, mercurial, melancholy mind as revealed in the soliloquies. The actor must be allowed space in the early speeches ('O that this too too solid flesh' and 'O what a rogue and peasant slave am I') to burst out of pent anger, barely contained by melancholy, into positive rage. He must be encouraged to use the studio: now acting close to the microphone so that we are in his head, now restlessly pacing away, occasionally shouting a line in anguish. This demands careful rehearsal so that actors and studio managers understand each other's intentions. Act 3 scene 1 of *Hamlet* is very difficult and will be examined in more detail later. Focusing for the moment on the 'To be or not to be' speech, the actor playing Hamlet should work very close until his train of thought runs out and he turns. 'Soft you now, the fair Ophelia' will still be quiet, before the painful confrontation.

Hamlet is closest of all to the microphone in the 'Now might I do it pat' soliloquy, when he comes upon Claudius ostensibly at prayer. This introduces an important and by no means simple consideration on radio: who are we 'with'? Claudius believes himself to be alone in what is presumably a very private corner of the palace: so the whole of 'O my offence is rank' to 'All may be well' is thinking aloud, however quietly spoken. There should be silence as the king prays for absolution for a few seconds before a vocal start makes us aware of Hamlet as he comes upon Claudius. And the perspective demands that we are 'with' him. In such scenes the relative intimacy of the actors is important.

Now to some problems. It is often necessary, especially during long speeches, for other significant players to register their presence without distracting attention from the immediate content. Gertrude's impatience with Polonius and his circumlocutions in the 'Brevity is the soul of wit' scene is easily expressed on the stage, but must find some vocal equivalent in radio without being overplayed. Now comes the interesting production point: does Hamlet overhear Polonius planning to trap him by setting Ophelia in a place where he is known to walk daily? If he does, this would account for his cruelty to her in act 3 scene 1 and would add dramatically to the scene if he is speaking not only to her but to the king and Polonius, whom he knows to be concealed. Some critics insist that there is no textual evidence that Hamlet overhears the plot, but surely a certain dramatic licence is permitted. Easier said than done on radio. In the theatre it is easy enough to have the king, queen, and Polonius grouped downstage while Hamlet enters upstage, pauses to listen a moment before reappearing where he will be noticed: 'But look where sadly the poor wretch comes reading'. In cinema, a similar effect may be achieved by the camera tracking away and upward from Polonius and the others, whether or not Hamlet's presence is made obvious. On radio, this must all be done by perspective with perhaps very short and careful interpolations, so that we are 'with' Hamlet and the other players are further off-mike, projecting slightly. Act 3 scene 1 is, I have said, difficult: Hamlet must rouse himself out of meditation, remember that Ophelia is to be set upon him, and – goaded by the return of his remembrances – work himself into a rage. The poor young woman, hurt by his insults and bullying, must retain enough calm for 'O what a noble mind is here o'erthrown'. Only then, when Claudius and Polonius emerge, ignoring her except for a callous throw-away

line, can she break down. Her discreet sobbing will emphasize the king's self-centred indifference and Polonius' insensitivity.

The transmogrification of Bottom in sound is also quite difficult. Radiophonic effects help greatly, but much must be left to the actor playing Bottom and the other hempen homespuns. Perhaps Bottom can contrive something like an ass's bray on his reappearance before he speaks his line, to be greeted with wails, shrieks, and general consternation. He must also react (but be careful not to over-react) to Titania's wooing. There are no words, so Bottom must do what he can with luxurious grunts and blissful sighs. This can be remarkably funny and effective. In the early scenes where the mechanicals meet and rehearse, before Bottom is transformed, it is a good idea to suggest the mutual exasperation of Quince and Bottom by half-interruptions, groans, and other impatient noises; but again these should not be overdone. A good actor can do wonders with little Flute, but it is also important for the producer to get every gentle laugh he can from Snug, Snout, and Starveling.

Music, in my opinion, should be used sparingly and perhaps not at all in most of the tragedies and histories. Ideally any music should be specially written, so that the setting of songs is entirely compatible with incidental music at the beginning and end of the play and between scenes. This can be an expensive business, however. Where music already recorded is used in conjunction with standard settings of songs in plays like *Twelfth Night*, *The Tempest*, or *Cymbeline*, the producer must select most carefully so that there is no 'period' disharmony. Renaissance music, for example, should not be used with Victorian song. Feste's songs and those of Ariel are essential to the action, but quite often songs on radio seem to go on for a very long time, when there is no accompanying visual picture, and a producer might find it expedient to prune or cut altogether.

So to silence and swordplay. Comparatively long silences are highly effective in the theatre, suggesting exhaustion or defeat, regulating the tempo of lyrical despair – as in *Richard II*, act 3 scene 2 in the 'of comfort no man speak' sequence of speeches. On radio a silence of more than a few seconds becomes 'dead air' and anything really prolonged sets up all sorts of unfortunate alarums at the transmitter. The pace of silences must accordingly be regulated or else the pause may be filled and the dramatic effect heightened by birdcalls, a cold wind, the sea. Mad Lear meets blind Gloucester on cliffs high above rushing waves; ravens croak over Dunsinane; a nipping and an eager air whistles around the turrets of Elsinore.

Sword-fights on stage are often elaborately set and carefully arranged so as to generate maximum excitement. Even so, however spectacular, they may last too long. Without the spectacle, the clashing of metal accompanied by grunting, gasping, and suppressed curses is soon boring: so however hot and angry the exchanges before combat in the last act of *Henry IV Part 1*, or *Macbeth*, or *Romeo and Juliet* (between Mercutio and Tybalt), the actual fight must be fierce and very brisk. Such effects may be pre-recorded and the actors cued by lights, especially if an over-enthusiastic 'spot' studio manager provides a sort of additional industrial hazard to the actors: but often the combatants prefer to do their own effects or leave it to another member of the cast who will take cues from the producer.

Visual devices, readily resolved in the theatre or cinema, can become problems in sound. Titania's passion for Bottom, given clever playing by both actors, is not difficult to represent; but what of Olivia's growing infatuation for Cesario/Viola, or Viola's for the duke? How is the likeness of the twins, Sebastian and Viola, to be put across? Much depends upon the skill of the actors. In one production of *Twelfth Night* in which I was involved, Viola and Sebastian took the trouble to study each other's voices and tricks of speech. Sebastian had a naturally light, young voice, and the actress playing Viola, as feminine as anyone could wish, happened to be able to simulate the tones of an adolescent youth – to excellent effect, indeed, in the 'smiling at grief' scene with Orsino, where at times she fell out of her Cesario role and became – just for a line or a few words – Viola. What, then, of *As You Like It*? It may be argued, with reference to the text, that Orlando knows quite soon that Ganymede is Rosalind – see act 4 scene 1 and, significantly, act 5 scene 2 ('And greater wonders than that'). Now this is obviously no dogmatic assertion, but it is a viable interpretation. And fashionable though it may be to play Orlando as bisexual, it is a lot more fun if he isn't and knows or guesses who Ganymede is. In the theatre this may be gradually achieved in the best traditions of high comedy. On radio it would be very difficult, calling for considerable skill on the part of the players without anyone being sure that the point had been made. Away from comedy, there is the moment of high drama in *Hamlet* where the prince confronts the queen: 'Look here upon this picture and on this'. Many productions use a comparison of lockets: Hamlet carrying the miniature portrait of his father, Gertrude that of Claudius. Easy enough on stage; but curiously effective on radio if Hamlet snatches the chain around his mother's neck and jerks it roughly, causing her to cry out in pain, so that physical distress and fear add to the intensity of her emotional disturbance.

It will be apparent that much depends upon the skill and application of the actors. Although radio actors are deprived of touch or contact playing and limited in their use of space, visitors to a studio are often surprised by the amount of physical expression the actors (who are, of course, widely experienced in the theatre and often in television or cinema) give to their performances. This is most noticeable in eye-contact, and, except in an intimate scene between two or three players, old hands will stay around the microphone responding to the players who have the important lines as they would on stage. Some actors give a great deal from the first read-through; others prefer to build a part slowly. I had the good fortune and immense pleasure to work over many years with a company of about thirty players who came to know each other well. When they were sent their scripts, they knew who else was playing whom and studied their own parts accordingly. Nevertheless, it was interesting to note that the first read-through was sometimes hesitant until each player had ascertained how someone with whom he or she was involved in major scenes was approaching the part. Occasionally there would be distinguished guest players, always welcomed and assimilated. The function of the producer, as I see it, is to regulate the performance, notably the ad-libbing, without interfering with immediate rhythms. Nevertheless, the overall flow of a production is his or her responsibility. The producer's knowledge of the text must be thorough, with particular attention to difficult passages of verse or prose and necessary (but not too much) background information. The producer may offer a brief preliminary sketch of the way he or she sees the play in question, but should never be inflexible. If an actor interprets a part in a way which is likely to upset the general lines of a production, this must be corrected or adjusted tactfully at the earliest moment. Accents must be agreed. For example, the mechanicals in *A Midsummer Night's Dream* may be played with Cockney accents or the vague west-country approximation known as 'Mummerset'. We found in one version of the play that four of our mechanicals were native northerners and the others could do the accent. Puck, as it happened, was also from the north, so that with a hint of his native accent, we were able to distinguish a 'folk-spirit' from the imperious royalty of the fairy kingdom. One of the essential duties of the producer is to see that a day's work runs efficiently with the minimum

of delay. Effects and music should be exactly decided before the actors come to the studio, where necessary pre-recorded, however long this may take. In stereo productions it may be necessary to call the actors for an additional 'rehearsal' day. Stereo is obviously more complicated than mono recording and takes a great deal more time. If radiophonics are to be used, it is a good idea if the composer is present at rehearsals and is then given a free hand. He will know the intentions of producer and actors and will fashion his work in the spirit of the presentation.

Working with an experienced company who know each other's work and are probably friends has more advantages than the saving of time and money or added efficiency. The camaraderie and support become an essential part of successive productions. There is real and genuine respect for the performances of others. While it was always a delight to work with celebrated actors, my own preference was to offer major parts to different members of the regular group. Confrontation scenes work wonderfully on radio. It was splendid to see the supporting cast all grouped and working as the furious Paulina flew at the hysterical Leontes and to hear how their reactions moved the principal players. It was even more impressive, after careful private rehearsal, to see the cast watching and listening in the great scenes between Hamlet and Ophelia, Hamlet and the queen, Brutus and Cassius, Othello and Emilia, Othello and Iago, Angelo and Isabella, and on so many other occasions. They were not involved, but there was not a crossword or thriller or income-tax return in sight.

The ultimate benefit of such a spirit, carried over not for a season or a run but from year to year, is that newcomers are made at home, learn quickly, are helped, and that ensemble playing becomes a pleasure rather than a chore. It is amazing how much noise a dozen actors can make in a studio when backed by more distant crowd effects in (say) *Julius Caesar* or

*Coriolanus*. It is delightful when the assembled revellers at the Boar's Head respond with such real mirth to the antics of Falstaff and (up to a point) the Prince of Wales. But when the actors have a studio arranged so that they can play as in a theatre, the genuine laughter in the Pyramus and Thisbe drama presented to Theseus and his court creates an atmosphere among the players themselves which lifts individual performances and transmits an enthusiasm which (I hope) is infectious.

---

*Note*: A useful pamphlet which appeared while this volume was in proof is Janet Clare's *Theatre of the Air: A Checklist of Radio Productions of Renaissance Drama 1922–1986, with an Appendix of Television Productions (excluding Shakespeare), Renaissance Drama Newsletter* Supplement 6 (Summer 1986).     S.W.W.

# THE DISMEMBERMENT OF ORPHEUS: MYTHIC ELEMENTS IN SHAKESPEARE'S ROMANCES

## DAVID ARMITAGE

'As the soule of *Euphorbus* was thought to live in *Pythagoras*: so the sweete wittie soule of *Ovid* lives in mellifluous and hony-tonged *Shakespeare*, witnes his *Venus* and *Adonis*, his *Lucrece*, his sugred Sonnets among his private friends, &c.'[1] And so may the soul of Francis Meres be thought to live in critics who examine Shakespeare's debt to his favourite poet; since Ovid's influence is found largely in the early work it is, by implication, a youthful phase, which Shakespeare grew out of. Yet, as Ovid acknowledged through Pythagoras, 'All things doo chaunge. But nothing sure dooth perrish. This same spright/ ... never perrisheth nor never perrish can.'[2] Just so did the soul of Ovid live in Shakespeare throughout his career, to find its final expression in the four late romances. '[T]he most resonant echo of Ovid in the corpus'[3] occurs not in one of the works noted by Meres, but in *The Tempest* (as Prospero's invocation, 'Ye elves of hills, brooks, standing lakes and groves' (5.1.33–50), adapts the Latin original and Arthur Golding's translation of Medea's speech in *Metamorphoses*, 7. 197–209 (Golding, ll.265–77)), while it is in *Cymbeline* (2.2) that a copy of the *Metamorphoses* makes its second appearance in Shakespeare's works. Just as the book which Lavinia 'tosseth so' in *Titus Andronicus* (4.1.41) is an index of a major influence on the play, so does Imogen's bedside reading show that Ovid was much in Shakespeare's mind as he was engaged in a later, and very different, Ovidian phase.

Shakespeare's changing attitude towards his most important classical influence, as well as his developing use of myth, can be suggestively illustrated by his allusions to the story of Orpheus, which he took from Ovid, and supplemented with common interpretations and personal associations. Also, as a myth whose most striking motif is dismemberment, Orpheus may provide an image for the breaking and scattering of mythic elements in the romances, most potently from the Orpheus story itself. Northrop Frye is correct when he decides that 'Orpheus is the hero of all four romances',[4] but by failing to substantiate this characteristic perception by referring to Shakespeare's more abiding hero, he does not realize the full force of his speculation.

The Orpheus who haunts the romances is a composite figure, a cluster of associations which can be seen accumulating across Shakespeare's work. Two of the earliest references are symptomatic of Shakespeare's youthful attachment to Ovid as a stylistic master, as the

[1] Francis Meres, *Palladis Tamia, Wits Treasury* (London, 1598), pp. 281–2

[2] W. H. D. Rouse, ed., *Shakespeare's Ovid, Being Arthur Golding's Translation of the Metamorphoses* (London, 1904, rep. 1961), bk. 15, pp. 183, 187; all references to Golding are to this edition.

[3] Frank Kermode, ed., *The Tempest* (London, 1958), p. 147. All quotations from Shakespeare are taken from editions in the *New Arden Shakespeare* (London, 1951–82), unless otherwise noted.

[4] *A Natural Perspective* (New York, 1965), p. 147.

singer appears twice in passages of elaborate Ovidian conceit relating to rape:

> He would have dropp'd his knife, and fell asleep,
> As Cerberus at the Thracian poet's feet.
> (*Titus Andronicus*, 2.4.50–1)

and

> So his unhallowed haste her words delays,
> And moody Pluto winks while Orpheus plays.
> (*Lucrece*, 552–3)

Both allusions image the forestalling of a brutal assault by the sweetness of the victim's voice (though in *Titus Andronicus* the reference is cruelly ironic, since Lavinia has already been raped, and her tongue cut out), thus associating Orpheus with the calming of violent barbarism. The myth may be apt for the Roman setting of the works, but it is used decoratively – in contrast to the story of Philomel, for example, which has important thematic and structural force throughout *Titus Andronicus*. Just as decorative in its place is the striking image in *The Two Gentlemen of Verona*:

> For Orpheus' lute was strung with poets' sinews
> Whose golden touch could soften steel and stones,
> Make tigers tame, and huge leviathans
> Forsake unsounded deeps, to dance on sands. (3.2.77–80)

However, even when the conscious exaggeration of the passage, and its dramatic setting, are taken into account, Shakespeare may be seen to use Orpheus as symbolic of the poet's power to move his audience, in an early moment of poetic self-awareness. The lines are spoken by an exemplary shape-shifter, Proteus, yet this does not guarantee that Ovid is the sole inspiration behind the image, since the Virgilian account of Orpheus (in *Georgics*, 4.457–527) is narrated by the sea-god himself, who also mentions Orpheus' calming effect on tigers (*Georgics*, 5.510). In the absence of other reliable allusions to Virgil's pastoral poetry,[5] the connections between the *Georgics* and *The*

*Two Gentlemen of Verona* are more probably coincidental than significant. Nevertheless, the associations made here with art, dismemberment ('strung with poets' sinews'), calmed ferocity, and, most characteristically, the depths of the sea,[6] are to become more fertile as Shakespeare recalls them in the romances.

In Ovid's version, the story of Orpheus divides into three main scenes: his descent into Hades to rescue Eurydice; the power of his music over nature; and his death at the hands of the Maenads. Once Shakespeare has alluded to Orpheus' descent (in *Titus Andronicus* and *Lucrece*), and the potency of his music (in *The Two Gentlemen of Verona*), it only remains for him to conclude with his death. This he does in the play which is his most artfully Ovidian, yet also the one in which he first seems to question his enthusiasm for Ovid, *A Midsummer Night's Dream*. One of the entertainments proposed to Theseus by Philostrate is

> The riot of the tipsy Bacchanals,
> Tearing the Thracian singer in their rage.
> (5.1.48–9)

Theseus rejects this, and chooses instead

> A tedious brief scene of young Pyramus
> And his love Thisbe, very tragical mirth
> (5.1.56–7)

in which Shakespeare satirizes Golding's verse and vocabulary, along with that of other minor contemporaries. He will continue to rely upon Golding as a source of ideas, phrases, and stories (not least in the romances), but his burlesque shows that affectionate scepticism has replaced uncritical passion as his dominant attitude towards the translator.

But Shakespeare abandons neither Ovid nor

---

5 For doubts about Shakespeare's knowledge of Virgilian pastoral, see T. W. Baldwin, *William Shakspere's Small Latine and Lesse Greeke* (2 vols., Urbana, 1944), vol. 2, p. 464.
6 Images of unfathomed depths have been used by K. Wentersdorf as a positive test of Shakespearian authorship, in 'The Authenticity of *The Taming of the Shrew*', *Shakespeare Quarterly*, 5 (1954), 25–6.

Orpheus. His last allusion to the singer, before his final plays, may seem predictable, but only because it is so naturally integrated in its context. As part of his serenade on music to Jessica, Lorenzo details the power of music over wild animals; the exemplary mythological association then arises:

> therefore the poet
> Did feign that Orpheus drew trees, stones, and floods,
> Since naught so stockish, hard, and full of rage,
> But music for the time doth change his nature.
> (*The Merchant of Venice*, 5.1.79–82)

If the acknowledgement of '*the* poet' is not merely conventional, Shakespeare almost certainly means Ovid here, since he is the only poet dignified by such particularity in his work (as in *Titus Andronicus*, 4.1.57, 'Pattern'd by that the poet here describes'). However, if this is so, he misrecalls the *Metamorphoses*, since Ovid's Orpheus drew only trees and stones, not 'floods'. The additional waters may come from the prefatory 'Epistle' to Golding's translation:

> So Orphey in the tenth booke is reported too delight
> The savage beasts, and for too hold the fleeting birds from flyght,
> Too move the senselesse *stones*, and stay swift *rivers*, and too make
> The *trees* to follow after him and for his musick sake
> Too yeelde him shadowe where he went. By which is signifyde
> That in his doctrine such a force and sweetenesse was implyde,
> That such as were most wyld, stowre, feerce, hard, witlesse, rude, and bent
> Ageinst good order, were by him perswaded too relent.   ('Epistle', 517–24; my emphasis)

Wherever the addition came from, it is important in renewing the association in Shakespeare's mind between Orpheus' music and 'floods' – or 'unsounded deeps' – seen in *The Two Gentlemen of Verona*, and which is pregnant with meaning for the romances.

Lorenzo's speech also shows Shakespeare allegorizing the myth for the first time, as he glosses it with a conventional interpretation similar to Golding's. Yet he did not need Golding as a direct or sole source for this allegorization. It seems likely that he used an annotated Ovid at school, and had access to widely used lexicons,[7] but even so, at a time when myth was a major item of intellectual currency, such interpretations were commonplace. For example, when Shakespeare alluded to Actaeon in the opening scene of *Twelfth Night* – 'That instant was I turn'd into a hart,/ And my desires, like fell and cruel hounds,/ E'er since pursue me' (1.1.21–3) – he did not need to name the huntsman, since he could assume that the allusion would be recognizable, and that his audience would know the usual interpretation of the episode as an emotional turmoil.

The variety of allusions to Orpheus in Shakespeare's earlier work shows that he had a detailed knowledge of the myth, as found in Ovid and Golding, and of the common interpretations of it. These details are enriched by personal associations, and all return in those plays where mythologizing is combined with mythopoeia – the romances. Myth has become more integral to the poetic fabric of the plays, developing from decorative spangling in the early work to concealed fertile allusion (such as Actaeon in *Twelfth Night*). In the romances, the direct references are more pointed and resonant, the indirect ones more elusive and fruitful. Partly because of this skilful absorption of mythic elements, the romances seem to partake of the nature of myth, as has often been observed. G. Wilson Knight, for example, said of Shakespeare in this late phase, 'the author is moved by vision, not fancy; is creating not merely entertainment, but myth in the Plato-

---

[7] See e.g. D. T. Starnes and E. W. Talbert, *Classical Myth and Legend in Renaissance Dictionaries* (North Carolina, 1955), pp. 111–34; R. D. Drexler, 'Ovid and *The Tempest*', *Notes and Queries*, 28 (1981), p. 145.

nic sense'.[8] It is not necessary to agree with the assumptions of his criticism, or to examine too closely the connotations of 'in the Platonic sense', to concur with Wilson Knight in finding these plays mythic (in atmosphere, resonance, and indeterminacy, if not in intention); a more accurate, and suggestive, description of them might be 'myths in the Ovidian sense'.

In the *Metamorphoses*, stories are linked by a variety of factitious connections, but the thematic ties are vital, as sequences are established, and significances sprung across discrete narratives. As John Dean suggests, Shakespeare's 'use of the *Metamorphoses* may have contributed directly to his sense of romance structuring,'[9] and in the light of Ovid's practice the four late romances could be seen as a cycle, analogous to a section of the *Metamorphoses*. Book 10 and the opening of Book 11, for instance, are framed by the story of Orpheus, who is the narrator of Book 10, choosing the stories therein to reflect his mood or activities – stories of unhappy love, such as Venus and Adonis (which we can be sure Shakespeare knew), or the tale of an animative artist, Pygmalion. Shakespeare is the framing Orpheus of the romances – though his motives for writing them may be beyond conjecture – and he creates a series which forms the most integrated group of plays in his output,[10] save perhaps his earlier historical cycles. They may differ in style and setting, but, like Ovid's narratives, they are linked by a common atmosphere, recurrent motifs, and parallel thematic movements.

Ovid is often blamed for not being Virgil, particularly when their versions of the Orpheus myth are compared.[11] As can be seen from such a comparison, Ovid's ethos is that of romance, not tragedy. Virgil's Orpheus is the victim of tragic 'furor' (*Georgics*, 4. 495), who offends against the inflexible divine order, loses his wife, and descends into inconsolable grief, only to be torn to pieces by the Maenads. Virgil emphasizes fate (Eurydice is

doomed, 'moritura puella' (458)), high emotions, the seriousness of suffering, and obeisance to a vast, over-arching order; his Orpheus is demi-god, rather than semi-man. Ovid dissolves his predecessor's high seriousness and challenges the Virgilian *gravitas*, a style expressive of a world view comprehending tragic solemnity and punitive hierarchy. Ovid's outlook, as well as his subject matter, is metamorphic. He emphasizes regeneration and transfiguration; achieved possibility and relieved suffering; capricious gods and indistinct causality. Like Shakespeare in his late plays, Ovid goes beyond irredeemable tragedy to romance, which is always provisional in its catastrophes and promises reunion after division, life after death, and joy after disaster. 'The thrust of romance, as a genre, is the redemption of a world full of misfortune, a blossoming of new life out of loss and death, and an affirmation of the ultimate harmony that may follow, even proceed from, tragedy.'[12] Ovidian metamorphoses, and Shakespearian romances, are amply comprehended by such a definition. Ovid's sympathetic nature, harmonizing music, and patterns of transfiguration in his telling of the story of Orpheus are such stuff as romance – or a Shakespearian romance – is made on.

---

[8] 'Myth and Miracle' in *The Crown of Life* (London, 1965), p. 15.

[9] *Restless Wanderers: Shakespeare and the Pattern of Romance* (Salzburg, 1979), p. 199.

[10] Even if they are not a chronological group; for evidence that *Coriolanus* follows *Pericles*, see Gary Taylor, 'The Shakespeare Canon: New Evidence for Chronology and Authorship' (forthcoming). I am grateful to Mr Taylor for giving me details of his conclusions.

[11] E.g. W. S. Anderson, 'The Orpheus of Virgil and Ovid: *flebile nescio quid*' in *Orpheus: the Metamorphoses of a Myth*, ed. John Warden (Toronto, 1982), pp. 25–50; for a more sympathetic account of Ovid's version, to which I am indebted, see Charles Segal, 'Ovid's Orpheus and Augustan Ideology', *Transactions of the American Philological Association*, 103 (1972), 473–94.

[12] Peggy Ann Knapp, 'The Orphic Vision of *Pericles*', *Texas Studies in Literature and Language*, 15 (1974), p. 619.

While the generic similarities between the Ovidian narrative and the romances can be felt, the precise influence of the Orpheus episode can be detailed in the plays. In *Cymbeline*, Iachimo muses on

> The cloyed will –
> That satiate yet unsatisfied desire, that tub
> Both fill'd and running. (1.7.47–9)

Although the Arden editor is loath to see this as a definite allusion to the Danaides (who had to fill a bottomless vessel eternally as a punishment for killing their husbands), he refers to Marston's *The Fawn* – where the myth is mentioned twice, the vessel being called a 'tub' both times – and to Horace, *Odes*, 3.11.26, as the ultimate source.[13] Yet there is no need to invoke either Marston or Horace here, since Golding supplies both the allusion and the word 'tubbes' (which Shakespeare, a magpie for distinctive words and phrases, could have picked up). One of the eternal punishments halted by Orpheus' music on his descent to the underworld is translated thus:

> And *Danaus* daughters ceast too fill theyr tubbes
> that have no brink. (10.46)

The homely monosyllable 'tubbes' (translating 'urnis') is characteristic of Golding, who often takes Ovid's realism to excess. The ethical interpretation that supports Iachimo's image is a conventional one: Georgius Sabinus, for example, glosses the lines 'urnisque vacarunt/ Belides' (*Metamorphoses*, 10.43–4) with, among other information, this allegorization:

His urnis & huic dolio Plato in Gorgia assimilat animum incontinentem, qui effusis in omni intemperentia libidinibus agitatur.[14]

(In the *Gorgias*, Plato compares these urns and this jar to an insatiable disposition, which is aroused by desires that find their outlet in every excess.)

Similar ideas of sated insatiability are, of course, found elsewhere in Shakespeare, but the confluence of Golding's 'tubbe(s)' and the ethical slant suggests that Shakespeare was thinking of the Danaides, and that he had recently re-read Golding's translation of the Orpheus episode.

Evidence that he had re-read not only Golding's version but also the original Latin comes from the additions to his – and our – vocabulary in the romances. In *Metamorphoses*, 10.64, at the moment of losing Eurydice for the second time,

> stupuit gemina nece coniugis Orpheus

> (This double dying of his wyfe set *Orphye* in a stound.) (Golding, 10.69)

This typically Ovidian conceit 'gemina nece' (compare 'iterum moriens' (10.69)) is important for *The Winter's Tale*, as will be shown, and 'stupuit' seems to have excited resonances. It is solely in *Cymbeline* and *The Winter's Tale* that Shakespeare uses words with the Latin root 'stupere' – 'stupefy', 'stupefied', and 'stupid':

> Those she has
> Will stupefy and dull the sense awhile
> (*Cymbeline*, 1.6.36–7)

> which if you, or stupefied,
> Or seeming so, in skill, cannot, or will not
> Relish a truth
> (*The Winter's Tale*, 2.2.165–7)

and

> is he not stupid
> With age and alt'ring rheums?
> (*The Winter's Tale*, 4.4.399–400)

'Stupid', in *The Winter's Tale* (4.4), is cited by *OED* as its first use in the sense 'Having one's faculties deadened or dulled; in a state of stupor; stupefied, stunned',[15] while 'stupe-

---

[13] J. M. Nosworthy, ed., *Cymbeline* (London, 1969), n. to 1.7.48–9.

[14] *Metamorphoses seu Fabulae Poeticae* (Frankfurt, 1589), sig. Y1ᵛ (my translation); cf. e.g. Jacobus Pontanus, *Metamorphoseon* (Antwerp, 1618), p. 393 (quoting Lucretius, *De Rerum Natura*, III,1003–10); Geffrey Whitney, *A Choice of Emblemes* (Leyden, 1586), p. 12 ('Frustra').

[15] *OED*, s.v. *stupid*, adj. A,1.

fied', in *The Winter's Tale* (2.1), as a participial adjective, antedates *OED*'s first citation (from John Taylor, the Water Poet, in 1639) by twenty-eight years[16] (assuming the play was written in 1611). Both 'stupid' and 'stupefy' had been in the language, with other senses, and used in different ways, before Shakespeare wrote the romances, but that he should so innovatively and sparingly re-use them is perhaps attributable to the prominence of the root at the crucial moment in the Ovidian narrative.

As well as these suggestive, though previously unnoticed, influences from *Metamorphoses*, 10, some larger, better attested borrowings from Book 11 deserve notice. The best known occurs in *The Winter's Tale*, where Shakespeare snaps up the name and thievish disposition from the son whom '*Chyone*' bears to Mercury,

> hyght *Awtolychus*, who provde a wyly
> pye,
> And such a fellow as in theft and filching had
> no peere.            (Golding, 11.360–1)

While here Book 11 helps Shakespeare's naming and characterization, elsewhere it affects his plot and imagery, as he recalls the story of Ceyx and Alcyone. Steevens noted that Imogen and Pisanio, when discussing Posthumus' departure in *Cymbeline* (1.4.8–22), echo Ovid's moving description of Ceyx's ship dwindling into the distance as Ceyx looks on; Shakespeare had also remembered this passage in an acknowledgedly Ovidian work, *Venus and Adonis*, and had conflated it with an important image from later in Ovid's version which he returned to repeatedly in the romances (none of these reminiscences has, I think, been remarked before):

> as one on shore
> Gazing upon a late embarked friend,
> Till the wild waves will have him seen no
> more,
> Whose ridges with the meeting clouds
> contend            (*Venus and Adonis*, 817–20)

The image in line 820 comes from Ovid's extended account of a storm and shipwreck, which also seems to have provided material for the sea-plays, *Pericles* and *The Tempest*, and for *The Winter's Tale*, a coastal work:

> The surges mounting up aloft did seeme to
> mate the skye,
> And with theyr sprinckling for too wet the
> clowdes that hang on hye.
>                 (Golding, 11.573–4)

One of Shakespeare's favourite images in storm passages in the romances is this Ovidian one of the coalescence of sea and sky:

> the brine and cloudy billow kiss the moon
>                 (*Pericles*, 3.1.45–6)

But I am not to say it is a sea, for it is now the sky; between the firmament and it you cannot thrust a bodkin's point            (*The Winter's Tale*, 3.3.83–6)

and

> the sea mounting to th' welkin's cheek.
>                 (*The Tempest*, 1.2.4)

These unnoticed recollections reveal the persistence of certain parts of the *Metamorphoses* throughout Shakespeare's career, from his earliest phase of Ovidianism to his last, as do the allusions to Orpheus. Also like the Orpheus story, the narrative of Ceyx and Alcyone is an Ovidian romance (as Chaucer may have recognized when he called it 'A romaunce' in *The Book of the Duchess*, 48), and so may have had a less tangible influence on the nature of Shakespeare's romances; drowned Ceyx and grief-stricken Alcyone are reunited after death, as are Orpheus and Eurydice, when both are metamorphosed into birds, tragedy[17] thereby being redeemed to become comedy.

As here an episode with a strong marine element influences the romances – in detail and, possibly, in spirit – so the more personal

---

16 *Ibid.*, s.v. *stupefied*, ppl. a.

17 For Ceyx and Alcyone as tragedy, see Julius Caesar Scaliger, *Poetices libri septem* (Heidelberg, 1617), III, xcvi.

association between Orpheus and the depths of the sea returns. In these plays, the sea becomes an analogue to Hades in the Orpheus myth. His descent is a purgatorial journey, a defeat of death, and a successful challenge by the apostle of harmony to the forces of disharmony and destruction. While Orpheus returns from the depths of the underworld, Thaisa, Ferdinand, and Alonso (the first in fact, the other two in fancy) return from the sea. When Pericles casts Thaisa overboard, he regrets that he

>                       straight
> Must cast thee, scarcely coffin'd, in the ooze;
> Where, for a monument upon thy bones,
> And e'er-remaining lamps, the belching whale
> And humming water must o'erwhelm thy corpse,
> Lying with simple shells.    (*Pericles*, 3.1.59–64)

In Ariel's song, 'Full fadom five' (*The Tempest*, 1.2.399–405), the sea is seen as the agent of Alonso's metamorphosis; though in the song the sea-change is physical, his metaphorical immersion does seem, by the end of the play, to have exercised a purgatorial change in his attitude towards Prospero. Alonso himself expresses the Orphic association of music and the sea-bed:

> Methought the billows spoke, and told me of it;
> The winds did sing it to me; and the thunder,
> That deep and dreadful organ-pipe, pronounc'd
> The name of Prosper: it did bass my trespass.
> Therefor my son i' th' ooze is bedded; and
> I'll seek him deeper than e'er plummet sounded,
> And with him there lie mudded.    (3.3.96–102)

This imaginative connection between music ('sing', 'organ-pipe', 'bass') and the depths of the ocean is characteristically Shakespearian, and returns in Prospero's valedictory invocation (whose rich Ovidian echoes were noted above), where the words formerly given to Alonso are re-used:

>                 and, when I have requir'd
> Some heavenly music, – which even now I do, –
> To work mine end upon their senses, that
> This airy charm is for, I'll break my staff,
> Bury it certain fadoms in the earth,
> And deeper than did ever plummet sound
> I'll drown my book.    [*Solemn music*] (5.1.51–7).

Orpheus is a shadowy presence in this passage by virtue of an association within Shakespeare's mind. However, his metaphorical tutelage extends over all the romances in one of their more noticeable (and noticed) features – music. The musical richness of these plays far exceeds anything in Shakespeare's previous work, and may partly be explained by the King's Men's acquisition of the Blackfriars – whose musicians had a considerable reputation – in 1608. The virtuosity of the Blackfriars musicians certainly presented the playwright with greater opportunities than before, but this alone cannot account for the peculiar potency and privilege granted to music in the romances. Shakespeare had presented it as a regenerative force in the Quarto version of *King Lear*, when the Doctor asks, over the sleeping Lear, 'Please you draw neere, louder the musicke there'[18] (the character and his line are omitted in the Folio), but it is in *Pericles* – another play presumed to date from before the acquisition of the Blackfriars – that he dramatizes its power fully; when Cerimon revives Thaisa, music is one of his major restorative agencies:

> The still and woeful music that we have,
> Cause it to sound, beseech you. [*Music*]
> The viol once more; how thou stirr'st, thou block!
> The music there!    [*Music*] (3.2.90–3)

While here, the enlivening power of music is realized dramatically in the restoration of the mother, the restitution of the daughter finds music being used as the background to a metaphorical harmonization:

---

[18] Q1 (London, 1608), sig. K2ʳ (4.7.25 in the Arden conflation).

*Pericles.* . . . But hark, what music?
   Tell Helicanus, my Marina, tell him
   O'er point by point, for yet he seems to doubt,
   How sure you are my daughter. [*Music*] But what
      music?
*Helicanus.* My lord, I hear none.
*Pericles.* None?
   The music of the spheres! List, my Marina.
*Lysimachus.*
   It is not good to cross him; give him way.
*Pericles.* Rarest sounds! Do ye not hear?
*Lysimachus.*
   Music, my Lord? I hear.
*Pericles.*                    Most heavenly music!
                                    (5.1.222–31)

The highest and most natural symbol of harmony, the music of the spheres, is a perfectly imagined background to such a reunion, providing an image of accord – as earlier it was the agent of it – at a crucial moment of dramatic and personal resolution.

   The literal and metaphorical capabilities of music are realized more comprehensively in *The Tempest*, which contains more songs than any other play by Shakespeare, and requires instrumental music as well. On 'the isle . . . full of noises, / Sounds and sweet airs, that give delight, and hurt not' (3.2.133–4), the Orphic power of music as an harmonic agency is inescapable; for example, in 2.1, the courtiers are halted in their wrangling by 'Ariel . . . playing solemn music' (SD, 179), while it is Ariel's redemptive 'music and song' (SD, 292) which forestall the plot against Alonso, and restore political harmony. Ferdinand provides a more precisely Orphic image, when he describes how

   This music crept by me upon the waters,
   Allaying both their fury and my passion
                                    (1.2.394–5)

combining the emotionally ameliorative power of music (exemplified by Orpheus in *The Merchant of Venice*) with its ability to calm the sea (which Shakespeare associated with Orpheus in *The Two Gentlemen of Verona*). *Pericles* and *The Tempest* allegorize and image the force of music as they enact it – and as they realize some of the implications of the Orpheus myth.

   Such implications are dramatized most powerfully in the final scene of *The Winter's Tale*, where there is a scattering of dismembered elements from the myth. A suggestively Ovidian metamorphosis marks the presence of Orpheus in the statue scene (5.3), in which Shakespeare, like Ovid, combines the myths of Orpheus and Pygmalion. The parallel between Hermione and Galatea has often been drawn:[19] both are statues transformed into living women in return for their lover's patient devotion. Yet in *Metamorphoses*, 10, it is Orpheus who tells the story of Pygmalion and Galatea as a hopeful expression of the generative power of the artist and the hard-won rewards of love; Pygmalion's art can give life to inanimate material, like Orpheus', but it exacts no cost so painful as the loss of Eurydice. Ovid's framing of the two narratives is designed to point up the thematic connections between them, and it is these that Shakespeare dramatizes in this climactic scene. As the 'statue' is brought to life, the instrument of metamorphosis called for by Paulina recalls Orpheus' lute in *The Two Gentlemen of Verona*, 'Whose golden touch could soften steel and *stones*' (3.2.78; my emphasis):

   Music, awake her; strike!
   'Tis time; descend; be stone no more.
                                    (5.3.98–9)

Hermione's return to life, and the reunion of the characters, are Shakespeare's major departures from his source, Greene's *Pandosto*, in which the queen remains dead, and the king commits suicide. By ending with a triumph over seeming tragedy, he turns the prose romance into an Ovidian one, such as the story of Ceyx and Alcyone, or that of Orpheus and Eurydice (in which the lovers' shades are

---

19 Most fully by A. H. R. Fairchild, *Shakespeare and the Arts of Design* (Missouri, 1937), pp. 71–4.

happily reunited in Elysium). The play's resolution is precarious, and the tragic possibilities still latent in this closing scene are signalled by a more precise echo of the Orpheus myth. As Hermione descends, Paulina urges Leontes:

> Do not shun her
> Until you see her die again; for then
> You kill her double.          (5.3.105–7)

This conceit of double dying is typically Ovidian, and, as noted above, it comes at the most poignant moment in Ovid's version of the Orpheus story ('stupuit *gemina nece* coniugis Orpheus' (10.64; my emphasis)). Paulina's advice is a test of Leontes' steadfastness and repentance, as Orpheus' lethal solicitude for Eurydice is inverted: Orpheus killed his wife 'double' with a loving look, while Leontes may do the same to his if he does not give her such a look.

The presence of Orpheus in the statue scene can be further illuminated by a comparison with two contemporary analogues, in Beaumont's *Masque of the Inner Temple and Gray's Inn*, and Campion's *The Lords' Masque*. In his practical essay, 'Of Masques and Triumphs', Bacon counsels:

Let *Antimasques* not be long; They have been commonly of Fooles, Satyres … Cupids, Statua's Moving, and the like.[20]

Bacon would almost certainly have seen the 'Statua's Moving' in Beaumont and Campion's masques, since both were written for the celebrations surrounding the marriage of Princess Elizabeth in February, 1613; he could also have seen *The Winter's Tale* – which may have begun the theatrical fashion for moving statues – for it, like *Much Ado About Nothing*, and *The Tempest*, was presented during the festivities by the King's Men. Orpheus is present alongside the moving statues in both of the masques. As the statues enter dancing in the *Masque of the Inner Temple*, Mercury observes:

> See how they move, drawne by this
>      heavenly joy,
> Like the wilde trees, which follow'd
>      *Orpheus* Harpe.          (ll. 163–4)[21]

The image is apt, but, like Shakespeare's early references to Orpheus, it has been applied rather than absorbed. Campion's use of Orpheus is more elaborate and explicit, as the singer is the masque's controlling figure. The most spectacular *coup de théâtre* in the piece is the scene change which reveals 'foure Noble women-statues of silver, standing in Severall nices',[22] who have been petrified by an angry Jove. When Jove's aid is solicited to reanimate the statues, the prayer is, in fact, an '*Invocation in a full Song*', since Prometheus' advice has been taken:

> Let *Orpheus* decke the Hymne, since pray we
>      must.          (p. 256)

The music exercises its softening power and, as Orpheus notes,

> *Jove* is pleas'd; Statues have life and move:
> Go, new-borne men and entertaine with
>      love
> These new-borne women…
>                    … Court them faire:
> When words and Musicke speak, let none
>      despaire          (p. 256)

Art's power, and the prospect of a loving union, are dramatically united in the transformation, as in *The Winter's Tale*. Yet, in the masque the effect is spectacular, rather than mysterious and climactic as in the play. While Shakespeare charges the atmosphere of the drama with an imaginative absorption of the myth, Campion loses mythic resonance and creates a lesser dramatic illusion. Nevertheless, a sensitive courtly spectator who saw the two masques – especially Campion's – and *The*

---

[20] *Essayes* (London, 1625), p. 225.
[21] Ed. Fredson Bowers in *The Dramatic Works in the Beaumont and Fletcher Canon* (Cambridge, 1966–  ), vol. I.
[22] *Works*, edited by Walter R. Davis (London, 1969; page refs. are to this edn.), p. 255.

*Winter's Tale* together in 1613 must have been struck by *déjà vu* occasioned as much by sympathetic Orphic resonances as by 'Statua's Moving'.

Shakespeare's most radical dismemberment of the myth is in *Cymbeline*, where, decked in a cluster of images and associations, Cloten masquerades as Orpheus. The boorish prince is the instigator of the play's most noticeable musical episode, when he uses 'Hark, hark, the lark' (2.3.19–25) as a seductive aubade to Imogen. While he is obviously inharmonious, in his illiterate speech, as in his lumpen bearing, he can understand that Imogen may be moved by the music he controls:

I am advised to give her music a mornings, they say it will penetrate. [*Enter musicians.*] Come on, tune: if you can penetrate her with your fingering, so: we'll try with tongue too                    (2.3.11–14)

yet the crudity of the word-play belies the sweetness of the music, and renders it impotent. Later, like Orpheus, Cloten is murdered by 'mountaineers' on a wild, pastoral hill-side. If Cloten is identified with Orpheus, in Golding's baffling moralistic reading, he gets his just deserts for attempting to seduce his step-sister:

The death of Orphey sheweth Gods just
    vengeaunce on the vyle
And wicked sort which horribly with incest
    them defyle.            ('Epistle', 224–5)

A more relevant allegorization of Orpheus' death is the political one supplied by George Sandys, in which the Maenads are

*taken for the heady rage of mutiny and Sedition, which silence the authority of the law; and infringe that concord (the musicke of Orpheus) which had reduced wild people to civility; returning now to their former pravity and naturall fiercenesse.*[23]

Just as Cloten is an ironic Orpheus, so are the 'mountaineers' ironic Maenads; Guiderius and Arviragus may be living a wild existence, but they are nevertheless more civilized, and more royal, than Cloten. His death could be inter-preted as a return to harmony, as the wild man from the ruling family is killed by the resurgent representatives of natural 'civility' and the blood line.

The ironic reworking of the Orpheus myth around Cloten comes to a head in a striking, unremarked image:

I have ta'en
His head from him: I'll throw't into the creek
Behind our rock, and let it to the sea,
And tell the fishes he's the queen's son, Cloten
                    (4.2.150–4)

repeated in:

I have sent Cloten's clotpoll down the stream
In embassy to his mother.        (4.2.184–5)

Only the memory of Orpheus' head, floating down the river Hebrus, prophesying as it went, could have allowed this head to go 'In embassy' and to 'tell the fishes he's the queen's son, Cloten'. The source usually cited for 4.2.150–4 (from *The Mirror for Magistrates*) describes dismemberment, but the head is not specifically mentioned, as Hamo relates how

In flight I taken was, and hewde in pieces
    small:
Which downe the cleeves they did into the
    waters cast.[24]

That the reference in 4.2.184–5 is immediately followed by 'Solemn music' also suggests an association between the severed head and music that may recall Orpheus' head being accompanied by his harp on its river journey.

Shakespeare finally recollects the myth in *Henry VIII*, in which the song 'Orpheus with his lute' (3.1.3–14) may be seen as his farewell to Orpheus – and thus, by association, to Ovid – as he moves away from the dramatic romance. Despite the teasing similarities between the lyric and an undistinguished passage in Beaumont and Fletcher's *The Cap-*

---

[23] *Ovid's Metamorphosis Englished* (Oxford, 1632), p. 387.
[24] Lily B. Campbell, ed., *Parts Added to the Mirror for Magistrates* (Cambridge, 1946), p. 314.

*tain*,[25] there is little reason to assume that it is not by Shakespeare. The description of Orpheus' power over nature – even over 'the billows of the sea' – may not be uniquely Shakespearian (as comparison with *The Captain* shows), but it is characteristically so; when combined with the statement of music's power over the emotions,

> In sweet music is such art,
> Killing care and grief of heart
>    Fall asleep, or hearing die     (3.1.12–14)

the song provides a summary of a myth which has suffused the romances, and of its implications. Orpheus may seem to have been irreparably dismembered in these plays, but this envoi shows conclusively that Shakespeare does remember him.[26]

---

[25] 3.1.32–8; edited by L. A. Beaurline in *The Dramatic Works . . .*, vol. 1; in both passages trees 'bow' (cf. *Capt.*, 3.1.34–5 and *HVIII*, 3.1.3–5), and in both the waves of the sea have 'heads' (cf. *Capt.*, 3.1.36–7 and *HVIII*, 3.1.10–11), for example.

[26] I am particularly grateful to Jonathan Bate and Anne Barton for help with earlier versions of this essay.

# REMEMBERING 'HAMLET': OR, HOW IT FEELS TO GO LIKE A CRAB BACKWARDS

## EDWARD PECHTER

Whatever else it is, *Hamlet* is a well-made play. The first scene engages our immediate and deep interest. The play then efficiently establishes the central conflict between·the prince and Claudius and gives us in act 2 some very enjoyable cat-and-mouse, as strategies beget counter-strategies. After the richly exciting climax sustained through the latter half of act 3, we are given the kind of abatement we expect in Shakespearian fourth acts. Finally, the play sweeps us to the revenge catastrophe in the most splendidly thrilling ending that Shakespeare, or probably any other playwright, has ever given an audience. No wonder, then, that many commentators have over the years expressed admiration for *Hamlet* as a piece of dramatic craftsmanship, testifying eloquently to the play's solider Aristotelian virtues.[1] Still, it probably seems perverse to begin with an appreciation of *Hamlet*'s structural qualities. As we all know, the chief interest of the play is the protagonist, and although we have dutifully learned not to abstract the prince from the play, his fascination for us doesn't really seem to depend essentially upon the play's formal excellence. Moreover, this formal excellence itself has not been universally acknowledged: is the play in fact so well made? Johnson can show us our crooked way here, for after praising the play's variety of incident, diversity of mood, and 'continual succession' of new and interesting characters, he feels compelled to qualify: 'The conduct is perhaps not wholly secure against objections,' he tells us. 'The action is indeed for the most part in continual progression, but there are some scenes which neither forward nor retard it.'[2] Let's put this more simply, in the words of wise Polonius: 'This is too long.'[3]

Is *Hamlet* too long? – that is the question. None of us wants to be guilty of Polonius's smugness, but his remark about the player's speech provides a base from which any theatrical discussion of the play itself should proceed. Shakespeare's company probably used a shorter text than the modern conflation from which most of us work, and they probably performed it more quickly than we tend to do. But having thus twice abridged the play, we find ourselves left with the same problem, for it is the consequence not merely of the quantity of the action in *Hamlet* – the sheer mass of the text, the length of time required to perform

---

[1] Dr Johnson, Bradley (in *Shakespearean Tragedy*), and Harley Granville-Barker (in the *Preface to 'Hamlet'*) so admired it. For more recent examples, see J. K. Walton, 'The Structure of *Hamlet*', in *'Hamlet'*, Stratford-upon-Avon Studies 5, eds. J. R. Brown and Bernard Harris (1963; rpt. London, 1972), 44–89; John Russell Brown, *Shakespeare's Plays in Performance* (Harmondsworth, 1969), pp. 146–66; Mark Rose, *Shakespearean Design* (Cambridge, Mass., 1972), pp. 95–125; and Bertrand Evans, *Shakespeare's Tragic Practice* (New York and Oxford, 1979), pp. 76–114.

[2] Samuel Johnson, *Dr Johnson on Shakespeare*, ed. W. K. Wimsatt (Harmondsworth, 1969), p. 140.

[3] All quotations from *Hamlet* are from the Riverside Edition, edited by G. B. Evans *et al.* (Boston, 1974). In view of the familiarity of the play, I have not cited act, scene or line.

it – but of its quality. It's the old problem of delay, though not the prince's but the play's delay that we must wonder about. Delay, to be sure, is intrinsic to all narratives of any significant length, furnishing (even in jokes) an exquisite pleasure in postponing the inevitable conclusion. In revenge drama, moreover, a rather substantial delaying element was already conventional well prior to *Hamlet*. But the delays in *Hamlet* far exceed normative expectations, and are of a much more perplexing kind, as Johnson astutely suggested in objecting not to scenes that retard the action, but to scenes that *neither* forward *nor* retard the action. As a number of recent commentators have pointed out, it seems demonstrably to be a strategy of *Hamlet* throughout to frustrate us with delay, to withhold from us the sense of a coherently complete action, to *seem* too long. In Stephen Booth's witty version of Olivier's voice-over: '*Hamlet* is the tragedy of an audience that cannot make up its mind.'[4]

I have now presented two very different – apparently contradictory – *Hamlets*, one a conventionally satisfying play, the other a play that interests us in its continual frustration of our conventional expectations. Which of these plays shall we take – both, one, or neither? In these days of hermeneutic indeterminacy, *mises-en-abîmes*, and self-consuming artefacts, it is the unconventional *Hamlet* that we tend to see and value, and in what follows I shall be content largely to be absorbed into this flow. But focusing on the play's action in terms of frustrated purposes, loss of impetus, and the like, can sometimes make *Hamlet* sound suspiciously like Beckett, and this is not the impression that the play can make, and seems designed to make, in the theatre. Though *Hamlet* buffets us about right from the beginning, and plays fast and loose with our expectations, its demands upon our confidence are always justified in time. Even as we are made to wonder where it is going, the play re-engages our trust in its own energy and coherence of purpose. And of course the ending,

well performed, redeems all sorrows we may have felt.

I am suggesting that we must acknowledge both the well-made and the unconventional *Hamlet*, and further that our interest should be in the relationship between the two. How does the play both sustain and frustrate our sense of its ongoing movement towards dramatic closure? How can we be made to feel both that we are sweeping towards revenge and going like a crab backwards? And, finally, we might ask why it is that the experience of such a contradiction is one that we should value. But these larger concerns are rather too large for me here. I will limit myself to the unconventional *Hamlet*, especially its opening movements – with this last proviso, that such a focus can reveal at best about half the truth of the play, or half of the part I can see.

I

We can begin with one of the most important constituents of the play's delaying strategy: repetition. Repetition figures significantly in the first action of any appreciable magnitude performed in *Hamlet*, the changing of the guard. At the very beginning, to be sure, our sense is not of delay but of indecent haste. Francisco's 'Nay, answer me' functions –

[4] 'On the Value of *Hamlet*', in *Reinterpretations of Elizabethan Drama*, ed. Norman Rabkin (New York, 1969), p. 152. Other commentators in this line include Robert Hapgood, '*Hamlet* Nearly Absurd: The Dramaturgy of Delay', *Tulane Drama Review*, 9 (1965), 132–45; Michael Goldman, *Shakespeare and the Energies of Drama* (Princeton, 1972), pp. 74–93; J. Philip Brockbank, '*Hamlet* the Bonesetter', *Shakespeare Survey 30* (1977), pp. 103–16; Barbara Everett, '*Hamlet*: A Time to Die', *Shakespeare Survey 30* (1977), pp. 117–24; James Calderwood, *To Be and Not To Be: Negation and Metadrama in 'Hamlet'* (New York, 1983); and Terence Hawkes, 'Telmah: To the Sunderland Station', *Encounter*, 60, 4 (April 1983), 50–60. Hawkes is particularly relevant, since he too sees the play as a compound of recursive and successive structures, and also makes much of Dover Wilson's need to enclose the play within a stable interpretation, though in a way with which I shall want to disagree later on.

many have noted this – as an emphatic assertion of *his* right to the sentry's role. In 'Who's there?' Barnardo had prematurely assumed the sentry's responsibility – usurped the office, one might say. Nonetheless, by Barnardo's ''Tis now strook twelf. Get thee to bed, Francisco', the time is in joint, the roles rightly sorted out, and the valediction, along with Francisco's grateful acknowledgement, consummates the ritual. But Francisco cannot, or will not, leave the stage. It takes two more cues, first from Barnardo again ('Well, good night'), and then from Marcellus ('O, farewell, honest soldier'), and two further acknowledgements by himself ('Give you good night', and again, an exact repetition, 'Give you good night') before Francisco can finally get some rest. In all, during the course of twelve lines he is three times bidden and must himself twice bid good night. Fifth time lucky.

What happens at the beginning of *Hamlet* happens throughout *Hamlet*. Valediction delayed by repetition, or valediction whose delay is expressed through repetition, is the business of the stage over and over again. Here are five instances in the first three acts:

(1) Laertes's first line in 1.3 ends, 'Farewell', but he stays to deliver a forty-line speech to Ophelia, culminating in a catalogue of four maxims, all saying the same thing. 'I stay too long', he says as his father enters, at once to chastise him for his tardiness and prolong yet further his departure with his own catalogue of conventional aphorisms, all repeating each other and Laertes earlier. Free finally to go ('Most humbly do I take my leave, my lord'), Laertes holds himself up, rather like Francisco earlier, to remind Ophelia again of the precepts he has tried to character in her memory: 'Farewell, Ophelia, and remember well / What I have said to you'; and only after Ophelia's assurance that it's in her memory locked does Laertes's last 'farewell' (the third time he has used this word, the fifth time he has used one or another valedictory formula) become suited to the action.

(2) In 1.5, it is the ghost whom we hear repeating his valedictions: 'Adieu, adieu, adieu! remember me.' Hamlet, after a speech about memory, repeats the repetition: 'Now to my word: / It is "Adieu, adieu, remember me".'

(3) Two scenes after this, we have Ophelia's description of the wordless but nonetheless prolonged departure from her of Hamlet, who is at first unable to let go of her with his hand, and who is to the last unable to let go of her with his eyes.

(4) In 3.1 we are actually present at an interview between Hamlet and Ophelia, during which, in the space of about thirty lines or perhaps three minutes' playing time, Hamlet 'has said Farewell four times in three speeches'.[5] After the last two of these, Ophelia's speeches, 'O help him, you sweet heavens!' and 'Heavenly powers, restore him!' make dramatic sense only if she is alone; Hamlet must therefore actually twice depart, or at least move to depart, but both times he roars back to order *her* to depart. In all, during the same brief period of playing time, Hamlet dismisses her five times: 'Get thee to a nunn'ry ... Go thy ways to a nunn'ry ... Get thee to a nunn'ry, farewell ... To a nunn'ry, go, and quickly too. Farewell ... To a nunn'ry go.'

(5) At the end of act 3, it is Hamlet again, but with a different woman. 'Good night,' he tells Gertrude. The afterthought, 'but go not to my uncle's bed', is perfectly natural, and the injunction to refrain (a version of both his and Laertes's earlier advice to Ophelia) culminates in a repetition, of which he himself is aware, of the parting words: 'Once more good night.' Once more, however, he is not quite done, although the afterthoughts again flow naturally on an easy 'and', culminating now in a self-conscious conclusiveness:

---

[5] Nevill Coghill, *Shakespeare's Professional Skills* (Cambridge, 1965), p. 17.

> So again good night.
> I must be cruel only to be kind.
> This bad begins and worse remains behind.

These lines confirm Hamlet's motivation retrospectively; they project the consequences of his action into the future; and they rhyme. In all these respects, the effect is of decisive scenic closure. The effect, though, is surprisingly shattered in 'One word more, good lady'. Many words follow in fact, thirty lines of them, including yet another terminal-sounding but medial-proving couplet, before the third repetition of the closing formula: 'Mother, good night indeed.' The Q2 pointing here is much preferable to F's 'good night. Indeed', for it emphasizes the playfulness, reflecting Hamlet's and our own consciousness of the sequence of repetitions; but even its definitive promise of closure is broken as we find ourselves treated to still more words of afterthought. These include a third non-terminal couplet and another self-conscious bit of play from Hamlet about terminations ('Come, sir, to draw toward an end with you') before closure is at last really achieved, 'Good night, Mother.'

Or is it achieved? In the Folio, Gertrude remains on stage and Claudius enters to her; the scene continues. Even if we follow the Quarto directions, the final 'Good night, Mother' will still not satisfy completely, for by now, as the king says of the poisoned cup, it is too late.

## II

Repetition isn't particular to *Hamlet*; as Paul Krieder demonstrated forty years ago, it is common to Shakespeare.[6] But there are special qualities to the repetition of *Hamlet*; it is thematically relevant, for one thing, pointing to the difficulty of completing an action. As Barbara Herrnstein Smith points out in *Poetic Closure*,[7] repetition is a force primarily for continuing rather than completing a poetic structure. Closure, by contrast, usually requires a deviation from the established, sustaining pattern. The use of the rhymed couplet at the end of a blank-verse scene is an obvious conventional example, and, as I've suggested, it's a convention that *Hamlet* honours more in the breach than the observance. Maurice Charney points out that, though the play's scenes usually include a rhymed couplet near the end, 'Significantly, the couplet is not usually the very last line of the scene. Shakespeare seems eager to avoid a too-formal close by adding a few extra-metrical words.'[8] The examples Charney cites, along with some he doesn't, all point towards the same thing: the business is apparently completed, but a supererogatory imperative ('go' or 'come') or hortatory ('nay let's follow' or 'nay, come, let's go together') is required to get the actors to depart. Like the repeated farewells, these stalled exits, woven into the fabric of *Hamlet*, act out the play's condition, that of the puzzled will.

The puzzled will in *Hamlet* is, of course, inseparably bound up with the puzzled mind. A complete action is one whose limits are fixed, whose meaning can thus be stabilized, whose name is not lost. It is precisely this sense of stability that the play puts into question, in denying the neat categories by which conceptual topics, either ethical or ontological, may be defined and understood. Hamlet's inability to leave Gertrude in the closet scene reflects the pursiness of a time when 'virtue itself of vice must pardon beg', and when moral exhortation must take the form of its own contrary ('not this, by no means, that I bid you do'). Cruelty and kindness seem interchangeable in the scene, like heroism and villainy just earlier, with Claudius kneeling at the *prie-dieu* and Hamlet postponing killing him for reasons (in Johnson's words) 'too horrible . . . to be

---

6 *Repetition in Shakespeare* (Princeton, 1941).
7 *Poetic Closure: A Study of How Poems End* (Chicago, 1974).
8 *Style in 'Hamlet'* (Princeton, 1969), p. 204.

uttered'.[9] It is an appropriate climax to an act that begins with a soliloquy in which the mighty opposites of being and not being dance repeatedly round to the other side of the disjunctive 'or' that should be keeping them in their proper places.

In emphasizing the puzzled mind I am queuing up behind the long line of critics, headed by Schlegel and Coleridge, who recognize that the paralysis of action in *Hamlet* develops out of a difficulty in the consciousness. It is the play itself that establishes this priority right from the beginning, in Hamlet's plea to the ghost:

Haste me to know't, that I, with wings as swift
As meditation, or the thought of love,
May sweep to my revenge.

Action follows knowledge here as the night the day, in the sequence prescribed by the efficient bucket brigade of contemporary faculty psychology: first reason, then will. But the priority of reason to will does not make an end to the play's search for the origin of action. In Hamlet's words after the ghost's revelation, we are made to acknowledge a kind of double regression, from reason or thought in some general capacity to what was conceived of as the first faculty of the rational soul, the memory:

Remember thee!
Ay, thou poor ghost, whiles memory holds
    a seat
In this distracted globe. Remember thee!
Yea ...
... thy commandement all alone shall live
Within the book and volume of my brain,
Unmix'd with baser matter.

As Nigel Alexander points out, 'The entire design of the play's opening has led to this moment of the special creation of Hamlet's memory.'[10] Hamlet is nothing if not true to his 'word', moreover; he is a great rememberer, vast in his capacity to store experience.[11] And not only this, but eagerly seeking out experience, extraordinarily energetic in his capacity to discriminate among its various forms, and throughout motivated by the consistent intention to use his knowledge as a basis for significant action, 'struggling all the time', as G. K. Hunter says, 'for purposive mastery over the chaos of his perceptions'.[12] Hunter is right to suggest that it is the whole quality of Hamlet's mind that engages us, his heroic struggle to assume the full burden of his wide-ranging consciousness.[13] He resists the temptation to

---

9  Quoted by Horace Howard Furness, ed., *A New Variorum Edition of Shakespeare. 'Hamlet'* (2 vols., 1877; rpt. New York, 1963), vol. 1, 283.

10  *Poison, Play and Duel* (London, 1971), p. 49.

11  Others who have emphasized the importance of the memory in *Hamlet* include: Harold Fisch, *Hamlet and the Word: The Covenant Pattern in Shakespeare* (New York, 1971); Richard Helgerson, 'What Hamlet Remembers', *Shakespeare Studies*, 10 (1977), 67–98; James P. Hammersmith, '*Hamlet* and the Myth of Memory', *ELH*, 45 (1978), 597–605; and Jill L. Levenson, 'Dramatists at (Meta) Play: Shakespeare's *Hamlet*, II, ii, ll. 410–591 and Pirandello's *Henry IV*', *Modern Drama*, 24 (1981), 330–7.

12  'The Heroism of Hamlet', in *'Hamlet'*, Stratford-upon-Avon Studies, 5, eds. J. R. Brown and Bernard Harris (1963; rpt. 1972), p. 104.

13  For this reason I have deliberately avoided any very technical consideration of the position of memory in Elizabethan psychology. My contention above, that the memory is conceived of as the first faculty of the rational soul, is based on Frank Manley, who in the notes to his edition of Donne's *Anniversaries* cites Bernard and Peter Lombard from the *Patrologia* as well as passages from Donne's *Sermons* (Baltimore, 1968, p. 124). E. M. W. Tillyard, by contrast, places the memory as the last constituent of the middle faculties, rather than the first of the higher – *Elizabethan World Picture* (London, 1943), p. 65. Perhaps the Elizabethans were less consistent and systematic than we tend to assume, and perhaps all we can say about the special prominence of memory in the play is that it derives from a position somewhere in the middle: mediating between the impressions of objective reality and the more strictly intellectual faculties that are meant to decide upon action, the memory participates in all the actions of the mind, and thus may stand as a synecdoche for the mind as a whole.

In a similar spirit, I cannot go along with Nigel Alexander and Jill Levenson (*op. cit.*) in seeing much relevance to *Hamlet* in the memory systems discussed by Dame Frances Yates in *The Art of Memory* (London,

reduce this burden to some more manageable core of awareness – though the prospects of such delimitation (in the different versions provided by Horatio, Laertes, Fortinbras, and the player) are all obviously appealing to him. And he resists the ultimate temptation of shedding the burden altogether. Before Ophelia appears, to our eyes but not Hamlet's in the fourth act, it is the Player King who defines the prospect of oblivion most fully. 'Purpose is but the slave to memory,' he says, and for him such forgetfulness is both inevitable and desirable: 'Most necessary 'tis that we forget / To pay ourselves what to ourselves is debt.' The Player King is himself a shadow, more of a ghost than the ghost. His affectless couplets suggest the eerie, inert indifference of the lifeless. In more ways than one, the speech of the Player King is the dead centre of the play. Yet in what we all know to be the vital centre of the play, 'To be or not to be', Hamlet moves not to reduce or annihilate but rather to enlarge the scope of his consciousness, assuming a knowledge of 'fardels' that seems to go beyond his uniquely personal experience, thereby enabling himself to speak for all of us, on stage and off, who are forced by this play to wait in the shadowy interim between conception and action.

### III

It is to us off stage now that I wish to turn, thinking not so much of the crisis endured by Hamlet in the play, as of the one that we as an audience share with him. Consider again Hamlet's phrase after the ghost's departure, 'whiles memory holds a seat / In this distracted globe'. The distracted globe, of course, is Hamlet's head; he is cudgelling his brains, as Harry Levin says.[14] But at the same time his words, if not his hands, gesture outwards towards us seated in the Globe. And for all the excitement on stage – even the groundlings, we are told, stopped cracking nuts when the ghost appeared – we are moved to distraction,

tempted mentally if not actually to look away from the stage to the members of the audience around us, to ourselves really. It is a moment that defines our existence as an audience, like Hamlet's on stage, as an anxious introspection, a distracted self-consciousness, whose name is memory.

What is more important than this pun, the active exertion of the memory is central to the response that the play demands of us right from the beginning, from the first scene. I have already made much of the repetition in the first action of *Hamlet*, but I doubt any audience is aware of it as such. It represents the extreme jitteriness of the sentries, and we are

1966). The star of Dame Frances's cast is a sixteenth-century 'mnemotechnician' called Giulio Camillo, whose Memory Theatre is described by a contemporary as concerned with 'all things that the human mind can conceive'. Perhaps, but it does not seem to be concerned with the relationship of such conceptions to anything external to themselves. Any potentially useful theory of memory must try to explain how the mind first of all acquires and then stores information about the reality construed to be external to itself. But Camillo's Memory Theatre is a wholly self-contained structure of mental forms, perfectly invulnerable to any interference from external phenomena, and therefore devoid of any cognitive value or content.

If this is relevant to *Hamlet*, it is only to that relatively minor but interesting part of the play called Polonius. Polonius loves his 'foolish figures' dearly, and they usually fall neatly into place, each term following the other as the night the day, as in the 'declension' by which he demonstrates Hamlet's madness. The trouble is that the sequences go round in circles ('to define true madness, / What is't but to be nothing else but mad?') without reference to any reality external to themselves. Both Polonius and Camillo work within the elegant though inert systems of scholastic thought which so infuriated Bacon, the 'degenerate learning [that] did chiefly reign amongst the Schoolmen'. Like the Ptolemaic model of the cosmos to which Polonius predictably subscribes (just after his self-satisfied 'declension'), the memory systems described in *The Art of Memory* are the product of human wit turned in upon itself, rather than working 'according to the stuff', and thus 'bring ... forth indeed cobwebs of learning, admirable for the fineness of thread and work but of no great substance or profit'.

[14] *The Question of 'Hamlet'* (New York, 1961), p. 18.

much too absorbed in the action – wondering why they are so anxious – to be conscious of the means by which the anxiety is conveyed to us. The repetition functions mimetically, in other words, describing qualities of the world external to ourselves, in those anxieties we can scarcely be said self-consciously to participate.

In the business that follows, however, we are brought towards such self-conscious participation, again primarily through the phenomenon of repetition. The word is 'again':

> What, has this thing appear'd *again* tonight?

> Sit down a while,
> And let us once *again* assail your ears . . .

> Peace, break thee off! Look where it comes *again*.

The repetition of 'again' is particularly significant, since the word itself signifies the perception of repetition. They have seen 'this thing' twice before. They have described it to Horatio before; it is not specified how many times, and the weary 'once again' gives a sense of stretching out into infinity. But it is only a momentary sense; the development here is clearly towards a calm poise, as the characters relax and sit down to hear Barnardo's retrospective exposition. Barnardo's speech, moreover, invites us to relax as well. Not only does its syntax promise extensive elaboration; theatrical convention promises the same thing. Retrospective expositions are conventional to drama, and an even minimally sophisticated audience will, remembering its dramatic experience, respond to the cue and relax.

All this shatters with the ghost. Entering on an emphatic 'again', the ghost undermines the protective structure articulated by the repetitions. 'Those who cannot remember the past are condemned to repeat it.'[15] Santayana's maxim has become a universal cliché probably because of the reassurance implied by its converse: those who *can* remember the past thereby acquire control of the present and, perhaps, the future. It hasn't worked out that

way for Horatio and the others, however; remembering has in no way diminished their vulnerability to the present terror. And we are clearly intended to share their defencelessness; the cover of 'yond same star' is meant to distract us, make us look the wrong way, so that the ghost surprises us.[16] It's an interestingly expressive theatrical trick, for our vulnerability too is realized in the frustration of expectations derived from past experience. It is memory that has let us down, and the theatrical trick is a momentary realization of this, not in conceptual but in spatial terms – what Stephen Dedalus calls 'the ineluctable modality of the visible'. The wrong way we've been looking is backwards.

But this is rushing things. Though some such intuition may be available to us, it is premature to claim any systematic awareness. After all, for us it is only the first appearance of the ghost. And before we have much of a chance to consider what has happened to us, we are encouraged to direct all our attention to the figures on stage, hard at work trying to master their own chaotic perceptions. The process begins even in the moment of terror, in Barnardo's repeated perception of likeness: 'In the same figure like the King that's dead', and 'Looks 'a not like the King?' In the presence of the ghost, this perception of similarity to a known past does not diminish anxiety; but when Marcellus later reaches for Barnardo's straw, 'Is it not like the King?', the similarity is amplified by Horatio's memory 'Such was the very armor he had on . . . So frown'd he

---

[15] George Santayana, *The Life of Reason* (New York, 1954), p. 82.

[16] In discussing the ghost's appearance in 1.4, Kenneth Burke points to the same kind of strategy. At the appointed time of twelve, we are assaulted by a sudden blast of noise – but not the ghost. Then, once we become distracted with the 'vicious mole of nature' speech, the ghost enters: 'this ghost, so assiduously prepared for, is yet a surprise'. This is from a chapter in *Counter-Statement* called 'Psychology and Form', to which I owe a great deal in terms of general methodology (2nd edn. (Chicago, 1957), p. 30).

once . . .' – and the temperature sensibly cools. Before long, they can re-enact the gesture of an earlier relaxation ('Good now, sit down'), and we find ourselves actually hearing the retrospective exposition we thought we were going to get earlier, an elaborately detailed description, full of legalistic precision, of an event from the distant past: the chivalric duel between old Hamlet and old Fortinbras.

As Horatio's long exposition develops, a connection begins to emerge between the two invasions: perhaps the ghost has manifested itself *because* of Fortinbras's illegitimate claim to repossess the lost lands. It is Barnardo who catches up with and confirms this understanding:

> Well may it sort that this portentous figure
> Comes armed through our watch so like the
>     King
> That was and is the question of these wars.

'Was and is': the fundamental gesure of the historical intelligence at work. The time is now in joint. Though Barnardo is still tentative, Horatio very nearly regains his earlier complacency: 'A mote it is to trouble the mind's eye.' The speech that follows about the most high and palmy state of Rome is smooth and decorated, wholly self-possessed and secure. Horatio moves beyond Barnardo's perception of immediate analogy between past and present to a broad frame of historical reference. The portents surrounding mighty Julius' assassination are famous and familiar, every schoolboy's property. And every spectator's property as well: Caesar's death was an immensely popular dramatic subject, and no doubt Shakespeare's own version of a year or so earlier was fresh indeed in the memory of some among *Hamlet*'s first audiences.

But the ghost re-enters to repeat his earlier shattering effect. His cue words are a repetition ('But soft, behold! lo where it comes again!'), except that 'again' now belongs as fully to us for we too have seen it before – as to the figures – on stage, substantiating whatever intuition we may have felt earlier of a betrayal by our memory. Those who *can* remember the past are condemned to repeat it? Heaven and earth, must we remember?

Yet, to the mind that seeks understanding, what alternative is there to the large discourse, looking first of all before? The question is prompted by the speech of Horatio that follows. The syntax and rhythm of the speech suggest the stage directions. Four times Horatio uses an 'if' clause before 'speak' in the imperative. Each corresponds to a movement on stage to intercept the ghost, and to a shifting of conceptual grounds as well, as Horatio moves from one philosophical position to another in an attempt to achieve satisfaction. He begins with a scepticism consistent with contemporary Protestant views of ghosts: 'I'll cross it though it blast me. Stay, illusion!' When this doesn't work, he changes his terms to conform roughly to the more traditional Catholic attitude: 'If there be any good thing to be done /That may to thee do ease, and grace to me, / Speak to me.' Failing this, he retreats to a particularly classical idea, the political portent, such as the unnatural omens at the time of Caesar's death mentioned just earlier: 'If thou art privy to thy country's fate / Which happily foreknowing may avoid, / O speak!' And finally he appeals to folklore, the wisdom of an unspecifiable 'they', derived from a lost source, an ur-auctoritas antecedent to historical record:

> Or if thou hast uphoarded in thy life
> Extorted treasure in the womb of earth,
> For which, they say, your spirits oft walk in
>     death,
> Speak of it, stay and speak!

Though the shifts are subtle, the direction of the movement is clear enough: this is going like a crab backwards. Horatio's words regress endlessly, enlarging the globe's memory into a seeming infinity, yet cannot contain the ghost: ''Tis here!' ''Tis here!' ''Tis gone!' To use Stephen Dedalus's words again, a *Hamlet-*

obsessed character in a *Hamlet*-obsessed book, history has become a nightmare from which we are trying to escape.

IV

Myth, according to P. J. Aldus, involves us 'in a constant regression into prehistory ... and ... more deeply, into elusive human experience not available to factual record.'[17] In this sense, *Hamlet* is a play with extraordinary and perhaps even unique powers to activate a consciousness of myth in its audience. (This isn't all that makes *Hamlet* itself extraordinary. The mere presence of archetypes does not by itself confer much literary value; if so, *The Hairy Ape* would be a masterpiece. But this brings me back to the well-madeness of *Hamlet*, which I promised not to talk about.) Not only does it tell an old, old story: it tells us that it does so, consistently thrusting upon us a sense of its own antiquity of origin. Consider the Player's speech in act 2. The speech has been the occasion of much throwing about of brains: Marlowe, or Nashe, or Marlowe/ Nashe, or Kyd, or some lost play, or Shakespeare's own juvenilia, or Ovid, or Virgil, or indeed Homer himself in whom the legend in a sense originated – just which of these antecedents furnishes the echoes for us here?[18] Though much of this speculation may strike us as rather desperate, it seems to me likely that it reflects the (also somewhat desperate) experience of Shakespeare's first audiences, or what we can imagine any of them familiar enough either with recent theatre or the classics or both to feel, hearing words at once so familiar and so old-fashioned, so provocative of an elusive sense of *déjà entendu*.

One measure of the play's extraordinary mythic weight is the presentation of the protagonist as embodying a traditional heroic and sacrificial role. More than any of the 'major four' tragedies, and perhaps more than all Shakespeare's other tragedies, *Hamlet* presses home upon us this sense of the protagonist

right from the beginning. The fourth scene shows Hamlet going too far, exceeding the limits of all kinds of conventional boundaries – physical, prudential, ontological. Along with the invocation of fate ('My fate cries out') and the indirect allusion (in 'the Nemean lion') to Hercules, the scene insists that we recognize a kind of paradigm of heroic action in the tragic mode, the realization of a familiar pattern. Mythic approaches to the protagonist, however, have tended to be interested more in Oedipus than in Hercules, and surely in response to real pressures from the play. The first words that Hamlet utters, 'A little more than kin, and less than kind', point to an unnatural family romance; the first thing he says about himself, 'O that this too too sallied flesh would melt', expresses a suicidal guilt; and throughout the play – in his delay, his madness (real and/or feigned), his attitude towards his mother and/or Ophelia, his sense of his father as a bigger man than himself – Hamlet reveals profound internal pressures for which the available commonsense explanations seem inadequate, and which even he often finds inexplicable.

If we turn to Freud to account for this, we come again to remembering – for Freud's version of a guilty conscience is virtually coterminous with a guilty memory, either of the child's aggressive and erotic impulses towards his parents or, in the later Freud, the inherited memory of an actual deed, the putative murder of the primal horde's father-

---

[17] *Mousetrap: Structure and Meaning in 'Hamlet'* (Toronto, 1977), p. 8.

[18] The earlier comments are amassed by Furness, *op. cit.*, vol. 1, 180–6. The argument was brought into this century by W. M. A. Creizenach, *The English Drama in the Age of Shakespeare*, trans. Cecile Hugon (London, 1916), pp. 315–16 and p. 331; C. F. Tucker Brooke, 'Hamlet's Third Soliloquy', *Studies in Philology*, 14 (1917), 237–42; and it flurried again in 1928 in the *TLS* exchange among Middleton Murry, Wilson Knight, Poel and Fripp (520, 568, and 593). Recent commentators on the classical antecedents include Levin, pp. 138–68, and Aldus, p. 57, *op. cit.*

leader. Though this hypothesis has never been accepted (unlike Adam and the apple), the effect is the same, for guilt seems equally competent to flourish whether or not an impulse has been transformed into a deed (hence Jesus's words about lusting after a woman in your heart). Psychoanalysts have invented a term to account for this – 'par-amnesia', a distortion of memory in which fantasy and actuality are confused. Part of the horror of this sort of Hamlet-like guilt is that its source is intangible: the memory of an action so remote in time, or so deeply buried in the subconscious, that it may have no objective existence – or whose relation to any actual event is, as Freud says in his essay on 'The Uncanny', 'a matter of indifference':

Among instances of frightening things there must be one class in which the frightening element can be shown to be something repressed which *recurs*. This class of frightening things could then constitute the uncanny; and it must be a matter of indifference whether what is uncanny was itself originally frightening or whether it carried some other affect . . . if this is indeed the secret nature of the uncanny, we can understand why linguistic usage has extended *das Heimliche* . . . into its opposite, *das Unheimliche* . . .; for this uncanny is in reality nothing new or alien, but something which is familiar and old-established in the mind and which has become alienated from it only through the process of repression.[19]

This comes very close to *Hamlet*: the admix-ture of strangeness and familiarity, of fear, guilt, and repetition. 'Look out kid / Some-thing you did / God knows when / But you're doing it again.'[20]

Again, the point I want to emphasize is not just Hamlet's problems, but the capacity of the play to make them ours as well, to involve us in the protagonist's guilty memories. These can sometimes surface surprisingly in the least likely places. I am thinking now of the play's second scene, whose formal splendour and elegant costumes serve, we all know, as con-trast to the dark and jagged anxieties of the

opening on the ramparts. Claudius begins it with a gorgeous speech, balancing the memory of old Hamlet with 'remembrance of ourselves', and moves then to specifics:

Therefore our sometime sister, now our
    queen,
Th' imperial jointress to this warlike state,
Have we, as 'twere with a defeated joy,
With an auspicious, and a dropping eye,
With mirth in funeral, and with dirge in
    marriage,
In equal scale weighing delight and dole,
Taken to wife.

In part what makes this so impressive is the heaping up of rhetorical antitheses in the middle, then as now the staple of political rhetoric,[21] but what makes the speech truly effective is Claudius's masterly orchestration of the materials in the great period as a whole. By crowding our mind with adverbial details (the way in which he acted), he leaves us little room to contemplate the nature of the act itself. Still better and still worse, by with-holding the verb, Claudius manages to get us to accept the act without our noticing it. 'Our sometime sister, now our queen' – it's all there, in that illicit apposition. We don't notice it because we're made to exert our minds in anticipating possible verbs that will allow us to identify the syntax of these apposite nouns in the overall structure (are they subjects? Is this a very formal direct address to Gert-rude?). Just as in the first scene, we find our-

---

19 *The Complete Psychological Works of Sigmund Freud*, ed. James Strachey, 24 vols. (New York, 1963), vol. 17, p. 241.
20 The lyric of a Bob Dylan song called 'Subterranean Homesick Blues'.
21 John Kennedy was fond of it ('Ask not what your country can do for you, ask rather what you can do for your country'), and so was Mackenzie King, the Cana-dian Prime Minister who assured his divided country in the Second World War that they would have 'conscrip-tion if necessary, but not necessarily conscription'. (As F. R. Scott said about MacKenzie King, 'He never let his on the one hand / Know what his on the other hand was doing'.)

selves distracted, looking the wrong way, though here it is looking after rather than before. By the time the verb comes to allow us to sense that we've been fooled, again it is too late.

It is at this point that Claudius delivers (with a bland smile, I assume) the remark that has figured so fundamentally in the debate surrounding the Danish succession: 'nor have we herein barr'd / Your better wisdoms, which have freely gone / With this affair along.' Claudius refers to some kind of council meeting that occurred prior to the action of the play, and many have lamented the play's withholding from us the details of that meeting. Not so Dover Wilson however, who in *What Happens in Hamlet* claims that he and Shakespeare's first audiences had access to the minutes, so to speak.[22] Wilson's contention, that Shakespeare's audience would assume the play's politics conformed to the (presumably) stable definition of the Elizabethan constitution, has been refuted;[23] yet in a curious way Wilson is right. We do know what happened at that meeting, since it has just been re-enacted in front of us. Claudius's words apply to us as well as to Polonius and the others, for haven't we freely gone along with the affair? 'Freely' is debatable; there's no effective defence against skilful rhetoric in the act. We need time to dismantle Claudius's speech, as I did earlier, and the theatre doesn't give us time. In the theatre, as Kenneth Burke once implied, we are all more or less members of Antony's mob.[24] The 'more or less' is a significant qualifier; we can at least sense we're being taken in, if we can't actually prevent it. But back then to 'freely': how can we feel responsible for something that could not have been otherwise? Such responsibility must be not for something that we did, but for something we are – namely, guilty creatures sitting at a play.[25]

Still another surprising reminder of our complicity comes in the nunnery scene, which has provoked by far the most famous of Dover Wilson's clarifying interventions in his edition of the play. Empson argued years ago in '*Hamlet* When New'[26] that the whole Hamlet–Ophelia relationship seemed designed to make us angry both with Hamlet for his puritanism and with ourselves for partly sharing it. Booth is getting at a similar thing, in describing the shocking effect by which the scene suddenly disrupts our sense of Hamlet as merely feigning madness; 'The audience', Booth says, 'finds itself guilty of Polonius's foolish confidence in predictable trains of events . . . They

---

22 (1935; rpt. Cambridge, 1971), pp. 26–38.

23 See E. A. J. Honigmann, 'The Politics in *Hamlet* and "The World of the Play"', in '*Hamlet*', Stratford-upon-Avon Studies, 5, eds. J. R. Brown and Bernard Harris (1963; rpt. London, 1972), 129–47.

24 See 'Antony in Behalf of the Play', in *The Philosophy of Literary Form* (Berkeley and Los Angeles, 1973), pp. 329–43.

25 If it is asked what we are guilty of (or complicit in, or at least what we have allowed ourselves to condone – these distinctions don't seem to me very important finally), one answer is: our memories. This is an inherited guilt. For Elizabethan audiences, the memories might include the shenanigans by which Henry got a dispensation first to marry Katharine and subsequently to annul the marriage in order to marry Anne Boleyn. (For an unblinking account, see James Gairdner, *A History of the English Church in the Sixteenth Century from Henry VIII to Mary* (London, 1912).) Like the Hales case evoked in the graveyard scene, which as Malone pointed out (Furness, vol. 1, 376–7) must have been based rather on overheard stories than on documentation, this is the sort of vintage memory, going back a generation or two, that one can imagine either Shakespeare or his audience picking up as children, listening in on parental conversation – where one learns so much, after all. (Think of Joyce's Stephen again, listening in from under the table at the beginning of the *Portrait*: 'Pull out his eyes / Apologize'.) Beyond the questionable political morality, there is, as Jason Rosenblatt demonstrates, the ambivalence in scriptural tradition and canon law about marrying one's deceased brother's widow, and ultimately of course the incest taboo, the sexual act that has the primal eldest curse upon it – a memory available, presumably, to modern as well as to Elizabethan audiences. (See Jason Rosenblatt, 'Aspects of the Incest Problem in *Hamlet*', *Shakespeare Quarterly*, 20 (1978), 349–65.)

26 *Sewanee Review*, 61 (1953), 15–42, 185–205.

both overestimate the degree of safety they have as innocent onlookers'.[27] For Wilson, however, the problem is registered as wholly external to the audience's own self-consciousness. 'Something is lost,' he says about the nunnery scene, 'some clue to the relationship' to account for Hamlet's otherwise 'perplexing' and 'outrageous' behaviour. 'And what is lost', he continues, 'is a very simple thing – a single stage direction.'[28] So he invents one, by which Hamlet overhears Polonius's plot to loose Ophelia to him, and can thereby be seen to play his rant in the nunnery scene to the spies he knows to be lurking behind the arras. Problem solved.

'Something is lost' – no truer words exist to describe the effect of the nunnery scene or the play as a whole upon us. What more natural response to such a painful acknowledgement of absence than the felt need to fill it with a clarifying presence? The question, though, is how legitimately we may act upon this felt need. Wilson wishes to distinguish his clarification from that of the psychologists ('sex-nausea as induced by his mother's behaviour') and the historians ('an ill-digested lump of the old play by Kyd'), both of which, he says, 'fail to satisfy'.[29] But they satisfied their proponents. Historians and psychologists like historical and psychological explanations, just as editors like editorial ones. A holograph, a source, a primal instinct, the author, the speaking subject, nature – our explanations vary but they are all of them grounded in origins. It is not just *Hamlet* we desire so to explain, of course, but *Hamlet* is special in the way its workings – making us feel that 'something is lost' – constantly reinforce the desire. When our explanations take the objective form of narrative, we call them myths. In this sense Wilson's great work of editing and commenting upon *Hamlet*, taken together the most brilliant sustained endeavour of our time and probably of any time to demythologize the play, turns out to be itself something of a myth. For, not unlike Freud with his primal horde, Wilson invents a story in order to make what is felt to be an intolerable experience comprehensible and therefore more tolerable.

My point is not to go on bashing Dover Wilson. He is far more often right than he is wrong, and he may even be called right here, in the sense that his endeavour, to establish a reliable and detached perspective upon *Hamlet*, is one in which we all have a share. Ever since Plato distinguished between mere opinion and knowledge, the latter defined with reference to a stable realm of being outside nature and history, we have invested heavily in the idea of an independent, objective reality that controls and validates interpretation. Why this heavy investment? It reflects the anxious intuition that without such a transcendental or 'foundational' control upon consciousness and action,[30] human purpose and dignity is lost, and we are left at best with the brute facts of sleeping and feeding, or at worst with madness and suicidal despair. According to Terence Hawkes, Wilson's desire to get *Hamlet* right reflects an obsessive and unconscious fear of revolutionary politics,[31] but neurotic self-interest isn't the whole story or even, I think, the main one. After all, Wilson's desire to solve the problem of *Hamlet* by gaining (regaining, he believed) access to some putative origin is not unlike Hamlet's own desire to solve his problems within the play. Hamlet too has his neurotically self-interested side, but his enormous appeal to audiences throughout history should suggest how profoundly the

27 'On the Value of *Hamlet*', p. 159.
28 Editor's 'Introduction', *The Tragedy of Hamlet, Prince of Denmark* (Cambridge, 1934; repr. 1971), p. lvi.
29 *Ibid.*
30 'Foundational' is Richard Rorty's term, though his pragmatism is 'anti-foundational' in nature. For a full version of the history of philosophy I allude to here, see Rorty's *Philosophy and the Mirror of Nature* (Princeton, 1979), and *Consequences of Pragmatism (Essays: 1972–1980)* (Minneapolis, 1982).
31 'Telmah', *op. cit.*

play makes us not only acknowledge this desire for 'perfect conscience', but honour it.

The honour seems to me essential to any response to *Hamlet*. Without generating in us such profound desires for access to a controlling order of being to which our interpretations can refer, then the play's frustrations of those desires would be meaningless. The need, and the frustrating of the need, are parasitic upon one another – the contradictory purposes about which I wrote at the beginning. I have been emphasizing the frustrations in this essay, and I shall end with emphasis upon them now. Hamlet's father is lost. Whatever he was – Hyperion; the doer of foul crimes while in his days of nature; a man, take him for all in all – he is now no more. In *The Margins of Philosophy*, Derrida describes writing as an 'essential drifting . . . cut off from all absolute responsibility, from *consciousness* as the authority of the last analysis, orphaned, and separated at birth from the assistance of its father'.[32] The words can apply both to Hamlet and to the play's audiences; for no amount of human effort can restore the objective authority that we seek. This authority is irretrievably lost, even if we could find it. Unlike Freud's primal horde or Claudius's business meeting, which perhaps never occurred, and unlike Hamlet's father, who though he must have existed did so only in whatever sense dramatic characters we never get to see are said to have existed – unlike these, there must really have been a Shakespearian manuscript and probably an ur-*Hamlet*, for that matter, as well. Somewhere, moreover, it may still exist, and we'd love to find it, but among the mysteries it would solve it could not reach the heart. The real ur-*Hamlet* is *Hamlet* itself, in the play's capacity to make us mix memory with desire, in the imagination of a condition of clarity, not to say innocence – the cessation of those bad dreams that prevent us from being kings of infinite space. The lost play by Kyd is merely the reified object of this desire. If the historical details did not exist to tell us that there was a Kyd play, we'd simply have to invent it. But it works the other way round as well. If we found the Kyd play, we'd have to *dis*-invent *it*, for something would *still* be lost. We would no doubt then need to hypothesize another reification, and so beat on, boats against the current, or like a crab going ceaselessly backwards into the past towards, as we suppose (along with Milton's Satan), the ultimate priority – the origin of ourselves.

---

[32] Translated, with additional notes by Alan Bass (Chicago, 1982), p. 316.

# 'THEN MURDER'S OUT OF TUNE': THE MUSIC AND STRUCTURE OF 'OTHELLO'

## ROSALIND KING

> O, you are well-tuned now,
> But I'll set down the pegs that make this
>    music,
> As honest as I am.           (2.1.177–9)

Iago's commentary on the reunion of Othello and Desdemona on the island of Cyprus is more than just a fanciful statement of his intentions. Iago as a character deliberately sets out to destroy the harmony of love, but Shakespeare, the dramatist, presents his words and actions as part of an extensive pattern of musical images and effects. This pattern works integrally as a structural theme. It unites and expands the ideas of the play and provides the essential terms of reference for both aesthetic and moral judgement.

*Othello* probably makes more use of music than any other Shakespeare tragedy. Iago's two songs and Cassio's wind music are essential to the plot, while the 'willow song' expresses Desdemona's situation and her state of mind with accurate and agonizing economy.

Previous studies have demonstrated that Shakespeare knew and was using well-established musical theory.[1] They show that the play contains passages which spring from such commonplaces as the superiority of string over wind instruments, the existence of 'music that cannot be heard' (the music of the spheres), and the continuing debate as to whether the performance of music was a suitable occupation for anyone who claimed to be a gentleman.[2]

Renaissance ideas of musical harmony were inextricably bound up with order and structure. Following the ideas of Pythagoras and Plato, Renaissance scholars believed that the simple mathematical proportions 1:2, 2:3, 3:4, which result in the intervals of perfect harmony in ancient music – the octave, the perfect fifth, and the perfect fourth – were also responsible for the beauties and numerical structure of the universe, from the 'dancing' of the tuneful planets to the form and constitution of man. Discounting folk-song and ballads, audible music on earth was considered as falling into two categories – public, outdoor ceremonial music played on 'loud' instruments by professional musicians and bandsmen (military trumpeters, drummers, and the like) and private, indoor music played on 'soft' stringed instruments (virginals, lutes, viols etc.), sometimes by professional musicians but often by members of the upper classes for the

---

All Shakespearian references are taken from the *Complete Works*, ed. Peter Alexander (Glasgow, 1951).

[1] F. W. Sternfeld, *Music in Shakespearian Tragedy* (London, 1963); Lawrence Ross, 'Shakespeare's "Dull Clown" and Symbolic Music', *Shakespeare Quarterly*, 17 (1966).

[2] Much of the confusion stems directly from Aristotle, *The Politics*, e.g. 'We think it not manly to perform music, except when drunk or for fun' (Book 8.4.7). 'it is plain that music has the power of producing a certain effect on the moral character of the soul, and if it has the power to do this, it is clear that the young must be directed to music and must be educated in it' (Book 8.5.9): trans. H. Rackham (London, 1932).

amusement of themselves and their friends. The music in *Othello* exists in all these forms: actual and metaphorical, public and private, folk-song and art-song. It is an essential part of the way Shakespeare illustrates both the initial harmony of Othello's and Desdemona's love and the manner in which they combine their official public roles with their private lives.

As a military commander and general, Othello's life is punctuated by musical sounds – mostly played on trumpets and drums – designed to regulate life in the garrison and give orders on the battlefield. During the course of the play, the trumpets announce the arrival of first Othello and later the Venetian senator, Lodovico, before summoning all the characters to a state dinner. The trumpet is a reminder of state, ceremonial, and duty. A public instrument, it was used for broadcasting information to large numbers of people and in contemporary art and iconography it had understandably become the identifying symbol for personifications of Fame.[3]

The first reference to trumpets in the play, however, comes from Desdemona. She uses it with the connotations of both 'fame' and the 'military life' to express her love for her husband and to convince the Venetian Senate that it is fitting that she should accompany him to Cyprus:

> That I did love the Moor to live with him,
> My downright violence and storm of fortunes
> May trumpet to the world.     (1.3.248–50)

The daughter 'never bold' that her father has described, demonstrates instead that she is the true partner of a man of action. She is no simple retiring maiden but a woman who is well aware of the consequences of her actions. She knows that Othello is a public figure and that by marrying him, particularly in such a 'violent' manner, she is likely to attract public attention to herself. She is not prepared to stay at home, a 'moth of peace', but is anxious to share her husband's life and to take an active

role in it. Indeed, both lovers see their relationship as a reciprocal one, a partnership of mutual help and interest, and in these early scenes their descriptions of each other find similar and complementary expression:

> She loved me for the dangers I had passed,
> And I loved her that she did pity them.
>                                (1.3.167–8)

Just as Desdemona demands to share her husband's life, so Othello – perhaps even more remarkably – is willing for her to do so. Throughout the first half of the play in every speech of more than half-a-dozen lines, he manages to combine with perfect ease the most earnest consideration of state affairs with equally earnest and loving reference to his wife. He too is anxious that she should accompany him on his expedition to Cyprus, and adds his voice to her request:

> And heaven defend your good souls that you
>     think
> I will your serious and great business scant
> For she is with me.          (1.3.266–8)

Shakespeare twice adopts the point made in Cinthio's Introduction to *Gli Hecatommithi*,[4] the major source of the play, that 'he who wishes to form a true judgement of beauty must admire not only the body, but rather the minds and habits of those who present themselves to his view'. Thus, while Desdemona 'saw Othello's visage in his mind' (1.3.252), Othello wishes that the Senate be 'free and bounteous to her mind' (1.3.265) by allowing her to go with him to Cyprus. It is the similarity of thought and outlook, the bounty, the generosity, and the courage which each finds in the other that is important. This sharing of roles is further indicated when they meet after the storm on the island of Cyprus. He greets her as the soldier-hero and she him as the

---

[3] Cf. Geoffrey Chaucer, *The House of Fame* Book 3; ll. 1237ff, ed. F. N. Robinson (London, 1957).

[4] Ed. Geoffrey Bullough, *Narrative and Dramatic Sources of Shakespeare*, vol. vii (1973), p. 240.

supporting lover: 'My fair warrior ... My dear Othello' (2.1.180). The rarity of their thinking is emphasized by observations made by other characters on the same theme which are markedly rooted in sexual stereotypes. Cassio's description of Desdemona as 'Our great Captain's Captain' (2.1.74) is a recognition of Desdemona's powers in the terms of perfect woman-on-a-pedestal which in no way detracts from Othello's purely masculine authority, whereas Iago's very similar line, 'Our General's wife is now the General' (2.3.305), has exactly the opposite effect – and deliberately so. Instead of a unity in partnership, Iago depicts for his audience just another henpecked husband, harassed by an appalling wife.

From his observations about women to his thoughts on reputation, Iago consistently follows and exploits conventional beliefs about the way the world works. He thinks as Everyman thinks and Everyman is therefore bound to hold him in respect: 'It would be every man's thought, and thou art a blessed fellow to think as every man thinks' (2 Henry IV, 2.2.52). It is this that makes him so powerful. Audiences do not stop to disapprove of his scheming – they are too excited by it – and every character in the play (not just Othello and Desdemona) is taken in by it because in the context of normal social behaviour everything he says appears reasonable and credible even when it is most lying and pernicious.

> And what's he, then, that says I play the villain?
> When this advice is free I give and honest,
> Probal to thinking. (2.3.325–7)

In supporting Desdemona's request to accompany him to Cyprus, Othello quite clearly is not thinking like Everyman, and it is Iago's constant task throughout the long scenes of 3.3 and 3.4 to manipulate him into thinking that way. Even after vowing to kill her for the personal injury supposedly done to him, Othello is still able to appreciate not only Desdemona's charm but also her immense capability – although, because now obsessed with her body, he can only regard her as a concubine:

> O, the world has not a sweeter creature; she might lie by an emperor's side and command him tasks. (4.1.181)

It is evident from Iago's relationship with his own wife and from his views expressed in the rhyming game he plays with her and Desdemona that his ideas on what might be possible within marriage are very different from Othello's. In his own marriage, petty wrangling and jealousy are the norm and he is thus understandably determined to destroy the harmony and accord that his black commanding officer has found. His manner of doing this is evidenced by his behaviour in the landing-in-Cyprus scene, which in many respects is a paradigm of the entire play since it shows the acute strategy with which he responds to different but similar situations. The stage picture of an overly courteous Cassio taking Desdemona 'by the palm' and kissing his fingers (in a manner still practised by Italians wishing to impress and still regarded with suspicion and derision by Englishmen) is instantly replaced by that of Othello and Desdemona in each other's arms. Iago is the commentator on both. He perverts the former innocent though overdone courtesies to a gross anal sexuality:

> Yet again your fingers to your lips? Would they were clyster-pipes for your sake. (2.1.175)

However, when he likens the embrace between Othello and Desdemona to a well-tuned string instrument in the passage with which this article began, he is describing no more than the truth. He demonstrates that he is capable of appreciating the extent and quality of Othello's and Desdemona's love – an essential prerequisite to attempting to destroy it.

God's hand tuning the string of the universe

is a fairly common Renaissance and Shakespearian emblem. In *Troilus and Cressida* (1.3.109) Ulysses uses the image of an untuned string to express political anarchy, and in *Richard II* the deposed king languishing in prison, considering the 'music of men's lives' (5.5.44ff), mentions the discord which results from a 'disordered string' – one that is plucked out of time with the others. Iago does not mention a specific instrument, but the lute, a solo instrument with courses of strings tuned in consonant pairs so that two strings are plucked together and sound as one, lends itself admirably to an image of union in marriage. Such an instrument also forms the central image in Sonnet 8 – one of the initial sequence urging love, marriage, and procreation – because the sound produced when both identically pitched strings are plucked together is far fuller and more resonant than either would produce singly:

> Mark how one string, sweet husband to
>   another,
> Strikes each in each by mutual ordering;
> Resembling sire and child and happy mother,
> Who, all in one, one pleasing note do sing.

The difficulty of tuning a lute and the horrible sound that can result even when only one string in one of those pairs is out of tune had become commonplace by the time Webster was writing *The Duchess of Malfi*:

> 'twas just like one
> That hath a little fingering on the lute
> Yet cannot tune it.           (2.4.34–6)

One of the ways in which Iago cultivates his appearance of honesty is by pretending to the practice of harmony, and it is through music that he effects the vital first stage of his plot, the undoing of Cassio. Despite Iago's disparaging remarks, Othello has undoubtedly made the right decision in appointing Cassio to the lieutenantship. As an 'arithmetician' (1.1.19) he should know something about recent revolutionary developments in the art of fortification.[5] The defence of Mediterranean

islands at this time centred on their fortified ports, thus, rather than requiring a soldier who can 'set a squadron in the field' (1.1.22), Othello needs someone to design and build the new star-shaped defences and to calculate the track of tunnels for the laying of mines. Cassio is not, however, completely 'bookish', for during the course of the play he proves himself to be an accomplished swordsman. Both Othello and the Venetian Senate have the greatest confidence in him, and at the end of the play the governorship of the island falls to him quite naturally. Unfortunately, he has two weaknesses – a bad head for drink and a basic insecurity regarding his position in society. He presents himself as a gentleman from Florence but is slightly uneasy in the role. In his description of Desdemona to Montano (2.1.61–87), and in his manner of greeting her when she lands in Cyprus, he is seen striving just a little too hard to be courtly, and it is this excess which gives Iago his chance: 'Ay, smile upon her, do. I will gyve thee in thine own courtship' (2.1.170). This social unease is further emphasized by his ambivalent attitude to Iago's songs on the Court of Guard. He is beguiled by the music but he is also wary of it. He is not sufficiently sure of himself and his own social standing to risk behaving in what some might consider to be an improper manner.

> *Cassio.* Fore God, this is a more exquisite song than the other.
> *Iago.* Will you hear't again?
> *Cassio.* No; for I hold him to be unworthy of his place that does those things.           (2.3.91ff)

Roderigo has already drunk 'potations pottle deep', and Iago has 'flustered with flowing cups' the three remaining guards (2.3.47ff). By persuading Cassio to accept a drink, staging a

---

[5] E.g. the bastioned trace developed by Italian engineers at the beginning of the sixteenth century – extremely thick walls with projecting bastions able to withstand artillery bombardment.

rowdy drinking song and organizing a fight, Iago has corrupted the entire 'Court and Guard of safety'. A single drunken man might be overlooked but not a noisy brawl involving all members of the watch. Othello has decreed that the island should be free to celebrate both the sinking of the Turkish fleet and his own marriage – again a perfectly balanced combination of the public and private life – but the islanders can only do this in safety if those on watch are keeping to their duty. The decree is made in the form of a direct address by Othello's herald to the audience – not a stage rabble as in most eighteenth- and nineteenth-century editions[6] – thus bringing that audience into some measure of active involvement in the situation.

The original audience cannot have been ignorant of the spectacular advances of the Turks in the Mediterranean, as they were a matter for public concern and well documented.[7] Cyprus had in fact fallen to the Turks in 1571 and Hakluyt's *Voyages* includes an eyewitness account written by a Venetian nobleman.[8] He tells how the Venetian garrison of Famagusta eventually surrendered after a siege lasting nearly six months on promise of a safe conduct to Candy (Crete), but that the promise was not kept. Almost the entire garrison was murdered or taken as slaves and one of its commanding officers skinned alive.

Appended to *The Mahumetane or Turkish History* published in 1600 are two short tracts, 'The Narration of the Wars of Cyprus'[9] and 'The Causes of the Greatness of the Turkish Empire'. This last attempts an analysis of the reasons for Turkish success and concludes that, in contrast with the Turkish forces, the Christians at all levels of command were badly disciplined and too preoccupied with their own differences and jealousies:

we are desperately diseased, even to the death, our soldiers being mutinous, factious, disobedient, who fashioned by no rules of discipline, contained in duty by no regard of punishment ... which is as common to the captains and commanders as the private soldiers, a number of whom studying their particular revenge, their private ambition or (than which with men of war there is naught more odious) their servile gain, betray their country, neglect their princes' command and without executing aught worthy their trust and employment cause often impediments through malicious envy of another's glory, to whatsoever might be worthily executed.

In this context, it becomes clear that Shakespeare's play is very much more than the 'most famous story of sexual jealousy ever written'.[10] Othello's and Desdemona's love is presented as quite inseparable from their management of state affairs, while Iago's jealousy of both Cassio and Othello, and the factious quarrel which he engineers on the Court of Guard, is part of an examination of the ways in which personal rivalries can affect and be affected by wider political issues. This marks a departure from Cinthio's story, in which the geographical change of scene from Venice to Cyprus is incidental and bears no stated military or political significance, and where no mention is made of the Moor's ability in his public life. Shakespeare presents a man who has been entrusted with a large measure of the safety and commercial interest of the Venetian state, and who, for the first half of the play, seems capable of fulfilling that trust. Iago's plan demands a reversal of Othello's values of love and loyalty, and the first stage of this plan is effected by the drinking song directed against Cassio.

The song instructs the drinkers to forget

---

6 Cf. Capell, 'A street. People moving in it. Trumpets. Enter a Herald attended.' Malone, 'Enter a Herald with a proclamation; People following.'

7 Richard Hakluyt, *The Principal Navigations, Voyages and Discoveries of the English Nation* (London, 1589, enlarged 1598–1600); *The Mahumetane or Turkish History*, trans. R. Carr *et al.* (London, 1600); Richard Knolles, *The General History of the Turks* (London, 1603; subsequent editions 1610, 1621, 1631, 1638).

8 Hakluyt, vol. 2.1.121ff (1599).

9 *The Mahumetane or Turkish History*, Hh 4ᵛ.

10 Publicity for RSC production of *Othello*, 1985.

their public duty to the wider issues and longer time-scheme of the state and to concentrate instead on the personal pleasure that one man can snatch during a single lifetime:

> A soldier's a man;
> O, man's life's but a span;
> Why, then, let a soldier drink.  (2.3.66–8)

Cassio makes one last attempt to refer back to the public situation by proposing 'the health of our General', which Montano is quick to second; but Iago prevents the drinking of the toast by launching into a second song, 'King Stephen'.

This song is a single stanza from the middle of a traditional ballad entitled 'Bell, my wife' or 'The old cloak' and survives in Bishop Percy's manuscript. The nineteenth-century editors of the manuscript, Furnivall and Hales, describe 'a controversy between the spirits of Social Revolution and Social Conservatism. The man is anxious to better himself, no longer content to tend cows and drive the plough; his neighbours are rising and advancing around him; the clown is not now distinguishable from the gentleman.'[11] The song takes the form of a conversation between the shepherd and Bell, his wife. She wants him to get up and tend the cow, taking his old cloak about him; he wants to improve his attire – and his social standing – and go to court. Eventually, to save an argument, he gives in.

It is one of Bell's stanzas stressing the need for order and degree that Iago is singing, but in the ballad the king in question is King Harry.[12] Iago's change to King Stephen is interesting. Holinshed stresses that Stephen was a generous king but that he was directly responsible for the terrible civil wars that raged throughout his reign, 'having usurped another man's rightful inheritance'. He had sworn an oath of allegiance to King Henry I's queen, the Empress Maud, but broke this oath because of an 'ambitious desire to reign'. His arrival in England had been marked by a terrible thunderstorm which 'seemed against nature and therefore it was the more noted as a fore-

showing of some trouble and calamity to come'. Holinshed also explains Stephen's unusual generosity and his decisions not to collect taxes as a deliberate policy of buying support in preparation for the inevitable wars with Maud.[13] Stephen's reign was, and still is, notorious as a time of civil strife and anarchy, yet Stephen himself has been placed within Bell's format of modesty and worthiness. Iago has turned Bell's words into a praise of anarchy and dubious virtue, while as always retaining his appearance of honesty. Thus Iago uses apparent harmony in order to start the process of setting down the pegs that make the music between Desdemona and Othello. By this time almost half the play has passed, and as yet Iago has not even started to work on Othello himself.

Having been undone in music, Cassio ironically reinforces his fall from favour in an attempt to create harmony. He takes it upon himself to provide the traditional musical awakening for the bride and groom on the morning after the wedding night and has hired musicians to perform this aubade. These musicians are playing wind instruments or 'pipes'. This is a neat visual and aural pun on the 'clyster pipes' that Iago has already said should be at Cassio's lips, and the bawdy jokes made by the Clown on the nature of anal wind music in this scene indicate that the connection is deliberate:

Clown. O, thereby hangs a tail.
Musician. Whereby hangs a tale, sir?
Clown. Marry, sir, by many a wind instrument that
    I know.  (3.1.8–11)

Whatever the exact identity of these musical pipes – and this of course would depend on the

---

11  Ed. J. W. Hales and F. J. Furnivall, *Bishop Percy's Folio Manuscript* (London, 1867–8), vol. 2, p. 320.
12  Another version of the ballad, printed in Allan Ramsay's *Tea Table Miscellany* (London, 1740), pp. 105–7, gives 'King Robert'.
13  Raphael Holinshed, *Chronicles*, 2 vols (1577), pp. 365–94.

particular resources of the company – the instruments must have double reeds (like modern oboe reeds) which produce a nasal sound: 'Why, masters, ha' your instruments been in Naples, that they speak i' th' nose thus?' (3.1.3). Instruments of this kind might be blown directly, or attached to a bag (i.e. a bagpipe). The latter might be implied by the Clown's line 'put up your pipes in your bag' (3.1.19), while the phallic imagery could be emphasized visually by means of the distinctive upturned shape of the crumhorn.

Cassio behaves correctly in considering that music is necessary for the occasion, but he displays an inordinate lack of taste in his choice of such music. The Clown's comments indicate that it is coarse and crude and not suitable as an aubade for the newly married pair, and reports that the General would only be happy if the musicians could play music that cannot be heard. Of course neither the Clown nor the musicians take this to mean any more than that they should pack up and go away, but the line refers back to Othello and his wishes. He enjoys music. Even at the height of his rage he can be moved by the recollection that his wife 'sings, plays and dances well' (3.3.189). In desiring music that cannot be heard he is demanding the music of the spheres which is inaudible to the ears of fallen man but which alone would be a suitable accompaniment to his love for his wife.[14]

As the audible music in the play gets noticeably falser, so both Othello and Desdemona find it progressively more difficult to effect the harmony of true partnership. As her husband becomes unaccountably difficult and distant, she admits to Cassio that her 'advocation is not now in tune' (3.4.124). Similarly, as Iago drives in the wedge that alienates him from his wife, Othello finds that without her the very sounds intrinsic to his life no longer have any meaning for him:

> O, now for ever
> Farewell the tranquil mind, farewell content,
> Farewell the plumed troops and the big wars

> That makes ambition virtue. O, farewell.
> Farewell the neighing steed and the shrill trump,
> The spirit-stirring drum, th' ear-piercing fife,
> The royal banner, and all quality,
> Pride, pomp, and circumstance, of glorious war.
> And O ye mortal engines whose rude throats
> Th' immortal Jove's dread clamours counterfeit,
> Farewell. Othello's occupation's gone.

(3.3.351–61)

The farewell to the type of music which, according to classical theory,[15] had been thought capable of raising men to noble acts, the 'spirit-stirring drum, th' ear-piercing fife' emphasizes Othello's rejection of his public duty and demonstrates that just as with Cassio on the Court of Guard, the attack on the private man is resulting in the destruction of the public one. The terror of his situation lies in the fact that he and Desdemona had been so close that they had become indeed the 'beast with two backs', the hermaphrodite image of perfect love of which Aristophanes speaks in Plato's *Symposium* (189ff) and which Iago parodies in sexual terms in the first scene of the play (1.1.118). Thus casting off Desdemona is like trying to cut himself in half – it inevitably leads to his own destruction. Everything that he had ever lived for, including his public life established before he met Desdemona, is gone. He feels that he no longer exists, and refers to himself in the third person as 'Othello'. The long 'temptation' scene in which this speech occurs is preceded by a deceptively short and seemingly insignificant scene (3.2) in which Othello enters with his aides, dispatches a letter to the Senate, and then departs to inspect

---

[14] Ross, *Shakespeare Quarterly*, 17, pp. 117–18. I am grateful to Mr Andrew Pinnock for drawing my attention to the fact that the Musician's reply 'We have none such' is also a contemporary musical joke, since 'Nonesuch' was the name of a popular tune.

[15] Modes, rhythms and instruments were all considered to be capable of affecting the human spirit either for good or bad; cf. Aristotle, *Politics*, 8.5.8–9.

the fortifications. This is his last act of official business in the play, and it now becomes apparent that this six-line scene has marked the climax of Othello's career and that its position as the central scene of the play is a fitting one.

The fact that we, the audience, have already witnessed Iago's skilful manipulation of Cassio and Roderigo enables us to accept that his successful transformation of Othello is possible. The internal construction of act 3, scene 3 as a whole dramatizes the difficulty of Iago's task and shows the tightrope of expediency and luck on which he is walking. This scene is the longest in the play, and consists of constantly varying groups of characters: Desdemona, Cassio, and Emilia, with Othello and Iago entering later; Othello and Desdemona with Iago looking on; Othello and Iago; Othello; Othello and Desdemona with Emilia; Emilia with the handkerchief; Emilia and Iago; Iago; Iago and Othello. Throughout the scene, Othello keeps reiterating his belief in his wife's fidelity, a belief which is always first welcomed and then deftly punctured by Iago. By the end of the scene, the man who had been seen combining his domestic and public life with such ease – receiving and giving orders with Desdemona by his side, controlling his men and inspecting defences with a quiet because absolute authority – can now think of nothing except his wife's body and her supposed faithlessness, which eventually he comes to 'see' as clearly as if he had indeed the 'ocular proof' which he demands from Iago. He is tortured as much by the true picture of her virtues as by the false picture of her adultery, for, as Iago implies, those very qualities which attracted him must now be being used to attract others.

> *Othello.* Hang her. I do but say what she is: so delicate with her needle, an admirable musician – O, she will sing the savageness out of a bear – of so high and plenteous wit and invention.
>
> *Iago.* She's the worse for all this.     (4.1.183–7)

Iago's disparagement and suspicion of Desdemona's musical and other qualities is almost immediately challenged by the sound of a Venetian trumpet. Desdemona enters, fulfilling both her official duties and her family ones by having received Lodovico who has brought a letter from the Venetian Senate and who is also her kinsman. The entire incident and her precedence is a threat to Iago's plan, and he abruptly interrupts their conversation, thus demonstrating that he now has Cassio's place and rank. The situation then turns back to Iago's advantage, for Desdemona seizes the opportunity to talk about Cassio, and Othello, whose language even while accepting the letter consisted of words with normally sexual connotations – 'I kiss the instrument of their pleasures' (4.1.213) – now uses *this* 'instrument' merely as a prop to cover his eavesdropping on Desdemona's and Lodovico's conversation. Finally, private passion conquers duty altogether as Othello strikes his wife in public.

Desdemona is now naturally distraught. Their next meeting, the so-called 'brothel scene' (4.2), ends with an agonizing promise of reconcilation in which for a few moments it seems that Othello was about to accept Desdemona's protestations of innocence. His simple insult, 'Impudent strumpet' (l. 82), gives way to a progression of questions – 'Are not you a strumpet?', 'What, not a whore?', 'Is 't possible?' – which seems to display an increasing uncertainty concerning her guilt. This then prompts Desdemona's plea to heaven to forgive them *both*, which is probably best delivered as a renewed attempt to stress the equality of their relationship and the truth of their mutual love. For a brief moment he seems to concur in this image of forgiveness – 'I cry you mercy, then' – but this is an illusion. The admission of his mistake is merely ironical and the phrase which follows is a rejection of her and everything that she has just said: 'I took you for that cunning whore of Venice / That married with Othello' (4.2.90–1). For a second time he casts her away, and for a second time he calls himself by his name 'Othello'. After he has gone, she summons Iago and asks him to mediate for her. The trumpets sound for an official dinner and he prompts her back to her public role with the promise 'all things shall be well' (4.2.172). The biblical echoes in this phrase are ironic. She has just been kneeling to him as Othello had knelt earlier,[16] and Iago enjoys the role of father confessor.

In the next scene, as Lodovico takes his leave, Othello 'looks gentler than he did', but Desdemona, still with no clear conception of what is wrong, is haunted by the old song her mother's maid Barbary sang when her lover 'proved mad, / And did forsake her' – the 'willow song'.

The major significance of this scene is not so much that the song is sung as that it is broken off. The story of the song is too close to Desdemona's own situation to be borne, and she first muddles the order of the stanzas before finally stopping altogether, unable to go on. By this stage in the play, Desdemona is the only character who is still 'in tune'. It is vital therefore that her song should be well performed. She is an accomplished musician and must be seen to be so, otherwise the double collapse of her song is meaningless or merely embarrassing.

One of the two possible settings of the song identified by Sternfeld[17] – and the one which bears the closest resemblance to the words as given in the Folio – contains some striking harmonic modulations in the lute accompaniment which greatly increase the impact of the tune, while cadences in the lute part sound through rests in the vocal line to give the effect of sighs. The music therefore performs the task of expressing Desdemona's misery. The boy actor is not required to contribute his own emotions. All he is asked to do is to sing and play – the music will do the rest.

The song has two important dramatic functions. It displays Desdemona's emotional state and manipulates the audience's response to her. In her previous conversation with Emilia she has reiterated her beliefs concerning her marriage to Othello, but the audience, who

alone have the benefit of knowing exactly what is happening, may well be feeling that Emilia's worldly view is more sensible and pragmatic. The song has the effect of stripping away the accidentals in the current situation and reminding us not only of what love might be but also of the nature of Othello's and Desdemona's love before Iago set to work. It speaks directly to the hearts and minds of the audience, and has the effect of making us appreciate the absolute truth of what Desdemona represents as opposed to the worldly truth of Emilia's observations. This reaction to her is exactly the same as that which Othello has always experienced. He recognizes that she can 'sing the savageness out of a bear' and is afraid of the power of her words. He refuses to allow the rational force of words to interfere with his irrational passion. He is afraid that she will render him incapable of performing the task that he has set himself – the necessary, rightful killing of a woman who has wronged him: 'I'll not expostulate with her lest her body and beauty unprovide my mind again' (4.1.200). But it is not her body and beauty which weaken his resolve, for he comes to her while she is asleep and kisses her, exulting in her beauty but still quite firm in his intentions. The act of expostulation of course necessitates talking to her, and this he is not prepared to risk. When she wakes, he stops her expression of pity and tenderness for his overwrought state and prevents her explaining her motivations and actions. She realizes her danger, and her line 'Kill me tomorrow, let me live tonight' (5.2.84) is a last attempt to restore sanity to the situation. She knows that if only she could talk to him, all things would indeed be well, a brief moment is all that is needed, 'But half an hour ... But while I say one prayer' (ll.86–8). But the entire play is organized so that there is not one scene which presents the two of them talking privately

---

16 3.3.464.
17 *The London Book*, British Library Add. MS 15117, f. 18.

together, and part of the horrific quality of the 'brothel' scene arises from the fact that he has set up the interview in order to prove her guilt and is not talking *to* her but *at* her.

Othello takes his revenge, only to learn immediately that it is not after all complete and that Cassio is not dead: 'Not Cassio killed? Then murder's out of tune / And sweet revenge grows harsh' (5.2.118–19). For Othello at this instant, imbued with Iago's false music, harmony could only be achieved if both adulterous lovers had died.

It is left to Emilia, whose part is greatly strengthened in the Folio, to take over the feminine strength of the play after Desdemona's death[18] to bring Othello to a recognition of the truth. With the dawning of understanding, Othello's language reverts to normal. For the first time since he came to suspect his wife he considers himself as a soldier rather than simply an aggrieved husband. Now, again, he is able to talk with some ease about the two things which were dearest to him – his profession and his love – but this time his rejection of Desdemona has been absolute and irreversible and for a third time he refers to himself in the third person: 'Man but a rush against Othello's breast, / And he retires. Where should Othello go?' (5.2.273–4), and then again some ten lines later: 'That's he that was Othello; here I am.'

The very construction of Othello's final speech serves to underline all that is lost in the tragedy. His reminder that he has done the state some service gives way to personal thoughts both of Desdemona, the 'pearl' he has thrown away, and of his own nature. These are then combined as he repeats the service to the state which he had once performed in Aleppo by killing a foreigner who had harmed a Venetian.

> And say besides that in Aleppo once,
> Where a malignant and a turbaned Turk
> Beat a Venetian and traduced the state,
> I took by th' throat the circumcised dog,
> And smote him – thus.          (5.2.355)

On one level this is a vengeful triumph for Iago's white racism: the 'old black ram' has been justly punished for tupping the white ewe (1.1.90). On another, Iago as devil has achieved his ends, for according to conventional Christian belief both of his victims are damned – she for perjuring herself in laying claim to the sin of suicide (5.1.127) and he for the double sin of murder and self-murder. But neither of these possible views can be uppermost in the audience's mind. Emilia's swan-song, the 'willow, willow' refrain, reminds the audience of Desdemona's song and the dramatic reality which it created. The fact that love is unrequited is also proof that love exists. The protagonists of the play may be dead, but for those left alive – including those members of the audience who did not hang up their brains along with their hats on entering the theatre – the possibility of love remains. The tune that Iago was calling – the declaration that love is 'merely a lust of the blood and a permission of the will' (1.3.333) – is broken not with the torture that Lodovico has ordered but by the results of what he himself has engineered. The 'tragic loading of the bed' is a positive reminder not only of what might have been, but of what might be.

18 E. A. J. Honigmann, 'Shakespeare's revised plays: *King Lear* and *Othello*', *The Library* Series 6, vol. 4 (London, 1982), p. 159.

# THE 'AENEID' IN 'THE TEMPEST'

## ROBERT WILTENBURG

Even those sympathetic to source studies may well feel that enough has been said about the sources of *The Tempest*. More than most of the plays, it seems to be a rich confluence of elements drawn from Shakespeare's diverse reading, conversation, and theatrical experience. So many things float to the surface here: contemporary excitement over the exploration and colonization of the New World; bits of Italian and Spanish history and fiction involving usurpations, flights, islands, and returns; scenes and techniques from the ongoing human comedy of *commedia dell'arte* improvisations; some of Montaigne's reflections on nature and society, anger and restraint; and a fascination with magic, man's power to influence, and perhaps control, nature outside and inside himself and others, by the power of his 'art'.[1] Yet no one of these predominates, or presents a sufficiently strong matrix of incident and character to constitute a primary source. Kenneth Muir spoke for many readers, I suspect, when he concluded that, whatever the variety of his materials, 'it seems . . . likely that for once he [Shakespeare] invented the plot'.[2]

Others, however, have felt that something is still missing in our account of the play and its sources; among them, Muir himself, who twenty years earlier had voiced the opposite opinion that, although 'there were . . . a number of minor sources . . . it is highly probable that there was a main source as yet unidentified'.[3] Indeed, Shakespeare character-istically writes in response to a story. He does sometimes take inert lumps of chronicle history or philosophic speculation and transform them into things rich and strange, but his most frequent way with sources is to take an old story, badly or somehow inadequately or incompletely told, and tell it again. I believe the *Aeneid* is the main source of the play in this sense, not the source of the plot (though it does provide many incidental and verbal details and parallels), but the work to which Shakespeare is primarily responding, the story he is retelling.

The claims for the *Aeneid* in this respect have not been much considered, in part perhaps because they were so obvious. Source hunters instinctively prefer the secret, the subtle, and the arcane, but even groundlings have heard of Dido and Aeneas, and one needs not to be much of a classical scholar to spot the allusion to Virgil in Ariel's harpy-like entrance in act 3. Critics have not made much of this material: Muir speaks of the 'curious echoes' from the *Aeneid*; Frank Kermode feels 'that Shakespeare has Virgil in mind'; Geoffrey Bullough, in his authoritative account of the narrative and dramatic sources, does not even bother to

---

[1] For accounts of the sources, see Frank Kermode's new Arden edition (Cambridge, Mass., 1958); Kenneth Muir's *The Sources of Shakespeare's Plays* (London, 1977); and Geoffrey Bullough's *Narrative and Dramatic Sources of Shakespeare*, vol. 8 (London and New York, 1975).

[2] Muir, *Sources*, p. 283.

[3] *Shakespeare's Sources* (London, 1957), p. 261.

mention the *Aeneid*.[4] Some critics may have felt, with Chesterton, that 'a debt to Virgil is like a debt to Nature'. Others seem to have contented themselves with the reflection that since the *Aeneid*, at least in its first four to six books, was a chief text of contemporary education, it could be regarded as a common quarry of ideas and effects, requiring no special attention.[5]

The true significance of the *Aeneid* for the play may also have been obscured for a time by the misguided enthusiasm of Colin Still's *The Timeless Theme*.[6] Colin Still, a theosophical crank, was interested in *The Tempest* only insofar as it could be interpreted as an allegorical illustration of the 'timeless theme' he perceived as underlying all religions and all great literature, including (but not limited to) the Bible, Homer, Virgil, Dante, the mystical texts of the Zohar, Shakespeare, and Milton. Yet, for all the crude forcing of the evidence to very narrow preconceptions, Still made some valuable connections between the poem and the play. He noticed the exchange between Adrian and Gonzalo (2.1.79–84) concerning the identity of Carthage with Tunis (Gonzalo is wrong of course, Tunis is only near what had been Carthage), he remarked the general similarity of the interrupted voyage from Tunis to Naples to that of Aeneas' voyage from Carthage (near Tunis) to Cumae (near Naples), and he suggested that the experiences of Alonso's party in the enchanted island are comparable in several respects to those of Aeneas in the underworld.

Much useful work was done by J. M. Nosworthy, who identified several structural and verbal parallels, and demonstrated that Shakespeare has drawn directly upon the description of the storm and landing in *Aeneid* 1, both for general inspiration and for many specifics. He noted that both poem and play open with a storm and shipwreck in the present, then introduce the antecedent action, or 'causal plot' as he calls it, through Aeneas' narrative to

Dido, and Prospero's to Miranda, before beginning the present action or 'effectual plot'. He further demonstrated in detail that 'Shakespeare's tempest and Virgil's storm are analogous in origin and outcome. Both are provoked by supernatural means to ensure that a certain character shall arrive at a certain requisite locality and there be brought into relation with other characters.' He cited parallels between furious Juno and angry Prospero as authors of the storms, between Aeolus and Ariel as their agents (one of whom, we may note, will be rewarded with a wife, the other with his freedom); between the isolation of Ferdinand to effect his meeting with Miranda, and the relative isolation of Aeneas (he never loses his *fidus Achates*) to effect his meeting with Dido; and finally, between the supernatural preservation of mariners and ships in both. Beyond the storm and its consequences he cited verbal borrowings from *Aeneid* 1 and 4, the most significant of which go to form part of Ceres' speech to Iris in the masque of act 4, and Ferdinand's first encounter with Miranda, palpably based upon Aeneas' recognition of his mother Venus ('O dea certe') in *Aeneid* 1.[7] My intention here is not to multiply specific parallels, useful as that might be (though I will suggest one later), but to assess what Nosworthy calls the 'pervasive influence' of the poem on the play. In what follows, I will argue that Shakespeare has imitated, with important differences, the main pattern of Virgil's poem in its beginning, middle, and

---

[4] Muir, *Sources*, p. 282; Kermode, new Arden, p. xxxiv, n. 2.

[5] T. W. Baldwin, *William Shakspere's 'Small Latine & Lesse Greeke'*, 2 vols (Urbana, 1944), vol. 2, pp. 495–6. Baldwin remarks (p. 479) that 'there can be no doubt that Shakspere knew a great deal about [the *Aeneid*]. He refers frequently to characters and incidents, but these would be known to almost everyone. They were in the air as it were.'

[6] *The Timeless Theme: A Critical Theory Formulated and Applied* (London, 1936).

[7] J. M. Nosworthy, 'The Narrative Sources of *The Tempest*', *Review of English Studies*, 24 (1948), 281–94.

end; that is, in its situation, development, and resolution.[8]

Shakespeare takes as his 'given' for the play what we may call the Virgilian situation, a situation characterized by tempests, defiled banquets, and 'widowhood'. First in both poem and play is the tempest itself. In the play, it reflects the state of moral disorder occasioned by the usurpation, now dramatized as a physical disorder to effect Prospero's present purpose. But in the poem the tempest expresses a continuing relation between man and the gods, Juno in particular, whose hostility makes man's voyaging, man's history, a continual series of tempests – physical, personal, and social – the end of which remains, in the poem, promised but not achieved. The effect of these tempests, whether within man or outside him, is not so much ruin as separation. As Shakespeare's mariners cry out in the first scene when the ship appears to be lost:

> Mercy on us! –
> We split, we split! – Farewell, my wife and
> children! –
> Farewell, brother! – We split, we split, we
> split! (1.1.59–61)[9]

This is also Aeneas' situation in the first half of the *Aeneid*. His narrative of his voyage is punctuated with painful, helpless splittings and farewells. First of all to Troy itself; as Panthus says to him while they are still within the burning city:

> venit summa dies et ineluctabile tempus
> Dardaniae. fuimus Troes, fuit Ilium et ingens
> gloria Teucrorum; ferus omnia Iuppiter argos
> transtulit. 2.324–7)

This is the hour which no effort of ours can alter. We Trojans are no more; no more is Ilium; no more the splendour of Teucrian glory. All now belongs to Argos; it is Jupiter's remorseless will.[10]

Then there is Aeneas' farewell to his wife Creusa, inadvertently left behind in the escape from the city. Aeneas returned to search for her and reports:

> ausus quin etiam voces iactare per umbram
> implevi clamore vias, maestusque Creusam
> nequiquam ingeminans iterumque iterumque
> vocavi. (2.768–70)

I even risked shouting through the darkness. Again and again I filled the streets with my cries in useless repetition, as in my grief I called out Creusa's name.

He refuses to be consoled when her spirit argues the divinely ordained necessity of their separation: 'lacrimantem et multa volentem / dicere deseruit, tenuisque recessit in auras' (2.790–1) ('though I wept and longed to say so much, she forsook me and vanished into thin air'). Similar are the losses or leavetakings from many companions and friends, culminating in the loss, just when destiny seemed within reach, of his father Anchises:

> hinc Drepani me portus et inlaetabilis ora
> accipit. hic pelagi tot tempestatibus actus
> heu! genitorem, omnis curae casusque
> levamen,
> amitto Anchisen . . . hic labor extremus
> (3.707–10–14)

At last I found a harbour at Drepanum, but there was no joy for me on that shore. For here, after all the persecution of the ocean-storms, O bitterness! I lost my father, lost Anchises my solace in every adventure and care . . . This blow was my last anguish.

---

[8] Gary Schmidgall, in *Shakespeare and the Courtly Aesthetic* (Berkeley, 1981), has argued that *The Tempest* represents 'a highly compact version of Virgil's epic of a lost civilization rewon' (p. 75), another 'symbolic chronicle of the ascendancy of *imperium* over *violentia*' (p. 173), in which the heroes are 'subjected to the same tensions' and achieve similar resolutions (p. 169). While I would agree with much of what Schmidgall says, I believe that he overstates the similarities, and ignores the vital differences through which we can observe Shakespeare's *response* to Virgil.

[9] All quotations are from the new Arden edition.

[10] All citations from Virgil are taken from the Loeb Classical Library text of H. Rushton Fairclough, rev. ed. (London, Cambridge, Mass., 1935). The translation, unless otherwise noted, is that of W. F. Jackson Knight (Baltimore, 1958).

Throughout his journeys, Aeneas searches for a home, a place to rest. He prays at Delos, 'da propriam, Thymbraee, domum, da moenia fessis / et genus et mansuram urbem' (3.85–6) ('Apollo, grant us a home of our own. We are weary. Give us a walled city which shall endure, and a lineage of our blood') Yet without the gods' permission, and without full knowledge of their intentions, he finds only a series of false havens. Immediately after the departure from Troy he attempts to build the city of Aeneadae, only to be driven from the place by the shocking discovery of the bleeding bush, his old comrade Polydorus. His settlement on Crete also begins well, until 'subito cum tabida membris, / corrupto caeli tractu, miserandaque venit / arboribusque satisque lues et letifer annus' (3.137–9) ('falling from some poisoned part of the sky, a heartbreaking pestilence attacked and rotted trees, crops, and men, and the only yield of that season was death'). Aeneas' experience in the Strophades, the Turning Islands inhabited by the Harpies, follows the same pattern. He and his men make no attempt to settle there, but raid herds of cattle and goats, invite the gods to 'share their plunder', and '[build] seats of turf along the curving shore and [start] on a rich feast'. Suddenly the Harpies are upon them, defiling the food with their filth, and cursing Aeneas and his men as usurpers of their possessions and place. Their leader cries:

> bellum etiam pro caede boum stratisque
>     iuvencis,
> Laomedontiadae, bellumne inferre paratis
> et patrio Harpyias insontis pellere regno?
> accipite ergo animis atque haec mea figite
>     dicta.          (3.247–50)

You would fight for these slaughtered bullocks? And drive us innocent Harpies from our rightful realm? Attend then to my words.

– whereupon she prophesies a hunger so great that they will some day 'eat their tables'.

Shakespeare imitates this episode in 3.3 to make a similar point about pleasant delusions and false security to the 'three men of sin', Alonso, Antonio, and Sebastian. Ariel presents, and then harpy-like removes, a spectral banquet, emblematic of the delusive pleasures their forgotten crime against Prospero, their usurpation of his possessions and his place, has apparently secured. As the Harpies rebuke Aeneas for his misperception of what is pleasing to the gods, so Ariel reminds the three of their crime and of the superintending powers, which may delay, but do not forget.

Both ideas, that of the tempest, of man buffeted and isolated by forces he does not control, and that of the defiled banquet, of finding his desires and perceptions delusive, come to their most poignant focus in the idea of 'widowhood'. The passage in the play in which this idea appears has long been a puzzle:

*Adrian.* Tunis was never grac'd before with such a paragon to their Queen.
*Gonzalo.* Not since widow Dido's time.
*Antonio.* Widow! a pox o' that! How came that widow in? widow Dido!
*Sebastian.* What if he had said 'widower Aeneas' too? Good Lord, how you take it!
*Adrian.* 'Widow Dido' said you? you make me study of that: she was of Carthage, not of Tunis.
          (2.1.71–9)

Kermode would defend this passage against those who find in it only 'dreary puns' indicative of Shakespeare's 'fatigue', but concedes that the 'apparently trivial allusions to the theme of Dido and Aeneas [have] never been properly explained', and holds out the hope that 'our frame of reference is badly adjusted, or incomplete, and that an understanding of this passage will modify our image of the whole play'.[11] The immediate effect of the exchange is clear enough. We are given yet another example of the contrasting perspectives of the pompous and conventional Adrian and Gonzalo, and the cynical and ironic

---

[11] Kermode, new Arden, pp. 46–7, nn. 74–8.

Antonio and Sebastian. Gonzalo's phrase is pedantically correct (Dido was, in fact, the widow of Sychaeus), but also attempts to cast a mantle of respectability over this most notorious example of *indignus amor*. Antonio and Sebastian take the brutal view, widows being proverbially lustful, and (as Kermode suggests) they may even be indulging in familiar puns hinging on Dido – die, do; and Aeneas – any ass.

Yet I believe Shakespeare intends a further point for the reader of Virgil who is neither a fool nor a cynic. Rightly understood, the phrases 'widow Dido' and 'widower Aeneas' touch Virgil's presentation of the human situation at a vital point. In the view that dominates the first half of the poem (and still continues in the second), all are widows, all are widowers. All are necessarily bereft of, or separated from, what they most want, need, or love, whether in the form of a lost friend, brother, father, wife, husband, or city; or of a destiny promised but nowhere apparent. As Aeneas pitifully complains to Venus in Book 1:

quid natum totiens, crudelis tu quoque, falsis
ludis imaginibus? cur dextrae iungere dextram
non datur ac veras audire et reddere voces?

(1.407–9)

Ah, you are too cruel! Why again and again deceive your own son with mocking disguises? Why may I not join hand to hand, hear you in frankness, and speak to you in return?

In this situation, all desires, whether for knowledge, rest, intimacy, or consolation, must go unsatisfied or (what is often worse) incompletely satisfied, leaving men 'split' or 'widowed' from their own good. Virgil stresses the pathetic quality of this condition, and the tragic paradox whereby man's desperate attempts to find satisfaction merely drive him further from his best self and from his destiny. Both the pathos and the paradox are most fully explored in the story of Dido. She has fled to Africa and founded Carthage in the wake of her brother's brutal murder of her husband, Sychaeus. When Aeneas arrives, she has already proven herself as a builder and lawgiver, a shrewd and beneficent queen. An important condition, perhaps even source, of her purposefulness and self-sufficiency is that she has, as she says, 'Been irrevocably resolved never again to desire a union in wedlock with any man, since the time when death's treachery cheated me of my first love ... For he who first united me with him took all love out of my life' ('si mihi non animo fixum immotumque sederet, / ne cui me vinclo vellem sociare iugali, / postquam primus amor deceptam morte fefellit ... ille meos, primus qui me sibi iunxit, amores / abstulit', 4.15–17 ... 28–9). Yet now, Venus and Cupid have 'poisoned' her and Aeneas has 'stirred [her] heart to wavering' for the first time. She resists as best she can, but finally her own intemperate desires and the inflammatory counsels of her sister, 'set Dido's heart, already kindled, ablaze with new access of love, gave new hope to tempt her wavering intention, and broke down her scruples' ('his dictis incensum animum inflammavit amore / spemque dedit dubiae menti solvitque pudorem', 4.54–5). Virgil touchingly portrays her hesitations and indirections in revealing this love to Aeneas. But finally, with the connivance of Venus and Juno, they are driven together and make love in the cave. Virgil comments:

ille dies primus leti primusque malorum
causa fuit. neque enim specie famave movetur
nec iam furtivum Dido meditatur amorem;
coniugium vocat; hoc praetexit nomine
culpam.                                    (4.169–72)

On that day were sown the seeds of suffering and death. Henceforth Dido cared no more for appearances or her good name, and ceased to take any thought for secrecy in her love. She called it a marriage; she used this word to screen her sin.

Through this sad self-deception and Aeneas' subsequent desertion, Dido becomes a 'widow' twice over, and the chief example of the broken relations throughout the poem.

Worst of all, in losing Aeneas she loses not only her love but also herself, for she can no longer hide from herself that, in her dream of a satisfying love and 'marriage', she has violated the sense of 'honour and its laws' that had sustained her. Only suicide, one final 'widow-hood', remains. This sense of 'widowhood', of continual bereavement, underlies the famed Virgilian sadness. It leads to the 'pity for a world's distress, and a sympathy for short-lived humanity' ('sunt lacrimae rerum et mentem mortalia tangunt', 1.462) that Aeneas is so moved to find when he first sees Troy's story, the recurring story of men and civili-zations, depicted in the temple at Carthage.

That Shakespeare was sensitive to this aspect of the *Aeneid* is clear from his extended treatment of the Dido and Aeneas story, or rather of the originals for the story, in *Antony and Cleopatra*. There, too, the Virgilian conflict between love and destiny, subjective desires and objective necessities, is at the centre of the play, though it is resolved in a quite un-Virgilian fashion. There, too, the principals are described as 'widow' and 'widower', and the question is even raised whether Antony's relation with Cleopatra does or does not amount to a 'marriage' (2.2.119–23). In *The Tempest*, most of the characters are also 'widowed'. Sebastian reproaches Alonso for 'making widows' in Milan and Naples by his ill-advised African marriage and voyage. All are separated from country or friends, fathers from sons, each from the others, and, as Gonzalo retrospectively remarks at the end, 'no man was his own', each is in some way separated from himself and his own good. Most obviously 'widowed' is Prospero himself, who, like Aeneas, is in fact a widower (though nothing is made of it), but more significantly, is separated from his place, his rights, his proper self. As he says to Miranda in act 1:

*Prospero*. Thy father was the Duke of Milan, and a
    prince of power.
*Miranda*. Sir, are you not my father?    (1.2.54–5)

Only at the very end will he be able to say:

*Prospero*.                know for certain
    That I am Prospero, and that very duke
    Which was thrust forth of Milan . . .
                              (5.1.158–60)

Yet in the play it is clear that while these separations may be common, they are neither normal nor inevitable; the powers may delay, but do not forget, and will assist in reuniting the 'widowed'.

Granted, then, that the initial situations in play and poem are overwhelmingly similar, what can men, particularly the heroes Aeneas and Prospero, do in these circumstances? What enables them to act at all? What do they attempt and achieve? What price do they pay for their achievement?

At the centre of the *Aeneid* is Aeneas' visit to the underworld. Book 6 begins with Aeneas weeping for the loss of his friend and steers-man Palinurus; it ends with his determination to pursue a glorious vision of the future Roman civilization. This change is effected by a vision of the continuity of human life and effort that compensates for the inevitable pain of 'widowhood'. In the underworld, the sense of bereavement is even more intense than in ordinary life, for here Aeneas must relive all at once the loss of his Trojan comrades, see for himself the pain he has inflicted on Dido, and feel her unrelenting hatred. Most painful of all is the encounter with his father, Anchises; in his joy at finding him, Aeneas cannot restrain himself and pleads:

> da iungere dextram,
> da, genitor, teque amplexu ne subtrahe nostro.
>                              (6.687–8)

Father, oh let me, let me, clasp your hand! Do not slip from my embrace!

Virgil comments:

> sic memorans largo fletu simul ora rigabat.
> ter conatus ibi collo dare bracchia circum,
> ter frustra comprensa manus effugit imago,
> par levibus ventis volucrique simillima
>     somno.                    (6.699–702)

As he spoke his face grew wet with the stream of tears. Three times he tried to cast his arms about his father's neck, but three times the clasp was vain and the wraith escaped his hands, like airy winds or the melting of a dream.[12]

Balancing this confrontation with the past, with all that has been suffered and lost (or never possessed) is the vision of his children, of Rome, of a new civilization greater than Troy, great enough to make his sufferings worthwhile. Anchises, his father and guide, having reviewed many figures from the coming 'glory', and having contrasted the genius of other cultures with that of Rome, concludes:

> tu regere imperio populos, Romane,
> memento
> (hae tibi erunt artes) pacique imponere
> morem,
> parcere subiectis et debellare superbos.
>
> (6.851–3)

But you, Roman, must remember that you have to guide the nations by your authority, for this is to be your skill, to graft tradition onto peace, to show mercy to the conquered, and to wage war until the haughty are brought low.

Here he finds, in the idea of that civilization and world order, a conception of his destiny worth sacrificing himself for, worth sacrificing others for. He emerges, purged of his grief, prepared for the struggles that follow.

*The Tempest* possesses no fully comparable 'centre', though as Still and, more recently, Jan Kott have suggested, the enchanted island itself is like the underworld: both are places set apart, divorced from the mainland or the upper world, providing a magical ground where past and future are brought together, to heal and to begin anew.[13] Moreover, several characters in *The Tempest* have central experiences similar in various respects to those of Aeneas. Alonso, 'bereft' of his son, experiences a sharp grief and later guilt strong enough to reawaken in him a sense of 'kindness', a sense of his connection with other men analogous to Aeneas' discovery of a sense of

connection in time. His son Ferdinand, who is 'something stain'd with grief . . . [and] . . . hath lost his fellows, and strays about to find 'em' (1.2.417–19), is, like Aeneas, prepared by grief and isolation for the vision of a better world in the person of Miranda.

Most important is, of course, Prospero himself, whose superiority depends, like that of Aeneas, upon his greater awareness of the continuities of the moral life. What sets him apart from the other characters and makes him their proper governor – though every major character, except Miranda, either wishes, imagines, plots, or claims to be a 'king' – are his greater capacities for memory and conscience, the moral bases of his art. Even the best of the others are, in comparison, a trifle obtuse: Miranda is unaware of her noble birth, and has only the faintest memories of her life before her exile; Ariel and Caliban both attempt rebellion and must be reminded of who they are, who they have been, and their consequent obligations to Prospero. Self-forgetfulness is also the problem of Alonso and his party, and the quality of their crime against Prospero. Their usurpation involved a forgetting and violation of the better part of their nature, the familial and social bonds of 'kindness'. Antonio forgot his brother, Alonso his brother prince. 'Kindness', meaning not only benevolence but an awareness of man's social nature, of his connectedness with other men, and the fulfilment of his natural obligations to them, cannot be created or imposed, but like the alchemist's gold 'within' the lead must be drawn out, realized, recovered. The recovery of 'kindness' in turn makes possible the transmutation of past experience. This is Prospero's method in reclaiming Alonso. He first separates father and son in order to expose Alonso's 'kindness', his overwhelming affection for Ferdinand. He then presents the accusatory

---

[12] Cf. 'We are such stuff as dreams are made on.'

[13] Kott, '*The Tempest*, or Repetition', *Mosaic*, 10, 3 (1977), 9–36.

harpy-like vision of 3.3 in which the 'three men of sin' are called upon to 'remember' their crime; and Alonso is specifically directed to interpret the loss of his son as retribution. His contemplation of that past action, now understood through a revived conscience, a revived and vivifying 'kindness', transmutes the crime to the penitence which Prospero defines as the condition of personal reunion and political restoration. Thus Prospero confronts, and enables others to confront, both the past and the future, and intertwines them in a living knot, devoted as he is to the causes of both justice and love.

While similarities predominate in the delineation of the human predicament, the differences come to the fore here, in the response to it. Aeneas begins the founding of the new city with his proposed marriage with the daughter of King Latinus, much as Prospero constructs his hopes for renewal on the marriage of Ferdinand and Miranda. But in the *Aeneid*, the marriage abrogates the previous understanding with Turnus, and provokes the disruptive intervention of Juno. Both possible marriages – Aeneas and Lavinia, Lavinia and Turnus – reflect the same painful division seen in the 'marriage' and separation of Aeneas and Dido, and elsewhere in the poem. The one is a marriage of state, the cold requirement of destiny, the other a marriage of passion, supported by the furious, possessive subjectivity of Turnus, and of Lavinia's mother, Queen Amata. Between these fatal extremes there is no middle ground. The result is the long warfare that occupies the rest of the poem and kills so many of Aeneas' friends, allies, and noble enemies.

The marriage Prospero promotes between Ferdinand and Miranda serves many of the same purposes as Aeneas' proposed marriage. It too is a marriage of state, uniting the rival powers of Naples and Milan, re-establishing order and providing for continued order and vitality. But this is also a marriage based in nature, in what Prospero calls the 'Fair encounter / Of two most rare affections'. And Prospero, like a wise gardener, takes great pains to manage this natural attraction, not denying their passion, but restraining it with the masque, with the 'sanctimonious ceremony' that prevents the 'weeds' of 'barren hate / Sour-ey'd disdain and discord'. His aims are modest. He hopes for no new world (only the naive Miranda and the perpetually naive Gonzalo could imagine that), but only for a fresh start. His project wins the favour of that same Juno who had implacably opposed Aeneas; as she sings in the masque:

> Honour, riches, marriage-blessing,
> Long continuance and increasing,
> Hourly joys be still upon you!
> Juno sings her blessings on you.    (4.1.106–9)

For both Aeneas and Prospero, the resolution of the action depends finally upon the sacrifice or renunciation of something in themselves. Yet the nature and effects of their respective sacrifices could hardly be more different. Again and again, events in the poem reinforce the sense that human aspiration is irremediably tragic, that the city of law and reason must be built on blood, that, as Jupiter had decreed in Book 1, only in the distant future will the 'terrible Gates of War' be shut and the 'ghastly Lust of Blood' chained up (1.293–6); until then, the establishment of civilization requires the sacrifice not only of man's weakness, but also part of his tenderness, his humanity. Aeneas must accept a guilty world and a guilty destiny, in which his public purpose requires the sacrifice of his private affections: to lead and to overcome, he must deny himself. But that sacrifice, the sacrifice of what one loves, exacts a terrible psychological price in Dido, in Turnus, in Aeneas, for it causes fury, the loss of reason, the loss of oneself, in which all the accumulated sadness and bitterness are destructively vented. The *Aeneid* ends not in triumph (though we know the cause of Rome has triumphed), but in fury and dismay:

stetit acer in armis
Aeneas, volvens oculos, dextramque
    repressit;
et iam iamque magis cunctantem flectere
    sermo
coeperat, infelix umero cum apparuit alto
balteus et notis fulserunt cingula bullis
Pallantis pueri, victum quem volnere Turnus
straverat atque umeris inimicum insigne
    gerebat.
ille, oculis postquam saevi monumenta
    doloris
exuviasque hausit, furiis accensus et ira
terribilis: 'tune hinc spoliis indute meorum
eripiare mihi? Pallas te hoc volnere, Pallas
immolat et poenam scelerato ex sanguine
    sumit,'
hoc dicens ferrum adverso sub pectore condit
fervidus. ast illi solvuntur frigore membra
vitaque cum gemitu fugit indignata sub
    umbras.                         (12.938–52)

Aeneas stood motionless, a fierce figure in his
armour; but his eyes were restless, and he checked
the fall of his right arm. And now at any moment
the plea of Turnus, already working in his mind,
might have prevailed on his hesitation, when suddenly, there before him, he saw slung over his
shoulder the accursed baldric of Pallas and his belt,
inset with the glittering rivets, which he had known
of old when they had belonged to his young friend
whom Turnus had brought low with a wound, and
overcome. This baldric Turnus was wearing now
over his own shoulder, and the trophy was fatal to
him. Aeneas' eyes drank in the sight of the spoils
which revived the memory of his own vengeful
bitterness. His fury kindled and, terrible in his rage,
he said: 'Are you to be stolen hence out of my grasp,
you who wear spoils taken from one whom I loved?
It is Pallas, only Pallas, who by this wound which I
now deal makes sacrifice of you; he exacts this
retribution, you criminal, from your blood.' Saying
this and boiling with rage he buried his blade full in
Turnus' breast. His limbs relaxed and chilled; and
the life fled, moaning, resentful, to the Shades.[14]

Prospero too must perform a renunciation, a
sacrifice of some part of himself (two of them,
in fact), yet his renunciations produce not
bitterness and fury, but peace within himself
and reconciliation with others. First is the

renunciation (which Aeneas could only
imagine) of his fury, in this case, his justifiable
anger at those who had imposed the long
separation upon him. Throughout the play he
has sought justice: restoration for his wronged
self and suffering for the guilty. But now the
prosecution of justice becomes for Prospero,
as earlier for Alonso, not an end in itself, but
the necessary preparation for the recovery of
kindness. As he says to Ariel:

> Hast thou, which art but air, a touch, a
>     feeling
> Of their afflictions, and shall not myself,
> One of their kind, that relish all as sharply
> Passion as they, be kindlier mov'd than thou
>     art?
> Though with their high wrongs I am struck
>     to th' quick,
> Yet with my nobler reason 'gainst my fury
> Do I take part: the rarer action is
> In virtue than in vengeance: they being
>     penitent,
> The sole drift of my purpose doth extend
> Not a frown further. Go release them, Ariel:
> My charms I'll break, their senses I'll restore,
> And they shall be themselves.        (5.1.21–32)

Even more telling than the renunciation of
his anger, is the renunciation of his art, the
'rough magic', the power to constrain others
to share his 'fancies'. Although it has not, so
far as I know, been remarked before, this
second renunciation closely resembles an
episode in *Aeneid* 5 involving two boxers,
Dares and Entellus (5.362–484). Dares, the
younger man, defies all comers (there are
none) until Entellus, the old champion, is
finally persuaded to oppose him. Entellus
embarrasses himself by missing a punch and
falling down, then in furious shame and rage

---

14 William S. Anderson (*The Art of the 'Aeneid'*, Englewood Cliffs, 1969) comments:
    killing Turnus is a victory for the cause, but not for
    Aeneas. In this final struggle between aspects of *pietas*,
    Aeneas can only be the loser. Triumphant he should
    never be; angry, I feel that I understand him better. It is
    his final assertion against (enslavement to?) the destiny
    that has almost dehumanized him . . . (p. 100).

overcomes and humiliates Dares, threatens to kill him, and does in the end celebrate his victory by smashing in the skull of the prize steer. He concludes: 'Here victorious I lay down the gauntlet and my art' ('hic victor cacstus artcmquc rcpono', 5.484).[15] This story presents several similarities to the conflict between Prospero and his younger brother Antonio – the younger man boldly supplanting the elder, his aggressive boasting and over-confidence; the elder's delayed response, initial irresolution and need for external encouragement; and finally, the complete victory of the aroused elder, and the restoration of his claims. But what is most striking is the contrast between the two final renunciations of one's 'art' or strength, one's mastery over others. For Entellus, it is an equivocal victory: he has won once more, but he is defeated by age. His youth and strength are gone, and his farewell to his 'art' is also a farewell to his younger and better self, a farewell to his place among men. Prospero, however, bids farewell to his worse self, the desire for control, for a mastery of his fellows that stands in the way of his own recovery of 'kindness', and his renunciation is not a farewell, but a readmission to humanity.

It is often observed that there is something 'fundamental' about The Tempest, and that the editors of the Folio may have arranged things better than they knew when they placed it first. I think that this analysis of its relation to the Aeneid helps us understand why this should be so. Both works address the most fundamental questions raised by the enterprise of civilization: what is required to establish and to renew our life in common? Both agree that the answer is 'sacrifice', yet differ essentially on the nature of that sacrifice (is it to be a part of what is best in us, or a part of what is worst?) and on the consequences of that sacrifice for the individual (will it be fury or 'kindness'?).

That Shakespeare should, in addressing these questions in his last major play, have turned to a reconsideration and reworking of the Virgilian pattern seems peculiarly appropriate, for the Aeneid was not only the chief document of the Latin civilization the Renaissance inherited, but also, in its incorporation and transcendence of the Homeric patterns, the most frequently recommended model for imitation, the best way of using and responding to the past.[16] Jan Kott has suggested that in The Tempest 'The Virgilian myths are invoked, challenged, and finally rejected'.[17] I think it is more accurate to say that Shakespeare treats Virgil much as Virgil had treated Homer. What were ends for the first writer have become means for the second.[18] Just as Virgil subsumed the Homeric stories of men who fight primarily for themselves to the story of a man who fights primarily for his culture, his concept of civilization, so Shakespeare has subsumed the search for law, for justice, the story told so well by Virgil, into his own larger story of the search for 'kindness', a richer concept of civilization, in which, in Yeats's words:

> all hatred driven hence,
> The soul recovers radical innocence
> And learns at last . . .
> . . . that its own sweet will is Heaven's will.[19]

---

15 Loeb translation.

16 On this point see, for example, Baldwin, 'Small Latine & Lesse Greeke', vol. 2, 457.

17 Kott, 'The Aeneid and The Tempest', Arion, 5, NS 3 (1976), p. 444.

18 Brooks Otis, in Virgil: A Study in Civilized Poetry (Oxford, 1963) remarks that 'Homer gave him [Virgil] a form, something of a style, a great deal of content, but not the essential idea or meaning, not the ideological truth he wanted to convey' (p. 384). And Kenneth Quinn, Virgil's 'Aeneid': A Critical Description (London, 1968): 'though so much of the Aeneid is taken from the Iliad and the Odyssey, nothing is any longer the same. Virgil's words constantly recall Homer, only somehow to challenge, even to reject Homer' (p. 46).

19 W. B. Yeats, 'A Prayer for my Daughter', ll. 65–9. On the general movement from one idea of civilization to another, see Robert S. Miola's recent discussion of Cymbeline (Shakespeare's Rome (Cambridge, 1983)) as the 'conclusion of Shakespeare's Roman vision', in which 'Roman pride is balanced by humility, Roman courage by the qualities of mercy and forgiveness, Roman constancy by a capacity for flexibility, growth, and change' (p. 207).

# THE LIVING DRAMATIST AND SHAKESPEARE: A STUDY OF SHAKESPEARE'S INFLUENCE ON WOLE SOYINKA

## JAMES GIBBS

The student who sets out to examine the influence of Shakespeare on a living playwright can study texts, read the critics, and follow the biography of the living playwright. He can develop theories and postulate possibilities, but his surest guide is the acknowledgement by the living writer of his debts. For such an acknowledgement a student will travel miles, and it was in the hope of such an acknowledgement that I travelled to Stratford-upon-Avon in August 1981 to hear Wole Soyinka talk about 'Shakespeare and the Living Dramatist'.

Soyinka is an artist who works in several traditions and who has defined himself in relation to those traditions. Among his poems are those which are composed 'after' James Simmons, Thomas Blackburn, John Cowper Powys or Wilfred Owen; he has written adaptations of plays by Euripides and Bertolt Brecht; he has incorporated masquerade dances, *Agemo* rites and a New Yam Festival into his plays. He is allusive and eclectic; he borrows, commandeers, steals or requisitions as suits his purpose. He knows that there is a limit to originality and that the way material is used is more important than its source. However, those, like the present writer, who listened to Soyinka on 'Shakespeare and the Living Dramatist', hoping for an auto-biographical account or for comments which would make plain the complexities of his own plays, were, initially at least, disappointed. Surprisingly, the Nigerian playwright addressed himself to the impact of Shakespeare on Arab drama – a subject on which he has done no original research and on which he is not an expert. Unpromising on the surface, the talk was, in fact, of considerable interest for those who sought illumination about Shakespeare's influence on Soyinka and were prepared to dig for it. I will return to the paper repeatedly in the pages which follow, in which I consider part of the relationship between Shakespeare and Soyinka.

Some work has already been done on this subject. For instance, Martin Esslin has pointed out the resemblance between *A Dance of the Forests* and *A Midsummer Night's Dream*; Ian Watson has compared the setting for the dance in the same play with the settings of Shakespearian tragedies and has drawn attention to the similarity between Shakespeare's Triplets and Soyinka's; Peter Lewis and Gerald Moore have noted the Shakespearian qualities of some of the language used in *The Lion and the Jewel*; Alison Love has written at greater length and in more detail on the Elizabethan usages in some of Soyinka's poems; I have briefly suggested some of the parallels between *Henry IV*, Parts 1 and 2, and *Kongi's Harvest*; the Shakespearian quality of *Death and the King's Horseman* was remarked by some of those who saw the Chicago (1979) production.[1] In this essay, I intend to draw

---

[1] Martin Esslin, 'Review' in *Black Orpheus* (Ibadan), 19 (March 1963), 33–9; Ian Watson, '*A Dance of the Forests*',

attention to some of the ways in which Shakespeare influenced Soyinka, building on the work I have just mentioned, and following up lines of investigation prompted by my own reading and by 'Shakespeare and the Living Dramatist'.

Soyinka has a long and intimate knowledge of Shakespeare's plays. He read and studied them while at school, at University College, Ibadan, and at the University of Leeds, where he earned a BA in English Literature between 1954 and 1957 and worked on an MA from 1957 to 1958. Since then he has lectured at Nigerian universities in departments where Shakespeare's plays are taught. He has seen Shakespearian productions in, at least, London and Stratford, and, as his critical writing, including 'The Living Dramatist', indicates, he is a lively, sensitive and informed analyst of Shakespeare's plays.

At several points, particularly in the comments on *Antony and Cleopatra*, the Stratford paper indicates that Soyinka sometimes approaches Shakespeare's plays along routes similar to those travelled by Wilson Knight. The relationship between Soyinka and Knight must be established at the outset since it clarifies the relationship between Soyinka and Shakespeare. At Leeds, Soyinka took Knight's World Drama and Ibsen courses, showed him short stories, and became a friend. Although Knight did not lecture on Shakespeare when Soyinka was at Leeds, the influence of interpretative criticism on undergraduates studying English was strong: Knight's books were recommended and quotations from them were used in examination questions. But the 'influence' was not all 'one way': Knight read Soyinka's 1958 MA thesis when preparing his Shakespeare essay for *The Golden Labyrinth*, and in the Preface to his book wrote that the essay 'touched and clarified [his] plans, both in that essay and elsewhere'.[2] The point made by Soyinka which Knight found useful was – to plunge into the complex interweavings of influence – that Lear was 'most royal when on

the heath'. This idea was not, in fact, new to Knight,[3] and Knight might more accurately have indicated that Soyinka 'reminded' him of it. For his part, Soyinka might have encountered the idea about Lear's royalty on the heath in Knight's writings, or have arrived at it by himself, perhaps as a result of independent thinking, perhaps by extending lines of analysis which he had encountered in Knight's work.

The idea that Lear is most royal on the heath, or, more generally, that essential qualities are revealed when a protagonist is responding to a challenge and stripped of excrescences, did not appear only in Soyinka's student assignments; it is present in his play *A Dance of the Forests* and in an essay, 'The Fourth Stage', subtitled 'Through the Mysteries of Ogun to the Origin of Yoruba Tragedy'. Demoke in *A Dance* is reduced to his naked humanity and confronted with a situation where he can either deny his humanity or assert it.[4] 'The Fourth Stage' introduces another complicating factor into the relationship between Soyinka and Knight since it was written for a *Festschrift* in honour of Wilson Knight. Despite the fact that the 'occasion' might have encouraged a 'Knightian' piece, there is good reason to see it as a significant and permanent part of Soyinka's critical canon, since it contains ideas central to his theory of

*Transition* (Kampala), 27 (1966), 24–6; Peter Lewis, 'As the Bard himself might have put it', *The Daily Mail*, 13 December 1966; Gerald Moore, *Wole Soyinka* (London, 1978); Alison Love, *The Language of Nigerian Poetry*, M.Litt. thesis, University of Bristol, 1969; James Gibbs, *Study Aid to 'Kongi's Harvest'* (London, 1972); Soyinka's paper was delivered at the Shakespeare Institute on 17 August 1981 and appeared in *Shakespeare Survey 36* (Cambridge, 1983), pp. 1–10. See also Philip Brockbank, ('Tragic Ritual from Aeschylus to Soyinka', in the same issue.

[2] G. Wilson Knight, *The Golden Labyrinth* (London, 1962), p. x.

[3] I corresponded with Knight on this matter in 1970–1 and talked to him about it in September 1982.

[4] Wole Soyinka, *A Dance of the Forests* in *Collected Plays II* (London, 1973), p. 71.

tragedy, and since he has included it as an appendix to a collection of published lectures.[5] Nevertheless, 'The Fourth Stage' reveals an acute sense of Knight's approach to drama. For instance, in it Soyinka refers to Nietzsche and employs the terms Apollonian and Dionysian in a manner which recalls Knight. The argument of the essay is partly a challenge to Aristotle and the Western tradition, but the image of the protagonist which emerges – a striving Ogun asserting himself and expressing his quintessential character in the chthonic realm – recalls the image which haunts English tragedy of a king bereft of the accoutrements of majesty on a blasted heath. Soyinka has gone a long way round and through some unusual mysteries to arrive back, more or less, where Shakespeare and Knight left off. This is not to suggest that his defiant Ogun is Lear simply blacked up and hurled into the middle of an African festival. It is rather that, with an awareness sharpened by reading Shakespeare and Knight, with a sensitivity to similarities and a determination to explore human rituals, festivals, myths, and archetypes, Soyinka drew attention to a figure who was recognizable to those interested in European drama. From time to time in the course of this essay I shall return to Knight, who remains for Soyinka, as for many others, a valued interpreter of Shakespeare and a penetrating analyst of tragedy.

Soyinka began his career as a playwright with the 'usual sketches' for performance by his school friends and with short, comic scripts for the Nigerian Broadcasting Service. By the time he started writing plays 'seriously' he was already a Leeds graduate and an experienced actor, a short-story writer and polemicist. His first substantial work was a tragedy about apartheid and it may have been *A Dance of the African Forest*, some of which was presented at the Royal Court's Theatre Upstairs during November 1959 and parts of which were incorporated, with very few changes, into a play first presented at the time of Nigeria's

Independence (October 1960), *A Dance of the Forests*.[6] Only the latter text is available *in toto* and, because of its possible links with the first 'serious' play, I shall examine it at this point.

Esslin's comparison of *A Dance of the Forests* (hereafter *A Dance*) with *A Midsummer Night's Dream* is not very fruitful. It may be that Soyinka was encouraged by Shakespeare's play to write about the interaction of humans and spirits in a forest setting. But the distance between the themes of the two works and the abundant precedents for Yoruba narratives set in bushes of ghosts and forests of daemons make direct influence unlikely. A slightly stronger case can be made for linking Soyinka's play with *The Tempest*, a work of particular interest to a student from a British colony; and one in which the guilt of a wicked man is purged by his harrowing experiences in a world ruled by a magician, Prospero, who shares certain qualities with Soyinka's Forest Head. But even there the parallels are faint and it seems far more likely that, while Shakespeare showed that watching spirits at work makes good theatre and that masques can be mixed with dialogue drama, he exerted no greater influence.

The debt to *Macbeth* is obvious. Watson pointed out that the judgement scene is 'set in that *locus classicus* of magic pronouncements from *Macbeth*, a blasted heath'. He also invited readers to 'Note . . . the succession of freakish Triplets reminiscent of *Macbeth* with its three apparitions.' The Triplets, he pointed out, represent 'the most dehumanized abstractions of *real-politik*'. This is helpful, but to determine how Shakespeare influenced 'the living play-

---

5 Wole Soyinka, 'The Fourth Stage', is in *The Morality of Art*, ed. D. W. Jefferson (London, 1969), and in Soyinka's *Myth, Literature and the African World* (Cambridge, 1976). The dialogue continued: Knight referred to some of Soyinka's plays in *Neglected Powers* (London, 1971), and an essay is in a forthcoming collection edited by Henry L. Gates, Jr, *The House of Osugbo*.

6 See James Gibbs, 'The Origins of *A Dance of the Forests*', *African Literature Today*, 10,3 (1976), 33–45.

wright' it is necessary to draw attention to the differences as well as to the similarities between the two sets of Triplets. While it is true that Soyinka seems to have been struck by the dramatic impact of three apparitions, he transformed them even while he incorporated them into his play. He changed their shapes, an easy enough alteration and one to be expected from a playwright with any claim to originality. He also changed their prophecies so that they no longer addressed themselves to one man but to a nation and, as Watson said, they represent 'the most dehumanized abstractions of *real politik*'. Just how original *this* was is a moot point, for, while generations of critics have stressed the relevance of the prophecies for Macbeth, one influential critic has argued that, with the procession of future kings, they lay bare 'the inward mechanisms of time and history': in effect, that they represent 'dehumanized abstractions'. That critic was Wilson Knight, who also argued that the Triplets symbolized iron destruction, life born out of conflict, and creation victorious respectively.[7] Soyinka, I suspect, built on Knight's analysis almost as much as on Shakespeare's original device: he took an incident as interpreted by Knight, reworked it, and eased it into his own, highly original, theatrical context. The message of Soyinka's Triplets emerges with stark clarity from a comparison with Shakespeare's apparitions. Soyinka sounds a series of warnings to a people about to come under the sway, as he sees it, of ruthless, ambitious, unscrupulous rulers. He foresees Machiavellian monsters emerging, eager to argue that the end justifies the means and to excuse 'the crimes of today for tomorrow's mirage'. His final Triplet, *'fanged and bloody'*, says 'I find I am posterity', and asks 'Can no-one see on what milk I have been nourished?' The overt challenge to the Nigerian public represented by the Triplets was not matched by anything in the original: it reveals Soyinka's campaigning spirit, his open defiance of prevailing moods and his pessimism about the future.

The Shakespearian qualities of *The Lion and the Jewel* (drafted 1957–8), as perceived by Lewis, were reflected in the title of his review of the Royal Court production, 'As the Bard himself might have put it', and are essentially qualities of language. Within the play there is a richness of imagery and a rhetorical flair for which there are few contemporary and numerous Shakespearian precedents. Exploring a somewhat similar line of enquiry, Gerald Moore drew attention to the echoes of Hal's 'I know you what you are' in Lakunle's 'I know him what he is', and suggested that 'they are generally at variance with the pattern of Lakunle's language'.[8] 'Generally' perhaps, but not exclusively or inappropriately, since Elizabethan influences are apparent in the schoolmaster's language at several points, including the climactic moment when, in a 'speech of fire', he says

> Oh heavens strike me dead!
> Earth, open up and swallow Lakunle.
> *(Collected Plays, 2.54)*

Soyinka is capable of writing in a wide variety of styles and Lakunle uses several of them; one, illustrated here, is neo-Shakespearian. Its use is carefully controlled throughout the play. Soyinka clearly wrote in the expectation that some, at least, of his audience would bring an awareness of Shakespeare's plays to their listening and reading. He was aware that passages and lines from the British dramatist's plays had become part of the everyday discourse of Nigerians, indeed he knew that Nigerian schoolchildren commit long speeches from Shakespeare's plays to memory.

At the level of character and structure it is

---

[7] G. Wilson Knight, *Principles of Shakespearean Production* (Harmondsworth, 1949), pp. 148 and 178. See also *The Shakespearean Tempest* and *The Christian Renaissance*.

[8] Moore, *Wole Soyinka*, p. 24. Moore refers to a number of issues raised in this paper, including the Shakespearian qualities of *A Dance* and the influence of Wilson Knight on Soyinka.

possible to suggest further links between *The Lion and the Jewel* and some of Shakespeare's characters and dramatic construction. It is, for instance, possible to see Lakunle as a Holofernes-type and to find Falstaffian characteristics – to look for a moment to the histories – in Baroka. Both Soyinka's wooing scenes and his 'festive comedy' may be linked with Shakespeare. The evidence does not suggest any particular or specific debts, but, in view of Soyinka's exposure to Shakespeare, it can be asserted that in character and construction, as well as language, he wrote with an awareness of Shakespearian precedents.

Two plays from the mid-sixties, *The Road* and *Kongi's Harvest*, indicate that Soyinka's search for Yoruba dramatic forms did not preclude the use of Shakespearian elements. Indeed, Shakespeare was, in the terms of the Stratford paper, 'a liberating, even a revolutionary, force'. In both cases it is the chronicle plays, *Henry IV*, Parts 1 and 2, which have left their mark – in the first instance a hardly perceptible, but still revealing, mark.

*The Road* draws on *Agemo* rites and a drivers' Ogun Festival for basic structural elements. It is, with its single, highly symbolic set and its movement backwards and forwards in time, fundamentally un-Shakespearian. One sequence, however, seems to take off from a Shakespearian moment: it is that in which Samson, enthroned upon a table, pretends to be an African millionaire. This sequence fits effortlessly into the play and comments effectively on the values of Nigerian society; it also recalls the scene in which Falstaff plays the king in the Boar's Head (*1 Henry IV*, 2.4). The recollection is fleeting and suggests only that Soyinka had been struck by the powerful stage image of a man seated majestically, pretending to be supremely powerful. From that image his dramatic imagination took wing. The Nigerian playwright may also have been impressed by Shakespeare's use of histrionic characters who deepen the texture of the plays in which they appear by indulging in play-acting. If this idea did indeed come from Shakespeare – or was reinforced by Shakespeare's practice and concern with 'seeming' – it is certainly totally absorbed and used with complete confidence. Shakespeare may have provided a point of departure; his practice was not an end to be imitated.

The links between *Kongi's Harvest* and *Henry IV* are both more numerous and more complex. They begin on the surface, on the level of language, but are also found on the levels of structure and theme; an analysis of the links brings into focus both Soyinka's technique and his concerns. In 'Hangover', the Organising Secretary half-quotes Henry IV when he says, 'Contented? That is one uneasy crown / Which still eludes my willing head' (*Collected Plays*, 2.136). This is an allusion to a line ('uneasy lies the head that wears the crown') which Shakespeare bequeathed to those who use the English language and which is both wise saying and quotation. The speech is in character for the Organising Secretary and an illustration of Soyinka's manipulation of an element of a literary tradition, a playing with inherited phrases akin to that enjoyed by Yoruba orators.

The theatrical idiom on which *Kongi's Harvest* is constructed is partly derived from African Festival Theatre: it builds on the variations of movement, rhythm, and mood which are found in such celebrations as the Oshun Festival at Oshogbo, and it employs the ritual of a New Yam Festival. The structure also has an affinity with that of *Henry IV* in that both plays make a significant impact through the juxtaposition of scenes and through the contrasts and comparisons which are established between individuals and groups. Furthermore, Soyinka, like Shakespeare, uses distinctive kinds of language to heighten contrasts, and he locates one group in a night club, Segi's Bar, which has points in common with the Boar's Head.

Soyinka's play, like Shakespeare's history

plays, takes a political sequence as its raw material and gives it a distinctive shape. In the process a particularly significant role is created for the male protagonist and an ending, after a crisis has been reached and passed, takes the audience through a climax to a scene in a relatively relaxed mood, an epilogue of sorts. The concluding scene presents history at what could be a turning point: the forces at work in a community have been shaken up and a new phase may be about to begin. Soyinka is sometimes accused of leaving issues in the air at the end of his plays but there are obvious Shakespearian precedents for his 'open' conclusions.

At the centre of *Kongi's Harvest* is a concern with legitimacy, power, and leadership which has striking similarities with, and also significant differences from, Shakespeare's interests in *Henry IV*, Parts 1 and 2. Soyinka introduces three major contenders for power into his play: Danlola, Kongi, and Daodu. Danlola, the legitimate ruler, is in detention, but even there his ebullience and vitality are undiminished. Kongi, a politician who wants to usurp Danlola's religious functions without taking his responsibilities, is a repressive and authoritarian figure, a life-denying force. Daodu has a legitimate claim to Danlola's title by virtue of his birth, and a claim to leadership of Kongi's modern state of Isma since he is the leader of a successful farming co-operative. Even from this brief account of three characters similarities with *Henry IV* suggest themselves. Moreover, to accentuate the similarities, it should be pointed out that Kongi, like Bolingbroke, is a vulnerable usurper, and Daodu, like Hal, is a prince who keeps dubious company. If we hold the Shakespearian precedents in mind and stay alert to contrasts, distinctive qualities of Soyinka's political drama become clear. Kongi is not, like Bolingbroke, sucked into a power vacuum, but an arrogant monster; Daodu is not, like Hal, a calculating youth but a radical political leader; Danlola, the detained *oba*, is not a meditative prisoner contemplating a

hollow crown in solitary confinement, a Richard II. He is an irreverent wit, a very astute politician with loyal supporters and Falstaffian vigour. From comparisons Soyinka's sense of the strength of the past, the tyranny of the present, and the need for rebellion emerge with stark clarity.

The last scene of *Kongi's Harvest*, 'Hangover', is in the nature of an epilogue, a feature of Shakespeare's tragedies which Knight emphasized. But, whereas Shakespeare generally suggests that a moment of 'supernal insight' and a period of order will follow conflict, the final stage directions of the epilogue to *Kongi's Harvest* suggest that Kongi's rule will be imposed more repressively and widely than before. There is little or no insight and the 'order' promised is strictly on Kongi's terms. In all this, in the literary, thematic, and structural influences, Shakespeare appears to be for Soyinka, as he has been for generations of European – and for some Arab – writers, a liberating force, a stimulator of thought and creation.

The social and political problems reflected in *The Road* and *Kongi's Harvest* contributed to the increase in tension in Nigeria during 1966 and 1967. The activist impulses which Soyinka favoured – and glamorized – in *Kongi's Harvest* drew the playwright to comment publicly on Nigeria's drift towards civil war. One of his poems from this period, 'Malediction', dedicated 'For her who rejoiced', indicates the intensity of his feelings and his readiness to express himself in invective which recalls Shakespeare. The opening, 'Unsexed your lips / have framed a life curse',[9] strikes a distinctive note and one which is continued throughout. The poem, however, differs from any writing by Shakespeare – Lear's 'Dry up in her the organs of increase' comes to mind – in being a poet's curse upon an identifiable individual. Soyinka seems to be prepared to be

---

[9] Wole Soyinka, *Idanre and other Poems* (London, 1967), p. 55.

inspired by Shakespeare in certain respects, but his concept of the function of a writer is substantially different.[10]

At this point and in relation to this poem, it is necessary to take into account the opinion of those who draw very different conclusions from mine about the Shakespearian influence on Soyinka. Chinweizu, Onwuchekwa Jemie, and Ihechukwu Madubuike, who campaign for the 'decolonization of African literature', regard Soyinka as a cultural mercenary working in the service of imperialist forces; they see his use of Shakespearian elements as evidence of an alienated and subversive sensibility. They describe the language of 'Malediction' as 'a blend of Shakespeare and the Victorian English poets', and criticize the writer for 'not cursing the way his forefathers cursed, nor the way his contemporaries curse'. They find him guilty of 'voluntary cultural suicide' and of blocking the channel of cultural transmission.[11] Their haste to condemn Soyinka and their narrow understanding of 'Malediction' prevent them from responding to the vigorous, creative, independent voice of the poet, whose use of English is profoundly informed by Yoruba habits and who is a nationalist and pan-Africanist as well as an independent-minded heir of the language of Shakespeare.

Soyinka was detained for twenty-seven months during the civil war, partly because of his articles for the Nigerian press, partly because of his activities on behalf of a Third Force. He was able to write a certain amount while in prison and shortly after his release he published a collection of poems, *A Shuttle in the Crypt*. This contained a sonnet, entitled 'Hamlet', which must be considered in the present context. The poem appears beside three others in which Soyinka analyses his experiences in terms of figures from what may be called 'Western literature'. The choice of Hamlet and the other archetypes (Ulysses, Joseph and Gulliver) was bound to be condemned by those, like Chinweizu, who were

committed to 'the decolonization of African literature' and to those, like Adamu Ciroma, who saw in Soyinka's prison writings 'the influence of colonial and foreign education *par excellence*'.[12] 'Hamlet' reveals Soyinka's knowledge of *Hamlet* and his interpretation of the protagonist's role in terms of a 'prince of doubts', an approach familiar from William Hazlitt and Samuel Taylor Coleridge to Laurence Olivier's film. In the course of the poem, in which, incidentally, 'told by an idiot' is quoted from *Macbeth*, Hamlet, the dithering, doubting intellectual, fails to take action until confronted by Laertes's treachery. The final lines are 'It took the salt in the wound, the "point / Envenom'd too" to steel the prince of doubts'.[13] These lines illustrate Soyinka's view of Hamlet, his delight in the manipulation of familiar idioms ('salt in the wound') and his pleasure in word-play ('to steel the prince of doubts'). His choice of the sonnet form indicates his sense of decorum: he expressed his poetic response to a Shakespearian character in a poetic mode which Shakespeare had used. In view of the evidence produced in this essay, the whole idea of defining himself and explaining his position in terms of a Shakespearian protagonist is not surprising; a variation on the approach has already been observed in relation to *A Dance* and *Kongi's Harvest*. Soyinka appropriated a figure 'from an alien land' in order to communicate and not because his sensibility was irredeemably alienated. His originality is apparent when critics move from source-spotting to the more demanding task of determining what he has done with what he has borrowed – or stolen.

An analysis of the contact between Africa

---

10 See Love, *The Language of Nigerian Poetry*, p. 183.

11 Chinweizu, Onwuchekwa Jemie and Ihechukwu Madubuike, *Toward the Decolonization of African Literature* (Enugu, 1980), pp. 170–1.

12 Adamu Ciroma, 'Review of *The Man Died*', *New Nigeria*, 5 April 1973.

13 Wole Soyinka, *A Shuttle in the Crypt* (London, 1976), p. 22.

and Europe is central to Soyinka's play *Death and the King's Horseman*. Written at Cambridge during 1972–3 and based on the interrupted ritual suicide of the King's Horseman at Oyo in 1945, the play combines an examination of colonial issues with a study of suicide.[14] Soyinka exposes the shallowness of the British District Officer, Simon Pilkings, and of his wife Jane, and the arrogance and insensitivity with which they intervene in the Yoruba community around them, particularly in the life and death of Elesin Oba, the King's Horseman, who, having enjoyed power and privilege during the reign of his master, the *alafin* of Oyo, is duty-bound to follow him into the passage of death.

Soyinka's play has a fluid, Shakespearian construction. It develops through contrasts and juxtapositions, moving from the market-place to the DO's bungalow, back to the market, on to the Residency – where a masked ball is in progress – and finally draws to an end in the prison near to the Residency where, in an earlier age, prisoners were held before being sent down to the coast. The play is written largely in prose, with praise songs and chants from Elesin's Praise Singer, and with richly textured, image-filled speeches from Iyaloja, the Queen of the Market, and from Elesin Oba himself. Elesin, accompanied by his Praise Singer, dances into the market on his way to embrace death. He pauses, first to demand the attention and gifts due to him from the market women and then to ask for a young woman, the Bride, as a final 'bridge' to help him cross the abyss which separates life from death. While Elesin 'breaks the virgin-knot', news of his intention to commit suicide reaches Pilkings. To avoid trouble on an evening when the Prince of Wales is being entertained in the Residency and out of a desire, presented as misguided, to preserve a life which is forfeit, Pilkings despatches a force which is eventually able to apprehend the Horseman. Having heard of the *alafin*'s death and anticipating that his father will have willed himself to death,

Elesin's son, Olunde, returns from his medical studies in England. When Olunde finds Elesin is still alive, he commits suicide in his father's place – thereby restoring the family's honour to a certain extent. Olunde's body is brought to Elesin in prison and the Horseman strangles himself with the chains attached to his wrists.

The play follows, very roughly, a brief account, hardly more than an anecdote, about the historical episode. The source was filled out by the playwright with a series of contrasts and with comparisons on themes such as honour, duty, and self-sacrifice. These themes are handled so as to reveal how flippant, insensitive, and narrow-minded British colonial officers and their wives could be and to show the holistic quality of the Yoruba world view. In his Author's Note to the play, Soyinka warns the would-be producer against 'a sadly familiar reductionist tendency', which would centre the play on the 'clash of cultures'. However, the action and dialogue certainly bring out elements of contrast between Europe and Africa and between the British and the Yoruba world view. There are also, as Olunde makes Jane Pilkings realize in his talk of sacrifice and duty, points of departure for a rewarding dialogue.

*Horseman* is Soyinka's most obvious examination of the colonial encounter and is easily accessible to British audiences. Writing in England, Soyinka seems to have considered it appropriate to have borne his hosts in mind and written in a convention to which they – or at least the relevant, theatre-going minority of them – were accustomed. The sense of dialogue between England and Yorubaland, Europe and Africa, is apparent at linguistic, thematic, and structural levels; the dialogue between Soyinka and Shakespeare which the

---

[14] Soyinka seems to have relied on Ulli Beier for an account of the historical episode. His play shows no evidence of independent research or of examination of Beier's source which was Pierre Verger, who had made enquiries at Oyo.

play embodies is less apparent. The Stratford paper points the student in the right direction, for in that paper, arguing for the Arab–African quality of *Antony and Cleopatra* and treading once again a path taken by Wilson Knight, Soyinka described 'the physical terrain' of Shakespeare's play as 'the meeting point of the Orient and the Occident'. He claimed that 'Cleopatra [imbued] the approach of death with a measured ritualism that is suffused with the palpable shadowiness of the crypt', and he wrote of the way 'ritual transformation steps towards the mystic moment of transition'.[15] These sentences, with the substitution of 'Africa' for 'Orient' and of 'Elesin' for 'Cleopatra', could be applied to *Horseman*, and draw attention to the play's 'threnodic essence' – on which the Author's Note lays emphasis.

Elesin, to complicate matters, is a figure of majestic proportions, 'a man of enormous vitality [who] speaks, dances and sings with that infectious enjoyment of life which accompanies all his actions' (p. 9).[16] In his own society, he is an Antony. This 'triple pillar of [Oyo is] transformed' by his desire for 'that goddess through whose lips / [He sees] the ivory pebbles of Oya's river-bed' (p. 19). Dallying, and then arrested, Elesin fails in his bid to think and die; he is captured by his enemy, preserved, much to his dismay, alive. Unlike Shakespeare's Enobarbus he cannot pass over easily into death, for, like Antony, having abandoned his life's purpose for a 'goddess', he botches his suicide attempt; he then, briefly, suffers the fate, which Cleopatra fears, of being led captive by enemies.

Shakespeare's Egypt in which Eros, Iras, Charmian, Enobarbus and Cleopatra die is a bourne in which the worlds of the living and the dead nudge and jostle one another; in this respect it is similar to the Yoruba world in which Olunde and Elesin exist. The similarities are so marked that Soyinka's play, like his Stratford paper, compliments Shakespeare for his perception of an African attitude to death and invites contrast and comparison. On occasions, even the language and imagery of *Horseman* reveal a debt to – or at least an affinity with – *Antony and Cleopatra*. Enobarbus, about to die of melancholy, addresses the moon as his 'sovereign mistress' and invites her to 'disponge upon' him 'the poisonous damp of night'. In his cell, contemplating the same moon, Elesin speaks to Pilkings about the white man's 'twin brother'. He says:

The moon was my messenger and guide. When it reached a certain gateway in the sky, it touched that moment for which my whole life had been spent in blessings. Even I do not know the gateway. I have stood here and scanned the sky for a glimpse of that door but I cannot see it. Human eyes are useless for a search of this nature.[17]  (p. 62)

Yet even when the two plays come closest together in terms of language and invite comparison in terms of character, action, theme, and world view, Soyinka's remains a distinctive voice and vision. He articulates a genuinely Yoruba and more general African perception. Far from being a cultural mercenary, he is fiercely and subtly opposed to the values carried to the frontiers of their empire by Simon and Jane Pilkings.

Shakespeare has sometimes been an inhibiting or debilitating influence on playwrights writing in English. In the case of Soyinka, because of the combination of a strong personality, a firmly apprehended, vigorous, dynamic culture and a stimulating teacher,

---

[15] There were precedents for challenging the pattern of ritual suicide at Oyo in the last century. In the interests of dramatic clarity Soyinka makes no reference to this or to the growing opposition to the practice during this century. In the interests of dramatic mystery, he suggests that the Horsemen died by an effort of will. Dr Samuel Johnson, the Yoruba historian, made it clear that assistance was available for the intending suicide and that Horsemen could be strangled or given poison. *The History of the Yorubas* (London, 1921).

[16] References are to the London, 1975 edition.

[17] The manner in which the moon is regarded in *Horseman* and the imagery used to describe the sky are significantly similar to those used by Ezeulu in Chinua Achebe's *Arrow of God* (London, 1964).

Shakespeare inspired rather than overawed. The Elizabethan's influence acted, as it had on German romantics and Arab innovators, as a revolutionary and liberating force. The ambition, eloquence, subtlety, and range of Soyinka's works are partly the result of his experience of Shakespeare's plays.

Soyinka could have told his audience at Stratford about his own response to Shakespeare in a plain, straightforward manner. But this was not his dramatist's manner and whatever he said in that line would inevitably have been misconstrued and twisted by those with very simple ideas about what 'decolonization' means. Soyinka is truly a 'decolonized' writer and this shows itself in the confidence and originality of his use of material from Britain and elsewhere. By indicating the influence of Shakespeare on Arab dramatists and by his analysis of *Antony and Cleopatra* Soyinka was, in fact, revealing this much about himself. To appreciate it, one has to approach 'Shakespeare and the Living Dramatist' in an Egyptian rather than a Roman manner, and, following Shakespearian precedents, 'by indirection find direction out'.

# SHAKESPEARE AT STRATFORD, ONTARIO: THE JOHN HIRSCH YEARS

## ROGER WARREN

My previous report on the Canadian Shakespeare Festival at Stratford, Ontario for *Shakespeare Survey* covered the 1980 season, the final year of Robin Phillips's regime.[1] The extraordinary series of confusions and intrigues which followed almost wrecked the festival altogether;[2] and the first task facing John Hirsch, Artistic Director 1981–5, was to keep the festival going at all. But he did much more than that. He created a young company within the main ensemble to work at the Third Stage, a small-scale replica of the Festival Stage, where promising young actors are trained to cope with the arduous demands of the main theatre; and he offered some striking interpretations of Shakespearian comedy and romance.

John Hirsch is particularly interested in the late plays, and expressed frustration that his dream of staging all four in one season was impossible for box office reasons. After his remarkable production of *The Tempest* in 1982 I share his frustration, for this was the first coherent version of the play I have seen, the only one to weld the disparate elements of the play into a unity. In the process, it provided solutions to areas of the play which often prove intractable in performance, particularly the masque and the so-called clowns' scenes. It made full use of Stratford's huge thrust stage in order to evoke Prospero's magic powers, especially when Ariel suddenly appeared on the upper level as a harpy with gigantic wings, or when the entire vast stage gradually filled up with singing spirits during the masque. Mr Hirsch is a master of such breathtaking effects, but in his hands they are never just effects: they serve a larger interpretative purpose. Taking a hint from Prospero's words to Ferdinand before the masque begins, 'All thy vexations / Were but my trials of thy love', he began masque itself with an interpolated song for Ariel which, by alluding to Aeneas' voyage to the underworld in the *Aeneid* and to Tamino's trials of fire and water in *The Magic Flute*, made it clear that the masque was the happy outcome of Prospero's trials of Ferdinand, just as the appearance of the harpy at the banquet was the climax of his trials of the 'men of sin', with Ariel as the presenter in each case. Ferdinand had been purified by his trials, for which his reward was Miranda, and their wedding took place there and then. This provided a firm focus for the visual and musical celebration which followed, so that the masque did not degenerate, as it so often does, into an uneasy jumble of classical goddesses and sunburnt sicklemen.

More successful still were the Stephano/Trinculo/Caliban scenes, because, for the only time in my experience of the play, they were integrated into the main plot's world of poli-

---

[1] *Shakespeare Survey 34* (Cambridge, 1981), pp. 155–60. My visit to the 1984 festival was made possible by a Research Award from the British Academy.

[2] These are chronicled in Martin Knelman's *A Stratford Tempest* (Toronto, 1982).

10   *The Tempest*. Stratford, Ontario, 1982. Len Cariou as Prospero

tical power. Stephano's resolve to be 'king o' the isle' became a striking parallel to the conspiracies of Antonio and Sebastian against Prospero and Alonso. The most experienced Shakespearian actor in the company, Nicholas Pennell, was strategically cast as Stephano, whom he played as a servant who suddenly saw the chance of becoming a master, expressing his 'bloody thoughts' with a twisted sneer; yet this bully-boy collapsed in terror at the sound of Ariel's 'invisible' tabor, so that Caliban had to take him in his arms and reassure him with 'Be not afeard. The isle is full of noises'. Such preparation for the famous

speeches, so that they are properly integrated into the action rather than seeming isolated set pieces, is very characteristic of Mr Hirsch's direction, as his treatment of Prospero also demonstrated.

The emphasis on trial in the harpy and masque scenes, and on power struggles in the Stephano scenes, recurred in the interpretation of Prospero. A vigorous figure of not more than middle age, this Prospero clearly resented his loss of political power and therefore relished all the more the different kind of power which his magic art gave him. So his renunciation of that power, the decision to choose virtue rather than vengeance, and the implementing of that decision – 'I do forgive thee, / Unnatural though thou art' – seemed to cost him everything. Irving Wardle in his review exactly caught the effect of the renunciation speech:

if there is one passage that confirms Prospero's powers it is at the moment when he abandons them. Trembling from head to foot in a gradually intensifying circle of white light, Len Cariou at last nerves himself to address his Ovidian farewell to the island's spirits. I have heard it better spoken, but never with a stronger sense of what Prospero was giving up.[3]

It was extraordinary that this effect should have been achieved with an actor of only moderate powers as Prospero: Len Cariou was loud and clear, but lacked subtlety. The director's vision was so strong that it came across nevertheless, a spiritual journey from darkness to light for some characters (Ferdinand, Alonso) but not others (Antonio, Stephano) and only with great effort, and without any certainty of future happiness in Milan, for Prospero himself.

The movement from darkness to light was also central to John Hirsch's production of *As You Like It* in 1983, but this time the interpretation could not be fully realized because the actress playing Rosalind did not rise to the demands of the part or of the staging. But the very fact that this production only partly worked served usefully to expose the bare bones, as it were, of Mr Hirsch's approach to Shakespeare's comedies and romances. The first half was very dark indeed, starting with a Dickensian street scene in the snow, where a ragged urchin sang 'Under the greenwood tree' in a cracked voice. This was the village over which Oliver held harsh sway. Duke Frederick's black-clad court was harsher still. Le Beau's reference to 'a better world than this' took on an extra edge when his remarks to Orlando were noted down by a sinister figure in dark glasses and a greatcoat, attended by armed guards. Jaques was not just a cynic or a

solitary but a shattered, fragmented personality, an extreme interpretation so brilliantly executed by Nicholas Pennell that it seemed perverse of the director to cut the speech that most justified it, the Timon-like outburst: 'What woman in the city do I name . . .' The first half ended with Orlando hanging his verses on the trees, so that the last words were about Rosalind, 'The fair, the chaste, and unexpressive she': the way seemed prepared for a second half to be dominated by Rosalind.

This sharp division of the play, which deliberately exaggerated both the constraints of the court and the liberty of the countryside, strongly recalled Michael Elliott's treatment at the Royal Shakespeare Theatre in 1961, in which a wintry first half gave place to a sunlit Arden in full leaf, fit setting for Vanessa Redgrave's radiant Rosalind to take control of the play. The problem with John Hirsch's version was that Roberta Maxwell's Rosalind failed to do this. Neither the mock wooing nor the mock wedding ever seemed more than a game; and this Rosalind seemed incapable of responding to Andrew Gillies's firm but gentle Orlando. Other Orlandos have made 'I can live no longer by thinking' a frustrated outburst, or merely dismissive; Mr Gillies spoke the line quietly, reasonably, almost unwilling to spoil Ganymede's fun. But Roberta Maxwell seemed unable to catch his tone; she could do nothing with Rosalind's reply 'I will weary you, then, no longer with idle talking', which Vanessa Redgrave made suddenly serious. Again, Vanessa Redgrave had relished the formality of the final scene, caressing every word, slowly sighing out 'To you I give myself, for I am yours': she could risk this delivery because she had laid the emotional foundations so firmly in her earlier scenes with Orlando. Since Roberta Maxwell had not, the words were of virtually no use to her; and so the formality of the final scene seemed so much empty ritual – which was precisely the

---

[3] *The Times*, 1 July 1982.

impression that Mr Hirsch had avoided so successfully in his staging of the masque in *The Tempest*. But the clear aim of the production – harsh discord resolved in a forest setting – which did not work out properly here, was superbly realized in Mr Hirsch's *A Midsummer Night's Dream*, the outstanding success of the 1984 season.

Whereas he had exploited the characteristics of the Stratford stage just as it was to create a sense of Prospero's magic in *The Tempest*, Mr Hirsch and his regular designer Desmond Heeley completely transformed the stark platform into a forest for the *Dream*. This was not only extremely beautiful in itself, it also subtly mirrored the text: the stage and balcony were filled almost from floor to roof with tall, slender saplings; but the brown leaves on those midsummer trees perfectly reflected the confusion of the seasons which Titania describes and which in turn reflects the chaotic relationships in both the fairy kingdom and the mortal world. This chaos was established right at the beginning of the play, which opened with Theseus and his army of conquistadors defeating Hippolyta and her Amazons in pitched battle. The tension was echoed in the fairy quarrel, where Oberon's attendants threatened Titania's with spears. The fairies' costumes were variations on the Elizabethan styles worn

11   *A Midsummer Night's Dream*. Stratford, Ontario, 1984. Titania (Patricia Conolly), Oberon (Nicholas Pennell), Puck (Diego Matamoros)

by the mortals, but in addition Oberon's branched head-dress carried the suggestion of a tree-spirit. These designs exactly matched the combination of courtly and rural elements in Shakespeare's presentation of the fairies.

The emphasis upon tension, far from spoiling the lyrical beauty of the verse, intensified its impact, especially in Patricia Conolly's accomplished double performance as Hippolyta and Titania. As Hippolyta, her comparison of the moon to a 'silver bow / New-bent in heaven' had additional resonance in a context which emphasized that she was an Amazonian queen. As Titania, her pale beauty was a reminder that in Ovid the name Titania is a synonym for Diana, the moon goddess;[4] her phrase about the moon, 'pale in her anger', was a description of herself as well, and she delivered her extended account of the seasonal chaos with an impassioned intensity and involvement. Not since Judi Dench at Stratford-upon-Avon in 1962 have I encountered a Titania who showed such concern for the effects of her quarrel with Oberon on both the natural world and the 'human mortals'. The whole speech was so rivetting that even the characteristically noisy Ontario audience actually shut up and listened to her.

Opposite her, Nicholas Pennell developed from a sternly dominating Theseus to an Oberon of imposing authority, and the particularly strong connections between the two couples in this production made a much better case than usual for the recently established tradition of doubling these parts. It inevitably causes technical problems at 4.1.99–100, where the exit of the fairy couple is followed without a break by the reappearance of the mortal one; but John Hirsch typically turned the difficulty to advantage. Slowly the 'fair blessed beams' of the sunrise warmed the trees, and hinted at the new mood of 'gentle concord' which resolves the preceding tensions, as huntsmen gradually assembled with Theseus' dogs. When Mr Pennell and Miss

Conolly finally appeared, the fresh green of their hunting robes, set against those brown leaves, reinforced that new sense of warmth and reconciliation, and so did Mr Pennell's very sure, witty pointing of Theseus' irony in lines like 'Good-morrow, friends. Saint Valentine is past', as he modified his previous severity towards the lovers.

The stress on the earlier tensions did not involve any loss of humour, either in the lovers' quarrels or in the relaxed, genial humanity of the mechanicals. Brian Bedford was a quietly confident Bottom and William Needles a Quince with more control over his cast than in most productions: he did not hesitate to correct their errors even during the course of the play scene itself. The basic comedy of situation in which the delicate fairy queen falls in love with the braying ass-headed weaver was all the funnier because both Titania and Bottom had been established as strongly characterized individuals. The production ended with one of Mr Hirsch's touches of theatrical magic: the shimmering light representing the 'field-dew consecrate' with which the fairies bless the palace not only spread across the entire huge stage but was reflected all over the roof of the theatre as well. This was an appropriately breathtaking conclusion to a production of stunning impact.

John Hirsch's productions, like those of his predecessor Robin Phillips, were imaginative, elaborate, carefully worked out reinterpretations of the plays. Neither director did things the simple way. But during both regimes there were also several very satisfying productions that used the Stratford stage in a more direct fashion. Robert Beard's *Merry Wives of Windsor* in 1982 was a case in point. It caught exactly that sense of an Elizabethan country-town community with a relaxed ease which did not need the elaborate external invention – children playing conkers or the wives going shopping when not gulling Falstaff – which Terry

---

4 *Metamorphoses*, 3, 173.

12   *The Merry Wives of Windsor*. Stratford, Ontario, 1982. Susan Wright as Mistress Page and Pat Galloway as Mistress Ford

Hands used to create the world of Windsor in his celebrated 1968–75 version for the Royal Shakespeare Company. Susan Benson, an exceptionally gifted designer who had conjured up the magnificent black and gold court splendour of Robin Phillips's *A Midsummer Night's Dream* in 1976–7,[5] was equally successful in creating sober but beautiful brown and russet costumes which reflected the prosperity of the Elizabethan middle class.

There was no set apart from furniture, and virtually no externally imposed business; the country-town atmosphere derived primarily from the firm grasp of individual, often eccentric character displayed by the whole cast from the opening exchanges: Shallow, Slender, and Evans got the play off to a tremendous start by making every word tell. Douglas Campbell is that extreme rarity, a natural Falstaff, and he virtually owns the part at this festival. Like the rest of the cast, this Falstaff was wholly unexaggerated, drawing laughter from his expert projection of the text. Even more successful, along the same lines, were Susan Wright's Mistress Page, whose verbal timing rivalled that of Brenda Bruce in Terry Hands's version and who never missed a verbal trick from start to finish; and especially Nicholas Pennell's Ford, who equalled Ian Richardson's spasms of jealousy without, like him, going over the top. When he first disguised himself as Brook he wore a black patch over one eye, but when he next appeared in disguise he was wearing a patch over the other eye. He was so consumed by his fantasies of cuckoldry that he neglected all practicalities, even when they were connected with the pursuit of his revenge. As Irving Wardle put it, this was 'no piece of directorial business: it is what this Ford would have done'.[6]

This was one of the most straightforward, and most delightful, productions of Shakespeare that I have seen. The difficulties of the Stratford stage seemed to fall away because the cast was so thoroughly at home on it, their confidence enabling them to concentrate on putting across text and character. But to unwary newcomers the stage can present pitfalls to which I have referred in previous reviews. The main problem is that it is virtually impossible to communicate with all the audience at any one time, unless the actor is standing still in the position of strength centre stage, just in front of the pillars supporting the balcony. This problem was recognized by Tyrone Guthrie from the start. After the opening season in 1953, when Guthrie created both the festival and its stage, he said: 'I think the solution is for the actor to keep turning slowly, facing now this, now that, part of the house . . . It is the producer's duty to see that all parts of the house get fair do's.'[7] This attempt to give everyone 'fair do's' creates more problems than it solves. The aggressive platform stage is thrust so far into the audience, who surround it in such a wide arc, that when an actor turns to address one side of the far-flung audience he often becomes inaudible to that third or even two-thirds of the audience from whom he has turned away. And even if he remains audible, turning away seriously endangers the continuity of the speech. Aware of this, many actors tend to resort to nervous gabbling, especially if their speeches contain verbal humour, or they disrupt them with restless movement. All these problems were illustrated in Mark Lamos's 1984 production of *The Merchant of Venice*.

Mr Lamos set the play in the context of an eighteenth-century Shrovetide carnival, filling the stage with *commedia dell'arte* figures, in order to isolate Shylock's austerity and severity from the Christians' prodigality and revelry. This contrast seemed imposed from the outside, with nothing like the impact of the charged moment at the end of the trial scene when Antonio dropped a crucifix round Shy-

[5] This production is described in *Shakespeare Survey 31* (Cambridge, 1978), pp. 143–4.

[6] *The Times*, 3 July 1982.

[7] *Shakespeare Survey 8* (Cambridge, 1955), p. 129.

lock's neck as he knelt in humiliation before the Duke. A sense of revenge mingled with Antonio's Christian mercy. But the moment had not been prepared for: the suggestion that Antonio shared Shylock's intolerance had not been sufficiently established earlier on. The production, and John Neville's performance as Shylock, both lacked a clear line. At first, with his mockingly varied 'well . . . well . . . well!', it seemed that Mr Neville was aiming at a sly, ironic Shylock; but any possibility of irony vanished when he gabbled the speech about Laban's sheep without any relish for its brilliant combination of biblical argument, dubious morality, and colloquial, garrulous phrasing, and it became increasingly apparent that Mr Neville was simply taking things as

they came. A straightforward approach did not work in his case because, unlike the cast of *The Merry Wives*, his lack of experience on this treacherous stage meant that many of his lines were simply inaudible.

The one completely successful performance in this *Merchant* was Domini Blythe's as Portia. She seemed particularly well served by Mr Lamos's elaborate eighteenth-century staging – or it may simply have been that, with her long experience of this theatre, she was able, as Mr Neville was not, to realize the director's intentions. In her first scene she was attended not merely by Nerissa but by a whole entourage of functionaries, as in the Marschallin's levée in *Der Rosenkavalier*. At first sight this seemed a rather desperate attempt by

13   *The Merchant of Venice*. Stratford, Ontario, 1984. Domini Blythe as Portia and Heather Macdonald as Nerissa

14   *Love's Labour's Lost*. Stratford, Ontario, 1984. John Neville as Armado

Mr Lamos to fill the huge space; but that entourage was turned to specific advantage later, when the great lady became an 'unlessoned girl' as she radiantly resigned her power and all her possessions to Bassanio. After her two previous suitors had made their wrong choices there was a long pause as Portia gazed at the leaden casket and realized, obviously for the first time, that it must be the right one. This strongly marked moment of realization meant that Domini Blythe could release much laughter later on when she said 'I could teach you / How to choose right', only to silence it instantly with the quiet integrity of her next phrase: 'but then I am forsworn; / So will I never be'. This Portia caught all the humour, tenderness, and authority of the part; and if the casket scenes lacked their full impact, that was largely because they fell victim to the company's restlessness. The caskets were constantly on the move, carried around the stage by Portia's ladies, a device inherited from earlier productions by Tyrone Guthrie in Ontario (1955) and by his disciple Michael Langham in Warwickshire (1960).

Mr Langham's 1984 production of *Love's Labour's Lost* was an expansion for the main stage of his studio version with the young company the year before. But his interpretation went back much further than that, to his production of the same play which the Ontario company brought to Chichester as part of the Shakespeare Quatercentenary celebrations in 1964. After John Barton's developing, ripening work on this play for the Royal Shakespeare Company between 1965 and 1979, it came as quite a shock to realize that, apart from changing the costumes from Caroline to Edwardian, Mr Langham's interpretation had not developed at all in twenty years: it had exactly the same virtues and vices as the earlier version.

There were two most effective climaxes, the multiple sonnet-reading and the gradual realization among the revelling courtiers that a messenger of death had, almost imperceptibly,

materialized in their midst. But elsewhere Mr Langham's fertile invention did not arise from character or situation. The most striking performance in 1964 was William Hutt's immensely stylish Armado, an elegant, ageing Don Quixote. John Neville in 1984 was clearly in the same tradition, but this time character was pushed towards caricature: this tattered Armado was not merely elderly, but positively falling apart with senility, his legs hardly able to sustain him. And in both productions Holofernes was sheer caricature, a cane-brandishing pedant without a trace of humanity. In the second version, assuming that the audience would not understand Holofernes's description of Armado as 'vain, ridiculous, and thrasonical', Mr Langham instructed Nicholas Pennell to fart before 'thrasonical' and then to flap his academic gown to disperse the smell. The audience laughed, of course; but when they are actively encouraged to respond to such diversions rather than to follow the text line by line, the inevitable result is that a human moment like Holofernes's 'This is not generous, not gentle, not humble' will go for nothing – which is just what happened.

Conclusive proof that Mr Langham was not primarily concerned to explore the text came in the final moments, when the spring and winter songs became a mere accompaniment to the ladies' departure, again as in 1964. The reduction of such an important passage to generalized background music for an elaborate stage spectacle, like the imposed gags, further discouraged the audience from attempting to follow anything but the most general outline of the story. Mr Langham comes from what seems to have been a more backward era of Stratford's history, and I find it alarming that such a director should have been in charge of training a young company. He seemed to be encouraging them in some very bad habits; but evidence of a more promising approach was provided by Joseph Ziegler's handling of Berowne's big speech about the power of love to justify broken oaths. He took the audience step by step with him through his long verbal argument, so that delighted laughter greeted his sophistical conclusion 'It is *religion* to be thus forsworn': if they hadn't been following, they wouldn't have laughed. This was heartening in two ways. Like the response to Patricia Conolly's Titania, and despite much depressing evidence to the contrary, it demonstrated that even such inattentive audiences as those in Ontario are prepared to listen to the text if encouraged to do so; and it suggested that directors may after all be teaching the young company, of which Mr Ziegler is a product, how to communicate the text. Further welcome evidence of this was provided by Leon Rubin's production of *The Two Gentlemen of Verona* in 1984.

It is obviously easier to communicate with the audience in the studio conditions of the Third Stage than in the wide-open spaces of the main house. Mr Rubin encouraged his young cast to adopt a much more deliberate pace than they would have dared to risk in the big theatre; and he was clearly determined to interpret the play, to make the verbal jokes very clear, and particularly to make the emotions very real. Unlike the updating in *The Merchant* and *Love's Labour's Lost*, the modern dress here had a clear purpose. Mr Rubin drew on the sexually ambiguous image of some contemporary pop singers for two chief reasons. First, it enabled him to get round notorious difficulties like the outlaws, who emerged as an aggressively ambidextrous rock group, choosing Valentine as their leader because he was 'beautified / With goodly shape'. Second and more important, the modern fashions helped to suggest the ado-

15　*The Two Gentlemen of Verona.* Stratford, Ontario, 1984. The Outlaws (John Moffatt, Kevin Anderson, Laurence Rosso) with Valentine (Rob McClure) and Speed (David Johnson)

lescent emotional confusions of the lovers. Julia and Proteus played their farewell scene in bed: their affair had gone so much further than in most productions that even more seemed at stake when Proteus subsequently betrayed her. That harsh experience made her hard-bitten and resentful. 'How many women would do such a message?' was bitter, and the surely humorous lines to Silvia's portrait, 'I should have scratch'd out your unseeing eyes, / To make my master out of love with thee' were venomous. This Julia was truer to the society created by the production than to the text. Valentine's speech of forgiveness was altered from 'All that was mine in Silvia I give thee' to 'All my love to Silvia I also give to thee', in order to make it clear that Valentine was not simply handing Silvia over to the man who had just attempted to rape her. The two friends embraced, watched distrustfully by the two girls. It became a dark ending, with no easy resolution. It did not wholly solve the problems of a difficult text, but at least it explored rather than evaded them; and in that respect Mr Rubin's approach was very much attuned to the Artistic Director's.

# SHAKESPEARE PERFORMANCES IN LONDON AND STRATFORD-UPON-AVON 1984–5

## NICHOLAS SHRIMPTON

This was a year of star performances and strong readings. Ian McKellen, Ben Kingsley, Anton Lesser, Irene Worth and Juliet Stevenson played major tragic roles for the two major companies, while Nicky Henson brought unusual distinction to the clowning at Stratford. Directors were equally self-assertive. Twelve years ago John Russell Brown argued, in *Free Shakespeare*, for a simplified actors' theatre which resisted 'one-sided interpretations, however subtle or well-informed'. A feminist *Troilus and Cressida*, a Jungian *As You Like It*, and an Ealing Comedy *Merry Wives of Windsor* in the space of a single season suggested that his ideas had yet to take root.

Distinctive acting and distinctive interpretation did not, however, always coincide. Ian McKellen's Coriolanus at the National Theatre in December 1984 was a bravura performance of the kind which Antony Sher's Richard III had reintroduced to the English stage six months before. Its effect, unfortunately, was rather different and it was so because Peter Hall's *Coriolanus*, though notionally the same production, was persistently at odds with it.

Hall's idea for the play, which opened during the bitterest phase of the miners' strike, was simply to stress its contemporary relevance. The stage of the Olivier Theatre was transformed by John Bury into a vast amphitheatre, open to the audience on one side and dominated at the rear by a huge pair of doors. Classical in style, yet punningly modern in its

notion of the play as a forum for debate, the set summed up the Ancient and Modern quality for which the production was striving. On the vertiginous rampart above the door stood a Roman soldier with a spear. Beneath him, however, some rash plebeian with an aerosol had spray-painted the slogan 'Corn At Our Own Price' and the 'company of mutinous Citizens' appeared to have wandered in from the streets of modern London.

As a matter of fact they had wandered in from the streets of modern London, for the box office sold forty tickets for every performance to customers prepared to sit and stand on stage. There a handful of actors cast as shop-stewards alternately roused them to mutiny and cowed them into clearing the stage when the principals needed it. Filling your set with extras who pay you for the privilege of appearing sounds like the best idea since vanity publishing, particularly when their modern dress contributes to the interpretation of the play. But Hall's spontaneous crowd proved to be a very mixed blessing. Smartly dressed, nervously clutching handbags and programmes, self-conscious and eager to please, they looked more like a coachload of tourists caught up in a coup than a revolutionary mob.

What they really were, of course, was an inappropriate importation from another kind of theatre. When, for example, the Théâtre du Soleil turned its audience into the *sans-culottes* for their production of *1789*, it did so with an improvised script which allowed the crowd to

16   *Coriolanus*, National Theatre, 1984. Ian McKellen as Coriolanus

answer back. Peter Hall's *Coriolanus* could permit no such intrusions into the text. The consequence was that a device originally intended to involve and liberate the audience here served to alienate and confine them. Stephen Wall supplied an appropriately modern metaphor for the effect when he commented that 'the audience remains stubbornly unintegrated in the action, despite the conscription of some of its number as on-stage hostages'.[1]

Other modernizing devices were more straightforward. Politicians wore academic gowns (to suggest togas) over grey suits (to indicate twentieth-century power and rank). The two Tribunes, indeed, had a specifically symbolic function as the old and new Labour Party: Sicinius Velutus was a bluff TUC baron, Junius Brutus a grim Welsh militant in a black polo-neck sweater. Coriolanus himself made his first appearance in a double-breasted suit and white trench-coat, with a sword slung casually over his shoulder. He looked like a pop star on his way to a Buckingham Palace soirée and behaved accordingly. On other occasions such contemporary detail vanished entirely. In act 1, scene 8, for example, Coriolanus and Aufidius fought in a sandpit with swords and shields, dressed only in loin cloths and helmets. Despite the loud electronic music by Harrison Birtwistle, we seemed suddenly to be in the world of a David painting.

Amidst this deliberately confusing décor Ian McKellen strove to make sense of Coriolanus. The noisy and picturesque qualities of the staging appeared at first to offer a fatal temptation to his weakness for romantic self-indulgence and in the early scenes he seemed merely an egotistical poseur. A hint of something deeper came with his first taste of suffering. Confessing weakness on 'Have we no wine here?'(1.9.92), his voice began to show us the man behind the snob, and by act 3, scene 2 ('Pray be content / Mother, I am going to the market-place') a tragic dimension was emerging. He remained a Coriolanus who

suffered better than he commanded, a sensitive romantic solitary rather than the heroically inflexible aristocrat which the military action of the play demands. World weariness and prickly awkwardness were his best effects. In moments of violence, defiance or decision the manner frequently seemed hollow.

Unfortunately, the semi-contemporary setting made this figure very hard to place. Not a general as we know generals, nor a politician of any kind we would recognize, he seemed to make sense only as a disappointed prima-donna. There is something of Coriolanus in this, but by no means enough. The production had no feeling for aristocracy, military virtue, patriotism or filial duty – the unfashionable values which Coriolanus embodies and on which the arguments of this difficult tragedy depend. As a consequence his sufferings appeared to be a private matter, with little bearing on the politics of the play.

Those politics were themselves very uncertainly handled. Frederick Treves was a weighty and moving Menenius and Irene Worth, though sometimes hampered by the awkward acoustics of the amphitheatre, a quietly powerful Volumnia. Elsewhere the mixture of periods frequently left actors at a loss. Heroic hints of the picket-line in the crowd scenes, for example, made the eventual come-uppance of the Tribunes more than usually difficult to play with conviction and the production's attitude to the people would be better described as indecisive than ambiguous. Modernization is not enough as a director's answer to *Coriolanus*, though, ironically, hindsight now suggests a rather more interesting contemporary parallel than Hall found for a production, during the miners' strike, of a tragedy about the indomitable hero of a hundred fights whose impatience with ballots leads him into disaster.

Humbler circumstances of every kind attended Sam Walters's production of the 1603

---

[1] *Times Literary Supplement*, 28 December 1984.

17 *Coriolanus*, National Theatre, 1984. Menenius Agrippa (Frederick Treves) with Volumnia (Irene Worth) and Virgilia (Wendy Morgan)

First Quarto of *Hamlet* at the Orange Tree Theatre, Richmond in March 1985. The text, the setting (a small bare room above a pub), and the limited cast (nine actors performed nineteen parts, then re-doubled themselves as the Players) all promised to present insuperable difficulties. Scholarly curiosity might be satisfied by such an enterprise, but could anything else be said for it? These fears were wholly unjustified. The tragic experience proved to be more vividly available here, in the modern equivalent of an inn-yard, than it had been on the stage of the National Theatre.

In part this was simply confirmation of the growing sense that *Hamlet*, in whatever text, is today most effective in studio performance. The cheek-by-jowl intimacy of the Orange Tree's tiny auditorium suited both the private processes of Hamlet's introspection and the conspiratorial closeness of public life at Elsinore. Sending Hamlet to England ('Lords Rossencraft and Gilderstone shall goe along with you'), Claudius received a whispered answer, full of soft and deadly irony: 'O with *all* my heart: farewel mother'. At the same time the spectacular aspects of the play, which might seem to be at risk in such circumstances, were very little harmed. Peter Wyatt's rapid and passionate ghost, for example, was played without smoke, gauzes, or even much of a lighting plot. It seemed all the better for it.

The text itself, for all its imperfections, contributed something to the freshness of the playing. Walters had, reasonably enough, made absolute fidelity subordinate to the needs of performance and tidied up a few of the more ludicrous or confusing variants. King Hamlet's sepulchre, accordingly, 'op'd' rather than 'burst' his ponderous and marble jaws, Hamlet spoke of 'country' rather than 'contrary' matters to Ophelia, and The Mousetrap took place in familiar Vienna rather than surprising 'Guyana'. This meant that the production was not a perfect test of the quality and status of the First Quarto. In larger matters, however, the actors were true to their distinctive script and the consequences were striking. The brevity of this text (2,154 lines against the 3,723 of the Second Quarto) proved ideally suited to the kind of small-scale performance

for which it was, very probably, originally intended. Regional repertory companies who shrink from the cost of a conventional *Hamlet* might well consider this alternative.

Even the oddity had its advantages. Listening to the First Quarto in performance proved to be an experience not unlike hearing the New English Bible read in church. It is commonplace but clear ('*Hamlet*. I never loved you. *Ofelia*. You made me believe you did'), prompting perpetual ghostly memories of the more familiar text but keeping the essential issues always in view. This can, of course, induce its own kind of confusion. But the benefits are also very real. Actors as well as audiences are stimulated by the newness of the

18   *Coriolanus*, National Theatre, 1984. Menenius Agrippa (Frederick Treves, centre) addresses the Tribunes, Sicinius Velutus (David Ryall, left) and Junius Brutus (James Hayes)

19 *Hamlet* (First Quarto), Orange Tree Theatre, Richmond, 1985. Peter Guinness as Hamlet

20 *The Merry Wives of Windsor*, Royal Shakespeare Theatre, 1985. The Host of the Garter Inn (Trevor Martin) and Falstaff (Peter Jeffrey)

lines. Peter Guinness's delivery of 'To be, or not to be, I there's the point' commanded an intense attention which I have rarely seen the uncorrupted text achieve in the theatre. After the second line ('To Die, to sleepe, is that all? I all') he took off his coat and began to exit. Then, suddenly, moved by a fresh thought, he stepped back and continued. Death was vividly in every mind long before he reached 'he may his full Quietus make, / With a bare bodkin', delivered with his dagger in position to cut his wrist.

This is, of course, at least as much a tribute to Guinness's playing as it is to the fortuitous oddity of his material. He was a gaunt and dangerous Hamlet, a pock-marked malcontent who refrained from action only because he chose to. This text is the only one to authorize a teenaged Hamlet. Walters and Guinness ignored such prompting and gave us a mature man whose extensive knowledge of the world only deepened his distress. The affected madness was powerfully handled (one of the incidental benefits of First Quarto proved to be that the court's worry on this score is so strongly indicated), and the early placing of the nunnery scene, whatever the arguments against its authenticity, served to establish the sense of a man who is from the first disgusted with life. First Quarto is a lesser text than its alternatives. But this production gave clarity, energy, and tension to the ideas which it does contain and offered the most entirely satisfactory piece of tragic acting of the year.

Productions at Stratford, though all by different directors, were consistently both less austere than the Orange Tree *Hamlet* and more coherent than the National Theatre's *Coriolanus*. The real star of *The Merry Wives of Windsor*, which opened in March 1985, was the set. By a slight but significant piece of juggling with numbers, the director, Bill Alexander, chose to move the play from the 1590s to the 1950s, thereby turning a Tudor citizen comedy into a neo-Tudor suburban farce. His designer, William Dudley, obliged him with a witty and striking series of period interiors for the semis and saloon bars of Elizabeth II's Windsor.

Between scenes, while these elaborate sets were manipulated, characters rushed about (sometimes in an open-topped Morris Minor) to incidental music in the manner of the Ealing comedies. This air of comic frenzy was in part intended to hide an actual slowness of pace and the verbal comedy often suffered from such interruptions. Once in position, however, the visual humour of the *mise-en-scène* provided appropriate compensation. The Garter Inn, for example, was a superb specimen of brewers' Tudorbethan, complete with brass hunting horns, framed sporting prints and a Sabrina-like barmaid. Here Falstaff propped himself on a bar stool to absorb his drinks, Nym played darts, and Robin (a truant Etonian) read *Eagle* on a settle by the door.

Characters were transposed with equal daring. Page looked like a bank manager. Ford might have been running a garage. Mine host of the Garter Inn sported a regimental blazer and handle-bar moustache, and Dr Caius became (to very good effect) a medical equivalent of Peter Sellers's Inspector Clouseau. The motive for this radical up-dating was not, I think, mere whimsy. Uniquely amongst Shakespeare's comedies, *The Merry Wives of Windsor* did not seek to transport its original audiences to foreign climes or (Falstaff's other incarnation notwithstanding) previous eras. Instead it gave them back an image of themselves. Bill Alexander's purpose was clearly to offer us the same opportunity.

Some details stubbornly resisted the translation. The presence of servants, for example, was hard to reconcile with the lower-middle-class suburban world which we were shown. More importantly, the concentration on a period style sometimes distracted actors from the delivery of Shakespeare's jokes and the winning of the audience. Peter Jeffrey's Falstaff, in his tweed suit and yellow waistcoat, was an acute character study of an unscrupu-

21　*The Merry Wives of Windsor*, Royal Shakespeare Theatre, 1985. Ford's house, act 3, scene 3. Dr Caius (David Bradley), Page (Paul Webster), Ford (Nicky Henson), Mistress Page (Janet Dale), Mistress Ford (Lindsay Duncan)

lous, post-war temporary gentleman. The result, however, was neither very warm nor very funny. Delivering a box of Black Magic to Mistress Ford he seemed in his element. Delivering a line like the immortal 'I'll no pullet-sperm in my brewage', he seemed strangely at a loss. This Falstaff functioned as a villain rather than a rogue, and was best in his most brutal moments.

Elsewhere there were signs of interpretative indecision. The Merry Wives themselves were played with marvellous panache by Janet Dale and Lindsay Duncan. Gossiping under the hairdrier in act 2, scene 1, giggling over gins on the sofa in act 4, scene 2, or acting out their 'overheard' dialogue in act 3, scene 3, as a piece of extravagant amateur dramatics, they were sharp, subtle and inventive. They suffered,

nonetheless, from a deep-rooted uncertainty. Were these wise and sympathetic heroines, taking a deserved revenge on that blundering creature, Man? Or were they satirical portraits of grotesquely vulgar, bourgeois housewives? The actresses were not sure and, as a consequence, neither was the audience.

Fortunately, in the latter part of the play such worries became less important. As the action became more farcical, and as Nicky Henson's Ford was able to infect the playing with more and more of his remarkable comic zest, the production came irresistibly to life. Henson's disguise as Brook (a Hitler moustache, gold-rimmed spectacles and a yellow cycling cape) was less than subtle. But his second appearance in the suburban doorway to confront, yet again, the notorious buck-basket, was a superb piece of humorous staging. Dressed in a Hollywood tough guy's trench coat, he froze momentarily on the threshold with his posse of friends behind him. Then, in sudden frenzy, he threw himself bodily into the dirty linen for a wild and vicious search. Emerging empty-handed, he paused again, before offering us, in the still, small voice of inconsequential conversation, the line 'Well, he's not here I seek for' (4.2.140). Control of pace and volume of this degree of precision is the essence of great farce acting. Stratford's season was the richer for it.

Beneath this tide of comic energy the love plot was rather washed away. Paul Spence played Fenton as a funny beatnik, periodically contorted with absurd spasms of existentialist *angoisse*. One sensed his need to compete with comic performances on the scale of Henson's Ford or Sheila Steafel's eccentric Mistress Quickly. The play's story suffered nonetheless. Shakespeare's comedy carefully balances the humiliation of Falstaff with the defeat of the citizens' schemes for Anne Page. If we cannot believe in her love affair, or even if we are too much distracted from it, the fundamental pattern of the drama is distorted.

Partly for this reason, I felt that the controversial curtain call was entirely appropriate. The romance plot (however slight) had long since been sacrificed to the needs of farce and the pointing up of period detail. Putting the entire cast on stage for a wild and wonderful jive routine was just the way to end a knockabout evening. This production suffered from some local misjudgements but possessed high spirits, comic relish and an authentic sense of fun. The dancing at the curtain call summed up those qualities to perfection.

Adrian Noble's Stratford production of *As You Like It*, in April 1985, was also in modern dress, though in a manner which was, deliberately, both less obtrusive and less consistent. The world of the first act was notable for its harsh weather and harsher social distinctions, rather than for any precise sense of period.

Orlando hunched himself against the wind in jeans and a donkey-jacket for the quarrel with his gentleman farmer of a brother, while at court a plutocratic gentry seemed still to be wearing Edwardian white tie and tails.

Indoors, too, environment seemed more significant than costume. Rosalind, in a debutante's party dress, was discovered in a cavernous room full of furniture under drapes. The banished Duke's apartments, one assumed, were closed up. But such literal reading was soon rebuked. Why does she wrap herself in one of the dust sheets? Why does Touchstone (a white-faced clown in evening dress) emerge from under the table? What on earth is going on?

The point of the scene was, of course, precisely to drive us to that question. Naturalistic assumptions were being steadily undermined in preparation for a move to the Forest of Arden which would have the magical qualities of a pantomime transformation scene. The process was continued by the wrestling match. On the surface this was very literal. By the light of four glowing braziers, gentlemen with brandy and cigars watched a witty pastiche of the modern grapple game, with Charles as Big Daddy. It was lively, violent, and amusing. Yet, at the same time, the lurid qualities of the scene somehow suggested that we were at the circus rather than the theatre, observing a spectacle which had more to do with fantasy than mimesis.

At the beginning of act 2, the reasons for such preparation became clear. Duke Frederick (with Joseph O'Conor doubling the roles) stepped through a mirror into Arden and became his moral opposite, Duke Senior. Adrian Noble was offering us *As You Like It Through the Looking Glass*. In the final scene Jaques would act out his reversal of philosophical temper in precisely the same way. Abandoning cynicism for a curiosity about the religious life, he stepped off stage through the identical pier glass. And the piece of furniture from which Rosalind removed the drape, when she wrapped herself in a dust sheet in act I, scene 2, was, of course, the very same object. What she would find on the other side of it was a mirror-image of her habitual sexual identity – reversed, by role-playing, into masculinity.

This Carrollian analogy for the transforming effects of Shakespeare's pastoral convention (perhaps suggested by Empson's inclusion of *Alice in Wonderland* in his *Some Versions of Pastoral*) was, of course, suggestive rather than exact. The Forest of Arden here started as the original palace covered with even more enormous dust sheets than those which we saw in the first act. This telling domestic image (akin to the effect of mirror reversal) of the familiar made strange also conveyed, by its icy whiteness, the 'churlish chiding of the winter's wind' in this houseless 'desert'. Rosalind, Celia and Touchstone struggled through it as if through snow. Adam fainted into its billows. After the interval, however, some more radical transformation was required, and the Forest became a Green World after all. Spring had clearly arrived. Green furniture kept us (just) in touch with the original notion of familiar things subtly altered. But a grassy stage-cloth and a large pool of water took us, inevitably, back to the conventionally pastoral image of a context in which the self could be transformed.

Despite its dwindling utility, the looking-glass motif had great initial force. Expressed in striking designs by Bob Crowley, it, at very least, preserved the production from the danger of prettiness which the stock greenwood image brings with it and made audiences think afresh about what the pastoral conceit implies. It did, however, also have a more extended purpose. As the quotations in the programme suggested, the idea of the ambiguous self was here being taken very seriously. Court and country, sinner and saint, cynic and convertite and, above all, man and woman were implied to be merely opposite sides of the same coin. The playing of Rosalind and

Orlando rested, throughout their courtship, upon the Jungian concept of animus and anima. Both sets of clothes, rather than just Rosalind's, were delicately shifted away from their original stereotypes towards an androgynous mean. When these lovers looked at each other they saw, not so much the possibility of a pastoral excursion into the opposite sexual identity, as a vision of the opposite sexual identity as a mirror image of their own.

Ideas of this degree of complexity are precisely what makes the work of Adrian Noble so exciting. They can also, it must be said, impose terrible burdens on actors. Juliet Stevenson's Rosalind was touching in her vulnerable moments but desperately unsure when she was required to be witty, flirtatious or high-spirited. It may be that this gifted actress is (like so many gifted actresses) simply not a comedienne. It may also be that the psychological lumber which she was required to carry in this production was too much, and was insufficiently appropriate, for any actress who simultaneously has to undertake the task of making an audience laugh at Rosalind.

Fortunately there were other players available to take up the slack. In particular the production reminded one that *As You Like It* has not one but two witty heroines. Fiona Shaw played Celia quite marvellously as a sparky deb with a sharp tongue, an even sharper sense of style and, eventually, a comprehensible weakness for a similarly upper-crust Oliver. Her heroic but horrified declaration 'I'll put myself in poor and mean attire' (1.3.107), spoken like a duchess contemplating a visit to an Oxfam shop, was one of the comic highlights of the year. In a broader style, Nicky Henson was once again conspicuous, this time as Touchstone. He performed smooth backchat with Celia, rough slapstick with Audrey and William, and a splendidly choreographed set-piece for the 'Retort Courteous' speech, in act 5, scene 4, which involved assembling the entire company (bar Rosalind, Celia and Jaques de Boys) into an energetic

22  *As You Like It*, Royal Shakespeare Theatre, 1985. Orlando (Hilton McRae) and Rosalind (Juliet Stevenson) in act 5, scene 2

chorus line. So powerful, indeed, was this comic climax that it was almost impossible to follow. The final scene strove hard for the kind of surreal serenity which Noble achieved so notably at the end of his production of *Measure for Measure* in 1983. It did not achieve it, offering instead the voice of Hymen over the tannoy and an elegant but insubstantial ballet.

One further feature of this *As You Like It* which demands to be recorded is Alan Rickman's Jaques. This was acting which divided the critics to a quite extraordinary degree. Irving Wardle, in *The Times*, described him as 'a no-saying figure so at odds with the production's line of thought that he is confined to a rat-like leer, and to over-elaborating his solos as unsupported arias'.[2] It seemed to me a strikingly intelligent performance: cool,

supercilious, and witty in ways which perfectly complemented (often, of course, by contrast) the other playing. Rickman was responsible for one truly astonishing moment when Orlando leapt upon Duke Senior's woodland dining-table for 'He dies that touches any of this fruit / Till I and my affairs are answered' (2.7.98–9). Jaques's response was not a comic aside but a piece of calm bravado. In entire silence he walked steadily from downstage to the table and, on 'An you will not be answer'd with reason, I must die', picked up an apple and bit it. Not all the detail was as good as this. Some of the ideas remained undigested, the conclusion was disappointing, and the erotic tension was

---

[2] *The Times*, 25 April 1985.

23    *Troilus and Cressida*, Royal Shakespeare Theatre, 1985. The Greek generals in conference: Nestor (Mark Dignam) and Agamemnon (Joseph O'Conor) seated, with Ulysses (Peter Jeffrey, standing right)

(perhaps inevitably) rather low. *As You Like It* remained a production which was fresh, funny and, above all, intellectually alive.

Setting was crucial once again in Howard Davies's production of *Troilus and Cressida*, which opened in June 1985. Ralph Koltai had designed a single set, consisting of the white interior of a nineteenth-century mansion three-quarters smashed by war. Peeling pictures, broken shutters, a chandelier and some fallen curtains hung crazily above a grandiose staircase. By turns Trojan and Greek, public and private, conference chamber and troops' taverna, it placed us on the shores of the Black Sea in the 1850s. This context had, of course, more than merely geographical appropriateness to recommend it. It invoked the Crimean War in order to make us think, simultaneously, of the heroic idealism of the Charge of the Light Brigade and the brutal reality of the wards at Scutari.

This was, in other words, a political reading of *Troilus and Cressida*, and one which kept its eye very firmly on public event. Peter Jeffrey's excellent Ulysses was a frock-coated, Gladstonian figure with the confident rhetorical manner of the Victorian House of Commons. Joseph O'Conor's equally impressive Agamemnon was an elderly general in a quilted smoking-jacket. First seen round a conference table, with a secretary taking minutes and a telegraph machine tapping out dispatches in the corner, they were entirely convincing portraits of powerful statesmen. The traditional uncertainty about the genre of this text – is it tragedy, history, problem play, comedy, satire, or burlesque? – was here decisively settled. In this production it was an energetic history play with strong political implications. The familiar story of the Trojan War was, as a consequence, given an unfamiliar degree of narrative impetus and conviction.

Private life could not, of course, be simply excluded, but that too was made the subject of energetic political analysis. This was, in a word, a feminist *Troilus and Cressida* which took Shakespeare's dual concern with 'wars and lechery' (5.2.194) as an opportunity to articulate that strand of contemporary feminist thought which sees militarism and male sexual oppression as the twin roots of patriarchy.

The obvious objection to such a reading of the play is what we have traditionally assumed to be its view of women. The flighty Helen is the original cause of the war; Cressida is the most notorious case of female fickleness in the whole of Western literature. Howard Davies defeated these objections by a combination of subtle re-emphasis and sustained playing against the text. Helen became a 'man's woman' – a sinister and brutal vamp, infected by the values of her Prussian Junker of a paramour (Sean Baker in high-necked uniform, monocle, and duelling scar). Cressida, more interestingly, was re-read as a serious nineteenth-century New Woman whose infidelity reflected, not moral weakness, but her status as the victim of an aggressively masculine culture.

To make such playing possible, Pandarus too has, of course, to be transformed. Clive Merrison was no salacious procurer but a sympathetic relative, more cousin than uncle, more sexual therapist than pimp. A slim, elegant and endearingly disillusioned figure, he was subjected to savage bullying in his scene with Paris and Helen and disassociated himself from the fighting of the final act by playing a piano in a corner of the battlefield. When, in the last line of the epilogue, he bequeathed us his diseases, it was for once not at all clear what they were meant to be.

Talking to such a figure, Cressida has no need to be a coquette. As Juliet Stevenson played it (very much more at home here than she had been as Rosalind), the speech 'Upon my back to defend my belly; upon my wit, to defend my wiles; upon my secrecy, to defend mine honesty' (1.2.252–4) was a serious feminist statement, spoken by a woman who had authentic reservations about the wisdom of a

24    *Troilus and Cressida*, Royal Shakespeare Theatre, 1985. Pandarus (Clive Merrison) and Cressida (Juliet Stevenson) in act 1, scene 2

25    *Othello*, Royal Shakespeare Theatre, 1985. Iago (David Suchet) and Othello (Ben Kingsley)

liaison with a man whose qualities she doubts. Stern, thoughtful, and persistently sceptical, she did her best to suggest that Troilus had been given fair warning of the relationship's dangers. Even more interesting was the transformation of act 4, scene 5. Her reception in the Greek camp was turned from the customary piece of coy flirtation into a cruel display of male sexual brutality. No tease, but a terrified victim, she was thrown from general to general in a manner which threatened to be the prelude to multiple rape. Ulysses' 'Her wanton spirits look out / At every joint and motive of her body' (4.5.56–7) became, as a consequence, the slanderous misrepresentation of a frustrated man.

Fascinating though this high-minded re-reading was, certain crucial joints of the play creaked a good deal under the strain. Pandarus was one such point of difficulty, Cressida's final scene with Diomedes another. Juliet Stevenson was obliged to patch up the latter by stooping to the desperate expedient of suggesting that terror had somehow driven Cressida mad. Shakespeare's plays will always mean more than we conventionally expect them to. But this does not imply that they will always mean exactly what we want.

The other substantial penalty of this interpretation was that one whole area of the play's life was suppressed. In this production *Troilus and Cressida* was no longer really a play about love, and its weakest moment was the normally intensely touching scene of the morning after the first night together. Feminists are perfectly capable of falling in love. But this Cressida's doubts about men were so considerable, and so explicit, that only a fool would ignore her hesitations. Anton Lesser's energetic and eloquent Troilus was, of course, obliged to ignore them and paid the inevitable price of seeming silly. In *The Taming of the Shrew* Petruchio has a spaniel called Troilus. After this interpretation of *Troilus and Cressida* one could not but see why.

Though the play's romantic interest van-

ished in a way which made it, on this occasion, tragic history rather than tragedy of love, a good deal of its comedy survived. Alun Armstrong supplied a gloomy northern batman of a Thersites, who appeared to be the original valet to whom no man is a hero. His slapstick was deft and his backchat lethal. He was, as a consequence, extremely funny, though there were times when his accent and his fierce intensity made him seem less a cynic than the voice of the Nonconformist conscience.

For all its strains, this was a singularly coherent and compelling account of a difficult play. Its elaborate atmospheric apparatus, grand crowd scenes and ample music (Pandarus even accompanied himself on the piano, with a Kurt Weill-like tune, for the song in his final speech) made it an uncomfortably long evening – 3½ hours without the interval – and many people will remain unpersuaded by its stresses. The production was, nonetheless, a milestone in the history of the play. Henceforth we will never again discuss this text in quite the same way.

The same, alas, cannot be said for the *Othello* which Terry Hands directed, also at Stratford and also with Ralph Koltai as his designer, in September 1985. Hands used, perhaps rashly, the Arden text, with its mass of Quarto variants, and based his image of the protagonist on the well-known portrait of the Moorish Ambassador to the court of Queen Elizabeth I. Ben Kingsley, accordingly, played Othello as a sensitive and scrupulous Arab intellectual. On a bare, black stage, occasionally broken up with rectangles of neon light, this delicate figure encountered a bulky and passionate Iago. David Suchet put much serious emphasis on Iago's own jealousy. This was no practical joker but a wounded man, driven by many of the same emotions that he chooses to exploit in his victim. 'I hate the Moor' (1.3.380) can rarely have been delivered with such venom, and his remark (of Desdemona) that 'Now I do love her too' (2.1.285) was stressed to an unusual degree.

Unfortunately this determined sense of psychological depth was hard to reconcile with his equal willingness to play to the audience as a chatty, stand-up comic. He did both things well but failed sufficiently to distinguish between them. His director, it must be said, provided very little help. Hands's idea of how to underline a point consisted, for example, of the decision to follow 'Hell and night / Must bring this monstrous birth to the world's light' (1.3.397–8) with an exit in which Iago strolled off stage amidst clouds of smoke, flashes of light, and thunderous organ music, while a gigantic crucifix was flown in above.

If such effects were vulgar, the blocking was often simply careless. From the point in act 1, scene 1 when Iago was left fully visible to Brabantio who is supposedly unable to see him, to the dreadful moment in the final scene when Othello was unable to reach the huge hanging lantern for 'Put out the light, and then put out the light', the staging lacked any real conviction. In such circumstances it would perhaps be unreasonable to expect a powerful performance from the protagonist. Certainly

Ben Kingsley did not supply one. Physically slighter than his Iago, he handled the access of disturbance with delicate skill. His timing, and his nervous toss of the head, on 'No, not much mov'd' (3.3.228) was a fine effect, and he gave an acute impression of the way in which dignity and self-confidence can collapse suddenly into merely outward composure. But the Othello music and the tragic grandeur of the later scenes seemed beyond his range. The oriental excitability, which he had so carefully established, dwindled all too easily into inarticulate gesturing, and the final scene, normally so tense, seemed strangely slow and vacant. This was a production full of nervous tension and emotional detail, but lacking a real sense of the tragic sadness of things. At the last it reasserted its notion of Othello and Iago as psychological counterparts, and one died clutching the other by the throat. Coherent conception of this kind is the indispensable basis for the intelligent production of Shakespeare. Careless execution is as liable in the Royal Shakespeare Company as anywhere else to let it all be in vain.

# THE YEAR'S CONTRIBUTIONS TO SHAKESPEARIAN STUDY

## 1. CRITICAL STUDIES
### *reviewed by* BRIAN GIBBONS

This year is marked by a new book, *Shakespearean Dimensions*,[1] from G. Wilson Knight, in his sixtieth (and, sadly, last) year of writing, worthy of welcome. Speaking for himself in a sprightly, brief and candid introduction, Wilson Knight affirms his faith in a Shakespeare saturated in idealism, says that he sees his own natural pursuit to have always been interpretation of Shakespeare, rather than criticism, and recalls a review he wrote of H. A. Mason's *Shakespeare's Tragedies of Love*. Mason had there objected that the almost superhuman status accorded to Antony in *Antony and Cleopatra* had no dramatic basis in what we see him do, and Wilson Knight demurely observes, 'Even so, is not the attempt somehow justified by its result? We cannot but admire the temerity with which Mr Mason offers clusters of the most mind-ravishing quotations as a logical part of his indictment.' Wilson Knight has always had the power to communicate to his readers the mind-ravishing quality of Shakespeare's dramatic language. The title of his book seems to recall *Twelfth Night*:

> A spirit I am indeed;
> But am in that dimension grossly clad
> Which from the womb I did participate,

but the high point for me is the essay on 'Caliban as a Red Man' which, though pre-viously published elsewhere,[2] feels somewhat different in this new context. The book's first chapter invokes the traditional terms 'soul' and 'spirit', since 'there is such a reality, beyond brain and all logical thought' which 'makes a large and determining part of what we mean by man and his universe' (p. 6). Wilson Knight simply sketches features of his spiritual auto-biography which he considers provide a context for his Shakespeare interpretation, so making it clear that he wants the focus to fall on the plays not on himself. In discussing Caliban he concentrates on his 'normal, clair-voyant' apprehension of nature and spirit (a finely paradoxical description); he compares the primitive consciousness of the North American Indian, using first-hand illustration. This approach makes Caliban's language vividly available, removing a layer of famili-arity as if it were a coat of varnish.

It is in this emphasis on the simultaneity of

---

[1] The Harvester Press, Brighton; Barnes and Noble Books, Totowa, New Jersey, 1984.
[2] In *Shakespeare's Styles, Essays in Honour of Kenneth Muir* (Cambridge, 1980). The other essays in *Shakespearean Dimensions* recently first published elsewhere are 'Glou-cester's Leap' (*Essays in Criticism*, 1972), '*Timon of Athens* and Buddhism' (*E in C*, 1980), 'Vergil, Shakespeare and the Seraphic' (University of Exeter, 1976), 'Society and the Cosmos', (*Critical Dimensions*, 1978). There are also separate essays on Lyly, Webster, and Ford.

sensory immediacy *and* supernatural strangeness, so well described by Wilson Knight, which few attempts in print or on the stage in the English-speaking world even try to convey. Perhaps their dismalness would have convinced the present generation that *The Tempest* is theatrically deficient, were it not for Giorgio Strehler, whose recent supreme production made one think of Wilson Knight. Its Titianesque courtiers, Callot-like Trinculo, and an African black Caliban, signalled the political dimension; a weightless flying Ariel (he/she), solid wood ship's deck subject to fluctuating transformations, and a wide surrounding volatile sea of silk moved by unseen real hands, united trance, fear and laughter: it was history as carnival transcended by rite.

Also ambitious, risking more than most literary studies, not excluding the radical and alternative, is the new Stephen Booth on indefinition and tragedy,[3] a readable book, at times a little off-the-cuff, light but intelligent, with much locally perceptive comment as it weaves in and out of its main topic, that tragedy gives a local habitation and a name to the most terrifying of things, 'a deed without a name', but does this 'without denying its namelessness, its incomprehensibility, its indefinition' (p. 118). The discussion explores the many kinds of pattern, from those woven in the verbal structure (semantic and grammatical) in the soliloquy 'If it were done' from 1.7 of *Macbeth*, to those of the plot of *King Lear*, and relates these structural patterns, with their limits, to the experience depicted – and hence to the audience's experience – which is not complete, not a closed unit with a beginning, a middle, and an end;

an audience's experience of *Macbeth* is of truth beyond the limits of categories. That experience, which I think is what we are labeling when we use the word tragedy, is made bearable by a vehicle, the fabric of the play, which has limits, has pattern, and is insistently man-made. The patterns of the play are made by the very elements whose disjunction takes

the mind beyond the usual limits of its tolerance.
(p. 117)

The notion of the mind's usual limits of tolerance is productive in Booth's argument; for him an audience is not merely relieved of physical involvement in the dangerous events enacted before it but is rendered 'genuinely, though temporarily ... superior to the helpless relativism in which the human mind is trapped and by virtue of which the human mind ordinarily requires itself to recognise one of the set of terms in which a perceived fact operates and to ignore or deny the others'. The thinking sometimes reaches for over-refined or over-tenuous formulations on the one hand, or impulsively exaggerates on the other; thus Booth asserts at one point that the tragedy of *Macbeth* occurs in the audience which, in persisting in seeing the play through Macbeth's eyes, 'cannot keep itself in the category dictated by its own morality' (p. 105), so that Shakespeare induces an audience 'virtually to be Macbeth for the duration of the performance' (p. 106). Eight pages later this is half-retracted, in fact; such exaggerations, reformulations, and retractions are less objectionable in a lively discussion than in a finished book, and so it may be to the point that there is something conversational in the whole procedure of these essays (hospitable as that procedure is to sudden thoughts injected at an angle to the main direction of argument), allowing a piece of analysis to proceed as improvised exploration, sometimes excitedly searching for a suppler means to register an impression and incurring excesses of various kinds along the way. At the book's centre is something genuinely difficult, genuinely worth getting at, which Booth gets clear:

[in *King Lear*] the intensity of patterning compensates for the equal intensity of its demonstration that ... all human perception of pattern is folly: the

---

[3] *King Lear, Macbeth, Indefinition, and Tragedy* (Yale University Press, 1983).

omnipresent, never-quite-circumscribable patterns testify – as faith in a religious metaphysic might – that a governing idea for the play, a lodestone for our values, exists just beyond our mental reach . . . That would explain our all-but-desperate need to believe that Lear learns something between Act I and his death. (p. 22).

The occasional exaggeration and erratic line of Booth's argument are worth putting up with.

In contrast to Booth, Robert Rentoul Reed Jr[4] lays stress precisely on the dramatic pattern and the category of morality in *Macbeth*, seen as the climax of a sequence beginning in the early histories. To Reed, modern critics become misleading when they use modern criteria to

reach conclusions that, in terms of Tudor criteria, are illogical or invalid . . . These [Tudor] concepts include the biblical principle of inherited guilt; the doctrine that God is the fountainhead of retribution and that man . . . is merely His worldly instrument; and third, and not necessarily least, the fundamentally divine function of the conscience, in particular when its Old Testament dictates are violated. (pp. 10–11)

Thus Reed can give an account of the hero of a Shakespearian tragedy in terms deriving from his reading of King James I or Timothy Bright or Perkins the author of *A Discourse of Conscience* (1596), and it is in adducing quotations from such contemporary figures that Reed sternly presents the received ideas of at least some dogmatic writers of Shakespeare's time. The question remains of whether a spectator's doctrinal beliefs, cast formally for publication with didactic as well as conscientious intent, are quite the same as the response during performance to a powerful work of Shakespeare's imagination. Something of the tone with which Reed writes of *Macbeth* seems not to accord with the play as an audience can know it:

The true victory in the play *Macbeth*, as in *Richard III*, is probably God's, for Richmond and, later, Macduff are but His agents. King James, speaking of the devil and those who consort with him, has

already confirmed God's part for us; 'God . . . drawes ever out of that evill, glorie to himselfe . . . by the wracke of the wicked in his justice.' And wherein, in the play *Macbeth*, is found this 'glorie'? If God find 'glorie' in His judgement upon Macbeth . . . the glory does not lie in the act itself; the act is too meager. It lies, more rightly (I think), in God's having relieved Scotland . . . The bringing by God of a merely wicked man to judgement is worthy perhaps of a perfunctory glory. (p. 197)

Recognition of the gap between a sixteenth- and a twentieth-century view of the world, between aspects of consciousness then and now, must of course abruptly strike us at the beginning of an encounter with Shakespeare, and must remain a fixed condition of it; but this is not to confine him to certain dogmas of his time, however widespread it is speculated that they may have been, while the special status of drama makes the identification of dogmatic conformity hazardous where it is not reductive. King James I, as cited by Reed above, shrivels one's sense of what it is to be human.

James P. Driscoll's *Identity in Shakespearean Drama*[5] approaches the plays in Jungian terms, reminding us that Jung's work on Renaissance alchemy and symbolism

give his work relevance to identity in Shakespeare, who so often intertwines and blends naturalistic and symbolic modes. By using myth, symbol and archetype to explore the human psyche, Jung has given us maps of psychic structure that are more detailed and more germane to Renaissance symbolism and ideals of identity than those drawn by any other modern psychologist. (p. 9)

In his Introduction Driscoll surveys the unhappy recent history of the word and concept ('The Identity of Identity', pp. 14–21). This establishes that he has read widely enough, and thought hard enough, to make his book worth reading. He offers four categories

---

[4] *Crime and God's Judgement in Shakespeare* (The University Press of Kentucky, Lexington, 1984).
[5] Bucknell University Press, Lewisburg, 1983.

or aspects of identity: *real*, what is revealed by plot and action; *social*, conceptions held by the society within the play as apparent in marriage, family, class and political expectations; *conscious*, referring to a character's ruling conceptions about himself; *ideal*, which is sought as a consequence of recognizing the tensions in and between the other types of identity, to be a unique individual whose wholeness is the love of self and others and truth to self and others.

If ideal identity can be said to have any function in earlier plays, it is only as the happiness to be gained from fulfilling social and political responsibilities, such as marriage and parenthood, and administering justice and maintaining order ... Cordelia is a salient example of truth and love's joining to create the wholeness that constitutes ideal identity.

Many of Shakespeare's major tragic heroes, in Driscoll's view, 'in their often confused or indirect ways are searching for this ideal', though Prospero

alone transcends all obstacles, and then only in old age, after long waiting and much suffering. Ideal identity is the aspect of identity in Shakespearean drama that poses the greatest challenges and opportunities for contemporary criticism. Modern man tends to be sensitive only to identity's naturalistic dimensions, but Renaissance man was keenly alive to both the naturalistic and the symbolic or ideal. We cannot understand how Shakespeare, Spenser, and their contemporaries saw Elizabeth I unless we realise that for them she was at once an immensely complicated real person and a powerful, almost numinous, symbol. Similarly, any character could be naturalistic one moment, symbolic the next, and both at the same time in varying degrees.

(pp. 22–3)

Driscoll relates Jung's terms 'persona' and 'shadow' to Shakespearian instances, and devises a flexible and productive plan for exploring the plays in terms of the four categories of identity; the overall scheme, seeing *King Lear* and *The Tempest* as the most complete and direct investigations of 'ideal wholeness', offers a somewhat familiar view of Shakespeare's oeuvre, but Driscoll is by no means indeed anxious to separate himself from a long, and important, traditional approach to Shakespeare; it is the clarity and scruple of his work which recommend it, not its innovatory potential, though in refurbishing the term 'identity' he has done a real service to current criticism as well as focusing the slackness and vagueness which have prevailed in much recent critical use of the term and concept.[6]

Especially in deploying the different categories of the term, Driscoll is able to do justice to the different modes and styles of different plays while developing his theme. It may be the case that interpretation of Shakespeare from the Jungian perspective does tend to move away from the distinct and particular in a play in seeking to uncover a parallel, but more complete, finally grandly unifying, work of philosophic discovery, a work of faith with its own independent value. Driscoll clearly does believe that *King Lear* and *The Tempest* form a kind of diptych bodying forth a representation of the value of ideal identity, established upon a paradoxical and tragic commitment to absolute truth and love; what makes this significant as literary criticism is his readiness to record the working of the plays, his responsiveness to awkward challenges presented to ideals of hope, integrity, closure of any kind. (Driscoll, like most good critics, takes Kermode's views on the sense of an ending in *King Lear* seriously and is stimulated by them.) On *The Tempest* he proffers the term 'metastance' to describe Prospero's transcendence of need for power, his freedom from the need to adopt Lear's Promethean stance, his achievement of a detachment which permits him to acknowledge 'the possibility of

---

6 An essay specifically engaged with selfhood and identity is Mark Bracher, 'Identity in *As You Like It*' (*Studies in Philology*, 225–40). Bracher says, 'By embracing her role as Ganymede Rosalind is ... able to get outside her monistic, habitual self and achieve a more inclusive, incohesive self that realises the folly of romantic ideals even while loving Orlando ... the ultimate nature of the self is a plurality and not a monistic unity' (pp. 236–7).

unavoidable defeat and irredeemable sorrows without such acknowledgement paralysing the will to act' (p. 157). This interpretation modifies Norman Rabkin's term 'complementarity', from which it differs in stressing a stage beyond the dialectical; Driscoll adduces alchemy, as interpreted by Jung in his work on Renaissance occult philosophy, and traces out a code of alchemical symbolism without too insistent pressure; for Jung, in any case, 'metallic transformation' was 'metaphoric for self-transformation'. Initiation by fire, purgation by grief, water, sleep – these Driscoll touches on lightly. His main stress is on the achievement by Prospero of acceptance of time, acceptance of evil in humanity and nature, acceptance of loss of identity, of death: 'Such freedom is neither old age's inevitable fruit, as Lear so painfully demonstrates, nor is it, as the maturing Hamlet illustrates, entirely denied the young. It comes to any who can attain metastance.' This is a reasoned example of Jungian interpretation.

Conceding that Shakespeare's plays have formal strength, John W. Blanpied is more interested in their dynamic process, as performed before and experienced by the audience. His subject is *Time and the Artist in Shakespeare's English Histories*,[7] a rather long (278-page) account of the two historical tetralogies plus *King John*. Blanpied thinks that in the histories 'the presumption of order in the plays' made by critics 'has deflected attention from the experimental quality of the disorder ... we are meant to experience that disorder with some immediacy, and not necessarily with any assurance of its coming clear'; again, in the early histories 'instability often seems both matrix and matter of the plays'. Blanpied knows the plays very well and can be a perceptive commentator in a quite straightforward way. His book, however, is influenced by the metadramatic approach developed by Calderwood and the stress on acting found in Goldman: 'in the histories [the] ethos is irresolution itself, a deep-rooted resistance to

endings, and indeed a survival instinct for pressing on toward a future that ultimately is embodied in *us*, in our active presence in the theatrical occasion' (p. 254). Blanpied wishes to resist interpretation that reads the perception of ultimate form back into the process that yields it, yet inevitably he himself comes to these relatively early works with a full knowledge not only of the later works of Shakespeare but also of many theories about the coherence, or otherwise, of that sequence of plays; and with a knowledge of much critical theorizing, of whole layers of progressively refined versions of Shakespeare prefiguring or self-reflecting, progressively 'managing' to 'transform his own inevitable presence in the histories into the means of sounding out their huge and elusive energies' (p. 13). Blanpied cites Sigurd Burckhardt's theory of the two voices through which he thinks Shakespeare acts in his plays, the fool who wantons words, the priest who 'redeems the word in a transcendent meaning'. On the one hand there are characters plotting towards a future revelation, aiming to bring all mere acting (machiavellian and other deception) to an end, cultivating disorder in the interests of another broader order; this type resides in the historical world where the final truth is the fully formed design and no single moment is completely real. On the other hand are performers, 'antics', at home in the theatre not history, 'thrusting the play's live energy outward to us, rupturing the fabric of time and continuity, revealing all the machiavel's works as theatrical illusion ... There is no past, he insists, and therefore no future, only this passing moment.' Thus Falstaff needs to be as formidable as he is because in the later histories 'the machiavellian fiction of temporal continuity becomes tenacious and compelling' (p. 15).

To indicate the broad outline briefly, as here, may suggest that Blanpied has a familiar

---

[7] University of Delaware Press, Newark; Associated University Presses, London and Toronto, 1983.

approach. In the book as a whole there is much good local insight into the plays, but the author is rather often prey to inspirational over-writing where lucidity would be preferable, and though he celebrates Shakespeare's alertness to the danger of spurious stability, he falls prey to over-simple formulations himself. His own definition of acting, as existentially committed to the moment, overlooks the fact that actors build a role out of a sequence of appearances and a coherent evolving relationship with an audience, who for their part even retain a memory of the actor in one history play when he appears in the next; both audience and actor respond to the moment-by-moment traffic of the stage, but a completed, acted role is analogous to the creation, in Blanpied's terms, of history. Falstaff's attitude to Hal's ambition is partly contemptuous (present mirth being proverbially preferable to what's to come, still unsure); but Falstaff's role is not to be simplified too far; he has his own ambitions; though they are not confessed in soliloquy, they *are* acted; the parallels as much as the contrasts with Hal are surely real, as acting brings home to an audience. Stress on the dynamic existential elements in a play is salutary; the difficulty with Blanpied's account is that it strives so insistently for refined formulations, combining already very sophisticated ways of discussing the plays.

If there are affinities in approach and in method between Blanpied and Booth, there are also affinities between Edward Berry's account of *Shakespeare's Comic Rites*[8] and the recent book by Marjorie Garber, *Coming of Age in Shakespeare*. Berry, like Marjorie Garber, is interested in the concept of rites of passage, as studied by van Gennep and his successors in anthropology. In the only reference to *Coming of Age in Shakespeare* in his book, a footnote on p. 203, Berry says Marjorie Garber 'focuses on characterisation not dramatic structure, and cuts across generic lines'. To say that she is not 'focused' on dramatic structure seems to imply that she is

scarcely interested in it, which is most misleading; and furthermore, the best parts of her book seem to me to be on the comedies.

Berry makes some use of sixteenth- and seventeenth-century English autobiographies and non-literary works on transition, courtship, and marriage, and he cites accounts of the behaviour of primitive tribes as studied by modern anthropologists. He also takes up a very large number of issues which have interested modern critics in Shakespeare's comedies. There is an uneasy air of hit-and-miss about the choice, and use, of the autobiographies, and a very large number of commonplaces are repeated from beginning to end of the book as a consequence of its need to collect examples to establish social–cultural attitudes on one hand; and, on the other, instances from many plays concerning some topic such as love's madness, or disguising, or the exchange of love tokens, or recognitions, or courtship rituals, or the relation of a play's symbolic geography to its concern with liminality. Many of these topics deserve, and have received, separate study by previous writers on the comedies, as Berry's footnotes indicate; but the somewhat rushed and crowded survey of so many complex and subtle issues is not satisfactory, and is further complicated by the rather loose attempt at association with anthropology. The central concern of the book does seem to be with liminality, and this is more interestingly handled in Marjorie Garber's book, which also handles the relation between anthropology and Shakespeare's plays more acceptably.

Some sharply pertinent discussion of Shakespeare, making use of socio-political writing contemporary with him to contrast him with his cultural context, is offered by Sarup Singh, who is also concerned to trace the relationship with Restoration dramatists in their treatment

---

[8] Cambridge University Press, 1984. Marjorie Garber's book was reviewed in *Shakespeare Survey 37* (Cambridge 1984), pp. 178–9. It came out in 1981.

of the common theme of the family.[9] Singh writes:

It is a painful fact that at the slightest provocation, Shakespeare's men have a tendency to denigrate the female sex and to treat as property even the women they claim to love. As Bernard Shaw has pointed out in his preface to *Getting Married*, even Antony and Othello, Shakespeare's most infatuated and passionate lovers, 'betray the commercial and proprietary instinct the moment they lose their temper' ... That Elizabethan husbands should treat their wives as property is not surprising if we remember, as Keith Thomas points out,[10] that under the contemporary law (which had come down from Anglo-Saxon times) a man was punished for adultery not for unfaithfulness to his wife but for violating the rights of another husband.

Singh cites a contemporary view: 'The law of England is a husband's law' (pp. 134–5).

Singh concludes that though Shakespeare remarkably gives most of his heroines very positive and often sparkling personalities of their own, he is 'reluctant to let them function on their own as individuals', and defers to the contemporary conservative world view. If there are marriages in Shakespeare which can be described as companionate, nevertheless, by comparison with the end of the seventeenth century, 'their *basis* is largely different' (p. 144). The restricted subject, and the admirable suppleness with which Singh treats it, make his book well worth consulting.

Marianne L. Novy's *Love's Argument. Gender Relations in Shakespeare*,[11] also makes use of the work of Lawrence Stone, though she makes rather more of the speculation that the ready expression of strong emotion was identified with women, men's ideal being reason and control: 'If establishing or admitting emotional ties was difficult for many in Shakespeare's audience partly because of their ideals of control and other social restrictions', the plays may have been attractive, thinks Novy, because they dramatize difficulties of trust and mutual understanding, the perils of expressing or denying passion.

She discusses the comedies, tragedies, and romances in terms of two pairs of antitheses, patriarchy–mutuality and control–emotion. The major part of the book sticks close to Shakespeare, rather than adducing information or theory from cultural anthropology or social history, and a number of plays are interpreted in terms of their depiction of sexual relations, with particular emphasis on two works, *Taming of the Shrew* and *Othello*. There are few surprises in this book, but the interpretation has the advantages of temperance, also; it may make the plays more simple and coherent, more sympathetic to today's moderate feminists (men and women) than the plays have been found to be by many modern readers, including Sarup Singh. Still, Marianne Novy does advocate civilized values for sexual relations, and this can only do good.

Jane Donawerth's *Shakespeare and the Sixteenth Century Study of Language*[12] is to be recommended for its clear exposition of important conflicting theories of language in Shakespeare's time, citing illustrations from grammar text-books, classics taught in school, and other works published at the time. The aim being to 'gain insight into Shakespeare's plays, not to write a history of linguistics', the author emphasizes ideas for what they reveal of the interests of the age, however fallacious, rather than concentrating on novel ideas implying progress in the study of language. The first three chapters are enriched by copious quotations to illustrate, and complicate, the view of Elizabethan thinking on the following topics: definitions of language, the connection between words and things, the

---

[9] *Family Relationships in Shakespeare and the Restoration Comedy of Manners* (Oxford University Press, Delhi, 1983).

[10] Keith Thomas, 'The Double Standard', *Journal of Historical Ideas*, 20 (1959), 199–200.

[11] The University of North Carolina Press, Chapel Hill, North Carolina, 1984.

[12] University of Illinois Press, Urbana and Chicago, 1984.

cause and history of language, the power of language, the purposes of speech, speech and death, voice, expression and gesture as language, doubtful words and trust in language, the Elizabethan love of words: *res et verba*. This is a central and succinct contribution in 140 pages to a field often rather neglected because the primary texts, even those in English by Ascham, Mulcaster, and company, are in various ways awkward of access. These chapters are also strongly recommendable for their intended audience of students of Shakespeare and his contemporaries, because reasonable connections are made with the plays through apt quotation and straightforward interpretation, using Elizabethan-based terms. That Jane Donawerth does not strive to be among the most adventurous in applying modern linguistics she is the first to assert, but I do not think her approach in the least naive; implicit in its unfaltering lucidity is a rebuke to irresponsible and unknowing theorizing about Shakespeare and about language:

The definitions taught in school and adapted by the English humanists emphasise language as human communication over language as an abstract system of symbols: significance does not inhere in words, but arises from the interaction of speaker and listener as they order and understand the words. We may infer the view of the dramatic medium resulting from this view of language: one would regard a play not as an artistic artefact made from words, with aesthetic value depending only on the verbal construct, but as a communiction through words, with aesthetic value depending on the experience the words engender in the audience. This, in fact, is the conception of his medium that Shakespeare presents in the choruses and epilogues where he speaks either on his own behalf as a dramatist or on behalf of the actors. (p. 23)

Citing Gower in *Pericles*, Jane Donawerth continues:

That a play is as transitory as the voices of its speakers Gower indicates near the end; 'Now our sands are almost run / More a little, and then dumb' (5.2.1–2). The words of the play are not meant to form an artistic artefact valuable in itself, according to Gower . . . At the end of the play, Gower, the characters, and the words are gone, but the sense wrought out of human experience remains.

This book is not reactionary; its reasoned and lucid discourse is in fact focused on the inventive, playful, and complex nature of Shakespeare's language; but it does point out that these features are not the discovery of modern theorists of language and can be understood from a Renaissance perspective. That this involves the author in refuting the notion of reflexity, of linguistic units being intro-referential in dramatic discourse, for instance, is a circumstance that she seems ready enough to endure. She quotes from Erasmus and Vives as well as Mulcaster, Ascham, and Tomkis's *Lingua* to show that love of language was fostered, and fostered to ensure the preservation of knowledge and making of wise and virtuous adults from young students:

We misunderstand Ascham, who is often advanced as the spokesman for the Elizabethan addiction to words, if we do not place him in this humanist context. The English educator is not praising words above matter; he is praising words as the major instruments to knowledge and virtue: 'Ye know not, what hurt ye do to learning, that care not for wordes, but for matter, and so make a deuorse betwixt the tong and the hart. For marke all aiges: looke upon the whole course of both the Greeke and Latin tongue . . . when apte and good wordes began to be neglected, and properties of those two tongues to be confounded, than also began ill deedes to spring . . . newe and fond opinions to striue with olde and trewe doctrine, first in Philosophie, and after in Religion' . . . Ascham thinks that words are neglected at the risk of anarchy and damnation, but only because knowledge of words leads to more important knowledge and so to virtue. Ascham's narrowness shows itself in his religious bias . . . But there is nothing narrow in his ideal. Those who do not love words, he argues, will never love ideas because they will never perceive them clearly; nor will they be moral, for moral action comes from hard thought and knowledge, not simply from intuition. For Tudor humanists, speech, truth, and right action are linked in a generative process:

knowledge of one stage opens the way for progress at the next stage ... For Shakespeare, the man who loved words alone became a favourite character, but one to be mocked by the wiser sort in his plays: it is the dearth of knowledge in Armado, Osric, and Parolles, as well as their multitudinous words, that make them splendid fools. (pp. 128–9)

Keir Elam's *Shakespeare's Universe of Discourse*[13] is also concerned with language; he supposes that modern speech-act theory produces, when applied to the plays, 'in the dialogic exchange ... no longer static "characters" represented by their "diction" but interpersonal forces responsible for carrying forward the narrative dynamic' (p. 7). Nevertheless, in practice he does not dispense with either the concept or the term 'character' in his discussion. He also says that the main motive force of Shakespeare's comedies is 'the game of the pure self-activity of the word'. The book has a large bibliography and salutes many modern linguistic theorists and ideas, although its basic premises are highly exaggerated, where their applicability is not in doubt, and the careless superficiality with which Elam dismisses critics such as Coleridge or Granville-Barker suggests that his polemical intent could have been made more penetrating by being more sober. The argument is extremely awkwardly structured in a very long sequence of very brief sections; the plays too are fragmented, small bits of dialogue being extracted from their full dramatic context (which is not sufficiently taken account of), and changes in the level and direction of analysis are peremptorily made. The main play under discussion is *Love's Labour's Lost*, about which Elam has many perceptive comments in detail, and some cranky large theories. There is a great amount of theoretical material gathered in the book, which could have been made very much more accessible, and perhaps illuminating. Perhaps it is consistent with the polemical cast of the work that the discourse should be so persistently disjointed, abruptly redirected, and wearisomely long-winded. The style, one can only say, is abominable, and only real stubbornness in a reader will get him through to the end. The manifest interest of the subject, especially the whole possibility of linking modern linguistics to literary criticism, deserved something better.

Two collections of critical articles are worth noticing this year, though there is not space to discuss every item. The *Festschrift* for G. R. Hibbard edited by J. C. Gray, *Mirror up to Shakespeare*,[14] reflects the wide range of interests for which Hibbard is well known, from the close scholarship demanded of an editor to the lively treatment of matters of general interest to playgoers; the emphasis overall is on Shakespeare the dramatist rather than the poet, philosopher, or the occasion to play self-regarding critical games. Of articles specifically devoted to staging and stagecraft there is a group: T. W. Craik on 'Endings', Ralph Berry on '*Richard III*: Bonding the audience', S. P. Zitner on 'Staging the Occult in *1 Henry IV*', and R. W. Ingram's account of music, sounds and noise, '"Their noise be our instruction": Listening to *Titus Andronicus* and *Coriolanus*'. Of these, all cogent and useful, I would pick out Zitner's for the force with which it stresses the dependence of dialogue on other elements. The supernatural music in *1 Henry IV*, called for by Glendower and ridiculed by Hotspur, divides critics. The New Variorum editor thought Shakespeare believed in Glendower's magic powers, and some Welshmen think so too; but Zitner's point is about staging: Glendower seems to be at his most boastful:

---

[13] Cambridge University Press, 1984; subtitled 'Language-Games in the Comedies'.

[14] University of Toronto Press, Toronto, Buffalo, and London, 1984. Eugene M. Waith's contribution is about Ceremonies in *Titus Andronicus*. Can it be only an accident that in the copy sent for review the words 'Titus's readiness to sacrifice everything to principle is painfully clear' were smudged, and one word in particular, 'everything', was entirely blotted out, by the crushed body of a real black fly?

those magicians that shall play to you
Hang in the air a thousand leagues from hence
And straight they shall be here.

Zitner supposes the lines call for 'an appropriate upward gesture', and this would be
directed at the uppermost gallery of the tiring-
house, where the company's familiar musicians
routinely stationed themselves. Thus self-
conscious exposure of theatre artifice is used to
make fun of Glendower. Since Hotspur's
response is 'Now I perceive the devil understands Welsh', we may take this as meaning
'what a cheap theatrical trick', 'who are you
kidding?', or we may wonder whether Shakespeare intends the musicians to play from
under the stage, infernal music ominously
anticipating act 5 where Glendower does not
arrive at the battle of Shrewsbury because he is
'o'erruled by prophecies'. If the appearance of
the musicians aloft is presented to accord with
Hotspur's scoffing reaction, as Zitner inclines
to believe it should be, it removes what many
think an important ambiguity about Glendower and his type: you simply cannot tell
when they are calculatedly lying, or when
they are genuinely, powerfully dangerous.
Whatever the 'real' reason for his absence from
Shrewsbury, its effect on the scoffing Hotspur
is fatal. It seems to me that to insult Glendower's person and nation *may* be ominous,
indeed, but Shakespeare's dramatic style in the
*Henry IV* plays gives less overt force than in
*Richard III* to omens or the comedy of evil.
Writing on the end of *2 Henry IV*, in a good
essay, C. E. McGee gives historical background, the royal entries of Elizabeth I,
famous for her readiness to receive without
imprudence petitions or gifts from the baser
sort of her people on such great ceremonial
occasions. McGee's adducing of historical
record sharpens awareness of how Falstaff's
leer, and impudent cry 'God save thee, my
sweet boy', give Henry V no chance. On a
wider canvas Alexander Leggatt considers
the relation between *Macbeth* and the last

plays, seeing that in a sense *Macbeth* offers
two kinds of drama: one, the tale of a villain
punished, is told through theatrical means
that

belong to the traditions of masque, romance and
folk-tale, the tradition of Shakespeare's last plays.
Spectacle and ceremony, processions and banquets,
riddles and prophecies, idealized visions . . . but this
tradition is introduced only to be broken, parodied,
and perverted so that Shakespeare can make way for
the other kind of drama, the one that really interests
him in *Macbeth* – the trip inside the mind.

Concluding the essays on ceremony, ritual,
and emblematic elements, Anne Lancashire
writes on the substantial topic of 'The
Emblematic Castle in Shakespeare and
Middleton', speculating on whether the
emblematic castle may have been a 'major
physical reality on the stage' in original performances of *Macbeth*. She gives extensive
information on emblematic castles in various
theatre forms, in verbal imagery, and as
large-scale metaphors for the settings of
dramatic stories. The material drawn from
earlier religious drama is well-found and illuminating, and the article is educative. Also
combining well-directed and wide-ranging
reading and critical acumen is the discussion
of *Coriolanus* by R. B. Parker, a penetrating,
maturely balanced analysis of the play's dialectic which concludes that Coriolanus' decision to put his feelings for his mother above
all else

is an affirmation of the familial link on which a
healthy society has to be built and which Shakespeare has come to see as the truly *political* core of
human society set against the constant flux of
history . . . it is this ideal, not his battles, that gives
Coriolanus ultimate victory over Aufidius's pragmatic cynicism.                          (pp. 275–6)

Yes, but – what of the actual depiction of
family in the play? Parker's response to this
riddling tragedy is worth reading.

Much less interest is found in either the
choice of subjects or the writing in Stratford-

upon–Avon Studies, 20.[15] This occasional series used, once upon a time in its early volumes, to be required reading for anyone interested in criticism of a fresh, coherent kind; the latest collection is drab, with two exceptions. A. R. Braunmuller offers a carefully developed account of rhetorical, narrative, and dramatic structures in his piece 'Early Shakespearean Tragedy and its Contemporary Context. Cause and Emotion in *Titus, Richard III* and *Lucrece*'. Braunmuller begins with illustrations of the nature of the changes made to *Tancred and Gismund* between the manuscript of about 1567 and Quarto of 1591; he demonstrates that they involve more, and more fluent, blank verse; more rhetorical figures of repetition; metaphor rather than simile; emphasis on showing an audience events in the play's action; more attention to imagined environment and character relations expressed through dialogue and verbal reaction; greater use of props to externalize and specify emotional states. These changes indicate lessons learned from developments in the art of drama, and Braunmuller speculates 'cautiously' that 'Shakespeare probably learned some of them from the same teachers, the working dramatists of the popular theatre', especially Marlowe, Kyd, and Peele. Of Richard III he remarks

As *Richard II* demonstrates, the kingship cannot be 'acted' because the role includes too many public constraints, too many national and even religious expectations. Even so adept an actor as Bolingbroke or Hal must finally accept that he that plays the king cannot really choose to play any other part, cannot dare to rule ironically. Richard III's vitality requires change ... As with his more obviously comic cousins, Volpone and Face, inescapable and undisguisable facts (of expectation, physique, moral physiognomy) impose their own shape on the shape-shifter.

The role of Shakespearian king, Braunmuller concludes, requires a mute, hieratic paragon. In the other interesting piece, D. J. Palmer discusses 'The Self-awareness of the Tragic Hero', considering that the heroes are not all introspective by nature and few if any actually achieve self-knowledge, but the crisis they experience precipitates an involuntary confrontation with the inner self: 'they share a capacity for self-definition, a consciousness of identity'.

Pursuing this question of identity in relation to the hero and king is an excellent essay by a critic whose work is always worth reading, Scott McMillin; he can be relied on to revive the reader on the point of despair at acres of sterile academic print. McMillin's approach to 'Shakespeare's *Richard II*: Eyes of Sorrow, Eyes of Desire'[16] is to examine Shakespeare's interest in the problem of presenting profoundly inward experience in a dramatic character, not merely because it is a central problem Shakespeare deliberately confronts in this play but because, McMillin thinks, 'Much of the last half of Shakespeare's career can ... be understood as an attempt to establish an oblique vision in the theatre which would make the normally hidden a matter of perception'. McMillin takes the question at a subtle and penetrating level: the writing of this play commits Shakespeare to follow Bolingbroke's fortunes in the next two plays, but here Shakespeare 'leaves at the centre ... an experience which remains impervious to showmanship'. McMillin considers that the problem of manifesting this sense of inner vacancy, or hollowness, that the queen and Richard II share, is neither deflected nor solved by the playwright. When Richard discovers this 'nothing' within himself in the deposition scene, it is something his queen 'seems to have known about all along'. Richard journeys towards loss, 'something that takes the form of being entombed, graved, walled from sight, immured'. Finally Exton presents his coffin, the problem of theatrical representation of this terrible dis-

---

[15] *Shakespearian Tragedy*, General Editors, Malcolm Bradbury and David Palmer (Edward Arnold, 1984).
[16] *Shakespeare Quarterly*, 35 (1984), 40–52.

covery wryly, provisionally stated by Shake-speare: 'At the heart of loss, there is nothing for the theatrical eye to see, and "I" and "no" are one'.

Though McMillin's is far and away the best essay in this year's *Shakespeare Quarterly*, it is worth relating to it a piece on *Cymbeline*, a play in which spectacularly adventurous means are used by Shakespeare to depict inner experience so that it is visible in the theatre. Judiana Lawrence's account of 'Natural Bonds and Artistic Coherence in the Ending of *Cymbeline*'[17] take a sceptical view of the interpretation of Wilson Knight, who thinks the vision of Jupiter 'our one precise anthropomorphic expression of that beyond-tragedy recognition felt through the miracles and resurrections of sister-plays and reaching Christian formulation in Henry *VIII*'. Judiana Lawrence stresses that, since Jupiter is a vision within a vision in the sense that he appears in response to the threatening demands made by the ghosts in Posthumus's dream, he is therefore 'several times removed from the audience's actuality'. Surely nobody who has seen the episode performed in the theatre could think Jupiter's presence anything other than supremely actual: what is seen is before our eyes.

Three studies offer traditional approaches to later Shakespearian tragedy, broadly concerned with moral issues rather than with questions of staging and representation, whether of the outward or the inward self. A. J. Smith[18] strives for balance, as he in turn sees Shakespeare in *Antony and Cleopatra* offering a grand and magnanimous view of humanity in the play: 'The play attests the power of the human spirit to rise out of the wrack of circumstance and defy time by its own inherent splendour', holding against Caesar's 'vision of a great work in time a quality of present being'. Smith goes on: 'The play resists easy alternatives as it resists simple choices, neither putting statecraft before love nor proving the world well lost'. This account identifies the play's stable moral point of view

in its keeping us keenly aware of the limits of success and failure in outward events which matter so much less than inward: 'Who are we to judge an Antony anyway? We are asked to see what it is to be human, what being human may mean' (p. 85). For J. Leeds Barroll *Antony and Cleopatra*[19] provides a point of departure to argue a general theory of Shakespearian tragedy. Barroll is interested in the supernatural in *Antony and Cleopatra*: the soothsayer, the God Hercules leaving Antony, the 'clown' who brings the asp, all instance Shakespeare's concern to 'surmount the complex disputatio of his tragedy by invoking the fiat of the supernatural'; he compares the ghost in *Hamlet*, the oracle in *The Winter's Tale*, the descent of Jupiter in *Cymbeline* (with the rider that such speakers in a tragedy are never so definite as in the romances, tending rather to the elliptical). The clown in act 5 of *Antony and Cleopatra* is especially well analysed, being shown to allude to the parable of the Wise and Foolish Virgins (pp. 246–8) as well as the devil: 'The Clown recalls to us what snakes represent in other countries of the mind . . . the porter of Macbeth has become an Egyptian.' Barroll would assent to Smith's view of the play's complex dialectic, except that his approach through literary history stresses the rhetorical basis of dramatic composition, making characters less likely to be vehicles for the poet's spiritual or philosophical discoveries, more likely to be 'artificial persons' created with a view to representing how certain events came about: the transcendent, overall view subdues *disputatio*.

---

17 *Ibid*, 440–60. A number of lively and interesting articles on teaching Shakespeare appear on pp. 517–656, and are like a breath of fresh air after much of what precedes them. This is in itself an important comment on the current state of critical publications on Shakespeare in the academic journals.

18 *Literary Love* (Edward Arnold, 1983), chapter 3. *Troilus and Cressida* is discussed in chapter 2. Other chapters deal with Webster, Donne and Milton.

19 *Shakespearean Tragedy, Genre, Tradition and Change in Antony and Cleopatra* (Folger Books, Associated University Presses, London and Toronto, 1984).

Thirdly, Joseph Wittreich[20] gives chapter and verse for his argument that Shakespeare seems to be allowing, 'well in advance of Camus, that while history may have an end our task is not to terminate but to create it' (p. 129). This is a dense scholarly explication of St John's Revelation and the apocalyptic tradition generally, seeing Shakespeare's response in relation to his predecessor, Spenser, and his successor, Milton. Since the apocalyptic tradition in English Renaissance poetry has recently begun to be taken seriously in relation to the politics of the period by more critics than it used to be,[21] this book is timely, though stronger on the apocalyptic tradition than on applying it to Shakespeare. Wittreich reminds his reader that apocalypticism was customarily 'a way in which contemporary political and social events were given religious validation by incorporation into a transcendent scheme of meaning' (p. 8); but although Wittreich notes typological elements, his exegesis is not wooden and insensitive, as previous experience with this sort of scholarship may lead readers to fear; with the interesting ideas offered here, readers will be better equipped to support a widespread modern view, also advanced by Wittreich, that 'in *King Lear* apocalyptic thought is implanted with existential insight' (p. 10). Prophecy is interestingly discussed in relation to the Fool, and a case is made out for the contemporary relevant application of the Fool's prophecy to James I's Britain. The case establishes obscurity and ambiguity as part of such prophetic tradition.

A lively and specific piece on *King Lear* by E. A. J. Honigmann appears in this year's *Jahrbuch der Deutsche Shakespeare-Gesellschaft West*.[22] When Edgar asks 'Alive or dead?' the answer should not be a foregone conclusion. Similarly, Honigmann says, there are several warnings that Lear may be permanently deranged if 'repose' is withheld. In both cases it is important that an audience believe Gloucester may be dead and Lear incurably insane because the magic of their rebirth is so important to the play, and of course these rebirths are intimately connected with Lear's last entry. We note that Q and F directions read 'Enter Lear, with Cordelia in his arms'. This by no means assures us that Cordelia is dead, it leaves open the possibility of another return to life. Honigmann suggests: 'She opens her eyes; now it is the father who hangs breathlessly over his child. She wants to speak, but the words do not come; father and daughter are locked together in a look' (p. 60).

The range of interesting topics and the prevailing high standards in this year's edition of the Shakespeare Gesellschaft's *Jahrbuch* are to be emphasized. Wolfgang Riehle has a judicious and informative account of Britten's opera *A Midsummer Night's Dream*, and Dieter Mehl, on 'Chaucerian Comedy and Shakespearian Tragedy', writes as interestingly on the first as he does on the second, and he can make sudden dextrous use of the Toledo: 'The still common view that Shakespeare has debased Chaucer's characters, as if he wrote a kind of *Shamela* to Chaucer's *Pamela*, rests on a misunderstanding of Chaucer's poem and Shakespeare's play' (p. 125). The ensuing discussion is as succinct and sharp as this, noting the altered patterns of emphasis Shakespeare gives the narrative material as a result of his decision to make the play focus on war, heroic values, time, and fame, rather than courtly love and friendship, as had Chaucer in his poem. Furthermore in Shakespeare's *Troilus and Cressida*, 'the un-

---

[20] *'Image of that Horror'. History, Prophecy, and Apocalypse in King Lear* (Huntington Library, San Marino, California, 1984). A book on a related discursive theme in part discussing Shakespeare is Judith H. Anderson, *Biographical Truth. The Representation of Historical Persons in Tudor–Stuart Writing.* (Yale University Press, New Haven and London, 1984).

[21] See for instance, David Norbrook, *Poetry and Politics in the English Renaissance* (Routledge and Kegan Paul, London, 1984).

[22] Edited by Werner Habicht (Ferdinand Kamp, Bochum, 1984).

expected shifts from comedy to tragedy and back are more sudden and, in a sense, more Chaucerian than in *Romeo and Juliet'*. No less concerned with the manipulation of narrative through control of audience point of view, alternation between public and private worlds and their respective rhythms and styles, is Russell Jackson in an essay on varieties of triumph in *Antony and Cleopatra*. Jackson makes some good points about the differing sorts of processional entry in Egypt (beginning with the beginning, intimate conversations in public) and Rome, where the military triumph is a specific procession of a victor returning to the capital. Extending the sense to spectacular celebratory events, Jackson discusses reported and imagined events, and makes it unusually clear that the entry of victorious Ventidius at the beginning of act 3 is important. The interwoven tensions between outward and inward, private and public, are seen in Antony's death: 'His leave-taking from Cleopatra, and the raising aloft of his body amount to a private enactment of the state funeral, in which the body would be placed on a "stage" of the kind promised by Fortinbras for Hamlet's lying in state ... for the theatre audience it is any case a public spectacle'; on the other hand Antony's obsequies take place privately within a monument, the privacy of which is emphasized, Jackson points out, by the 'stealthy invasion' of the Romans.

Kurt Tetzeli von Rosador follows Dr Johnson's precept, that critical remarks are hardly understood without examples, in giving close illustration to his theoretical adumbrations on 'Plotting the Early Comedies: *The Comedy of Errors, Love's Labour's Lost, The Two Gentlemen of Verona*'.[23] Tetzeli von Rosador wishes to see the term 'plot' rehabilitated as an accepted critical tool. This means going back to Aristotle, who like the later Terentian theorists conceived of plot as having 'a thematic dimension and an inexorable movement forward'. The protasis is not only intended to impart introductory information but awaken expectation, and from the dramatist this calls for an art of precipitation, preparing a concerted forward movement. The analysis of opening scenes adroitly brings out their establishment of plot patterns which are repeatedly employed through the play; this illuminates further plot strategies used in repeated patterns of counterpoint; in this way *The Comedy of Errors* is shown in very detailed terms of theme and characterization by way of attention to an ample definition of plot. Having made a persuasive case for this ampler sense of the term 'plot', at least (as here) in the hands of a sprightly, exceptionally alert, subtle critic, Tetzeli goes on to distinguish between the different kinds of plot in *Love's Labour's Lost* and *The Two Gentlemen of Verona*. Whereas *Love's Labour's Lost* is shown to be composed from an indissoluble link between plot and theme, announced and set at once in motion in the opening lines, *The Two Gentlemen of Verona*, instead of arousing the audience's attention and pitching it forward, 'sends it on various wild-goose chases'; yet these journeys have little thematic or emblematic significance: external only, they usurp the place of true plot and action. Convincing as this argument is, I remain saddled with the difficulty that this may mean not that *The Two Gentlemen of Verona* is weak theatre, but that it is another kind of theatre, deliberately of the surface. There is no disputing the strength inhering in the kind of plotting analysed in the other two plays, and the closely disciplined analysis, supported by subtle interpretation, is a lesson to many self-indulgent lesser practitioners. This rehabilitation of plot deserves to be influential and ought to do good.

The year 1984 is something of a prodigy for its new publications by famous critics of an earlier generation. L. C. Knights, who offers an interesting essay on 'Hamlet and the Perplexed Critics',[24] writes as follows:

---

23 *Shakespeare Survey 37* (Cambridge, 1984), pp. 13–22.
24 *Sewanee Review*, 92 (1984), 225–38.

Schlegel's view that [the ghost] is 'commissioned, it would appear, by heaven' to demand vengeance seemed to be demonstrably wrong ... there is no need to bring in scholarly information here [– like Eleanor Prosser –] all we need do is attend to the play, this time not to patterning but to language, tone and manner. The very way the ghost speaks – and there is a striking contrast between its sepulchral rigidities and the nimble movement of Hamlet's prose when he is momentarily free of its dominance – makes it clear that there is no question of straightforward endorsement.

Knights offers a more than timely warning that we critics should resist being enticed into 'making interpretation an intellectual exercise on something "out there" to which we have no full personal responsiveness in which thought, feeling and judgement are inseparable ... unless it is *my* interpretation and *my* judgement I am only a trained, even a sophisticated, parrot.' Knights emphasizes that *Hamlet* or any other work of art has its being in being constant and ever-changing, in its power to awaken the individual's thought, feeling and judgement afresh.

John D. Cox succeeds in keeping scholarly information under control in his good, temperate essay on 'The Medieval Background to *Measure for Measure*'.[25] Cox writes that if the Duke is humanized by being made less than divine, his opponents are humanized by being made more than abstractions; the medieval tradition absorbed into the play is softened by the preciosity and sophistication of a foreign courtly tradition and the warmth and generosity of a familiar if archaic popular mode. Cox considers *The Woman Taken in Adultery* in the Chester, York and N-Town versions, Mary Magdalene in the N-Town *Passion Play* and the Digby play of that name, also Wager's *Life and Repentance of Mary Magdalene*'. Reaching further back, to Virgil, John Pitcher considers 'A Theatre of the Future: *The Aeneid* and *The Tempest*'.[26] This approach could have been prompted by a reading of Eliot's poem *Marina*. Pitcher thinks the Virgilian presence in *The*

*Tempest* often of a spectral kind, 'a half-seen image of death, or damnation, or despair, at the back of an episode, a line, or even a single word'. Pitcher finds Virgilian vocabulary, and Virgilian despair, scarcely to be avoided in the play; he recalls the unburied dead who in Virgil 'crowd around the river bank held back by waters thick with sludge, and ooze, belching their mud (*eructat harenam*, 6.297) into the river Cocytus'. Gonzalo knows Dido's widowhood is important to her, 'and he begins to see (but darkly) how her tragedy has something to do with the present. Both Dido and Carthage were utterly destroyed by Rome and yet there was still some continuity, centuries later, which reached into the lives of Claribel and her African prince in the city of Tunis.' We may resist following Pitcher's claim that everything in the Masque of Ceres is a rewriting of Dido's tragic history. Some of the parallels are very strained (salmons in both) but there is little doubt that a real affinity in manner between Virgil and Shakespeare exists, and Pitcher's response to both is interesting, suggesting the ultimately impalpable, certainly deep imaginative effect of the supremely great predecessors Virgil, Ovid, and Chaucer on Shakespeare. Precisely because of the differences in detail, there is every likelihood that in essence Shakespeare remembered, as Pitcher suggests, how the Trojan ships built from the timber of a sacred wood, 'like dolphins dived to seek the deep; and then as many virgin shapes – amazing omen – rise up to ride the sea'.

Scott McMillin, in another comparison, this time with a dramatist who remembered Shakespeare, discusses '*The Revenger's Tragedy* and its Departures from *Hamlet*'.[27] McMillin begins with the endings, noting that in the later play there is an absence, comparatively speaking, of moral discrimination, and an

---

[25] *Modern Philology*, 81 (1984), 1–13.
[26] *Essays in Criticism*, 34 (1984).
[27] *Studies in Philology* (1984), 275–91.

addition of theatrical self-abandonment. There is no equivalent to Horatio, no narrative focus on the new ruler, as in *Hamlet*. In *The Revenger's Tragedy* we have a firm effect of closure, emphasis is shifted to the present. McMillin is interested in the repetition of the masque in the non-Shakespearian play, arguing that it dissolves difference, identity, into similarity. Vindice catches the de-individualized and concerted implications of revenge by urging 'be all of music'. McMillin writes about the closure in which *The Revenger's Tragedy*, unlike *Hamlet*, does not project its possible endings elsewhere but turns instead upon the theatre and its firm statement, pointed in Vindice's final trim couplet. Yet such certainty has already been subverted by the proliferating theatricality of the double masque, which turns the actor-revenger into repetitions of himself. 'The revenging Vindice firmly declares his identity, but when the hero was first overtaken by his allegorical name his unique accomplishment dissolved into a type: "'Tis I, 'tis Vindice, 'tis I": and now the type is repeated too in a burst of theatricality ... in which all revenge dancers act alike'. So if Hamlet's name derives from his father, Vindice's belongs to allegory. The comparison suggests that there is something surprisingly resistant to a view of *Hamlet* as self-referentially theatrical.

A more sustained work of comparison is Vincent John Cheng's *Shakespeare and Joyce, a Study of Finnegans Wake*.[28] This entertainingly, but no less methodically, collects the allusions in Joyce's work to Shakespeare, in order to help illuminate *Finnegans Wake*. Readers may find their taste-buds stimulated by the following excerpt, which in various ways is a kind of gloss on modern academic publications on literature:

Postmartem is the goods ... Toborrow and toburrow and tobarrow! That's our crass, hairy and evergrim life, till one finel howdiedow ... Ah, sure ... what a humpty daum earth looks our miseryme heretoday as compared beside the Hereweareagain Gaieties of the Afterpiece when the Royal Revolver of these real globboes lets regally fire of his *mio colpo* for the chrisman's pandemon to give over and the Harlequinade to begin properly SPQueaRking Mark Time's Finist Joke. Putting Allspace in a Not-shall. (*Finnegans Wake*, 455.11–29)

Cheng focuses on the obvious allusions to *Hamlet, Macbeth, As You like It* and *Julius Caesar*, and shows how the competing versions of the apocalypse can be inspected from an orthodox Christian or a Viconian position. Furthermore, Cheng notes of Jaun–Christ–Bottom's apocalyptical vision which I have quoted above,

'SPQueaRking' cleverly describes the pandemonium of the Last Day, like the day in Rome (SPQR) when Julius Caesar fell (on the Ides of March), when 'The graves stood tenantless and the sheeted dead / Did squeak and gibber in the Roman streets' ... 'Putting Allspace in a Notshall' could only happen on the Last Day; doing so would please the spatialist Jaun–Shaun–Bottom, who might, like Hamlet or Brutus, say, 'O God, I could be bounded in a nutshell and count myself a king of infinite space, were it not that I have bad dreams'. See also 'Omnitudes in a knutshedell' in 276.2). It is [concludes Cheng of the Joyce] a lovely passage.

(pp. 48–9)

Isn't it rather a nightmare vision, also, of what can happen in articles about Shakespeare?

Finally, a return to order with G. Walton Williams on 'Shakespeare's Metaphors of Health: Food, Sport, and Life-Preserving Rest'.[29] He shows that sleep, though not daytime sleep (Falstaff), and proper food (not cannibalism), and exercise, moderately taken, are the means to health in Shakespeare as in commonplace Renaissance belief, and

As a general rule in Shakespeare's dramatic language a character who exhibits disturbance in any one of the three medicatives (though the cause of that disturbance may be unknown or wrongly

---

28 Pennsylvania State University Press, University Park and London, 1984.
29 *Journal of Medieval and Renaissance Studies*, 14 (1984), 187–202.

identified) is seen to be distracted, mad, or melancholic; characters who exhibit a wholesome participation in the three are seen to be healthy; and on characters not healthy an imposition of the three produces health.

He finds illustrations from the whole of the canon, a pattern constant from *The Comedy of Errors* to *Antony and Cleopatra*. He might have

added a remark from an essay with the irresistible title 'The Ironing of George Herbert's Collar':[30] 'Readers who need elbow room for themselves will observe that I have made no attempt to elaborate on all the implications of these suggestions.'

---

[30] Dale B. J. Randall, *Studies in Philology* (1984), 495.

## 2. SHAKESPEARE'S LIFE, TIMES, AND STAGE
### reviewed by RICHARD DUTTON

The year's most substantial contribution to our thinking on the shape of Shakespeare's life and career is E. A. J. Honigmann's *Shakespeare: The 'Lost Years'*.[1] Professor Honigmann has resurrected the suggestion first made by Oliver Baker in 1937, and later supported by E. K. Chambers, that the 'William Shakeshafte' mentioned in the 1581 will of Alexander Hoghton of Lea (in Lancashire) is in fact William Shakespeare. Douglas Hamer supposedly refuted the theory in 1970, but Professor Honigmann certainly knocks enough holes in that refutation to make a reopening of the case worthwhile; and in establishing a plausible Lancashire connection for Shakespeare – John Cottom, one of the Stratford schoolmasters during Shakespeare's teens, was a native of Tarnacre, only ten miles from Hoghton's Lea – he offers a possible answer to one of the more awkward questions posed by the whole proposition: why should a Midlander born and bred seek employment in the wilds of Lancashire? A further decisive factor would almost certainly have to be Roman Catholicism, since there is no doubt that the Cottom and Hoghton families, and their principal neighbours, had strong Catholic connections. If 'Shakeshafte' really was Shakespeare, there could be little doubt that the dramatist was a covert Catholic, at least in his youth, which (as Professor Honigmann suggests) is a good reason to look again at

plays like *King John, Measure for Measure* and (bearing in mind Samuel Harsnet's *A Declaration of Egregious Popish Impostures*) *King Lear*, which have marked Catholic associations. Further, if the Lancashire connection is conceded, it increases the possibility that the young Shakespeare – whom we are to think of employed initially as a schoolmaster, but perhaps taking part in household theatricals – first entered the professional theatre under the patronage of the local magnates, the Stanleys, Earls of Derby, and most particularly of the charismatic heir to the title, Ferdinando, Lord Strange. Professor Honigmann looks in particular at *Richard III*, where the role of the then Earl of Derby may well have been polished up to please his descendants, and at *Love's Labour's Lost*, where some punning on 'strange' and the fact that the King of Navarre was apparently originally named 'Ferdinand' offer yet another solution to that play's enigmatic topicality. I am tempted to add that the word 'strange' is even more highlighted in *The Tempest*, a play with an undoubted Ferdinand – but here the dating surely defeats us, Ferdinando (by then 5th Earl of Derby) dying in 1595 and there being no record of the play before 1611. This is precisely the kind of will-o'-the-wisp that Professor Honigmann in fact avoids: his

---

[1] Manchester University Press, Manchester and Dover, New Hampshire, 1985.

speculations all fall within the parameters of scholarly fact and reasonable conjecture and, while there is room for disagreement about most of his hypotheses, this is a serious and compelling exploration of the paths Shakespeare may well have trod in his first twenty-eight years. It is a pity, and ironic, that in their rush to publish on Shakespeare's (mythical) birthday, the publishers made a number of glaring print blunders, for which amends have had to be made with an *errata* slip.

A name sometimes cited but never invoked by Professor Honigmann is that of S. Schoenbaum, author of *William Shakespeare: A Documentary Life*, which for many of us (often in its *Compact* form) is the standard life of Shakespeare. This coolness may be explained by the fact that the former is an adherent of the 'early start' theory of Shakespeare's career, dating some of the works as early as 1586, while the latter on the whole subscribes to the 'late start' theory – assuming, in the absence of documentation to the contrary, that not too much predates Greene's 1592 attack on the 'upstart crow'. In his collection of essays, *Shakespeare and Others*,[2] Professor Schoenbaum reinforces this reputation as the arch de-mythologizer of Shakespeare studies (and not only Shakespeare: Jonson, Chapman and Middleton come under the 'Others'). We find him, for example, in the light of new evidence, admitting that he knows less about the intentions behind Shakespeare's will than he had assumed in his *Documentary Life*, and preferring 'an agnostic conclusion' to 'a specious certainty' (p. 53). This may sound nit-picking, a stolid conservatism, but it is deployed with such sense, humanity, and dry wit ('One may say of him what his namesake said of the race of metaphysical poets: to write on Jonson, it is at least necessary to read and think. Anybody can write on Shakespeare, and everybody does' (p. 189)) that it commands attention and respect. Just how much we sometimes need such patient scholarship is underlined in Professor Schoenbaum's collection here of his

reviews of the Shakespearian works of Dr A. L. Rowse ('Shakespeare, Dr Forman, and Dr Rowse'), where the spirit of Job takes on one tribulation and false certainty after another.

By contrast, we have *Edward de Vere and the War of Words* by Elizabeth Appleton.[3] In fifty breathless pages Ms Appleton 'reveals' that the Puritan pamphleteer, 'Martin Marprelate', was Gabriel Harvey, while his opponent, 'Pasquill', was none other than Edward de Vere, 17th Earl of Oxford (who also turns out to be the original of Nashe's Pierce Penniless). Not content with this, she also 'establishes' that Oxford wrote at least four plays – *A Midsummer Night's Dream, Henry IV 1* and *2* and (of course) *Hamlet* – previously thought to be by Shakespeare. I am sorry to say that this is research without circumspection or historical perspective; for all her obvious enthusiasm, Ms Appleton has no sense of what constitutes real evidence in the pursuit of Elizabethan allusions.

G. M. Cameron's *Robert Wilson and the Plays of Shakespeare*[4] is a good deal more scholarly and marshals a clear argument, but Mr Cameron is obsessed with an *idée fixe*, which is that virtually all of Shakespeare's comedies and tragicomedies (excluding only *The Comedy of Errors* and *The Merry Wives of Windsor*) are reworkings of plays by the actor and dramatist Robert Wilson. To prove this is a tall order, since only one extant play, *The Cobbler's Prophecy*, is known to be by Wilson, and only two others, *Three Ladies of London* and *Three Lords and Three Ladies of London* (both printed as by R.W.), may be ascribed to him with reasonable certainty. But Mr Cameron proceeds, on the very narrow grounds of plot or linguistic similarity, to ascribe a range of texts to

---

[2] Folger Books, Washington: The Folger Shakespeare Library; and Scolar Press, London, 1985.
[3] The Elizabethan Press, Toronto, 1985.
[4] Published by G. M. Cameron, Riverton, New Zealand, 1982.

Wilson, including old Shakespeare apocrypha favourites like *Fair Em* and *Mucedorus*. Then, usually on plot analogies, he sees Shakespeare's comedies as reworkings of these or (not scrupling to invent totally unknown works) of lost works deemed to be similar. It is a prodigious misdirection of energies, but it does at least convince me that Robert Wilson himself, apparently a Puritan of the Earl of Leicester's faction, is worth pursuing further.

Happily, the year has produced some more convincing sources, analogues, datings, and identifications relating to Shakespeare. Glynne Wickham points out some striking parallels between *Love's Labour's Lost* and *The Four Foster Children of Desire* (1581), a courtly entertainment involving Sir Philip Sidney, staged in relation to negotiations over Elizabeth's possible marriage to the Duc d'Alençon;[5] it is a likelier source than many for this enigmatic play. Georgianna Ziegler has unearthed the only known reference to Giulio Romano in English prior to *The Winter's Tale*, in *The Necessarie, fit, and Convenient Education of a yong Gentlewoman*, a late sixteenth-century English translation of an Italian work by Giovanni Bruto; she makes rather a meal of turning the book into a source for details of the depiction of Perdita as well as the name of the artist, but establishes a fair case for Shakespeare having read it.[6] Richard Levin, more briefly, adduces yet more evidence for the identification of Marlowe as the Rival Poet of the Sonnets.[7] Rosemary Wright posits a credible link between the lime tree by Prospero's bower and the proverbial 'pedlar robbed by apes' emblem, associated with vanity.[8] Gary V. Manitto argues convincingly that Culmann's *Sententiae Pueriles* should have been included in R. W. Dent's (1981) index of Shakespeare's proverbs.[9] Eric Sams has a long and exasperated piece on the relationship between the anonymous *The Taming of a Shrew* (printed 1594) and *The Taming of the Shrew* (printed 1623), which is likely to send all editors of the play scurrying back to their textual apparatus;

the essence of his argument is that there is no evidence whatever for any Shrew play except 1594 in the sixteenth century (though most editors posit a Shakespeare original shortly before or after 1594), while for him the Folio text has the hallmarks of 1603–4. If his argument were accepted – and it will certainly need some refuting – it would entail the most radical re-dating of a Shakespeare text for many years.[10] William B. Hunter revives the question of *A Midsummer Night's Dream* being written for some specific nuptial celebration (as, incidentally, does Professor Honigmann, pp. 150–3; see above); Professor Hunter ingeniously argues that the text as we have it is confusing because it reflects adaptation of the play not merely for one but for two wedding celebrations.[11] Stranger things have no doubt happened but I wish that such conjectures were forced to carry a disclaimer to the effect that there is no *evidence* that any professional dramatist prior to 1610 actually composed a full-length play with other than public performance as its first objective.

W. W. E. Slights credibly posits Remigo Nannini's *Civill Considerations upon Many and Sundrie Histories* (English translation 1601) as a source not only of names (Alfonso, King of Naples, his son Ferdinand, Prospero and Fabritio Colonna) but also 'for the background history of Shakespeare's Duke of Milan and for

---

5 'Love's Labor's Lost and The Four Foster Children of Desire, 1581', *Shakespeare Quarterly*, 36 (1985).

6 'Parents, Daughters, and "That Rare Italian Master": A New Source for *The Winter's Tale*', *Shakespeare Quarterly*, 36 (1985), 204–12.

7 'Another Possible Clue to the Identity of the Rival Poet', *Shakespeare Quarterly*, 36 (1985), 213–14.

8 'Prospero's Lime Tree and the Pursuit of "Vanitas"', *Shakespeare Survey 37* (Cambridge University Press, 1984), pp. 133–40.

9 'Shakespeare and Culmann's *Sententiae Pueriles*', *Notes and Queries*, NS 32 (1985), 30–1.

10 'The Timing of the *Shrews*', *Notes and Queries*, NS 32 (1985), 33–45.

11 'The First Performance of *A Midsummer Night's Dream*', *Notes and Queries*, NS 32 (1985), 45–7.

the political observations in *The Tempest*.[12] Winifried Schleiner usefully reviews witch-lore for analogues/sources for Puck, though she concludes by confirming Shakespeare's creative originality with the character.[13] Joan Ozark Holmer has discovered, in Miles Mosse's *The Arraignment and Conviction of Usury* ... (1595), the only known sixteenth-century book to connect the Laban story with usury, as Shakespeare does; if this is accepted as a source, it will set a new *terminus a quo* for *The Merchant of Venice*.[14]

Levi Fox's *The Early History of King Edward VI School Stratford-upon-Avon* is a useful little pamphlet, outlining the origins and progress, down to about 1750, of what we assume to be Shakespeare's school.[15] Dr Fox's most original findings relate to the periods before and after the presumed education of the school's most famous pupil, but there is a compact account here of the kind of schooling that Shakespeare is likely to have received. One thing that emerges clearly is the radical effect of the Reformation on the people of Shakespeare's parents' generation, when the Guild of the Holy Cross that dominated Stratford was abolished, to be replaced by the chartered corporation, and the school that many assume was founded by Edward VI was merely renamed.

The brief reign of Edward VI, when radical Protestant ideas were voiced more freely in England than at any time before the Commonwealth, is a key period in David Norbrook's *Poetry and Politics in the English Renaissance*.[16] This is an important re-reading of poetry and poetics from More, through Spenser, Sidney, Greville, and Jonson, to the early Milton. Dr Norbrook identifies a neglected strain of prophetic verse running through the sixteenth and early seventeenth centuries, sometimes utopian in character, often radical and implicitly anti-courtly. Spenser's affinities with this tradition are, he argues, what give his poetry a radical edge, for all the overt political conservatism of *The Faerie Queene*, while Jonson's

resistance to it helps to explain his position in the Jacobean court; the whole argument helps to place Milton in a native prophetic tradition which is often ignored in standard histories of poetry. This is another timely nail in the coffin of E. M. W. Tillyard's Elizabethan World Picture (though see M. M. Reese's qualified defence of Tillyard[17]), all the more convincing for not being too aggressive in its theme – there is no attempt to 'radicalize' the era unrealistically. In propounding his own thesis, Dr Norbrook absorbs and synthesizes a great deal of recent Renaissance scholarship – his Introduction, for example, offers a persuasive outline of twentieth-century fashions in the reading of Renaissance poetry – and this helps to give the book considerable authority and conviction. It will become required reading in its field. (A note to the publishers: I know there is a cultural point to be made with unjustified right margins and uncommanding type-faces, but I really cannot see that it is a service to a book that should be read as widely as this one to produce it looking as if it were set on a portable typewriter.)

For years the principal focus of Elizabethan theatrical research has been the Lord Chamberlain's/King's Men and their two houses, the Globe and the Blackfriars, all for their associations with Shakespeare. It may be indicative of a general widening of perspective that John Orrell – whose *The Quest for Shakespeare's Globe* was such an exemplary piece of scholarship – has now turned his attention to

---

12 'A Source for *The Tempest* and the Context of the *Discorsi*', *Shakespeare Quarterly*, 36 (1985), 68–70.
13 'Imaginative Sources for Shakespeare's Puck', *Shakespeare Quarterly*, 36 (1985), 65–8.
14 '"When Jacob Graz'd His Uncle Laban's Sheep": A New Source for *The Merchant of Venice*', *Shakespeare Quarterly*, 36 (1985), 64–5.
15 Dugdale Society Occasional Papers, no. 29, Oxford, 1984.
16 Routledge and Kegan Paul, London, 1984.
17 ''Tis My Picture; Refuse It Not', *Shakespeare Quarterly*, 36 (1985), 254–6.

*The Theatres of Inigo Jones and John Webb.*[18] Much has been written, of course, about Inigo Jones's designs and stage techniques for the Stuart court masques, but much less about the theatres that he (and latterly his neglected kinsman and disciple, Webb) devised, both at court and in other privileged contexts, for more conventional dramatic performances – an omission all the more surprising in view of the wealth of documentation that has survived about them. These are the subject of Professor Orrell's new book – the 1605 theatre at Christ Church, Oxford; the Cockpit in Drury Lane (for which he establishes, beyond reasonable doubt, that we do have the designs – among the most detailed for any pre-Restoration theatre in England); the Cockpit-in-Court; and various royal theatres both at Somerset House and Whitehall. The careful exposition and analysis of information, as readable as it is elegantly presented, makes this in every way a worthy successor to his earlier work. Shakespeare may not be the unspoken Grail behind this research, but Professor Orrell stresses that, in most instances, these theatres were designed either in conjunction with professional actors and dramatists, or with their requirements and usual practices very much in mind (in a separate article he stresses the practical emphasis in Serlio's theatrical plans, which lie behind so much of the Jones/Webb work[19]); there was a cross-fertilization between these court theatres and their commercial counterparts that the costly exclusiveness of the masques precluded. So this is an illuminating book not only for students of the arcane, self-regarding world of Stuart court theatre, but for anyone seriously interested in Renaissance drama. Something similar might be said of Jerzy Limon's *Gentlemen of a Company: English Players in Central and Eastern Europe 1590–1660.*[20] The book does not attempt to tackle all that is known about English actors on the Continent during this period, but concentrates on a neglected aspect, their activities in states on the south and east of the Baltic,

Poland, Bohemia, and Austria – many of these being places where acting continued, as it could not in the more researched Germany, during the chaos of the Thirty Years War. Again, this may seem narrowly specialist, but Dr Limon's scrupulous research opens up many issues for the general reader. For example, he stresses that, at least until 1606, the actors performed with great success on the Continent, speaking in English. We can explain this in several ways – perhaps they heightened non-verbal elements of performances, such as music, dancing, acrobatic 'leaping', mime or lewd antics (the English players' reputation for excellent acting was apparently matched only by that for their 'scandalous obscenity'). Or does this suggest something about styles of acting – might this be fuel for the champions of 'stylized' Elizabethan acting over the 'naturalist' camp, implying a formality of gesture which communicated even to international audiences? Again, we currently think of Elizabethan theatre, albeit under aristocratic patronage, as very much a proto-capitalist enterprise. Dr Limon suggests that some English actors chose to work on the Continent (some, of course, were forced there by the plague or lack of success) because of relatively secure and rewarding noble patronage – perhaps our usual concentration on the entrepreneurial activities of such as Henslowe and Alleyn distorts our general view of the profession at the time. Dr Limon also identifies, in the Gdansk Fencing School, a theatre which resembles and may well be modelled on the Fortune in London (itself, of course, modelled on the Globe) – an identification which could usefully expand our knowledge of Elizabethan public theatres. It is

---

[18] Cambridge University Press, 1985. Portions of the book first appeared in *Shakespeare Survey 30* and *35*. The latter, on the 1605 theatre at Christ Church, Oxford, was reviewed here two years ago.

[19] 'Serlio's Practical Theatre Scheme', *Essays in Theatre*, 3 (1984), 13–29.

[20] Cambridge University Press, 1985.

altogether a very suggestive and rewarding book.

For some people, of course, foreign soil begins at the city limits of London, and our knowledge of Tudor/Stuart theatricals in the provinces remains very patchy. All the more welcome therefore is the volume on *Norwich 1540–1642*, edited by David Galloway, in the University of Toronto Press's altogether admirable series, 'Records of Early English Drama'.[21] This is a thorough and scholarly collection of research materials rather than an evaluation of them. Professor Galloway quotes from R. W. Ingram, the editor of the *Coventry* volume in the series, 'The aim . . . is to collect written evidence of drama, minstrelsy, and ceremonial activity, not to interpret it'; and adds himself: 'The time for extended discussion of the similarities and differences between the cities, towns, and villages of Britain will be when many more volumes of REED are published. Only then shall we be able to assess the pattern of entertainment in the country as a whole.' We wait impatiently. In the meantime, this volume gives us much to get on with digesting. It is inevitably a very mixed bag of information, including details of payments to the city waits and permissions to travelling players to perform (as elsewhere, sadly, names of plays are never given), but enlivened with fascinating details, such as for 9 June 1554: 'This daye Robert Gold was sett vppon the pillorye and his eare nayled to the same for devysing of vnfitting songs against the quenes maiestie' or the details of a brawl (15–17 June 1583). Old favourites like the 'dragon' keep appearing for amending or painting (the local guild was St George's), but more unusual surely was the request from 'Sir ffrauncys Drake' (25 January 1589) that 'the waytes of this Citie may bee sent to hym to go the new intendid voyage' – apparently wanting them to perform at the departure of the disastrous Portuguese expedition. But why bring the Norwich city waits all the way to London? My favourite mini-drama is an entry for 13 September 1600: 'The Widdowe Drye this day brought to mr mayor a wrighting from Richard Rogers a ballet synger that he myght have leave to marrye the said widdowe / mr mayor answered he had nothing to doe with making of marriages but willed hir to follow hir husbonde & that neyther of them after marriage shall tarry in Norwich / he being no better than a rogishe vagrante.' Comprehensive glossaries, translations and indexes are provided for those unfamiliar with Elizabethan language or Latin and for those who want to trace repeated references to the same thing. The appendixes contain the final part of Will Kempe's famous 'nine daies wonder', the account of his morris dance from London to Norwich in 1600, the whole of which is reasonably accessible elsewhere, but also full if unannotated versions of Bernard Garter's and Thomas Churchyard's descriptions of the Entertainment of Queen Elizabeth in 1578 – which are not otherwise available in modern editions. The book is a splendid piece of selfless scholarship and a credit to its publishers.

John R. Elliott Jr has been busy in the archives of Oxford colleges. In Corpus Christi he has unearthed early evidence of the theatrical interests of Ferdinando, Lord Strange (so central to Professor Honigmann's view of Shakespeare, see above) and also an embarrassment in the life of the Puritan President of the college, Dr John Rainolds, author of *Th'Overthrow of Stage-Plays* (1599) – some thirty years before he had acted as Hippolyta in a college production of *Palemon and Arcyte*, a veritable example of 'men in women's raiment'.[22] At Christ Church, he has discovered a new document relating to theatricals staged at prodigious cost (Inigo Jones was involved, but designs have not survived) for

---

21 University of Toronto Press, 1984.
22 'Entertainments in Tudor and Stuart Corpus', *The Pelican* 1982–83 (Corpus Christi College, Oxford), 45–50.

King Charles's visit in 1636. The same finding, with a transcription of the document, is published in two places.[23] The version in *Theatre Research International* is somewhat fuller, partly because a co-author, John Buttrey, has apparently added information on the music and musicians involved, and there is a photo-copy in addition to the transcription, but the substance of both pieces is the same.

S. P. Cerasano has set about the useful task of reviewing our total knowledge of Philip Henslowe,[24] while Roslyn L. Knutson has mined the entrepreneur's papers yet again to question the old assumption that Elizabethan plays had to be revised or added to (at a cost) to make them worth reviving; she concludes that plays *could* be restaged as they were, at virtually no cost to the company.[25] Richard Fotheringham reopens the issue of the doubling of roles in Jacobean drama, thinking not only of the manning implications but also of the effect on the audience of having, for instance, the Fool and Cordelia played by the same actor; he points the way for some further study.[26] Laurie E. Maguire looks at the limited information we have about the contractual obligations and restrictions placed on dramatists by the acting companies; much of the evidence falls outside our period but probably has retrospective implications.[27] Andrew Gurr examines the practical, critical, social, and aesthetic distinctions between the terms 'audience' and 'spectators' in relation to Elizabethan and Jacobean drama,[28] while Michael O'Connell intriguingly asks, 'What would it mean to our sense of the Elizabethan and Jacobean stage . . . that from [an] anthropological perspective it could be viewed as a competing – idolatrous – religious structure?'[29]

*Shakespeare, Man of the Theatre*[30] records the Proceedings of the Second Congress of the International Shakespeare Association, 1981. Echoes of that extensive celebration-cum-conference, dedicated to the 'theatrical' dimension of Shakespeare, are enshrined in the two opening pieces, a sermon by the Reverend

Professor W. Moelwyn Merchant delivered at a full Elizabethan sequence of Morning Prayer, Litany, and Ante-Communion (the distinction between literary criticism, particularly of Shakespeare, and theology diminishes daily) and a characteristically witty inaugural lecture by John Mortimer.[31] The remaining pieces are all academic fare of a kind we might encounter anywhere and it is perhaps a pious hope that the volume can 'give some idea to those who were not there of the present state of Shakespeare studies'. But there is certainly some interesting material: Stephen Orgel on what we know of Renaissance theatres and what this suggests about the dramatists' attitudes to their audiences;[32] Bernard Beckerman on two modes of time in the drama of Shakespeare and his earlier contemporaries;[33] an impassioned plea from Inga-Stina Ewbank not to allow 'literary' and 'theatrical' approaches to Shake-

---

[23] 'Plays at Christ Church in 1636: A New Document', *Theatre Notebook*, 39 (1985), 7–13. (With John Buttrey), 'The Royal Plays at Christ Church in 1636: A New Document', *Theatre Research International*, 10 (1985), 93–106.

[24] 'Revising Philip Henslowe's Biography', *Notes and Queries*, NS 32 (1985), 66–72.

[25] '*Henslowe's Diary* and the Economics of Play Revision for Revival, 1592–1603', *Theatre Research International*, 10 (1985), 1–18.

[26] 'The Doubling of Roles on the Jacobean Stage', *Theatre Research International*, 10 (1985), 18–31.

[27] 'A King's Men's Contract and Dramatic Output', *Notes and Queries*, NS 32 (1985), 73–4.

[28] 'Hearers and Beholders in Shakespearian Drama', *Essays in Theatre*, 3 (1984), 30–45.

[29] 'Iconoclasm, Anti-Theatricalism, and the Image of the Elizabethan Theatre', *ELH*, 52 (1985), 279–310. The quotation is on the final page.

[30] Edited by Kenneth Muir, Jay L. Halio and D. J. Palmer, University of Delaware Press and Associated University Presses, London and Toronto, 1984.

[31] 'A Sermon Delivered at Holy Trinity Church, Stratford-upon-Avon, Sunday, August 2, 1981', 15–17; 'Shakespeare and a Playwright of Today', 18–33.

[32] 'Shakespeare Imagines a Theater', 34–46.

[33] 'Historic and Iconic Time in Late Tudor Drama', 47–54.

speare to become divorced;[34] M. T. Jones-Davies on the metaphorical status of actors as revealers of truth in Renaissance plays;[35] Mary Judith Dunbar on icons and emblems in *Pericles*;[36] Emrys Jones, brief but suggestive, on night sequences in Shakespeare, linking them with the festive elements in the plays;[37] Harriett Hawkins applies Popperian methodology to the rights and wrongs of Shakespearian criticism;[38] Roger Warren examines theatrical responses to some of the thornier problems of *All's Well that Ends Well*;[39] G. R. Hibbard on the Platonically perfect enunciation of certain Shakespearian lines (amongst which he cites Donald Sinden's 1969 Malvolio; see below);[40] A. R. Braunmuller on the way styles of language contribute towards characterization in some early plays, using Peele as a comparative standard;[41] Philip Edwards reflecting on the absence of the ghost at the end of *Hamlet*;[42] H. Neville Davies on *The Maid's Tragedy* as a reworking of *Hamlet* – poor old Beaumont and Fletcher;[43] Robert Weimann on 'authority' in Shakespeare, in terms both of literary and theatrical traditions and of socio-political structures;[44] Jörg Hasler on the 'unusually dense theatrical notation in [the] playtext' of the statue scene in *The Winter's Tale*;[45] Jeanne A. Roberts confidently feminist on four eighteenth-century actresses in Shakespearian comic roles (which might usefully be read alongside Leigh Woods's book on Garrick; see below);[46] and Adele Seef's revealing account of Charles Kean's 1858 production of *King Lear*, a work of 'historical realism, lavish spectacle and illusionism'.[47] Finally, Anne Barton gives one of a sequence of curtain-raisers for what eventually became *Ben Jonson, Dramatist*;[48] Professor Barton's reassessment of Jonson's last plays as a belated acceptance by the old man of his mongrel (and Shakespearian) Elizabethan heritage has already been widely accepted and I do not want to challenge it, but I would like to take issue with her view of the role of *Bartholomew Fair* in the progress to this change of heart. The claim that 'It is the

memory of Edwards, Sidney, Marlowe, Fletcher, and Shakespeare . . . which effectively mock the triumph of appetite and aggression at the Fair' (p. 171) hardly does credit to the critical mauling to which Jonson subjects some, if not all of these, in the course of the play; and to cast Fletcher and Shakespeare as a 'memory', when their *The Two Noble Kinsmen* had been performed at court barely a year before, is surely stretching things.

*English Literary Renaissance*, 14, 3 (1984) is a special issue on 'Women in the Renaissance'. It is the first of its kind in this periodical and their new consulting editor, Kathleen McCluskie, makes the immodest claim that they have 'judiciously awaited the maturity of feminist scholarship in the Renaissance'. It is, however, a claim borne out by the uniform excellence and vitality of the contributions. The greater number of pieces relate to women writers (or, in some cases, authors masquerading as women) in the period: Betty Travitsky

---

34 'The Word in the Theater', 55–75.
35 '"The Players . . . Will Tell All", or the Actor's Role in Renaissance Drama', 76–85.
36 '"To the Judgement of Your Eye": Iconography and the Theatrical Art of *Pericles*', 86–97.
37 'The Sense of Occasion: Some Shakespearean Night Sequences', 98–104.
38 '"Conjectures and Refutations": The Positive Uses of Negative Feedback in Criticism and Performance', 105–13.
39 'Some Approaches to *All's Well That Ends Well* in Performances', 114–20.
40 'Between a Sob and a Giggle', 121–7.
41 'Characterization through Language in the Early Plays of Shakespeare and His Contemporaries', 128–47.
42 'Shakespeare and Kyd', 148–54.
43 'Beaumont and Fletcher's *Hamlet*', 173–81.
44 'Shakespeare and the Uses of Authority', 182–99.
45 'Romance in the Theater: The Stagecraft of the "Statue Scene" in *The Winter's Tale*', 203–11.
46 'Shakespearean Comedy and Some Eighteenth-Century Actresses', 212–30.
47 'Charles Kean's *King Lear* and the Pageant of History', 231–42.
48 'Shakespeare and Jonson', 155–72. The book was finally *Ben Jonson, Dramatist* (Cambridge University Press, 1983) rather than the one cited on p. 155.

pursues the *querelles des femmes* in the writings of six authors, whose works range from mild satire to virulent polemic, concluding that they are all sincere works by women, not male dabblings in a literary game;[49] Jean C. Cavanaugh offers us a text of a recently discovered *Defense of Poetry* by the little-known Lady Anne Southwell (1574–1636): it takes the form of a letter written to Lady Ridgway, defending poetry against that lady's apparent preference for prose and, while her arguments are not new (she is mainly concerned with the function of poetry and the kind of truths it can and should convey), she conducts her case with vigour and lively metaphor;[50] R. J. Fehrenbach has edited a rather more substantial text, the anonymous *A Letter Sent by the Maydens of London* (1567), an answer to Edward Hake's (lost) *The Mery Meeting of Maydens in London*: it is interesting for its insight into the lot of Elizabethan women, particularly ordinary maidservants, though (the editor concludes) it was probably written by a man;[51] Carolyn Ruth Swift goes a long way towards reviving the literary reputation of Lady Mary Wroth, who has been known to too many of us as a patron of men like Jonson and Chapman rather than an author in her own right;[52] Sylvia Bowerbank similarly takes on the task of recovering Margaret Cavendish, Duchess of Newcastle, less from neglect than from ridicule (the subject here is her poetical and philosophical works, rather than her biographical and autobiographical ones), urging a feminist explanation of her peculiar fanciful imagination.[53] There are also three essays on the depiction of women in overtly male writing, all relating their subjects to the ideology and social conditions of the age: Suzanne Gossett traces the development of the handling of rape as a theme in Jacobean drama;[54] Dale B. J. Randall assembles some fascinating information about the pseudo-science of chastity tests, relating it to the most notorious scene in *The Changeling*, seeing this as an example of how men can even exploit 'science' in their

subjugation of women;[55] Mary Beth Rose takes a socio-sexual look at the phenomenon of women in men's clothes, and the reactions it stirred up, comparing *The Roaring Girl* with the contemporary *Hic Mulier/Haec Vir* pamphlets and treating them as different kinds of historical evidence of a profound ambiguity in Jacobean responses to the question of female independence.[56] (It is a sign of the times that Sandra Clark has elsewhere also given these long-neglected pamphlets a thorough going-over, from a similar perspective but with different observations.[57]) Last but not least there is a very useful annotated bibliography of *Recent Studies in Women Writers of Tudor England* (1485–1603), divided between Mary, Countess of Pembroke (compiled by Josephine A. Roberts) – who has, probably deservedly, received the lion's share of feminist attention in the period – and all the others (compiled by Elizabeth H. Hageman). While these make no claims to be exhaustive, they offer a very clear and detailed account of the state of current studies, and should be of considerable help to future scholarship.[58]

Barbara Howard Traister's *Heavenly Necromancers: The Magician in English Renaissance Drama* usefully fills a gap for many students of

---

[49] 'The Lady Doth Protest: Protest in the Popular Writings of Renaissance Englishwomen', 255–83.

[50] 'Lady Southwell's Defense of Poetry', after page 284.

[51] 'A Letter Sent by the Maydens of London (1567)', 285–304.

[52] 'Feminine Identity in Lady Mary Wroth's Romance *Urania*', 328–46.

[53] 'The Spider's Delight: Margaret Cavendish and the "Female" Imagination', 392–408.

[54] '"Best Men are Molded out of Faults": Marrying the Rapist in Jacobean Drama', 305–27.

[55] 'Some Observations on the Theme of Chastity in *The Changeling*', 347–66.

[56] 'Women in Men's Clothing: Apparel and Social Stability in *The Roaring Girl*', 367–91.

[57] '*Hic Mulier/Haec Vir* and the Controversy over Masculine Women', *Studies in Philology*, 82 (1985), 157–83.

[58] *Recent Studies in Women Writers of Tudor England*: Part I, 'Women Writers, 1485–1603', 409–25; Part II, 'Mary Sidney, Countess of Pembroke', 426–39.

Renaissance drama.[59] There has been a good deal of scholarly work on magic in the period over the last few years – one thinks, for example, of the work of Frances Yates and Keith Thomas, in very different traditions. But much of this is remote from the popular drama which, moreover, had its own archetypes of the magician, in some ways independent of the intellectual traditions. Professor Traister has absorbed and synthesized all these strands in a balanced way and, after a brief general exposition, applied them to detailed readings of major texts: *Friar Bacon and Friar Bungay, Dr Faustus, Bussy D'Ambois, The Tempest*, and finally a selection of court masques where the magician is a key figure, culminating in *Comus*. Shakespearians will be particularly interested in her account of Prospero, which seems to me most judicious, less anxious than some to explain everything in terms of one brand of neo-platonism or another, determined to see him as also the culmination (since he was the last significant magician on the Stuart popular stage) of a long theatrical tradition. There may not be many intellectual fireworks in this book, but it has all the virtues of a patient overview, recognizing that custom – what we *expect* to see – is as important an element in a living theatrical tradition, if only to be played against, as conscious innovation.

Louise Schleiner's *The Living Lyre in English Verse (from Elizabeth Through the Restoration)* touches only marginally on Shakespeare, but does so from an unusual angle – claiming the sonnets as an example of what she categorizes as the declamatory mode of lyric verse (as distinct from the song mode, which she illustrates from the songs of *Astrophil and Stella* and explores in more detail in the works of Herbert, Herrick, Crashaw and Cowley, and the speech mode, illustrated in the sonnets of *Astrophil and Stella* and again particularly in Herbert).[60] The heart of the book in fact seems to lie in tracing the evolution of the distinct declamatory mode as one of the characteristic

voices of the seventeenth century, the mode of oratorio or recitative, such as we find in *Samson Agonistes*. Professor Schleiner claims that this 'is not a book for the "fit audience though few" of the musically trained: all are welcome', but this non-musician at least found it quite heavy-going. Part of the difficulty is that, as she explains, the distinctions between speech, song, and declamatory modes of lyric were first drawn by the Russian Formalists, and she sometimes uses modern linguistic terminology every bit as arcane as that of the musicologists; on the other hand, she insists that she came by these distinctions from her own reading of Renaissance verse and sticks mainly to 'the terminology of traditional grammar and rhetoric since it is close to the mentality of the poets being studied' (p. 10). At times, as a result, we veer without much warning between Renaissance and modern perspectives, neither of them easily assimilated at a single reading. Nevertheless, there are rewards for those who persevere: as she demonstrates time and again, the relationships between Renaissance words and music are more complex and sophisticated than much earlier, often impressionistic criticism has allowed; we need to make stricter distinctions between different modes. And Professor Schleiner does establish, just, that this can be a proper field of enquiry for *literary* criticism.

Which takes us, neatly enough, into *Verdi's 'Macbeth': A Sourcebook*, edited by David Rosen and Andrew Porter.[61] This handsome book is the fulfilment of Andrew Porter's dream 'of a volume that would gather and order *all* the material related to *Macbeth* that a student of Verdi, a conductor, director, or singer, an historian, or an ordinary enthusiast might like to consult' (xiv). In this collection

[59] University of Missouri Press, Columbia, Missouri, 1984.
[60] University of Missouri Press, Columbia, Missouri, 1985.
[61] Cambridge University Press, 1984.

of historical, biographical, textual, and musi-
cological material, it seems to me he has just
that. It will be of less direct interest to enthusiasts of Shakespeare, though valuable to anyone
concerned with adaptations of his work, particularly four of the papers reprinted here from
the 1977 Verdi Congress held at Danville,
Kentucky – those by William Weaver, Jonas
Barish, Francesco Degrada and Andrew Porter
himself.[62] One wonders whether even the five
hundred pages allowed here could contain
anything quite so authoritative on Shakespeare's *Macbeth*.

In his essay in the Verdi volume, Jonas
Barish reminds us that David Garrick was one
of those who adapted *Macbeth*, as he did so
many Shakespearian works, before the Italian
composer. Leigh Woods's *Garrick Claims the
Stage: Acting as Social Emblem in Eighteenth
Century England*[63] is yet another full-length
study of the influential actor-manager, but less
a biography or a study of his professional
achievement than an attempt to see him as a
representative phenomenon of the age which
accorded him so much success. As Professor
Woods put it, 'A great and popular actor such
as Garrick functions to unify and embody his
culture in ways that to some extent transcend
the ordinary divisions enforced by social class
or by narrow professional interest' (p. 5). Such
an approach is inevitably tendentious, and the
portrait of Garrick it produces will not please
everyone – it is markedly less charitable than
the Stone/Kahrl critical biography (1979), for
example – but here it carries conviction. The
book does not aim to give a sustained analysis
of his acting of particular roles, but it does
touch on all his major Shakespearian successes,
stressing the way 'he seems to have
approached all his roles in a resolute spirit of
sympathy' (p. 35). This, surprisingly enough,
even extended to Richard III, whom he
portrayed apparently 'with touches of vulnerability and weakness' (p. 34) – an interpretation followed by neither Edmund Kean nor
William Charles Macready, as we learn from

articles on both of these actors in the role by
London Green.[64] All three, of course, performed in Colley Cibber's melodramatic
version of the play, but Professor Green argues
for an 'impetus of psychological realism' in the
interpretations of both Kean and Macready, a
claim he is able to substantiate with a surprising quantity of eye-witness accounts and
analyses. Macready and Kean were amongst
the first to reject Nahum Tate's notorious
version of *King Lear* (though neither performed in anything resembling Shakespeare's
own text); it is interesting all these years later
that Doris Adler still detects the influence of
that adaptation on modern performances and
interpretations.[65]

It is less surprising, of course, to find so
much commentary on modern performances,
much of it from the actors themselves – usually
in interviews – but *Players of Shakespeare:
Essays in Shakespearean Performance by Twelve
Players with the Royal Shakespeare Company*,
edited by Philip Brockbank,[66] is out of the
ordinary in allowing a collection of distinguished actors to put together their own
accounts of how they went about creating
particular Shakespearian roles. Styles of
presentation vary greatly, from Gemma
Jones's breathless use of the historical present
in piecing together Hermione, to Sinead
Cusack's self-castigations ('I failed when I
played Portia'), to Tony Church's scholarly

[62] William Weaver, 'The Shakespeare Verdi Knew',
144–8; Jonas Barish, 'Madness, Hallucination, and
Sleepwalking', 149–55; Francesco Degrada, 'Observations on the Genesis of Verdi's *Macbeth*', 156–73;
Andrew Porter, 'Translating *Macbeth*', 245–8.

[63] Contributions in Drama and Theatre Studies, Number
10, Greenwood Press, Westport, Connecticut, and
London, 1984.

[64] 'Edmund Kean's Richard III', *Theatre Journal*, 36
(1984), 505–24; 'The Richard III of William Charles
Macready', *Theatre Research International*, 10 (1985),
107–28.

[65] 'The Half-Life of Tate in *King Lear*', *The Kenyon
Review*, NS 7 (1985), 52–6.

[66] Cambridge University Press, 1985.

sense of the possibilities inherent in Polonius; they are without exception illuminating. Most relate to quite recent (1979–81) productions which will be fresh in many memories, the exception being Donald Sinden's recollection of his 1969 Malvolio, which compensates by being the longest piece and in his inimitably over-the-top style, concluding: 'I believe there is but one thing for Malvolio – suicide.' It is a volume that will surely beget imitators, perhaps focused on single productions.

Dunbar H. and Paul W. Ogden report on an unusual experiment at the Shakespeare/Santa Cruz Festival, where a performance of *King Lear* was mediated to deaf members of the audience (of whom Paul Ogden himself was one) via signing interpreters.[67] Apparently the effect was not only to make the action more intelligible to the deaf, but also to heighten the sense of the verbal/theatrical event for those who could hear.

David A. Male has produced three volumes in a series, *Shakespeare on Stage*, which also revolves around the RSC. These booklets, each about thirty pages of A4-size text, are clearly aimed at school and college students of drama, emphasizing the-play-in-performance over the literary text. The format of each is the same, concentrating on a single play – we have *The Winter's Tale, Antony and Cleopatra*, and *Macbeth* so far, but more must surely be coming, perhaps following A-level examiners – and illustrating (both literally and metaphorically) its acting potential from three recent RSC productions. The approach is quite basic, but teachers will surely find the clear comparison-and-contrast of the different productions a useful starting point for discussion.[68] And, limited though stage stills are as a record of performance, they are surely a better spur to our imaginations (even junior imaginations) than some of the cartoon Shakespeares that have been appearing – though Hugh Howse has volunteered a defence of the phenomenon.[69]

*Form and the Art of Theatre* by Paul Newell

Campbell is an exploration of the ground-rules of dramatic theory and criticism.[70] It is in many ways a work of synthesis, borrowing extensively from thinkers as remote as Aristotle and Plato and as recent as Kenneth Burke and (especially) Suzanne Langer. Nevertheless, Professor Campbell does advance one central argument as his own, which is that the concept of form is the essential ingredient in all theory and criticism, not only of dramatic texts (which is hardly a new proposition) but also of theatrical experience (which may well be) – a proposition he carries through the usual categories of 'The Theatre Audience', 'The Performers and the Performance' and 'The Genres of Theatre' to a final section on 'Dramatic Criticism: Object and Method', in which *A Midsummer Night's Dream* is taken as one exemplum. It would be a tough book for a beginner, the argument remaining rather abstract a good deal of the time and the author presupposing a wide acquaintance with plays, persons, and performances; but it is a useful refresher course for the seasoned professional.

It is a pleasure to welcome the appearance of *New Theatre Quarterly*, or perhaps I should say the reappearance of *Theatre Quarterly* (1971–81), since *NTQ* makes no bones about being a reincarnation of the old journal, still edited by Simon Trussler and Clive Barker, and still looking pre-eminently for 'ways of documenting living performance' so that, even though the first issue has a preponderance of articles related to the theatre of the past, it investigates it 'not as a matter of dead and dusty record, but for its potential for inter-

---

67 '*King Lear* for the Hearing and for the Deaf – a Question of Distance', *On-Stage Studies*, 8 (1984), 1–7. The whole issue is related to the Colorado Shakespeare Festival, and the contents page suggests it would all be of interest to Shakespearians, but I have only seen this article.

68 Cambridge University Press, all three titles 1984.

69 'Shakespeare in Cartoons', *English Today*, Preview Issue, 9–11.

70 Bowling Green State University Popular Press, Bowling Green, Ohio, 1984.

action with work-in-progress'.[71] Perhaps it is enough to say that the lead article of the first issue is by Jan Kott, analysing Marlowe's *Dr Faustus* as a piece of 'polytheatrical' drama, a blending of different modes of theatre, including blank-verse tragic discourse, morality play, dumb show, masques and numerous others.[72] Shakespeare figures very strongly, though not the Shakespeare of the RSC – it is the Shakespeare of the Footsbarn *Hamlet* and *King Lear*;[73] the semiotic Shakespeare – Keir Elam less at pains to apply semiotics to Shakespeare's plays than 'to attribute a direct semiotic awareness to those plays themselves';[74] perhaps pre-eminently the Shakespeare of Peter Brook, whose Parisian translation/adaptation of *Timon of Athens* is approached here, alongside his other productions at the Bouffes du Nord (including *The Ik* and the conflated *Ubu* plays), as 'the least performed of Shakespeare's plays, yet thematically and structurally perhaps one of the most modern'.[75] Beside such pieces, and for all its impeccably current vocabulary, Roberta Mullini's article on Shakespeare's fools – which tries hard to infuse new life into an old topic – looks distinctly old-hat.[76] Well, Simon Trussler rates the power of theatre to 'disturb' over 'its power to reassure' (p. 5) and *NTQ* looks set to resume where *TQ* left off, championing what we used quaintly to call the avant-garde and raising conservative blood pressures.

There is just space to record a few contributions to Shakespearian and related studies in non-English-speaking contexts. In France, Jean Fuzier relates *King Lear* to plays with a madhouse theme in a wider European context than usual, though he also discusses a few English examples less commonly cited (e.g. *The Honest Whore, Northward Ho!*), while in the same volume Nadia Rigaud discusses depictions of insanity in *Bartholomew Fair, The Changeling* and, more briefly, Fletcher's *The Pilgrim*.[77] In a similar collection of essays, bound loosely together by the intractable theme of 'The Implicit in English Literature

and Thought', three authors on Jacobean drama find the common theme something of a handicap: Maurice Abiteboul, writing on Jacobean tragedy (including Shakespeare), tries to rework as 'the implicit' some well-worn ironies and indeterminacies; Nadia Rigaud looks at the contemporary view of forced marriage in relation to what happens to Isabella in *Women Beware Women*; and Simone Dorangeon contrasts the 'amoral' comedy of *The Alchemist* with the Horatian ideals expressed by Jonson in 'To Penshurst' and 'To Sir Robert Wroth', linking the two via his dedication of the play to Lady Mary Wroth (she is, incidentally, under the misapprehension that Sir Robert Wroth was 'maître de Penshurst'). She concludes that 'Subtle and Face are redeemed by comic genius and live, in the strongest sense of the term, in the imagination of all, when the sage and chaste Mary Lady Wroth has sunk without trace' (p. 56, my translation) – ironic in view of current attempts to resuscitate the good lady (see above).[78] Werner Habicht

---

71 *NTQ* is now published by Cambridge University Press. The quotation is on p. 4.
72 'The Two Hells of Doctor Faustus: A Theatrical Polyphony', 6–17.
73 Geraldine Cousin, 'Shakespeare from Scratch: The Footsbarn *Hamlet* and *King Lear*', 105–27.
74 '"Understand Me by My Signs": On Shakespeare's Semiotics', 84–96.
75 David Williams, '"A Place Marked by Life": Brook at the Bouffes du Nord', 39–74.
76 'Playing the Fool: The Pragmatic Status of Shakespeare's Clowns', 98–104.
77 In *Folie, folies, folly dans le monde Anglo-Américain aux XVIIe et XVIIIe siècles*, Publications de L'Université de Provence, 1984. 'King Lear et le théâtre de l'asile', 115–24; 'L'image du fou dans trois pièces jacobéennes: *Bartholomew Fair* (Ben Jonson), *The Changeling* (Middleton), *The Pilgrim* (Fletcher)', 125–32.
78 *L'Implicite dans la littérature et la pensée anglaises*, Publications de L'Université de Province, 1984. "Rituel et stratégie de l'implicite dans la tragédie jacobéenne', 25–40; 'La modification de l'implicite du mariage forcé dans *Women Beware Women* de Middleton', 73–84; 'Quelques poèmes horatiens de Ben Jonson, ou la définition d'une norme restée implicite dans *The Alchemist*', 41–58.

offers us a brief but extremely well-documented survey of recent German trends in Shakespearian scholarship and production, emphasizing the unique place Shakespeare has in German culture and enquiring usefully both why 'some of the Shakespearian experimentations in Germany have been slightly more radical than elsewhere' and why this has been less so of late.[79] Finally, I am indebted to Mr Neville Masterman, Honorary Research Fellow of University College Swansea, for the following notice of *Magyar Shakespeare – Tükör*, a Hungarian book on local reactions to Shakespeare; I have not and could not read it myself, but perhaps it should not go unrecorded:[80]

The book contains an introduction, describing how the Shakespeare cult spread not only among the Hungarians but to the Slovaks, Czechs, Rumanians, etc., as well as to the Russians. It consists of a number of extracts, dating from 1777 to 1981, on Shakespeare himself, his place in Hungarian and world literature, and a discussion of individual plays and performances, written by many different kinds of men and women: poets, critics, journalists, actors and actresses, politicians, etc. The rebel poet, Sándor Petöfi (1823–49), his most ecstatic admirer, insisted that Shakespeare was 'half of creation'. There was a reaction against the cult in the twentieth century, however, Tolstoy and Bernard Shaw being called in to assist in its demolition. Yet new Shakespeare enthusiasts appeared, who demanded a reinterpretation of the plays. The authors believe the book is the first of its kind anywhere. All the first edition of 3,000 copies were sold out in the year of publication, indicating how highly Shakespeare is regarded among Hungarians and the part he has played in their national life.

---

[79] 'How German is Shakespeare in Germany? Recent Trends in Criticism and Performance in West Germany', *Shakespeare Survey 37* (Cambridge, 1984), pp. 155–62.

[80] *Magyar Shakespeare – Tükör* (Survey), by Sándor Maller and Kálmán Ruttkay; Gondolat, Budapest, 1984.

## 3 . EDITIONS AND TEXTUAL STUDIES
### *reviewed by* MacDonald P. Jackson

'Editors engaged in modernisations of texts would be well advised to discuss their difficulties more fully in print for their mutual advantage and the formulation of some working conventions that will do the least damage.' So wrote Fredson Bowers in 1959.[1] In *Re-Editing Shakespeare for the Modern Reader*,[2] Stanley Wells draws on his experience as General Editor of the Oxford Shakespeare to further the open discussion advocated by Bowers a quarter of a century ago and promoted by Wells himself in *Modernizing Shakespeare's Spelling*.[3] At the same time, Wells challenges the view, implicit in Bowers's phrase 'the least damage', that modernized editions are inevitably less scholarly than old-spelling ones, doing greater violence to the meanings of Shakespeare's plays. Under the chapter heading 'Old and Modern Spelling', Wells argues that the disadvantages of modernization have been exaggerated, and shows how specific problems, including several over proper names, may be met by 'reasoned decisions'.

Chapter 2, on 'Emending Shakespeare', offers new solutions to old cruxes, and questions a few Quarto or Folio readings that have not previously been doubted. One of these latter falls within the line in F *The Taming of the Shrew* in which Petruccio (Wells favours the Italian spelling of the name) tells Gremio: 'My

---

[1] *Textual and Literary Criticism* (Cambridge University Press, 1959), p. 180. My line references to Shakespeare's plays are to editions under review or *The Riverside Shakespeare* (Boston, 1974), ed. G. Blakemore Evans *et al.*

[2] Clarendon Press, Oxford, 1984.

[3] Clarendon Press, Oxford, 1979.

father dead, my fortune liues for me' (1.2.191). The simple change to 'his fortune' creates far better sense, and, as Wells says, 'I do not think we should be inhibited from adopting a superior reading by a fear that we might be improving on Shakespeare rather than on the agents of transmission' (p. 42). His suggestion that in F The Two Gentlemen of Verona, 1.1.43, 'eating Loue' should be 'doting love' is equally attractive. Among Wells's emendations are some designed to restore regular verse, since 'the policy of refusing to mend metre can be, and I think has been, taken too far' (p. 50). He also proposes that in a modern-spelling text 'auld grey doe' should replace Q's 'haud credo' in Love's Labour's Lost, 4.2.12, because, as A. L. Rowse pointed out, 'auld grey doe' represents Dull's understanding of Holofernes's Latin phrase, and that when at 4.2.127 of the same play Holofernes (Nathaniel in Q and F) addresses Jacquenetta as 'Damosella virgin' he intends the medieval Latin domicella and adds a translation. These last two cases illustrate Wells's point that modernization may prove a stimulus to thoughtful interpretation of the text.

One particularly interesting suggestion is that a well-known difficulty in Love's Labour's Lost, 4.1.144 – where Costard's speech about his supposed discomfiture of Boyet suddenly and mysteriously switches its focus to Armado and Moth – may be cleared up when a new emendation is combined with a new interpretation: Q's 'ath toothen side' may be emended to 'ath toother side', modernized as 'o' th' other side', and glossed 'on the other hand', becoming, as Wells explains, 'the linking phrase between Costard's contempt of Boyet and his praise of Armado' (p. 55).

Shakespeare wrote his plays not for readers but for his acting company, and in the knowledge that he would be involved in the production process. So printed texts based on his foul papers often give inadequate or contradictory indications of how the scripts were to be realized in performance: many details remained to be established during preparation of the prompt-book and actors' parts and in the give and take of rehearsals. Wells's chapter on 'The Editor and the Theatre: Editorial Treatment of Stage Directions' helpfully addresses the issues raised by the skimpiness of Shakespeare's written instructions about action, sound effects, business, properties, and spectacle. In identifying 'points at which additional directions, or changes to those of the early texts, are necessary to make the staging intelligible' – 'intelligible' in terms of the Shakespearian theatre – we should not be hidebound by eighteenth-century precedent (p. 68). A principle worth keeping in mind is the theatrical one 'that the editor may sometimes be able to provide information at a point equivalent to that at which its visual correlative would be apprehended in the theatre' (p. 76). Wells packs his discussion with illuminating examples.

His final chapter is a detailed examination of Titus Andronicus, act 1, and in particular of the questions about staging that arise when the Quarto (1594), based on foul papers, is collated with the Folio text, probably based on a copy of Q3 (1611) bearing annotations derived from a manuscript prompt-book. Q1's directions are authorial but incomplete. F's are fuller, but their links with Shakespeare are more tenuous. Shakespeare would, however, have recognized that the meagre instructions of his original autograph required supplementation, and Wells shows that F's clues to the play's theatrical realization deserve respect. Indeed, a major theme of this stimulating little book is that it was in the collaborative enterprise of performance that a Shakespeare script 'fulfilled its destiny', and that twentieth-century scholars have tended to underestimate the authority and utility of the Folio when its theatre-derived readings supplement or alter a good quarto text. Wells's last few pages (pp. 110–13), though undogmatic and recognizing that plays 'are open to different kinds of editorial treatment according to the varying needs of those who read them', register a significant shift in emphasis in recent Shakespearian textual thinking.

Assessment of F departures from the text supplied by a good quarto is crucial to the editing of all three plays to have appeared in the New Cambridge series this year, and one of these plays, *Richard II*, is the subject of an important investigation by Wells's Oxford Shakespeare colleagues, John Jowett and Gary Taylor.[4] Q1 (1597) of *Richard II* was evidently based either on Shakespeare's foul papers or on a transcript of them. It has long been agreed also that F was printed mainly from a copy of Q3 (1598) that had been sporadically annotated – apparently by reference to the prompt-book, from which F also derived the deposition episode, suppressed from the early quartos and first published, in a version inferior to F's, in Q4 (1608). An authoritative playhouse manuscript was thus the source for a whole episode in F and for at least some of F's new readings. After first considering and rejecting claims for F's direct bibliographical dependence upon Q5, as well as upon Q3 (they show that Q5's influence was probably mediated through the prompt-book, one short passage in this manuscript having been transcribed from an exemplar of Q5), Jowett and Taylor set about determining the pattern and nature of the annotation upon the exemplar of Q3 that served as printer's copy for F. They are aided in this task by 'the large number of instances in which F restored a correct Q1 reading where Q3 had acquired an error, the latter originating either in the Q2 printer's copy for Q3, or in Q3 itself' (p. 161). A table in which F's seventy-six restorations of Q1 readings are plotted against its seventy-five perpetuations of Q3 errors demonstrates that some areas of Q3 were systematically corrected, while others were untouched. That this alternation of sustained correction with sustained failure to correct results from fluctuations in the annotator's recourse to the prompt-book is strongly suggested by a survey of other pertinent dialogue

readings: those in which F compounds an error in Q3, probable errors shared by F and Q1–3, manuscript misreadings, changes to lineation, expurgations or retentions of profanity, F cuts, and generally accepted F corrections of Q1–3 error. When those of the above types of readings that point to prompt-book consultation are tabulated against those that point to failure to consult a prompt-book, there emerges a pattern closely correlated to that formed by F's restorations of Q1 readings corrupted in Q3. The dialogue exhibits distinct 'areas of correction', which together account for about half the text. Jowett and Taylor find an 'irresistible association between (a) the most plausible emendations of Q1 and F and (b) other indications of annotation' (p. 176). Besides an intermittently efficient collation of dialogue variants, there was a more systematic collation of stage directions and speech prefixes, the prompt-book being the source of all annotations upon the copy of Q3 from which F was set. Analysing the most significant variants in the light of these findings, Jowett and Taylor argue that many of the new readings passed on to F from the prompt-book probably originated with Shakespeare himself. They conclude that F should be used more freely than it has been by twentieth-century editors.

Andrew Gurr adopts a few more F readings than did the Arden editor, Peter Ure, including the plainly superior 'cousin, cousin' (Q 'Cossens Coosin') at 1.4.20, a handful of colloquial contractions ('who's' where Q has 'who is', for instance) at 5.2.73–6 and 5.5.5, and, with an excellent supporting note, the transposition 'And long live Henry, of that name the fourth', where Q has 'And long liue Henry fourth of that name' at 4.1.112. His emendations of shared QF errors include Singer's

[4] 'Sprinklings of Authority: The Folio Text of *Richard II*', *Studies in Bibliography*, 38 (1985), 151–200. The new editions published by Cambridge University Press are *Richard II* (1984), ed. Andrew Gurr; *A Midsummer Night's Dream* (1984), ed. R. A. Foakes; *Hamlet* (1985), ed. Philip Edwards.

convincing 'reined' at 2.1.70, where Ure and other modern editors have obstinately adhered to QF 'ragde': Gurr notes that the line as emended may have been inspired by a passage in *The Mirror of Magistrates* that describes Richard as 'not raygning but raging by youthfull insolence'. He is willing to repair lines that suffer obvious metrical disturbance, as at 5.3.21, where he is the first editor to supply 'in him', a plausible stopgap. But he balks at the good suggestion by Steevens recorded in his collation and commentary at 2.2.110.[5] One of his notes on a metrical matter strikes me as odd. At 1.1.204 he reads, with Q and F, 'Lord Marshal, command our officers at arms', but joins Ure in wondering whether the extrametrical 'Lord' may be an interpolation. He then suggests that 'Marshal' (spelt 'Martiall' in Q) 'may have been pronounced as a trisyllable, which would certainly make the use of "Lord" redundant metrically'. But 'Lord' is more obviously extrametrical if 'Marshal' is disyllabic; if 'Marshal' is trisyllabic, 'Lord' contributes to a good alexandrine.

Gurr fully justifies his use of Q6 and F to tidy up Q1's inconsistency, perpetuated by Ure, at 1.4.23; his notes on the scene's opening stage direction and on the entry and cue following line 52 help clarify the difficulties. He is idiosyncratic at 3.2.29–32, where Carlisle admonishes Richard:

> The meanes that heauens yeeld must be
>     imbrac't
> And not neglected. Else heauen would,
> And we will not, heauens offer, we refuse,
> The profered meanes of succors and redresse.

So the lines appear in Q. They are absent from F. Their syntax is perplexing, and somebody may have deliberately cut the Gordian knot.[6] If so, that person is unlikely to have been Shakespeare, since, as Gurr notes, 'F's omission of Carlisle's compact theologising diminishes the mildly comic point of Aumerle's translation' in the next speech. Many editors follow Pope in adding 'if' to line 30 and punctuating:

> The means that heaven yields must be
>     embraced
> And not neglected; else, if heaven would,
> And we will not, heaven's offer we refuse,
> The proffered means of succour and redress.

Others prefer:

> . . . neglected; else heaven would,
> And we will not. Heaven's offer we refuse,
> The proffered means of succour and redress.

Without recording Pope's emendation in his collation notes or commenting on the syntax, Gurr reads:

> . . . neglected. Else heaven would
> And we will not. Heavens offer, we refuse
> The proffered means of succour and redress.

This makes 'Heavens' a nominative plural and 'offer' a verb. Another novelty in punctuation occurs at 3.2.84: 'Awake, thou coward! Majesty, thou sleepest', instead of the usual 'Awake, thou coward majesty! thou sleepest'. (Jowett and Taylor uphold F's substitution of 'sluggard' for 'coward' here.)

F variants that Jowett and Taylor would consider authorial Gurr categorizes among unauthoritative 'changes introduced by the players and recorded in the promptbook, or perhaps wilful adjustments made by a literary-minded editor of the copy prepared for the Folio printers' (p. 179). At 1.1.157, for example, Richard jests in Q: 'Our doctors say, this is no month to bleede'. F replaces 'month' with 'time'. Gurr remarks that F's variant 'reduces what is probably Richard's joke about astrological influence in medicine'. (Peter Ure had cited a passage in Fletcher's *The Chances*: 'all physicians / And penny almanacs allow the opening / Of veins this month'.) Jowett and

---

[5] It may be worth proposing another transposition: 'would true noblesse' at 4.1.119, where Q1 and modern editors read 'true noblesse would' and Q2–5 and F replace the noun with 'nobleness'.

[6] A compositor's or scribe's eyeskip from 'The meanes' at the beginning of line 29 to 'He meanes' at the beginning of line 33 is an alternative possibility.

Taylor (pp. 191–2) suspect that Shakespeare decided 'to remove the unfortunate suggestion of menstruation' in Q's line. At 5.1.44 Richard says in Q: 'Tell thou the lamentable tale of me.' F changes 'tale' to 'fall'. Gurr, regarding F's word as an unsanctioned 'normalization', points out that Q's 'tale' cannot be a compositor's recollection of 'tell thee tales' in line 41, since a new man took over at line 43. All the more reason, Jowett and Taylor would reply, for assuming authorial revision, because F eliminates repetition of the cliché collocation 'tell . . . tale(s)': in F. 'Richard relates himself to a specific genre of narrative, the Falls of Princes, and in doing so he heightens the extent of his self-dramatization' (p. 189). Some nice decisions will confront future editors persuaded by Jowett and Taylor that F contains Shakespearian second thoughts.[7]

Gurr's Introduction is divided into sections on 'Date', 'History', 'Sources', 'Structure', 'Imagery', 'Language', 'Staging', and 'Stage History'. Convinced that 'Richard II was designed from the start to launch a sequence of plays', through which 'Jerusalem' recurs as a leitmotif, he makes original remarks on the 'several verbal hints which link the alternatives of the militant journey to Jerusalem and the peaceable pilgrimage with the opposition between Christian patience and militancy in resisting an unlawful king' (pp. 4–5). Repudiating the emphasis given the idea of divine right by an earlier generation of royalist critics, Gurr argues that Shakespeare's handling of his sources was governed more by considerations of dramatic structure than by 'any political predispositions', and that the paramount structural principle is 'balance'. His own account of the play's symmetries acknowledges a wide range of critical response, but spurns 'the turgid theorising about Richard as an actor or poet which entered twentieth-century readings of the play under the promptings of Pater and Yeats' (p. 18). In a useful corrective to facile contrasts between Richard's highflown rhetoric and Bullingbrook's down-to-earth plainness, Gurr points out that 'Bullingbrook's speeches in 1.1 are like Mowbray's, bombastic, over-assertive, with formal rhyming. His subsequent speeches are structured with the rhetorical tropes of pleonasmus, macrologia, bomphilogia and pericrgia, all figures of inflation and elaboration. He no more uses a plain style than Richard' (p. 34). 'Most of the images of the play are organised in relation to the four elements: earth, air, fire and water' (p. 23). 'The four elements' sounds rather like one of those thematic holdalls (such as 'appearance and reality') mocked by Richard Levin in New Readings vs. Old Plays, but Gurr traces various threads of imagery and suggests how they interweave. In his authoritative discussion of the play's Elizabethan staging Gurr finds Richard II 'remarkable in the Shakespearean canon for its lack of movement on stage' (p. 37). His brief stage history includes a fine description of John Barton's 1973 Royal Shakespeare Company production, in which Richard Pasco and Ian Richardson alternated the two major roles.

A theatrical orientation is more obvious in R. A. Foakes's slim edition of A Midsummer Night's Dream. After a lively and judicious discussion of the composition date and source material, Foakes's Introduction moves straight into brief essays on 'The Play on the Stage' and 'The Play in the Mind'. Theatre productions

---

[7] Jowett and Taylor cite two separate lines in Richard II in which an attractive F variant renders less exact a Q echo of Richard III or 3 Henry VI. They suppose that Shakespeare revised to remove unconscious self-borrowing. This seems a better theory than the Brooks–Ure alternative (Arden Richard II, p. xix, note 3) that Q was printed from a memorially contaminated transcript of foul papers, the transcriber sometimes corrupting the text with memories of Richard III (and presumably 3 Henry VI). Yet the occasional association in Q of metrical irregularity with repetition of exclamations and tags – especially in scenes in which York is prominent – remains puzzling, even when maximum allowance is made for the compositorial carelessness demonstrated by Alan Craven in Studies in Bibliography, 26 (1973), 37–60.

range from a typical nineteenth-century mix of operatic and balletic spectacle, enhanced by Mendelssohn's incidental music, to Peter Brook's sinister erotic fantasy, set in a white box equipped with circus trapezes. 'Dreams open up areas of experience repressed by the conscious mind, but can also shade into nightmares in which the frustrations of uncontrolled passions lead to violence and madness' (p. 31). Foakes subtly explores the play's capacity to yield significances that run the gamut from sadomasochism to innocent pastoral charm. He sees *A Midsummer Night's Dream* as occupying the same position among Shakespeare's comedies as *Hamlet* occupies among the tragedies. 'The strength of the play lies in the way its delightful fictions and charming poetry, orchestrated superbly into an artistic whole, continually reverberate with profundities that are in the end as far beyond our grasp as Bottom's dream' (p. 41). Again 'balance' becomes a key word (p. 37). Critically this is a stimulating edition, and the commentary fulfils Foakes's promise to give the reader special help in visualizing the details of what is happening and where people are on stage.

Textually *A Midsummer Night's Dream* poses few serious problems, Q (1600) having been set from Shakespeare's foul papers, and the Folio text from a copy of Q2 (a straight reprint of Q1) 'that had been rather haphazardly corrected and expanded by an editor who was able to compare it with a manuscript marked up for use in the theatre' (p. 139). The expansions are mainly to stage directions. A few of F's corrections to the dialogue have been generally accepted – such as the insertion of 'passionate' to fill a gap at 3.2.220 and the alteration of 'knit now againe' to 'knit vp in thee', which satisfies the rhyme at 5.1.186. At 1.1.139 Lysander laments that the 'course of true love' is often obstructed by 'the choice of friends'. F replaces Q's 'friends' with 'merit'. Like most editors Foakes prefers 'friends' as much more appropriate to Hermia's exclamation in response, 'O

hell, to choose love by another's eyes!' But he gives contradictory explanations of how 'merit' got into F, proposing in his note on 1.1.139 that 'merit' was Shakespeare's superseded 'first thought' (presumably surviving along with its intended replacement, 'friends', in the foul papers and wrongly selected by the prompt-book scribe), and in his textual analysis that 'merit' was 'a revision incorporated into the prompt-copy' (p. 140): perhaps in this second context 'revision' means 'superseded first thought' and 'incorporated' implies 'taken over by mistake', but Foakes's formulation on p. 140 gives the strong impression that he is there making a case for accepting the Folio change.

He does accept F's correction to Q's version of Theseus' comment on the departure from the Pyramus and Thisbe episode of Tom Snout, who represents 'Wall': 'Now is the Moon vsed between the two neighbors' (Q, 5.1.201). F replaced the nonsensical 'Moon vsed' with 'morall downe', which most editors have followed Pope in interpreting as 'mural down'. One minor difficulty about this solution is that by the late sixteenth century 'mural' was an archaism in the sense of 'wall' and Shakespeare does not use the word elsewhere. A more telling objection is that Q's nonsense cannot have derived by any normal process of corruption from 'murall downe', so that F's variant could be authoritative only if it were to represent Shakespeare's revision of the foul papers phrase misread in Q. It seems prudent to attempt independent emendation of Q. In an appendix to his Arden edition (pp. 159–62) Harold Brooks suggested that Q's variant is a misreading of 'mure rased' and that F's is a compositorial misinterpretation of an editorial annotation on the Q2 copy. Brooks conjectured that the annotator wrote 'wall downe', which the F compositor misread as 'rall downe', imagining that 'rall' was intended to turn an imperfectly deleted 'Moon' into 'morall'. Brook thought that even if 'wall downe' was in the prompt-book, it is unlikely to have had Shakespeare's sanction. His discussion of this crux strikes me as admirable. 'Mure' appears in *2 Henry IV*, composed within two or three years of *A Midsummer Night's Dream*. Foakes claims that 'mure rased' 'makes poor sense, for Wall has simply walked off, and has not been "rased" – effaced or destroyed' (p. 140). But this literal-minded stricture upon 'rased' might just as readily be applied to 'down'; without some poetic licence Theseus could make no quip at all. Brooks's treatment (Arden edition, pp. 155–8) of the muddle at 3.1.65–6 over 'odious', 'odours', and 'odorous' also seems preferable to Foakes's, though in Bottom's 'flowers of odious sauours' (Q) 'of' is clearly a mistake, whether Bottom's oral solecism or the compositor's aural substitution, for 'have'.

In 5.1.44–60, a passage discussed by Wells in *Re-Editing Shakespeare* (pp. 60–1), Theseus in Q reads out a list of the entertainments prepared for his wedding celebrations, commenting on each of them in turn. F assigns the announcement of each item to Lysander, leaving Theseus the interspersed comments. Evidently by the time F was printed in 1623 the lines had been apportioned between the two speakers in the prompt-book used by Shakespeare's company. Was the modification, which has theatrical appeal, made while Shakespeare was still with the company, or after his retirement and perhaps even his death? Foakes, while recognizing that Shakespeare may have instigated, or at least approved, F's division, opts for the less questionable authority of Q, which undoubtedly reflects the playwright's 'original conception' (pp. 118, 141, 143).

A further crux occurs at 3.2.257–9, where Q reads:

> *Demetrius.* No, no: heele
> Seeme to break loose: take on as you would follow;
> But yet come not. You are a tame man, go.

F replaced 'heele' with 'Sir', while following Q2 in relining thus; 'No . . . loose / Take . . .

follow.' But Q1's lineation is clearly correct: the opening words of Demetrius' speech complete a verse line begun by Lysander – except that one more syllable is required. Foakes follows F's wording and Q1's lineation. But in a recent note Gary Taylor improves on this expedient.[8] He accepts F's 'Sir' as an authoritative addition to, rather than replacement of, Q's 'heele', which he emends to 'yield', so that Demetrius sarcastically exhorts Lysander: 'No, no, Sir, yield.' In the context of Demetrius' taunts this simple emendation, defensible on graphic grounds, creates excellent sense while regularizing the metre.

Foakes is almost certainly wrong in supposing that in the stage direction added by F to the end of act 3, '*They sleepe all the Act*', 'Act' means the action of 4.1.1–135, the sentence constituting 'a prompter's reminder that the lovers must remain on stage when Titania enters in 4.1' (p. 104). The traditional understanding that 'Act' here is the interval between acts 3 and 4, and that F's direction indicates a break in performance introduced at some revival, probably after the King's Men began playing at the Blackfriars in 1609, is confirmed in Gary Taylor's forthcoming investigation of act intervals in the London theatres during 1576–1642. Among oddities of punctuation in Foakes's *A Midsummer Night's Dream* are the question mark at 5.1.22, where an exclamation mark is needed, and the placement of the comma after 'presented' instead of 'sport' in 3.2.14. The insertion of a second 'fair' in 3.1.85 is not recorded in the collation. These are petty cavils at an edition of some vigour and flair.

The question of the provenance of Folio variations from a good quarto is particularly pressing in respect of *Hamlet*. Q1 (1603) is a bad text, concocted by actors who relied on their memories of the play as they had performed it. Q2 (1604/5) is based on Shakespeare's foul papers, and F on a tidier manu-

---

8 'A Crux in *A Midsummer Night's Dream*', *Notes and Queries*, NS 32 (1985), 47–9.

script, perhaps, as Philip Edwards believes, a playhouse transcript of the foul papers preparatory to the creation of the prompt-book.[9] Bibliographical links between Q1 and Q2, most frequent in the first act, indicate, at the very least, sporadic reference to a copy of Q1 by the Q2 compositors, and F's bibliographical dependence in some way upon Q2 has also been suspected. Edwards does not attempt a detailed examination of evidence for the physical relationship between the three texts. The novelty of his sketchily argued textual theory lies in the fascinating case he puts forward for believing that Shakespeare made significant adjustments to *Hamlet* as it neared production, and that F's substantial omissions and additions to the text of Q2 reflect this authorial revision. F omitted about 220 lines altogether and added close to one hundred.

'It seems to me the likeliest thing in the world', writes Edwards, 'that in creating a hero who is a tangle of conflicting tendencies Shakespeare would have written a lot of tentative material – passages relating to aspects of *Hamlet* [*sic*] and his mission which needed saying but whose final placing was uncertain – and that in the end some of this material would seem redundant or wrong, and not to belong anywhere' (p. 17). Particularly intriguing is Edwards's discussion (pp. 14–19) of F's removal of Hamlet's fourth soliloquy from 4.4, and its cuts and modifications to the dialogue connected with Hamlet's voyage to England and dispatch of Rosencrantz and Guildenstern. These F changes substantially affect Shakespeare's presentation of his hero's inner development. But F's cancellation of two reflective passages preceding entries of the ghost (1.1.108–25 and 1.4.17–38) and its less drastic tightening up of several other speeches also shift the balance, or accelerate the progress, of certain scenes.[10]

Edwards thinks that many of F's deletions were Shakespeare's 'composition cuts', indicated in the foul papers by enigmatic markings misunderstood or disregarded by the Q2 com-

positors, and that some marginal or interleaved insertions may also have been overlooked. But he tentatively assigns a few authorial revisions to the next stage in the evolution of the script – the preparation by a playhouse scrivener, assisted by Shakespeare himself, of a fair copy intermediate between foul papers and prompt-book.

He perhaps overestimates the amount of Q/F variation likely to have arisen in the first of these ways – through the Q2 compositors' unsuccessful, and a fair copyist's successful, efforts at divining Shakespeare's intentions as expressed in confusing foul papers (which were, in Edwards's view, defective and illegible in places by the time Q2 came to be printed). Edwards's acceptance of so many F expansions and rephrasings would more plausibly be justified by a theory that the majority were introduced by Shakespeare into some manuscript deriving (directly or through intermediaries) from the foul papers. At 2.1.49–54 Polonius, explaining to Reynaldo his devious strategy for learning about Laertes' behaviour in Paris, momentarily loses the thread of his explanation. Edwards, following F, reads:

*Polonius.* And then sir does a this – a does – what was I about to say? By the mass I was about to say something. Where did I leave?
*Reynaldo.* At 'closes in the consequence', at 'friend, or so', and 'gentleman'.
*Polonius.*
At 'closes in the consequence' – ay marry,
He closes with you thus: 'I know the gentleman . . .

---

[9] 'Based on' need not imply 'directly printed from'. Behind F Edwards postulates a further stage of transcription some time after 1606.

[10] However, I agree with Dover Wilson, whose view is rejected by Edwards (p. 14), that whether or not Hamlet's long 'dram of eale' speech before the ghost's entry at 1.4.38 has the choric value often found in it, it does serve the useful dramatic function of distracting audience attention from thoughts of the ghost, for which the group on stage is waiting, and so rendering the ghost's third appearance no less startling than its brilliantly handled first two.

Q2 lacks the last six words of Reynaldo's speech and 'with you' in the last line quoted. Edwards posits 'an accidental omission by the compositor' in Reynaldo's speech, but remains silent about the absence of 'with you' from Q2. To the Arden editor (1982), Harold Jenkins, Reynaldo's extra words in F 'have the air of an actor's elaboration. It is noticeable that Polonius ignores them in taking up the cue ... F's *closes with you* ... shows a similar expansion.' Jenkins adheres to Q. He seems to me right in referring both variants to a single process of accretion in F, rather than to accidental loss in Q2, but less convincing in his claim that F has somehow imported the concoctions of actors. F's version of Reynaldo's speech is more amusing than Q2's. Here, and in many similarly variant passages (often associated with entries and exits) it may be easiest to assume authorial tinkering as the play was freshly transcribed.[11]

To take a further example, at 4.7.35–41 Claudius' interview with Laertes is interrupted by a sudden entry. Q reads (with Claudius speaking):

> And that I hope will teach you to imagine.
> *Enter a Messenger with Letters.*
> *Messenger.* These to your Maiestie, this to the Queene.
> *King.* From *Hamlet*, who brought them?
> *Messenger.* Saylers My Lord they say, I saw them not,
> They were giuen me by *Claudio*, he receiued them
> Of him that brought them.

F reads:

> And that I hope will teach you to imagine –
> *Enter a Messenger.*
> How now? What Newes?
> *Messenger.* Letters my Lord from Hamlet. This to your Maiesty: this to the Queene.
> *King.* From *Hamlet*? Who brought them?
> *Messenger.* Saylors my Lord they say, I saw them not:
> They were giuen me by *Claudio*, he receiu'd them.

Edwards conflates the two texts without comment. Jenkins dismisses F's extra dialogue as 'a theatrical elaboration', since from 4.6.8–10 'it does not appear that the bearer of the letters knew the identity of their sender, and it is arguably better if the king is not thus forewarned', but, like Edwards, he includes Q's 'Of him that brought them'. Again, the simplest theory is that all the variants arose during the same stage in the evolution of the play towards performance, and that Shakespeare was responsible for the F adjustments, since they include not only 'theatrical elaboration' of the messenger's entry, but also excision of his redundant last five words,, which clumsily repeat the king's 'brought them'.

Concentrating on clues to the author's compression of his text within the foul papers, Edwards fails to confront the possibility that Shakespeare was himself the source for some of those notorious one-word variants – 'interr'd' and 'enurn'd' at 1.4.49, 'heated' and 'tristfull' at 3.4.50, for example – in which the comparative merits of the Q2 and F readings have been inconclusively debated. At 4.7.7 both Edwards and Jenkins have Laertes speak, as in F, of Hamlet's 'feats, / So crimeful and so capital in nature'. Q2's 'criminall', where F has 'crimefull', is unlikely to be corrupt, however, in view of the parallel to Laertes' line afforded by *Coriolanus*, 3.3.81, 'So criminal, and in such capital kind'. The editor who, recognizing that *Coriolanus* vindicates Q2, nevertheless prefers the unusual 'crimeful', which Shakespeare had used in *The Rape of Lucrece*, is logically driven to hold Shakespeare responsible for both readings. Jenkins cites another parallel with *Coriolanus* in support of his strong argument in favour of F's 'o're Offices' ('o'er-offices') at 5.1.67, justly describing the verb as 'in Shakespeare's finest manner, both inventive and exact' (Arden edition, pp. 59–60). Edwards

---

[11] Edwards does apply this explanation to F's addition of the phrase 'Let me see' as Hamlet takes Yorick's skull from the Gravedigger at 5.1.156.

defends Q2's 'ore-reaches', but does not guess at the origin of F's variant. Surely it cannot be a mere corruption of 'ore-reaches'? Again, there seems a good chance that both words are Shakespeare's, F's being his second thought.

Whether in this last instance the Q/F variant resulted from corruption or revision, Edwards has, in my opinion, chosen the wrong reading, and in his editorial decision-making he is on the whole less judicious than Jenkins. Among questionable choices (spelling modernized) are Q2 and F 'design' instead of F2's 'designed' at 1.1.94; F 'sanctity' instead of Theobald's 'sanity' at 1.3.21; F 'Roaming' instead of Collier's 'Running' at 1.3.109; Q2F 'bonds' instead of Theobald's 'bawds' (which Edwards calls a 'ludicrous emendation') at 1.3.130; F 'rots' instead of Q2 Q1 'roots' at 1.5.33; F 'the dear murdered' instead of a conflation of Q1 and Q2 to give 'a dear father murdered' at 2.2.536; Q2 'habits devil' instead of Theobald's 'habits evil' at 3.4.163; and F 'pierce' instead of Q2 ''pear' (appear) at 4.5.151. He opts for F's 'solid', not Q2's 'sallied' (sullied) flesh. And, with the concurrence this time of Jenkins, he accepts, as I cannot, Q2 F 'good' in preference to Warburton's 'god' at 2.2.179. At 5.2.73 he refuses to expand F's 'interim's' to 'interim is' for the sake of the metre, because 'there is no authority for this'. As both Q1 and Q2 lack the material within which line 73 occurs, 'authority' is quite beside the point: the sole pertinent question is whether it is more probable that Shakespeare intended a metrical irregularity or that an unwanted elision has been introduced by compositor or scribe. There is an error in Edwards's text at 1.2.168, where 'Horatio' has strayed in from line 164.

In his introductory section on 'The Play and the Critics', Edwards aims to provide not a survey of *Hamlet* criticism but 'a personal graph, linking together some moments in the history of the interpretation of *Hamlet* which I find important' (p. 32). His own essay on 'The Action of the Play' leads us from the opening scene 'full of perturbation and anxiety' to the havoc of the close. A clear-sighted guide, Edwards points out features we might have missed: 'Ophelia's tragedy, like Hamlet's, is a tragedy of obedience to a father. Only she really goes mad. And then – always going one step further than the prince – she doesn't stop at thinking about ending her life' (p. 46). His verdict on the play is subtly phrased, and the term 'balance' crops up yet again. Contrasting Shakespeare's drama with *The Spanish Tragedy*, Edwards concludes: 'Hamlet's own belief towards the end of the play that a benign divinity works through our spontaneous impulses and even our mistakes is neither clearly endorsed by the play nor repudiated in ironic Kydean laughter. Hamlet is a tragic hero who at a time of complete despair hears a mysterious voice uttering a directive which he interprets as a mission to renovate the world by an act of purifying violence. But this voice is indeed a questionable voice. How far it is the voice of heaven, how its words are to be translated into human deeds, how far the will of man *can* change the course of the world – these are questions that torment the idealist as he continues to plague the decadent inhabitants, as he sees them, of the Danish court' (p. 59). Bradley's final remark on the play was that 'the apparent failure of Hamlet's life is not the ultimate truth concerning him'. Edwards sagely adds: 'But it might be. That is where the tragic balance lies' (p. 61).

In 'Hamlet and the Actors' Edwards concentrations on 'the tradition of cutting and its effect on the *Hamlet* that was presented to audiences until the end of the nineteenth century' (p. 61). His commentary supplements his critical Introduction with many shrewd observations, besides a few that can best be described as provocative (3.2.351), and others that seem patently wrong-headed, such as the notion that Polonius is a sexual innocent (2.1.30), or that Shakespeare intends comic burlesque at 2.2.431–2.

One last word on the text: although convinced that many F cuts are authorial,

Edwards, perhaps under pressure from his publishers, shuns the logical editorial course of relegating to the commentary or an appendix the Q2 passages that Shakespeare supposedly planned to discard. Instead he places passages unique to Q2 within square brackets, which we may ignore with all the insouciance that he imputes to the Q2 compositors. He regrets that 'it is not always possible ... to have the courage of one's convictions' (p. 32).

'Sometimes my own instincts in favour of the status quo war with my sense of logic', admits Stanley Wells in Re-Editing Shakespeare, 'and then I have to examine my instincts and try to identify the part played in them by inertia' (p. 30). Gary Taylor's 'The Fortunes of Oldcastle' is designed to provoke within Shakespearian scholars a particularly painful struggle between the better angel of reason and the worser spirit of sloth.[12] His article patiently draws the logical conclusion from familiar facts. Falstaff owes his name in 1 Henry IV to the accident of censorship, Lord Cobham and his family having complained about Shakespeare's alleged libel upon their ancestor, Sir John Oldcastle. The evidence, rehearsed by Taylor, that Shakespeare originally christened his fat knight Oldcastle and was forced to rename him is abundant, diverse, and conclusive. Taylor's contention is that 'Oldcastle' should be reinstated – in 1 Henry IV, not in 2 Henry IV, where the character was evidently called, ab ovo, 'Falstaff'. He anticipates and rebuts every conceivable counter-argument – including those pleading for consistency between the two Parts and with The Merry Wives of Windsor – and his reasoning seems flawless. To the diehard who would retain the enforced substitution for the sake of convenience, since 'an entire tradition of criticism and performance has been based upon it', Taylor points out that 'This attitude creates a situation in which the results of textual scholarship are always trivial, because if the results are not trivial they will be disregarded' (p. 93). He ends his article with a

ringing challenge to editorial inertia. So much for Edwards's fear (p. 32) that were he to present readers with a Hamlet trimmed of several famous lines he might be judged arrogant and eccentric!

No such fears trouble A. L. Rowse, editor of the new Contemporary Shakespeare series.[13] Eleven volumes have been submitted for review. Each small paperback comes equipped with a jejune prefatory essay, one or two explanatory notes,[14] and a text subjected to modernization more drastic than any contemplated by Wells. Rowse's professed aim is to help put readers more at ease with Shakespeare's dialogue. Perturbed to hear that the study of Shakespeare is dying out in schools and colleges, he rushes to the rescue with a first-aid kit that turns 'hath' into 'has', 'thou' into 'you', 'writ' into 'wrote', and, more boldly, 'fardels' into 'burdens' and 'poor-john' into 'codfish'. The changes to Elizabethan grammatical forms are purely cosmetic, and the synonym substitutions are made so haphazardly that virtually all the real difficulties of Shakespeare's language remain. What student of Romeo and Juliet would flinch from 'thou art' yet require no help with 'carry coals', 'take the wall', 'heartless hinds', 'Abraham Cupid', 'prick-song', 'King Cophetua', or indeed 'die'? Modern readers, misled by cartoonists and comedians, even need to be told that when Juliet exclaims 'O Romeo, Romeo! wherefore art thou Romeo?' 'wherefore' means not 'where' but 'why'. Since Rowse prints 'wherefore are you, Romeo?' he perhaps needs the lesson himself. Or was the telltale comma inserted by an overzealous subeditor or typesetter and passed over in the proofs? Despite bluster about editors who 'don't write poetry and do not know how to scan', Rowse's tam-

---

[12] Shakespeare Survey 38 (Cambridge University Press, 1985), pp. 85–100.

[13] University Press of America (Lanham, Maryland and London). Publication began in 1984 and the last volumes are scheduled for release in Spring 1987.

[14] But Hamlet gets three, and some plays have none.

perings with the text damage Shakespeare's verse, as (in the first 250 lines of *Romeo*) 'The which' gives way to 'Which', ''ware' (aware) to 'wary', by no means equivalent in sense, 'coz' to 'cousin', 'ope' to 'open', and 'strucken' to 'struck'. In Montague's 'Who set this ancient quarrel new abroach?' the last word becomes 'abroad'. Is appreciation of Shakespeare served by this crude gutting of his metaphors? The school-teacher who really wants pupils to understand Shakespearian English should prescribe a properly annotated edition such as Roma Gill's excellent Oxford School Shakespeare. Rowse's project is misconceived and its execution shoddy.

If modernizing editors need to confer about their procedures, so also do editors who retain the spelling of the originals. *Play-Texts in Old Spelling* preserves a dozen papers from the 1978 Glendon conference on the theory and practice of producing text, apparatus, and commentary for old-spelling editions of Shakespeare and his contemporaries.[15] Some contributions are of special relevance to this survey. Randall McLeod's ingeniously titled 'Spellbound' 'differentiates old spelling from old typesetting, and asserts that editorial uses of the former concept lack philosophical rigor, and that its general application in so-called old-spelling editions has distorted the subtle texture of accidentals which they are designed to convey' (p. 81). With a wealth of illustration he demonstrates how in Renaissance books compositorial spelling may be affected by the desire to separate adjacent kerns, by the use of ligatures, and by other typographical exigencies. There are lessons here for all Shakespeare bibliographers, textual scholars, and editors. S. P. Zitner scrutinizes a page of the Arden *Othello*, pleads for 'brevity and immediate relevance' in explanatory notes, and lists five categories of 'excessive annotation'. David Bevington (to whom Stanley Wells acknowledges a debt in *Re-Editing Shakespeare*) urges editors of Renaissance plays, whether their spelling be old or new, to aim for greater consistency and helpfulness in adding stage directions and in commenting on 'how the Elizabethan stage is being utilized' (p. 112). He exposes anomalies in editors' treatment of business in Shakespeare's plays, and proposes some working rules. The most substantial item is by Paul Werstine, who adds a lengthy 'Afterword' to the reprint of his article 'The Editorial Usefulness of Printing House and Compositor Studies'. His main topic is William White's 1598 quarto of *Love's Labour's Lost*, about which he, George R. Price, and Manfred Draudt have been disconcertingly at odds. Werstine's meticulous analysis of the evidence adduced by the other two bibliographers and his deployment of a vast mass of data from his own thorough study of White's printing shop 'clearly point to the use of printed copy' throughout *Love's Labour's Lost* (1598). As he is careful to note, it does not necessarily follow that the quarto serving as copy for the extant edition was a bad one, as has sometimes been conjectured.

In their Introduction to the collection, Shand and Shady mention that during the third session of the Glendon conference 'doubts as to the very validity of editing in old spelling' were freely expressed. Philip Edwards declared, 'If it were to do again, I would never do an old-spelling Massinger.' Alan Somerset bluntly asked, 'What is the function of an old-spelling edition?' – a question that, according to the editors, 'was never definitively answered'. It is a pity that Fredson Bowers was not present to meet this challenge with the same incisiveness and stamina exhibited in his response to some obscure remarks by Claire Badaracco on 'The Editor and the Question of Value' at the first conference of the Society for Textual Scholarship held in 1981 in New

---

[15] *Play-Texts in Old Spelling: Papers from the Glendon Conference* (AMS Press, New York, 1984), ed. G. B. Shand with Raymond C. Shady. McLeod's paper is reprinted from *Renaissance and Reformation*, NS 3 (1979), 50–65.

York.[16] The transactions of the society have been published in a handsome new annual called *Text*, designed to provide an interdisciplinary forum for textual scholars of diverse backgrounds. Bringing into sharp focus the issues perceptible within Badaracco's paper, Bowers cogently reaffirms the traditional goals and principles of critical editing.

Reassured of our goals, we may be baffled by the complexity of our bibliographical and textual data. *King Lear* puts all scholars on their mettle. Since W. W. Greg published *The Variants in the First Quarto of 'King Lear'* in 1940, it has been widely believed that F *Lear* was set from a marked-up exemplar of Q1 (1608). In *The Textual History of 'King Lear'* (1980) P. W. K. Stone advanced compelling evidence that Folio Compositor E's copy was – or derived from – an exemplar not of Q1 but of Q2 (1619). Stone argued that E's exemplar of Q2 had been annotated by reference to a manuscript derivative from Q1, and that E's Folio *Lear* workmate, Compositor B, set directly from this manuscript. Gary Taylor strengthened Stone's evidence that Compositor E was working from Q2 and hesitantly endorsed his distinction between B's copy and E's.[17] Aided by the computer, Taylor now examines Compositor B's pages of *King Lear* more rigorously in the light of his treatment of known copy spelling and punctuation elsewhere in the Folio.[18] He concludes that in all probability 'B and E worked from the same kind of copy: an annotated exemplar of Q2' (p. 70). Positive evidence for quarto influence on F *Lear* falls mainly within E's stints or applies indiscriminately to Q1 or Q2. But Taylor argues that this is what we should expect: B's use of Q2 is less obvious than E's because B was always far less conservative in his treatment of copy, besides being wildly inconsistent from play to play. B's failure to reproduce Q2 semicolons, despite willingness to set semicolons in passages peculiar to F, remains somewhat anomalous; and Taylor's explanations of agreements between Q1 and

B's stints of F in mispunctuation corrected in Q2 leave niggling doubts. But it is in general terms more probable that F copy was homogeneous than heterogeneous, and we may provisionally accept Taylor's findings, based as they are on thoughtful analysis of more comprehensive data than have previously been available.

Since Taylor admits, in a more cautious formulation of his conclusions, the possibility that copy for F *Lear* was 'some sort of transcript which had been influenced by Q2 to an extraordinary extent' (p. 71), most of the criticisms that T. H. Howard-Hill levels at the hypothesis of mixed copy propounded in *The Division of the Kingdoms*[19] assail a position that Taylor has now abandoned.[20] Howard-Hill's own view, to which he is 'not wedded indissolubly' (p. 176), is that both Folio compositors did indeed have before them a transcript of Q2. He doubts that Q1 influenced F except by way of Q2. His review article on *Division* is important enough to warrant relaxation of this survey's policy of ignoring reviews.[21]

---

16 'The Editor and the Question of Value: Another View', in *Text: Transactions of the Society for Textual Scholarship 1* (AMS Press, New York, 1984), ed. D. C. Greetham and W. Speed Hill, pp. 45–73.

17 'The Folio Copy for *Hamlet*, *King Lear*, and *Othello*', *Shakespeare Quarterly*, 34 (1983), 44–61. In 'The Problem of Manuscript Copy for Folio *King Lear*', *The Library*, 6th series, 4 (1982), 1–23, T. H. Howard-Hill offered other reasons for thinking that E was not setting from Q1

18 'Folio Compositors and Folio Copy: *King Lear* and Its Context', *Papers of the Bibliographical Society of America*, 79 (1985), 17–74.

19 Clarendon Press, Oxford, 1983.

20 'The Challenge of *King Lear*' (review of *The Division of the Kingdoms*), *The Library*, 6th series, 7 (1985), 161–79.

21 Howard-Hill points out (pp. 177–8) that E's stints of *Lear* slightly more often agree with Q1 than with Q2 in what Paul Werstine described as 'a class of variants that lies between substantives and accidentals' (*Division*, p. 274), and argues that the apparent agreements with Q1 result from the binary nature of the variants and simply indicate *lack* of agreement with Q2 – agreement that one might expect if the conservative E were setting directly from Q2. Either Q2 was annotated by some-

The authors of *Division* set out to prove that F *Lear* is Shakespeare's revised version of the play preserved in Q. Reactions continue to vary. Sidney Thomas attacks 'the two-text school'.[22] R. A. Foakes, who finds the case for revision 'persuasively argued', re-examines the role of the Fool in Q and F.[23] In the Royal Shakespeare Company's 1982 production of *King Lear*, Antony Sher's Fool was a professional circus clown killed in act 3; in Grigori Kozintsev's 1970 film the Fool was a village simpleton kept alive through act 5. Foakes explores the middle ground between these extreme interpretations. He agrees with John Kerrigan (in *Division*) that Shakespeare was largely responsible for Folio changes affecting the Fool and that they emphasize his 'sardonically mocking side'. But he denies that a 'blathering natural' in Q is transformed into a 'canny rationalist' in F. 'It would seem rather that from the beginning Shakespeare had a kind of double-vision of the Fool, and that there is a radical indeterminacy in his conception of the role' (p. 40). In 'The Once and Future *King Lears*', Andrew Gurr is provoked by the recent studies of *Lear* into more general reflections on Shakespearian textual criticism.[24] As he says, 'Even in the relatively few cases where printed texts offer versions both with some claim to independent authority, the question of Shakespeare having second thoughts is complicated by the possibility that his fellows in the theatre had the thoughts for him. Most editors have not found that much of a problem, and have classed playhouse alterations more or less with the interfering habits of compositors and other transcribers. But it is inherently likely that a playwright who acted in his own plays and was a sharer in the company which performed them would have taken a hand in the tinkering, the cuts and other adjustments necessary to get a play off the page and onto the stage. Should an editor choose the first thoughts from the study or the second thoughts in the playhouse?' We are back with the questions raised by Stanley Wells. In confronting them himself while editing *Richard II*, Gurr must have decided that in the Folio text of that particular play any second thoughts were ones Shakespeare's fellows 'had for him'. Gurr ends with a fresh aperçu about F *Lear*'s transfer of the play's last speech from Albany to Edgar.[25]

Another Q/F variant in *King Lear* receives attention from Michael Warren.[26] At 4.6.83–4 Lear exclaims in F, 'No, they cannot touch me for crying. I am the King himselfe.' All modern editors assume that 'crying' is a mistake for Q's 'coyning'. Regarding both readings as authorial, Warren glosses 'touch me for crying' as 'cure me of my weeping', an allusion to the superstition that a monarch's touch could relieve such diseases as scrofula. Lear 'is the sufferer who should himself be the curer'. Warren thinks that in the context F's variant 'is neither superior nor inferior to the

---

body who concerned himself with a multitude of insignificant variants or E was setting from a scribal transcript. One interesting feature of Werstine's list of semi-substantive variants (*Division*, pp. 310–12) is not mentioned by Howard-Hill but cries out for explanation: the distribution of F Q1 and F Q2 links is clearly not random; from TLN 1189 to TLN 2959 of E's stints, for example, the agreements are overwhelmingly with Q1.

22 'Shakespeare's Supposed Revision of *King Lear*', *SQ*, 35 (1984), 506–11.

23 'Textual Revision and the Fool in *King Lear*', *Essays in Honour of Peter Davison: Trivium 20* (Saint David's University College, Lampeter, Wales, 1985), 33–47.

24 *Bulletin of the Society for Renaissance Studies*, 2 (1984), 7–19.

25 Randall McLeod could disabuse Gurr (p. 11) of his illusion that the setting of Shakespeare's name as the 'distinctly thespian "Shake-speare"' on the title page of *Richard II*, Q2 (1598) was a 'player's joke'. The printer was intent on avoiding the fouling of kerns. In 'The Uniqueness of *King Lear*: Genre and Production Problems', *Deutsche Shakespeare-Gesellschaft West Jahrbuch 1984*, 44–61, E. A. J. Honigmann points out the exciting possibilities that are opened up for interpretation when a producer rejects modern editorial additions of the word 'dead' to the QF stage direction that has Lear in 5.3 enter with Cordelia 'in his arms' (pp. 59–61).

26 '*King Lear*, IV.vi.83: The Case for "Crying"', *SQ*, 35 (1984), 319–21.

Quarto reading, merely different' (p. 321). His defence of F is ingenious, but Q's word seems much better to me.

If Shakespeare the playwright was not above fidgeting with the scripts that, according to Heminges and Condell, he had delivered to his company with scarce a blot in them, might not the lyric poet, warbling his native woodnotes wild, have sometimes changed his tunes? *The Passionate Pilgrim* (1599) printed Shakespeare's Sonnets 138 and 144 in versions different from those presented in the 1609 Quarto. Though some editors have dismissed *The Passionate Pilgrim* versions as memorial reconstructions of the Q text, others have considered them earlier drafts. Gary Taylor now argues that a variant text of Sonnet 2, preserved in eleven manuscripts of the 1620s and 1630s, also represents the poem as Shakespeare originally composed it.[27] The manuscripts 'speak a characteristically Shakespearean idiom'. Taylor extracts from them clues to the identification of Shakespeare's patron, to the dates of composition of the Sonnets, and to the authority of the 1609 Quarto. And he likens the variants between the two texts of Sonnet 2 to many of those between Q and F *Lear, Hamlet, Othello*, and *Troilus and Cressida*.

The 1609 Quarto of Shakespeare's Sonnets also offered to the world *A Lover's Complaint*, which some commentators have deemed spurious. Subjecting the poem to computer-aided 'stylometric' tests based on rates at which high-frequency words occur, M. W. A. Smith finds his own reasons to doubt its authenticity.[28] But his comparisons of *A Lover's Complaint* with *Venus and Adonis, The Rape of Lucrece, Hero and Leander*, and *The Tears of Peace* prove very little. Smith needs to look at more poems, including Shakespeare's Sonnets themselves, some of which are probably much closer in composition date to *A Lover's Complaint* than are *Venus* and *Lucrece*. Application of Smith's main tests to Sonnets 100–126, for instance, reveals that they are totally unlike his

first *Venus* sample (chi-square = 101.86) but quite like *A Lover's Complaint* (chi-square = 58.84). More convincing is Smith's exposure of the methodological inadequacies in Thomas Merriam's stylometric studies of *Henry VIII, Pericles*, and *Sir Thomas More*.[29]

Eric Sams's attacks on orthodoxies of Shakespearian scholarship require no help from the computer.[30] His chief weapon is forensic panache. Three recent editors have agreed that the anonymous *The Taming of a Shrew* (Q 1594) is indebted to Shakespeare's comedy. Sams argues that Shakespeare used *A Shrew* as a source when he wrote his own Folio play around 1603–4. He underestimates the strength of the metrical, lexical, and other stylistic evidence against this dating of *The Shrew*, but the Folio text may well have had a more complicated history than has lately been recognized.

Less contentious is a solid bibliographical article by S. W. Reid, who cites various spellings and mechanical features of Folio *1* and *2 Henry IV* which 'confirm Taylor's judgement that the non-B pages of these two plays were set by a single workman, one apparently distinguishable from the other compositors who served as B's partners elsewhere in F1'.[31] The

---

27 'Shakespeare's Sonnets: A Rediscovery', *Times Literary Supplement*, 19 April 1985, p. 450; a fuller version of this article is to appear in *The Bulletin of the John Rylands Library*.

28 'The Authorship of "A Lover's Complaint": An Application of Statistical Stylometry to Poetry', *Computers and the Humanities*, 18 (1984), 23–37. Smith (p. 23) distorts J. C. Maxwell's verdict in his New Shakespeare edition of *The Poems* (Cambridge University Press, 1969); Maxwell 'rather reluctantly' accepted the 1609 attribution, writing: 'I believe it to be a poem of Shakespeare's maturity' (p. xxxv).

29 'An Investigation of Morton's Method to Distinguish Elizabethan Playwrights', *Computers and the Humanities*, 19 (1985), 3–21.

30 'The Timing of the *Shrews*', *Notes and Queries*, NS 32 (1985), 33–45.

31 'B and "J": Two Compositors in Two Plays of the Shakespeare First Folio', *The Library*, 6th series, 7 (1985), 126–36.

new evidence 'also confirms Hinman's division of the pages of these plays between B and his partner' (p. 130).

Carol Marks Sicherman's claim is that in *Julius Caesar* 'the Folio short lines often provide eloquent implicit directions for stage-business, rhetorical emphases, and – above all – nuances of characterization'.[32] She explains that her concern is 'with genuine short lines, not with pentameters concealed in shared part-lines or disguised as short lines when the compositor split them on account of the Folio column or broke them to stretch copy' (p. 181). She has sane ideas about metre, and her sensitive analysis carries its message for editors wondering how best to arrange the verse.

In the Folio text of *Twelfth Night*, Sir Toby Belch remarks that Sir Andrew Aguecheek's hair 'will not coole my nature' (1.3.98–9). Gustav Ungerer conscripts a whole troop of Elizabethan notions about sex and hair in defence of this patent error, rejecting Theobald's admirable emendation, 'will not curl by nature', as 'an editorial fossil of the Augustan period' (p. 122).[33] Ungerer's explication of the Folio context loses the point of Sir Toby's jest, with its quibble on 'art' and 'nature'. Audiences laugh at the traditional text. As Ungerer interprets F's version, the passage is just so much theatrical dead weight.

R. F. Fleissner's repudiation of Theobald's most famous emendation seems equally wrong-headed.[34] In F *Henry V* the Hostess says of the dying Falstaff that 'his Nose was as sharpe as a Pen, and a Table of greene fields' (2.3.16–17). Re-examining the relationship between Falstaff's death symptoms and Hippocrates' *Prognostica* and its derivatives, Fleissner urges the superior claims of F's reading over Theobald's 'a' babbled of green fields'. He takes the Hostess to be describing the colour of Falstaff's face ('a Table of' meaning 'a veritable picture of, the very image of'). But F as it stands affords no warrant for attributing greenness to Falstaff's *face*: F unequivocally

and absurdly likens Falstaff's *nose* to both a pen and 'a Table of greene fields'. In a final footnote Fleissner regrets that he was unable to consult Gary Taylor's appendix on this crux in his new Oxford edition of *Henry V* (1982), but claims that Taylor's comments 'do not substantially affect my argument'. In fact Taylor raises telling objections to the unemended text – and to all attempts to connect the fields with Falstaff's appearance. Theatrically this moment calls for sentiment, as Theobald's instincts told him: it invites us to share the Hostess's grief, not boggle over her close encounter with a grass-green grotesque. Moreover, the Q reporters' recollection that, according to the Hostess, Falstaff 'talk't of floures' supports Theobald's guess that 'Table' results from the misreading of a verb of saying, without, however, proving that in the neutral 'talk't' they themselves had hit upon the right one.

Karl P. Wentersdorf explicates 'carded' in *1 Henry IV*, 3.2.60–4, and conjectures that 'cars' should be 'cards' (wool-cards with iron teeth, hence instruments of torture) in Fabian's 'Though our silence be drawne from vs with cars, yet peace' in Folio *Twelfth Night*, 2.5.63–4;[35] and Nancy C. Gutierrez cites 'Pearles low-prised in India' from William Warner's *Albion's England* (1586) in support of Q *Othello*'s 'Indian' at 5.2.347.[36]

The same issue of *Shakespeare Quarterly* includes Shirley Carr Grubb's long interpretation of the 'dram of eale' crux in *Hamlet*,

---

32 'Short Lines and Interpretation: The Case of *Julius Caesar*', *SQ*, 35 (1984), 180–95.

33 'Sir Andrew Aguecheek and His Head of Hair', *Shakespeare Studies*, 16 (1983), 101–33.

34 'Putting Falstaff to Rest: "Tabulating" the Facts', *Shakespeare Studies*, 16 (1983), 57–74. In 'Sir John's Flesh Was Grass: A Necrological Note on Falstaff and the Book of Isaiah', *American Notes and Queries*, 23 (1985), 97–8, Fleissner connects Falstaff's grass-green complexion with Isaiah's 'all flesh is grass'.

35 'Shakespeare and Carding: Notes on Cruxes in *1 Henry IV* and in *Twelfth Night*', *SQ*, 36 (1985), 215–19.

36 'An Allusion to "India" and Pearls', *SQ*, 36 (1985), 220.

1.4.36–8.[37] She summarizes: 'eale = oil (ME ele); noble substance = the soul, and one of the noble metals, gold or silver; scandle = stumbling-block, cause of offense in religion (L. scandalum), and disrepute; doth ... of a doubt = renders doubtful' (p. 202). Her exegesis, amply documented from theological sources and instructive about alchemical lore, implies a very different view from mine of what constitutes Shakespearian poetic sense.

---

[37] 'The Scandalous Dram of Eale', *SQ*, 36 (1985), 188–203.

# INDEX

(Proper names occurring in the filmography have not been indexed)

Abiteboul, Maurice, 235
Achebe, Chinua, 177n
Acker, Paul, 7
Adamaitis, R., 83n
Adler, Doris, 233
*Age of Kings, An,* 9, 19–21, 30,
  31, 94
Agee, James, 3
Aldus, P. J., 143
Alexander, Bill, 197
Alexander, Nigel, 139, 149n
Alexander, Peter, 86n, 94
Allen, Rod, 104n
Alleyn, Edward, 227
Allombert, Guy, 80
Anderson, Judith H., 219n
Anderson, Kevin, 189
Anderson, W. S., 126n, 167n
Andrews, Nigel, 85n
Anikst, Alexander, 85n
Appleton, Elizabeth, 224
Aquino, Deborah T. Curren,
  43n
Arendt, Hannah, 53n
Aristophanes, 155
Aristotle, 149n, 220, 234
Armstrong, Alun, 205
Ascham, Roger, 214
Ashcroft, Peggy, 95n
Avey, Wayne, 76n

Bacon, Francis, 131
Badaracco, Claire, 247, 248
Badel, Alan, 81n
Baker, Oliver, 223
Baker, Sean, 203
Balazs, Bela, 1n
Baldwin, T. W., 124n, 160n,
  168n
Ball, Robert Hamilton, 4, 53n,
  77n

Banham, Martin, 96n
Banionis, D., 83n
Barge, Gillian, 86n, 87
Barish, Jonas, 233
Barker, Clive, 234
Barroll, J. Leeds, 218
Barton, Anne, 133n, 230; *see
  also* Anne Righter
Barton, John, 13n, 47, 105, 188,
  240
Bass, Alan, 147n
Bate, Jonathan, 133n
Baur, Harry, 77n
Baxter, Keith, 42, 43
Bazin, André, 3, 39, 52, 91, 93,
  95, 96n
Beard, Robert, 183
Beauchamp, Gorman, 6
Beaumont, Francis, 131, 133,
  230
Beaurline, L. A., 133n
Beckerman, Bernard, 229
Beckett, Samuel, 136
Bedford, Brian, 183
Beier, Ulli, 176n
Belasco, David, 75n
Benjamin, Walter, 53
Bennett, Rodney,. 100
Benson, Peter, 106
Benson, Susan, 185
Berger, Thomas, 75n
Berlin, Norman, 79n
Berry, Edward, 212
Berry, Ralph, 215
Bevington, David, 56n, 247
Beylie, Claude, 3
Birkett, Michael,·79, 81
Birtwistle, Harrison, 193
Blackburn, Thomas, 169
Blakely, Colin, 89n, 90
Blanpied, John W., 211, 212

Blethyn, Brenda, 86n, 87
Bloom, Claire, 105, 108
Blumenthal, John, 6
Blythe, Domini, 186, 188
Bogdanov, Michael, 13n
Booth, Stephen, 136, 208, 209,
  212
Bothwell, Candace, 75n
Bourchier, Arthur, 7
Bowerbank, Sylvia, 231
Bowers, Fredson, 131n, 236,
  247, 248
Boydell, John, 77
Bracher, Mark, 210n
Bradbury, Malcolm, 217n
Bradley, A. C., 59, 63, 135n,
  245
Bradley, David, 198
Braunmuller, A. R., 217, 230
Brecht, Bertolt, 81, 82, 85, 169
Britten, Benjamin, 219
Brockbank, Philip, 170n, 233
Brook, Peter, 4, 6, 7, 9, 39, 79,
  80, 81, 83, 85, 86, 235, 241
Brooke, C. F. Tucker, 143n
Brooks, Charles, 76n
Brooks, Harold, 240n, 241,
  242
Brown, John Russell, 135n,
  139n, 145n, 191
Bruce, Brenda, 185
Bruto, Giovanni, 225
Bullough, Geoffrey, 150n, 159
Burckhardt, Sigurd, 211
Burke, David, 106
Burke, Kenneth, 141n, 145, 234
Burton, Richard, 86
Bury, John, 191
Buttrey, John, 229

Calder-Marshall, Anna, 89n

# INDEX

Calderwood, James L., 136n, 211

Cameron, G. M., 224

Camillo, Giulio, 140n

Campbell, Douglas, 185

Campbell, Lily B., 132n

Campbell, Paul Newell, 234

Campion, Thomas, 131

Capell, Edward, 153n

Caravaggio, Michelangelo Merisi da, 100

Cariou, Len, 180, 181

Carnovsky, Morris, 85n

Cavanaugh, Jean C., 231

Cavendish, Margaret, 231

Cerasano, S. P., 229

Chambers, E. K., 223

Chapman, George, 224, 231

Charles II, King, 229

Charney, Maurice, 95, 138

Chaucer, Geoffrey, 150n, 219, 221

Chekhov A. P., 94

Cheng, Vincent John, 222

Chesterton, G. K., 160

*Chimes at Midnight*, 19, 39, 40–5 *passim*, 50, 52, 53

Chinweizu, 175

Church, Tony, 233

Churchyard, Thomas, 228

Cibber, Colley, 233

Cinthio, Giraldi, 150

Ciroma, Adam, 175

Clark, Sandra, 231

Cobham, Lord, 246

Cobos, Juan, 43n, 44n, 50n

Coghill, Nevill, 137n

Cohen, Marshal, 1n

Coleridge, Samuel Taylor, 139, 175, 215

Condell, Henry, 250

Conolly, Patricia, 182, 183, 189

Cook, Ron, 106

Cooke, Alastair, 81, 82

Coronado, Celestino, 77

Cottom, John, 223

Coursen, H. R., 11

Courtenay, Tom, 76

Cousin, Geraldine, 235n

Cowie, Peter, 90n

Cowley, Abraham, 232

Cox, C. B., 96n

Cox, John D., 221

Craig, Edward Gordon, 5

Craik, T. W., 215

Crashaw, Richard, 232

Craven, Alan, 240n

Creizenach, W. M. A., 143n

Crowl, Samuel, 50n, 53n

Crowley, Bob, 200

Crowther, Bosley, 3

Cukor, George, 2, 77

Culmann, Leonhard, 225

Cusack, Cyril, 79n

Cusack, Sinead, 233

Czinner, Paul, 2

Dal, O., 83n

Dale, Janet, 198

Dante, 160

Davenport, Millie, 40n

Davies, Brenda, 86n

Davies, H. Neville, 230

Davies, Howard, 203

Davis, Walter R., 131n

Dean, John, 126

Degrada, Francesco, 233

Deistal, Edith, 76n

Dench, Judi, 183

Dent, Alan, 3, 76n

Dent, R. W., 225

Derrida, Jacques, 147

de Vere, Edward, Earl of Oxford, 224

Dieterle, William, 1, 2

Dignam, Mark, 202

Dollimore, Jonathan, 103n

Donawerth, Jane, 213, 214

Donne, John, 139n, 218

Dorangeon, Simone, 235

Dostoyevsky, F. M., 81n, 85

Drakakis, John, 7, 8

Draudt, Manfred, 247

Driscoll, James P., 209–11

Dudley, William, 197

Dunbar, Mary Judith, 230

Duncan, Lindsay, 198

Duncan-Jones, Katherine, 109n

Dylan, Bob, 144n

Eckert, Charles W., 1n, 6, 53n

Edward VI, King, 226

Edwards, Hilton, 40n, 48n

Edwards, Philip, 230, 243–7

Eisenstein, Sergei, 107

Elam, Keir, 215, 235

Eliot, T. S., 221

Elizabeth, Princess, 131

Elizabeth I, Queen, 216, 228

Elizabeth II, Queen, 197

Elliott, John R., 228

Elliott, Michael, 89, 90n, 181

Ellis, John, 104

Emelyanov, V., 83n

Empson, William, 145

Erasmus, Desiderius, 214

Esslin, Martin, 169, 171

Euripides, 169

Evans, Bertrand, 135n

Evans, Carol, 13

Evans, G. Blakemore, 42n, 81n, 135n, 236n

Everett, Barbara, 136n

Ewbank, Inga-Stina, 229

Fairbanks, Douglas, 79

Fairchild, A. H. R., 130n

Fairclough, H. Rushton, 161n

Farr, Derek, 106

Fehrenbach, R. J., 231

Felheim, Marvin, 76n

Fenwick, Henry, 86n, 93, 95–8, 105n, 106, 107n, 108n, 109, 110n

Finney, Albert, 76, 88

Fisch, Harold, 139n

*Five Kings*, 39, 41–6 *passim*, 49, 50, 52

Fleissner, R. F., 251

Fleming, Tom, 79n

Fletcher, Bramwell, 81n

Fletcher, John, 133, 230, 235, 239

Foakes, R. A., 238n, 240–2, 249

Forbes, Scott, 81n

Forbes-Robertson, Johnston, 75, 77, 79, 82

Fotheringham, Richard, 229

Fox, Levi, 226

France, Richard, 40n, 49n

Freud, Sigmund, 143, 144, 146, 147

Fripp, Edgar I., 143n

Frye, Northrop, 123

Furness, Horace Howard, 139n, 143n, 145n

Furnivall, F. J., 154

Furse, Roger, 3

Fuzier, Jean, 235

Gabel, Martin, 46, 49

Gabold, Anelise, 79n

Galloway, David, 228

Galloway, Pat, 184

# INDEX

Gance, Abel, 78
Garber, Marjorie, 212
Gardner, Carl, 104n
Gardner, James, 145n
Garrick, David, 230, 233
Garter, Bernard, 228
Gates, Henry L., 171n
Geduld, Harry, 4
Gerlach, John, 6
Giantvalley, S., 76n
Gibbs, James, 170n, 171n
Gielgud, John, 86, 105
Gielgud, Val, 7, 8n
Gill, Roma, 247
Gillies, Andrew, 181
Gogol, Nikolai, 81n, 85
Gold, Jack, 93, 94, 99–102
Golding, Arthur, 123–5, 127, 128, 132
Goldman, Michael, 136n, 211
Gossett, Suzanne, 231
Granville-Barker, Harley, 2, 7, 135n, 215
Gray, H., 39n
Gray, J. C., 215
Green, London, 233
Greene, Robert, 130, 224
Greetham, D. C., 248n
Greg, W. W., 248
Greville, Fulke, 226
Gricius, Jonas, 83n
Griffith, D. W., 75n
Grubb, Shirley Carr, 251
Guinness, Peter, 196, 197
Gurr, Andrew, 229, 238–40, 249
Guthrie, Tyrone, 185, 188
Gutierrez, Nancy C., 251

Habicht, Werner, 219n, 235
Hageman, Elizabeth H., 231
Hake, Edward, 231
Hakluyt, Richard, 153
Hales, J. W., 154
Halio, Jay L., 229n
Hall, Peter, 191, 192
Hallinen, Tim, 10n, 97, 104n, 109n
Hals, Frans, 109
Hamer, Douglas, 223
Hammer, Ina, 76n
Hammersmith, James P., 139n
Hands, Terry, 185, 205
Hapgood, Robert, 136n

Harris, Bernard, 135n, 139n, 145n
Harsnet, Samuel, 223
Hart, James, 2n
Hartnoll, Gillian, 75n
Harvey, Gabriel, 224
Hasler, Jörg, 230
Hawkes, Terence, 136n, 146
Hawkins, Harriett, 230
Hayes, James, 195
Hazlitt, William, 175
Heeley, Desmond, 182
Helgerson, Richard, 139n
Heminges, David, 250
Henslowe, Philip, 227, 229
Henson, Nicky, 191, 198–200
Herbert, George, 232
Herrick, Robert, 232
Hetherington, Robert A., 79n, 83n
Hibbard, G. R., 215, 230
Higham, Charles, 69n
Hill, W. Speed, 248n
Hirsch, John, 179–83
Hitchcock, Alfred, 2, 82, 116
Hodgdon, Barbara, 53n, 85n
Hogg, Ian, 79n
Hoghton, Alexander, 223
Holderness, Graham, 103
Holinshed, Raphael, 40, 42, 49, 154
Holman, Roger, 75n
Holmer, Joan Ozark, 226
Homer, 143, 160, 168
Honigmann, E. A. J., 145n, 158n, 219, 223, 225, 228, 249n
Hope-Wallace, Philip, 7, 76n
Hordern, Michael, 86, 88–90
Horsfield, Margaret, 7, 8n
Horton, Andrew, 39n
Houseman, John, 40
Howard-Hill, T. H., 248, 249n
Howell, Jane, 82, 92, 96, 100, 101, 103–6, 108–11
Howse, Hugh, 234
Hugon, Cecile, 143n
Huling, Lorraine, 76n, 78
Hunter, G. K., 139
Hunter, William B., 225
Hurt, John, 89n
Hutt, William, 188

Ibsen, Henrik, 94, 170
Ingram, R. W., 215, 228

Jackson, Russell, 13, 220
Jacobi, Derek, 93, 105
James I, King, 219
Jarman, Derek, 77
Jeans, H. R., 43n
Jefferson, D. W., 171n
Jeffrey, Peter, 196, 197, 202, 203
Jemie, Onwuchekwa, 175
Jenkins, Harold, 244, 245
Jensen, Soren Elung, 79n
Johnson, Celia, 105
Johnson, David, 189
Johnson, Richard, 108
Johnson, Samuel, 135, 136, 138, 177, 220
Johnson, William, 79n
Jones, David, 94n, 95–7
Jones, Emrys, 230
Jones, Gemma, 233
Jones, Inigo, 227, 228
Jones, James Earl, 86
Jones-Davies, M. T., 230
Jonson, Ben, 224, 226, 230, 231, 235
Jorgens, Jack, 4, 5, 11, 53n, 69n, 81n, 91, 94, 96
Jowett, John, 238–40
Joyce, James, 145n
Jung, Carl Gustav, 209–11

Kael, Pauline, 44n, 79
Kafno, Paul, 13n
Kauffmann, Stanley, 75
Kean, Charles, 230
Kean, Edmund, 233
Keith, Penelope, 105
Kempe, Will, 228
Kennedy, John, 144n
Kermode, Frank, 6, 80, 123n, 159, 160n, 162, 163, 210
Kerrigan, John, 249
Kettle, Arnold, 13n
King, Mackenzie, 144n
Kingsley, Ben, 97, 191, 204–6
Kitchin, Lawrence, 76, 91, 94
Knapp, Peggy Ann, 126n
Knelman, Martin, 179
Knight, G. Wilson, 57, 59, 125, 126, 143n, 170–2, 177, 207, 208, 218
Knight, W. F. Jackson, 161n
Knights, L. C., 220, 221
Knutson, Roslyn L., 229
Koltai, Ralph, 203, 205

255

Kott, Jan, 57, 60n, 81, 82, 165, 168, 235
Kozintsev, Grigori, 4, 5, 65, 75, 81, 83–6, 88, 94, 249
Krieder, Paul, 138
Kristiansen, Henning, 79n
Kurosawa, Akira, 4, 6, 13n, 65, 67, 70–4
Kyd, Thomas, 143, 146, 147, 217

Laffay, Albert, 91, 92
Lambert, J. W., 85, 86
Lamos, Mark, 185, 186, 188
Lancashire, Anne, 216
Langer, Suzanne, 1, 2n, 234
Langham, Michael, 188
Lawrence, Judiana, 218
Leaming, Barbara, 71n
Leggatt, Alexander, 216
Lesser, Anton, 191
Levenson, Jill, L., 139n
Levin, Harry, 140, 143n
Levin, Richard, 225, 240
Lewis, Peter, 169, 170n, 172
Limon, Jerzy, 227
Lindsay, Robert, 108
Lloyd, Robert, 79n
Lombard, Bernard, 139n
Lombard, Peter, 139n
Longhurst, Derek, 103
Love, Alison, 169, 170n, 175n
Lowry, Betty, 42n, 43n
Lucretius, 127n

McClure, Rob, 189
McCluskie, Kathleen, 230
McCowan, Alec, 105
McCullough, Andrew, 81n
Macdonald, Heather, 186
McDonald, N., 76n
McGee, C. E., 216
MacGowran, Jack, 79n
Machiavelli, Niccolo, 57, 58, 62
McKellen, Ian, 191–3
McKern, Leo, 89n, 90
Mackintosh, Mary, 75n
McLeod, Randall, 247, 249n
MacLiammóir, Micheál, 3, 4, 53n, 54n
McMillin, Scott, 217, 218, 221, 222
McRae, Hilton, 201
Macready, William Charles, 233
Madubuike, Ihechukwu, 175

Magee, Patrick, 79n
Maginley, Ben, 75n
Magretta, Joan, 39n
Maguire, Laurie E., 229
Male, David A., 234
Maller, Sándor, 236n
Malone, Edmond, 145n, 153n
Manitto, Gary V., 225
Manley, Frank, 139n
Manvell, Roger, 4, 5, 39, 53n, 75n, 76n, 81, 91, 92, 94
Marlowe, Christopher, 143, 217, 225, 235
Marowitz, Charles, 47
Marston, John, 127
Martin, Trevor, 196
Mason, H. A., 207
Mast, Gerald, 1n
Masterman, Neville, 236
Matamoros, Diego, 182
Matheson, T. P., 103n
Maurice, Clement, 77n
Maxwell, J. C., 250n
Maxwell, Roberta, 181
Mehl, Dieter, 219
Mendelssohn, Felix, 241
Merchant, W. Moelwyn, 229
Meres, Francis, 123
Merriam, Thomas, 250
Merrison, Clive, 203, 204
Merzin, L., 83n
Messina, Cedric, 94, 95, 105
Metz, Christian, 91
Meyerhold, Vsevolod, 5, 81n, 85
Michell, Keith, 105
Middlemass, Frank, 86n, 88
Middleton, Thomas, 224
Millar, Sylvia, 79n
Miller, Jonathan, 10, 86, 88, 95, 97–100, 102, 104, 109
Milton, John, 147, 160, 219, 226
Miola, Robert S., 168n
Mirren, Helen, 105, 108, 109
Mnouchkine, Ariane, 100
Moffatt, John, 189
Montaigne, Michel de, 159
Moore, Gerald, 169, 170n, 172
More, Sir Thomas, 226
Morgan, Wendy, 194
Mortimer, John, 229
Moshinsky, Elijah, 95, 99, 100, 103, 108–11
Moss, Arnold, 81n

Mosse, Miles, 226
Muir, Kenneth, 67n, 159, 160n, 229n
Mulcaster, Richard, 214
Mullini, Roberta, 235
Münsterberg, Hugo, 1
Murry, Middleton, 143n
Musa, Mark, 57n
Myerscough-Jones, David, 109n

Nannini, Remigo, 225
Naremore, James, 43, 69n
Nashe, Thomas, 143
Nearing, Barbara, 41n
Needles, William, 183
Nelligan, Kate, 105
Neville, John, 186–8
Nicoll, Allardyce, 2, 39
Nietzsche, Friedrich, 171
Noble, Adrian, 199, 200
Noble, Peter, 54n
Norbrook, David, 219n, 226
Nosworthy, J. M., 127n, 160
Novy, Marianne L., 213

Occhiogrosso, Frank, 90n
O'Connell, Michael, 229
O'Connor, John J., 89
O'Conor, Joseph, 199, 202, 203
Ogden, Dunbar H., 234
Ogden, Paul W., 234
Olivier, Laurence (Lord Olivier), 2–6, 39, 65, 75, 86, 89, 90, 95, 96n, 136, 175
Orbison, Tucker, 90
Orgel, Stephen, 229
Orrell, John, 226
Otis, Brooks, 168n
Ovid, 123–6, 143, 221
Owen, Wilfred, 169

Palmer, D. J., 96n, 217, 229n
Papp, Joseph, 86n
Parker, R. B., 216
Parry, Natasha, 81n
Pasco, Richard, 240
Pasternak, Boris, 83
Pater, Walter, 240
Peele, George, 217
Pennell, Nicholas, 180–3, 185, 188
Pennington, Michael, 108
Percy, Bishop, 154
Perkins, V. F., 85

Petőfi, Sándor, 236
Petrenko, A., 83n
Phillips, Margaret, 81n
Phillips, Robin, 179, 183, 185
Pickford, Mary, 79
Pinnock, Andrew, 155n
Pinter, Harold, 85
Pitcher, John, 221
Plato, 146, 149, 155, 234
Plowright, David, 89n
Poel, William, 143n
Polanski, Roman, 4, 65, 67, 69–71, 75
Pontanus, Jacobus, 127n
Pope, Alexander, 239, 241
Porter, Andrew, 232, 233
Powys, John Cowper, 169
Price, George R., 247
Prosser, Eleanor, 221
Pythagoras, 123, 149

Quayle, Anthony, 94, 98, 105
Quinn, Kenneth, 168n

Rabkin, Norman, 51n, 136n, 211
Rackham, H , 149n
Radzins, E., 83n
Rainolds, John, 228
Ramsay, Allan, 154n
Randall, Dale B. J., 223n, 231
Redgrave, Vanessa, 181
Reed, Robert Rentoul, 209
Reese, M. M., 226
Reeves, Geoffrey, 6n
Reid, S. W., 250
Reinhardt, Max, 1, 2, 65, 109
Reitel, Enn, 93
Rembrandt, 95, 99, 100, 109
Richards, Kenneth, 13
Richardson, Ian, 185, 240
Richardson, Ralph, 42, 95n
Richie, Donald, 74n
Rickey, Fred, 81n
Rickman, Alan, 202
Ridgway, Lady, 231
Riehle, Wolfgang, 219
Rigaud, Nadia, 235
Rigg, Diana, 89, 90
Righter, Anne, 75n; see also Anne Barton
Roberts, Jeanne A., 230
Roberts, Josephine A., 231
Robinson, F. N., 150n
Rorty, Richard, 146n

Rose, Billy, 40n
Rose, Lloyd, 90n
Rose, Mark, 135n
Rose, Mary Beth, 231
Rosen, David, 232
Rosenberg, Marvin, 9, 82
Rosenblatt, Jason, 145n
Ross, Lawrence, 149n, 155n
Rosso, Laurence, 189
Rothwell, Kenneth, 13
Rothwell, Talbot, 79n
Rouse, W. H. D., 123n
Rowse, A. L., 224, 237, 246, 247
Rubin, Leon, 189, 190
Rubio, Miguel, 43n, 44n, 50n
Ruby, Thelma, 43
Rutkay, Kálmán, 236n
Ryall, David, 195
Rylands, John, 250n

Sabinus, Georgius, 127
Sams, Eric, 225, 250
Sandys, George, 132
Santayana, George, 141
Scaliger, Julius Caesar, 128n
Schlegel, August Wilhelm von, 139, 221
Schleiner, Louise, 232
Schleiner, Winifred, 226
Schmidgall, Gary, 161n
Schoenbaum, S., 224
Scofield, Paul, 39, 79, 81, 83
Scott, F. R., 144n
Sebris, K., 83n
Seef, Adele, 230
Segal, Charles, 126n
Sellers, Peter, 197
Seltzer, Daniel, 51
Shady, Raymond C., 247
Shakespeare, William
  editions
    Arden, 67n, 123n, 127, 129n, 159n, 160n, 161n, 162n, 205, 238, 240–2, 244, 247
    Folio, 129, 138, 157, 168, 225, 236, 237, 238n, 239, 241, 242, 248–51
    New Variorum, 139n, 215
    Oxford, 251
    Quarto, 95, 99n, 129, 138, 195, 197, 217, 236, 237, 250
    Riverside, 42n, 81n, 135n, 236n

plays
  All's Well that Ends Well, 14, 95, 98, 99, 108, 109, 230
  Antony and Cleopatra, 10, 15, 90, 99, 170, 177, 178, 207, 218, 220, 223, 234
  As You Like It, 2, 15, 16, 95n, 96, 114, 119, 181, 191, 199, 200, 202, 203, 222
  Comedy of Errors, The, 7, 16, 220, 223, 224
  Coriolanus, 16, 17, 95, 108–10, 115, 120, 126n, 191–3, 197, 215, 216, 244
  Cymbeline, 17, 103, 104, 108–11, 118, 123, 127, 128, 132, 168n, 218
  Hamlet, 3, 5, 7, 17–19, 39, 75, 77, 79, 100, 107, 114, 117, 119, 135–47 passim, 175, 194–7, 218, 221, 222, 230, 235, 238n, 241–3, 245, 246, 250
  Henry IV, 40, 41, 43, 96, 216
  1 Henry IV, 19, 40, 42, 44, 45, 49, 51, 52, 113, 117, 119, 169, 173, 174, 215, 224, 246, 250, 251
  2 Henry IV, 19, 41–52 passim, 151, 169, 173, 174, 216, 224, 242, 246, 250
  Henry V, 2, 4–6, 13n, 19, 20, 40, 41, 75, 95, 96n, 251
  Henry VI, 92, 100, 105, 240n
  1 Henry VI, 20, 101, 106n
  2 Henry VI, 21, 105n, 106, 107, 110
  3 Henry VI, 21
  Henry VIII, 21, 75, 95n, 96, 113, 132, 250
  Julius Caesar, 9, 21–3, 40, 96, 115, 116, 120, 222, 251
  King John, 4, 23, 211, 223
  King Lear, 4–7, 9, 23, 24, 39, 75–89 passim, 100–2, 114, 116, 129, 208, 210, 219, 223, 230, 233–5, 248–50

Shakespeare plays (*cont.*)
  *Love's Labour's Lost*, 24,
    108, 109, 188, 189, 215,
    220, 223, 225, 237, 247
  *Macbeth*, 3, 4, 8, 24–6, 40,
    53, 67–74 passim, 75, 94,
    100, 101, 115, 116, 119,
    171, 175, 208, 209, 216,
    222, 233, 234
  *Measure for Measure*, 11, 26,
    98, 202, 221, 223
  *Merchant of Venice, The*, 26,
    27, 94, 100, 114, 130,
    185, 186, 189, 226
  *Merry Wives of Windsor,
    The*, 27, 96, 97, 183,
    186, 191, 196–8, 224,
    246
  *Midsummer Night's Dream,
    A*, 1, 2, 13n, 27, 28, 60,
    77, 95, 99, 108, 109, 115,
    120, 124, 169, 182, 185,
    219, 224, 225, 234, 238n,
    240–2
  *Much Ado About Nothing*,
    2n, 28, 29, 114, 131
  *Othello*, 3, 5, 29, 30, 53–5,
    58, 60, 64, 65, 82, 98, 99,
    149–58 passim, 205, 213,
    247, 250, 251
  *Pericles*, 30, 126n, 128, 130,
    214, 250
  *Richard II*, 30, 31, 40, 42,
    44, 100, 105n, 119, 152,
    217, 238, 240, 249
  *Richard III*, 31, 95, 100,
    105, 106, 108n, 216, 217,
    223, 240n
  *Romeo and Juliet*, 2, 31–3,
    39, 76n, 95n, 105n, 119,
    220, 246
  *Sir Thomas More*, 250
  *Taming of the Shrew, The*,
    4, 33, 34, 75, 79, 97, 99,
    124n, 205, 213, 225, 236,
    250
  *Tempest, The*, 34, 35, 95n,
    96, 115, 116, 118, 123,
    128, 130, 131, 159–68
    passim, 171, 179, 182,
    208, 210, 221, 223, 226
  *Timon of Athens*, 35, 235
  *Titus Andronicus*, 35, 104–8,
    123–5, 215, 217, 237
  *Troilus and Cressida*, 35, 58,

64, 113, 152, 191, 203,
    205, 218n, 219, 250
  *Twelfth Night*, 7, 35, 36,
    64, 96, 114, 118, 119,
    125, 251
  *Two Gentlemen of Verona*,
    36, 124, 125, 130, 189,
    220, 237
  *Winter's Tale, The*, 36, 37,
    60, 96, 100, 101, 104,
    106, 127, 128, 130–2,
    218, 230, 234
  poems
    *Lover's Complaint, A*, 250
    *Passionate Pilgrim, The*, 250
    *Rape of Lucrece, The*, 124,
      217, 244, 250
    *Venus and Adonis*, 250
    Sonnets, 250
Shallcross, Alan, 105n
Shand, G. B., 247
Shaw, Fiona, 200
Shaw, G. B., 158n, 213, 236
Sheehan, Patrick, 75n
Shelley, Percy Bysshe, 73
Shendrikova, V., 83n, 84
Sher, Antony, 191, 249
Shorter, Eric, 86
Shostakovich, Dmitri, 83n
Shreiber, Flora Rheta, 9
Sicherman, Carol Marks, 251
Sidney, Mary, Countess of
  Pembroke, 231
Sidney, Sir Philip, 226
Silviria, Dale, 5
Simmons, James, 169
Sinden, Donald, 230, 234
Sinfield, Alan, 103n
Singer, S. W., 238
Singh, Sarup, 212, 213
Slater, Ann Pasternak, 95
Slights, W. W. E., 225
Smith, A. J., 218
Smith, Barbara Herrnstein, 138
Smith, W. M. A., 250
Snodin, David, 105, 110
Somerset, Alan, 247
Sontag, Susan, 39n
Southwell, Lady Anne, 231
Soyinka, Wole, 169–78 passim
Spence, Paul, 199
Spencer, T. J. B., 4n, 77n
Spenser, Edmund, 219, 226
*Spread of the Eagle, The*, 9, 15,
    16, 22, 94

Stanley, Earls of Derby, 223
Stanton, Barry, 79n
Steafel, Sheila, 199
Steevens, George, 128, 239
Sternfeld, F. W., 149n, 157
Stevenson, Juliet, 191, 200–5
Still, Colin, 160, 165
Stone, Lawrence, 213
Stone, P. W. K., 248
Stoppard, Tom, 47
Strachey, James, 144n
Straight, Beatrice, 81n
Strange, Ferdinando, Lord, 223,
  228
Strehler, Giorgio, 208
Stride, John, 105
Styan, J. L., 6, 7n
Suchet, David, 204, 205
Sutton, Shaun, 86n, 94, 95n
Swift, Carolyn Ruth, 231

Taborski, Boleslaw, 57n
Tate, Nahum, 233
Tate, Sharon, 71n
Taylor, Gary, 126n, 238–40,
  242, 246, 248, 250, 251
Taylor, John Russell, 4, 8, 9,
  77, 128
Taylor, Sam, 4, 79
Tetzeli von Rosador, Kurt,
  220
Thanhouser, Edwin, 76, 79, 83
Theobald, Lewis, 251
Thomas, Keith, 218, 232
Thomas, Sydney, 249
Thomson, Virgil, 81n, 82
Tillyard, E. M. W., 139n, 226
Tolstoy, Leo, 236
Tomkis, Thomas, 214
Traister, Barbara Howard, 231,
  232
Traversi, Derek, 59
Travitsky, Betty, 230
Tree, Herbert Beerbohm, 4, 75,
  109
Treves, Frederick, 193–5
Trussler, Simon, 234, 235
Tutin, Dorothy, 89n, 90
Tynan, Kenneth, 47, 49n

Ultz, 109n
Ungerer, Gustav, 251
Ure, Peter, 238, 239

Vardac, A. Nicholas, 1, 75n

Vaughan, Henry, 83
Verdi, Giuseppe, 232, 233
Verger, Pierre, 176n
Vermeer, Jan, 109
Veronese, Paul, 95, 100
Virgil, 124, 143, 159, 160, 161n, 163, 164, 168, 221
Vives, Juan Luis, 214
Vokach, A., 83n
Volchek, G., 83n

Wadsworth, Frank, 9
Wager, 221
Waith, Eugene M., 215n
Wall, Stephen, 193
Walters, Sam, 193, 194, 197
Walton, J. K., 135n
Warburton, William, 245
Warde, Ernest, 76, 78–81
Warde, Frederick, 76–9, 82, 83, 88, 90
Warden, John, 126n
Wardle, Irving, 181, 185, 202
Warhol, Andy, 77
Warner, William, 251
Warren, Michael, 249
Warren, Roger, 230
Wars of the Roses, The, 20, 21, 31, 105
Watson, Ian, 169, 171, 172

Watteau, Antoine, 109
Watts, Richard, 1
Weaver, William, 233
Webb, Alan, 79n
Webb, John, 227
Webster, John, 152, 218n
Webster, Paul, 198
Weill, Kurt, 205
Weimann, Robert, 230
Welles, Orson, 3, 13, 39–57, 61–71 passim, 79, 81–3, 86
Wells, Stanley, 10, 11, 94n, 95, 105, 106n, 111, 236–8, 242, 246, 247, 249
Welsh, J. M., 85n
Wentersdorf, K., 124n, 251
Werstine, Paul, 247, 248n, 249n
White, William, 247
Whitney, Geffrey, 127n
Wickham, Glynne, 225
Widdowson, P., 103n
Wilders, John, 9, 11, 92, 96, 106
Wilds, Lilian, 80
Williams, David, 235n
Williams, G. Walton, 222
Williams, Raymond, 103
Williamson, Nicol, 102
Wilson, Dover, 136n, 145, 146, 243n
Wilson, Robert, 224, 225

Wilton, Penelope, 86n, 87
Wimsatt, W. K., 135n
Wittreich, Joseph, 219
Woods, Alan, 76n
Woods, Leigh, 230, 233
Worlock, Gloucester, 81n
Worth, Irene, 79n, 191, 193, 194
Wright, Rosemary, 225
Wright, Susan, 184, 185
Wroth, Lady Mary, 231, 235
Wroth, Sir Robert, 235
Wyatt, Peter, 194
Wyver, John, 104n

Yarvet, Yuri, 83, 84
Yates, Frances, 139n, 140n, 232
Yates, Peter, 76
Yeats, W. B., 168, 240
York, Michael, 105
Young, Filson, 8
Yutkevich, Sergei, 5, 85

Zeffirelli, Franco, 39, 65, 75
Ziegler, Georgianna, 225
Ziegler, Joseph, 188, 189
Zitner, Sheldon, P., 10, 86n, 215, 216, 247
Zohn, Harry, 53n